Assessing Academic Achievement

Assessing Academic Achievement

David E. Tanner
California State University, Fresno

Allyn and Bacon
Boston • London • Toronto • Sydney • Tokyo • Singapore

To Dylan, David, Gillian, John, and Suzanna, and to Susan.

Vice President and Editor-in-Chief: Paul A. Smith
Editorial Assistant: Shannon Morrow
Senior Marketing Manager: Brad Parkins
Production Editor: Christopher H. Rawlings
Editorial-Production Service: Omegatype Typography, Inc.
Composition and Prepress Buyer: Linda Cox
Manufacturing Buyer: Dave Repetto
Cover Administrator: Linda Knowles
Electronic Composition: Omegatype Typography, Inc.

Library of Congress Cataloging-in-Publication Data
Tanner, David Earl
    Assessing academic achievement / David E. Tanner.
      p.   cm.
    Includes bibliographical references and index.
    ISBN 0-205-28266-0 (alk. paper)
      1. Educational evaluation. 2. Academic achievement—Evaluation.   I. Title.
LB2822.75 .T36   2001
371.26—dc21
                                             00-023504

Contents

PART II   ASSESSING PERFORMANCE ACCORDING TO CRITERIA   45

3   Specifying the Standard and Focusing on the Outcome   47

4 Employing Authentic Assessment 72

5 Grading Students and Evaluating Instruction 99

Preface

Assessing Academic Achievement emerges from a feeling that one of the more important chinks in education's armor is assessment. My considered observation is that teacher preparation programs generally acquit themselves well when they instruct candidates in developing and presenting learning materials. I am unconvinced, however, that educators develop the same facility with documenting what students know and can do. This becomes particularly troublesome when one wishes to draw accurate inferences about what should come next in an educational program. Too often the business of grading becomes the only focus, and the opportunity to use assessment data to improve the quality of the educational experience is lost. A great deal more than just what students know is revealed in student performance data. Consistent with this premise, this book examines the many assessment tasks for which teachers are responsible as components of teaching, rather than as ancillaries. For someone who wishes to use assessment data to inform instruction, improve curriculum, and make sound judgments about students' progress, this book will be helpful.

As is the case in education generally, one's approach to assessment is grounded both in one's philosophy and in the practical exigencies of classroom life. Those who wish to pursue forms of assessment in which educators duplicate conditions beyond the classroom will find that I have dealt with authentic assessment in some detail, but not uncritically. Like all forms of assessment represented in the following chapters, authentic assessment procedures raise questions, just as they suggests answers. Those who must develop their own more traditional tests will find assistance in both test construction and in the data analysis that can reveal so much about the quality of the assessment and the progress of the student.

Because all educators deal with standardized test results, I have made an effort to help the reader understand something of the origin, the language, and the applications of those measures. This particular discussion will allow me to introduce topics in test theory and test development that one does not ordinarily find in an introductory textbook. I have raised these topics because the logical relationship between classroom assessment and the domain represented by formal educational measurement offers the potential for a fruitful discussion, particularly in the light of increasingly prominent high-stakes tests.

In this presentation, I will develop the discussion without imposing the burden of the highly technical analyses ordinarily associated with educational measurement. Indeed, I have tried to write for people who are intelligent but largely uninformed beyond their own experiences in primary and secondary schools. They, of course, will assess my success.

ACKNOWLEDGMENTS

As carefully as one might prepare written work, others' more objective and experienced eyes are invaluable resources. I am grateful for the expertise and comments from the following very helpful outside reviewers: Kathryn Alvestad, University of Maryland; George Johnson, Ohio University, Athens; James Koller, University of Missouri, Columbia; Leigh Garnet Lewis, Tarleton State University; Catherine McCartney, Bemidji State University; Patricia Pokay, Eastern Michigan University; Judith Speed, University of California, Davis; and Cathleen Stutz, Assumption College.

Paul Smith and Nancy Forsyth at Allyn and Bacon played pivotal roles in the structure and content of this book. I profited much from their experience and insight.

Dave Armstrong was my mentor many years ago at Texas A&M. He is a wonderful scholar, a prolific writer, and a good friend. I have never forgotten his example.

My most diligent editor is also my companion these 27 years. Susan's help and encouragement were irreplaceable. I am deeply indebted to her for her patience and interest.

D.E.T.

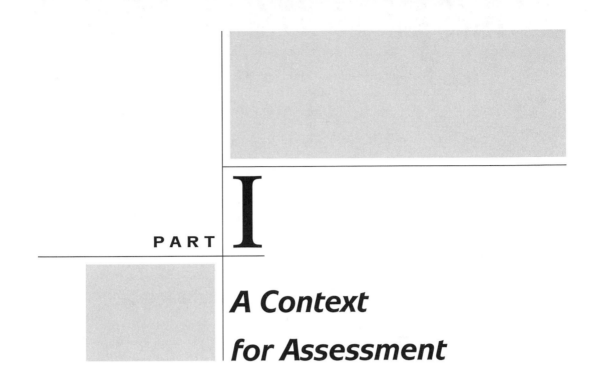

PART I

A Context for Assessment

No one who has any association with formal education is a stranger to assessment. In fact there is a natural connection between learning and assessment: The first task is to encourage students to acquire new skills and knowledge; the second is to document the student's progress and then use that information to improve the quality of teaching and learning. The connection between learning and assessment is not an equal partnership, however. Those preparing to teach typically spend the vast majority of their time learning to prepare and present the instructional materials and comparatively little time learning to assess students' learning.

There is a certain logic to this. People are rarely attracted to the primary or secondary school classroom out of a desire to evaluate student performance. It is teaching or helping that they enjoy, and that usually becomes their focus. This is probably also typical of most of the professors who work with teacher candidates during their preparation.

Equal time for assessment is not really the point of this discussion, by the way. Your author recognizes that, although assessment activities are pervasive in the educational setting, they share the stage with a number of other important processes. Rather, one must begin to view assessment as a component of the educational plan, a component that holds the potential to do much more than evaluate students. It also offers the opportunity to inform the other components of education so that *all* of the planning and execution activities are more effective. This point will be emphasized in Chapter 1 and pursued in greater detail in Chapter 2 as the role that assessment plays in the planning, preparation, and delivery of instruction, as well as in its modification for the future, is examined.

Chapter 1 also will describe a dichotomy that helps define assessment. The data gathered about students' performances have meaning because they can be compared to something. When teachers find meaning by comparing students to each other, they have employed a norm-reference. When teachers compare students to a standard, they have used a criterion-reference. There are arguments for and against both.

1

Assessment and Education

■ *Readers will recognize the integral role that assessment can play for those who wish to analyze and foster students' educational progress.*

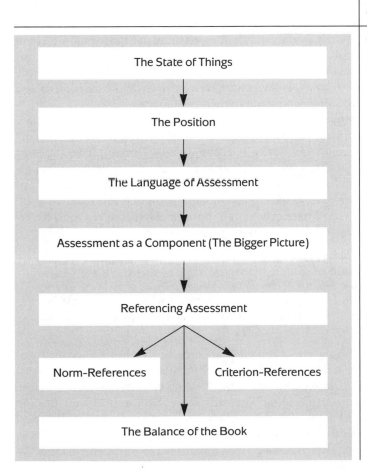

The State of Things

↓

The Position

↓

The Language of Assessment

↓

Assessment as a Component (The Bigger Picture)

↓

Referencing Assessment

Norm-References   Criterion-References

The Balance of the Book

The scholarly literature on classroom assessment provides its own rationale for a book on assessment. It suggests that, in some programs at least, assessment activities do not receive a heavy emphasis and that teachers, once confronted with the realities of classroom life, sometimes feel underprepared. Although the relevant elements of learning are sometimes difficult to observe directly, they can be examined and evaluated. This evaluation is most meaningful if assessment is an integrated part of the comprehensive educational plan rather than a stand-alone. Using an analytical approach, we can classify assessment techniques and procedures by whether they relate student performance to a set of objective criteria or to what is typical of the group. ■

Three decades ago, when Mrs. Harker began her teaching career, classroom assessment procedures were left to individual teachers, who functioned almost autonomously. Except for the battery of standardized achievement tests near the end of the school year, little was required in the way of procedure, and no one paid much attention to how she determined students' progress. This has changed. Increasingly, Mrs. Harker finds herself answering questions by administrators and parents about students' performance, class progress, and trends in literacy—assessment questions she feels ill-equipped to answer. How should she view assessment and instruction, as competing for her time or complementing each other in the classroom? ■

THE STATE OF THINGS

Evaluating students' progress must be at least as old as formal education, but, although it has a lengthy history, there is a good deal of evidence that we may not do it particularly well. Educational assessment often yields quite poor information about what students know and can do (Novak, 1998; Taylor and Nolen, 1996). Assessment data indicating that a student's math performance is below grade level are helpful only if the student is actually performing below grade level. Since we make decisions based on the data, we must have some confidence in their veracity.

There are probably many reasons why assessment performance falls short of what it ought to be, and recommended prescriptions are forthcoming in the succeeding chapters, but at least one source of difficulty is simply a lack of emphasis. Stiggins (1991) studied teacher preparation and noted that sometimes teacher preparation programs do not require formal course work in classroom assessment but include it as a component of some other course, such as curriculum. Although this makes a good deal of logical sense, it is out of harmony with important classroom realities. Referring to the state of things in assessment, Stiggins observed:

> These data are more troubling now than ever before because of our growing emphasis on outcomes-based education and our growing awareness of the critical role classroom assessment plays in determining the academic well-being of students. Our decade-long . . . analysis of classroom assessment, for example, reveals that teachers can spend a third to a half of their available professional time involved in assessment-related activities. (p. 7)

Although your author hopes for a broader audience, he developed this book primarily for the preparing teacher. It represents an effort to address the lack of assessment emphasis in teacher training. The attempt is to equip educators to deal with the realities of classroom assessment. The book will tackle specific problems dealing with the concepts and mechanics of different classroom assessment approaches and with the connection between assessment and other components of education. By the way, that connection is intended to be a unifying theme for the book. It will come up again later in this chapter and more particularly in Chapter 2, but know that it is a sort of hinge on which the assessment door is supposed to swing. Before continuing, we need to develop a context for assessment and provide comments on philosophy and terminology.

THE POSITION

Your author's approach to assessment is based on certain assumptions. One assumption is that although student learning—and those activities that are logically related to it—sometimes involves elusive processes and products, it can be identified and evaluated. The mechanisms must change with conditions, but the relevant evidence for assessment *is* observable. Classroom instructors often do not see the learners' analytical abilities directly, as an example, but with some care they can identify the evidence that indicates how well learners analyze.

A second assumption is that student assessment loses meaning when it is isolated from the other elements of the educational plan. Good teaching, for example, has a consistent effect on students' progress (Medley, 1985; Stodolsky, 1985), and, therefore, student performance cannot be understood in any comprehensive fashion without factoring in information about instructional quality.

A final assumption is that rather than assessment systems being good or bad, more accurately they are less or better suited to particular assessment circumstances. One need not look far to find a broadside leveled at standardized testing or criticism for a particular type of assessment item, but the issue is less "good versus bad" than it is a matter of the appropriate use of an approach and proper interpretation of the resulting data.

These three assumptions are central to the chapters that follow. They are summarized in Figure 1.1.

FIGURE 1.1   **Educational Assessment Assumptions**

1. **Student learning is assessable.** Although one may not be able to observe students' learning directly, the evidence for it is observable. Available techniques will allow one to assess students, as well as the other elements of the educational plan that are logically related to students' learning.

2. **Assessment should involve more than students' learning.** What the students accomplish is a product that reflects a number of components of the educational plan. The instructor's planning, the preassessment, and the instruction are all factors in students' performance. A comprehensive assessment plan is one that is developed to inform all the elements rather than just student performance.

3. **Good assessment is situation specific.** There is little point in criticizing an assessment form when the real culprit is poor application or misinterpretation of the data.

THE LANGUAGE OF ASSESSMENT

A variety of different audiences is involved in educational assessment discussions, not all of them educators. Students and their parents are interested, and even the popular press makes forays into this area from time to time. The language we use is not uniform, and, often, people use dissimilar terms as though they were interchangeable. Although these concepts occur later in the book, a few definitions will be helpful before we continue.

It is interesting to note that the Latin root for *assess* means "to assist in the office of a judge." Assess is related to the word *assize,* which refers to an action to be decided by judges' inquest (*Merriam-Webster,* 1994). This suits your author's approach very well. Educational assessment is a comprehensive process of describing, judging, and communicating the quality of learning and performances for those who are involved (Andrews and Barnes, 1990).

Assessment is the comprehensive term. It includes components that refer to **measurement, evaluation,** and **grading.** Referring to "those who are involved" in educational processes draws instructors into the equation as well. In Chapter 5 techniques will be examined that also assess teachers' performances.

Measurement is the descriptive part of the assessment process. It often involves assigning numbers to observations according to rules that fit the circumstances. In a simple example of measuring spelling ability, for example, one counts the number of words the student spelled correctly and assigns the corresponding number as a score. Measurement must be as objective as possible, but the truth is that it is never completely objective because elements of students' learning require a level of inference by the instructor.

Speaking of Assessment

Sometimes one must make a decision about what constitutes the relevant behavior of the learner, and those decisions require inferences. What behavior represents critical thinking, for example, or what is the difference between memorizing and comprehending? It is one thing to set out to measure critical thinking, and quite another to identify the behaviors that it represents.

Even the items one selects for an assessment instrument reflect a decision (which involves a subjective element) about what is most important to measure.

When your author was in the seventh grade, one of the classes was art. For one project we were to take an 8½ - by 11-inch sheet of paper and use a ruler to scribe any number of straight lines, as long as they stretched between any two edges of the paper. The lines intersected each other, of course, creating a series of smaller figures on the page. The task was to color each enclosed figure, but no adjoining figures could have the same color. Does it strike you that the completed assignment is a good indicator of artistic ability? Had the teacher drawn an inference that an observer might question?

If measurement has a subtle, subjective element, evaluation is more openly subjective. When we evaluate a performance, we make a judgment about its quality, but we

Assessing students usually has measurement, evaluation, and grading components. Measurement involves the observation required for data gathering; evaluation is the process of judging the quality of the student's performance; and grading is a brief representation of the evaluation.

base that judgment on the measurement. The student's spelling score of 14 reflects a measurement. Deciding that a score of 14 is "poor" or "good" spelling is the evaluative component. When we select a symbol to communicate the evaluation—an A, B, or C letter perhaps—we *grade* the performance.

ASSESSMENT AS A COMPONENT OF THE EDUCATIONAL PLAN

In the previous section, your author suggested that assessment involves much more than testing. Assessment is an integral part of the total educational plan, a connection that Novak (1998) outlined when he spoke of the relationship between the learner, the teacher, the knowledge, the context, and the evaluation. He wrote that each of the five elements "interacts with all the others, and all must be considered simultaneously" (p. 3). Koelsch, Estrin, and Farr (1995) explained the risk one takes when the different educational elements are approached piecemeal:

> *When assessment is disconnected from teaching and learning, students must respond to assessment demands that are devoid of a meaningful context or a familiar schema. That is, the ability of some students to respond is compromised, because the cues that they typically depend on in school are missing. Their chances for using their knowledge of the world and their own repertoire of strategies to accurately represent what they know are reduced; and because students cannot respond meaningfully, assessment outcomes are less useful to teachers for evaluating student learning and for planning instruction. (p. 20)*

The point is that whereas evaluating students' performance is an important component of the plan, it is one component. Assessment's potential is to inform all parts of the plan, including the instruction.

For Further Discussion

The concept of using assessment to inform instruction is simple, but it is often missed. There are shining exceptions, however. When your author was a graduate student, he took a series of statistics courses with doctoral students from various disciplines. Everyone did poorly on the first test. Your author was prepared for the professor to be very critical. He might have said something like, "How do you people expect to compete on a doctoral level?" or "You knew this test was coming; why did you not prepare more carefully?" Instead he said, "Everyone did poorly. It must be my fault."

Such a conclusion is possible when one is willing to use assessment data to evaluate more than the students' performance. In your experience, how common is it for teachers or professors to offer such an explanation?

REFERENCING ASSESSMENT

A measure of performance, aptitude, interest, and the like is meaningful only when it is compared, or referenced, to something else. There are two types of references common to educational assessment. **Norm-referenced assessment** lends meaning to the individual's score, grade, activity, and so forth, by comparing it to the scores and evaluations that others received. It is assessment by comparison to one's peers. With **criterion-referenced assessment** one compares the performance to an objective standard, or what Glaser (1994) called "an absolute standard of quality" (p. 6). Because very different assumptions and purposes are associated with each reference, the choice of whether to use a norm-reference or a criterion-reference is one we make carefully and well before the assessment is actually conducted.

> Norm-references give meaning to performance by comparing the learners' performances to those of their peers. Criterion-references compare the learners to a preestablished and objective standard.

The distinctions between norm- and criterion-referenced assessment provide some of the structure for the book. Therefore, they will be discussed briefly in the following sections.

Norm-References

In common language, the norm represents the level of performance that is typical among members of a group, and a norm-reference defines the level of an individual student's performance by comparing the student to the norm. An individual's score becomes meaningful when we know what score is typical for members of the comparison group. If data indicate that fifth-grade students average 50 points on a problem-solving measure, we know that a score of 57 is higher than average.[1] It is more than a matter of "above average" or "below average," however. Norm-references also indicate where the individual falls within the group. Indicating that someone scored in the top 10 percent or the first quartile reflects the use of a norm-referenced measure. The practice is particularly common in standardized testing.

Comparability is determined by ensuring that members of the norm group possess the same characteristics that are typical of all those who will be assessed. Depending on the type and purpose of the assessment, the relevant characteristics might be age, gender, ethnicity, grade in school, or particular social and economic characteristics. If the assessment is a nationally administered reading test for third grade students, the norm group is probably a group of third grade students whose gender, ethnicity, and social class characteristics represent children in the same proportions as children of that age throughout the country.

Besides a typical score, the scoring pattern may be very informative. If, for example, the scores on the problem-solving ability test are between 30 and 70, one would interpret a score of 57 quite differently than if all scores were between 43 and 57. In the first instance, the learner's score is somewhere near the middle of the distribution and, of course, in the second example, 57 represents the highest score.

Data indicating the average score and the most likely scoring distribution are usually published for the most common tests. They allow us to know before we examine a particular set of data what scoring pattern we might expect, so long as the group is typical. The size of the group and its representative characteristics are important qualifiers, however. Although we can make reasonable predictions about the characteristics of very large groups, predicting how students in one classroom will score is more than a little risky. Comparatively small groups may not be typical of the larger population for a variety of reasons. Perhaps the school is in a neighborhood where recent immigrants have gathered and where many of the children do not yet speak the primary language. In some instances, this could easily result in scores that are significantly lower than those of the comparable group.

As the size of one's group shrinks, it becomes increasingly difficult to make accurate predictions based on the characteristics of the norm group. Predicting individuals' performances based on the characteristics of groups is foolish at best. Information about what is typical of fifth graders usually reveals very little about one fifth-grade student in a class. Although we may know what the average will be, the range of scores, the interval from the lowest score to the highest, is often great. The probability is greatest that a student will score near the average for the group, but theoretically a student's score could fall anywhere from the highest to the lowest possible scores.

A norm-reference allows one to rank students—to identify who did best, and who did better than someone else. Settings in which assessment is norm-referenced are competitive by definition, sometimes more openly than others.

Speaking of Assessment

During your author's undergraduate days, he took a sophomore-level class in political science, his major. It was intended to be one of those classes that separate the students who are in earnest from those who are not. The instructor used a norm-reference to assess students, with a predetermined proportion to receive each letter grade. Having missed a previous class (the absence is sure to have been legitimate), this would-be political scientist naively said to the student who sat next to him, "I missed class Tuesday, may I borrow your notes?" The response was a curt and unapologetic "Nope!" Someone explained the classmate's mind-set when he observed, "It is not enough that I succeed; my friends must also fail."

This characteristic of placing students in competition with one another makes norm-referenced assessments objectionable to some and inappropriate in certain circumstances. Your author will neither defend nor reject them at this point, but just explain their use.

Criterion-References

The current usage of the term *criterion-reference* dates from work Glaser originally published in 1963 when he argued that, in assessment, frequently the issue is how well the learner's behavior matches a particular criterion. In these instances, educators are probably little concerned (or perhaps wholly unconcerned) with how learners compare to one another. The question is whether those assessed, for example, can write a coherent paragraph or solve an algebraic equation, rather than who can best perform those tasks (the normative approach). Criteria are important because they usually represent accomplishments that have independent value. In the case of authentic assessment, arguably considered a particular application of criterion-referenced assessment, the criterion is usually the real-world application of the learning. A criterion for judging whether third grade students can add and subtract could be their ability to make correct change for a purchase, for example.

Formal education is largely about helping students become literate people. To the degree that the transformation involves acquiring skills and abilities that can be stated as specific accomplishments, criterion-referenced assessment seems to suit many of our assessment needs. Comparing students to one another makes little sense if none of them learn to write coherent paragraphs, read good literature, speak the language clearly, solve problems, or do a host of other things that reflect literacy.

When we can define a particular educational outcome and that outcome reflects broad support, criterion-referenced assessment makes a great deal of sense. The task becomes a matter of determining which students can demonstrate the identified outcome. At this level of abstraction, criterion-references are very attractive. The difficulty comes in (a) establishing which particular outcome reflects the criterion and (b) determining how well the student must perform in order to be judged to have an adequate command of the material.

For Further Discussion

Criteria are easier to deal with when they are abstract than when they are immediate. For example, people will generally agree that one of the more important educational objectives is to learn to use the language well.

What should be the criteria for judging the language performance of a student graduating from secondary school?

Is it enough to speak the language well, or is writing required?
What should be the relevant criteria for judging each?
Is language ability something that someone has/does not have, or are there degrees of competency?

Sometimes the easiest way to view alternative systems is to contrast them. Norm- and criterion-references are contrasted in Figure 1.2.

FIGURE 1.2   Assigning Meaning to a Measurement

Selecting a Reference

Norm-References | **Criterion-References**

The reference is what is typical of the group. | The reference is objective standards.

However, group performance provides no absolute measure of performance (we know how one compares, not what one can do). | Although one has an objective measure of performance, sometimes the standards are arbitrary or chosen because they are convenient or easy to identify.

THE BALANCE OF THE BOOK

This book has five parts. Part I, consisting of this chapter and Chapter 2, was developed to create a context for assessment, a theme introduced as an integral part of a more comprehensive educational plan. The message is that education involves much more than instruction. That may seem to be a logical enough statement, but there is ample evidence that we often miss the point.

When lack of assessment experience is the problem, part of the fault may lie simply in the terminology we employ. The names *teacher, instructor,* and even *professor* emphasize presentation, not assessment (Stiggins, 1991). Educators must develop a broader view of educational tasks. Particularly in Chapter 2, your author will make a case for integrating assessment activities and assessment data in all components of the educational plan, from the earliest planning, through the actual teaching, to the final analyses of students' and teachers' performances.

Material in the earlier part of this chapter indicated that there are different references to use in judging students' performance. The distinction between criterion- and norm-references is a major element in the development of Parts II, III, and IV of this book. An increasingly important issue in recent years is assessing students according to specified achievement outcomes. Chapter 3 takes up the subject of identifying a standard by which to judge students' outcomes. Although the connection is often not clear in the literature, standards approaches are not new. They are related to the criterion-referenced assessment procedures of the past. One important difference—and a reason that advocates do not relate to criterion-referenced programs—is that some of the more contemporary standards models do not lend themselves to conventional testing procedures. Stiggins (1991) observed that teachers must come to know that many achievement outcomes do not work with the multiple-choice testing formats so common in the past. That matter will be a major focus in Chapter 4.

Chapter 5 takes up grading procedures and alternatives. Consistent with our theme of multiple educational components in Chapter 2, however, the discussion will extend to evaluating teachers' performance as well as the students'.

It should be clear by now that the educator's assessment role has many facets, but perhaps the most fundamental task is to evaluate the progress of one's students properly. No one will know your students better than you will know them. As the classroom instructor, you are in a unique position to conduct assessments because you will understand the students' circumstances. They often reflect conditions that are relevant to our interpretation of the assessment results. Stiggins (1991) observed, "In classrooms, assessment is virtually never a detached, scientific, objective laboratory act. Rather, it is . . . always an interpersonal act with personal antecedents and personal consequences. Experienced teachers sense this better than anyone" (p. 9).

However skilled outside evaluators may be, they will always lack information relevant to the proper assessment of your students. It is information that *you* will have. Consistent with this, Chapters 6 and 7 are planned to help you develop the rudiments of teacher-constructed paper and pencil assessment. In terms of the teacher's ability to construct classroom assessment for a particular group of students, these two chapters provide important supplements to Chapter 4 on authentic assessment.

With all of the discussion about authentic assessment and performance outcomes assessment, standardized testing is still a major influence in elementary and secondary school education. Chapters 8–10 in Part IV reflect that focus along with some technical elements of assessment that are so central to standardized testing. Besides validity issues and the basic assumptions involved in norm-referenced assessment, your author will look briefly at both aptitude and attitude scales in Chapter 8.

Data measurement and description are important elements of any type of assessment. In norm-referenced assessment there are particular procedures that are central to one's ability to understand and employ standardized test data. Chapter 9 will cover some of these procedures. Although some of the discussion has a statistical element, your author intends it to be straightforward and nonthreatening.

Chapter 9 is an important companion to Chapter 10, "Understanding Standardized Tests." Your author will examine what some of the more common test scores mean and how they compare to alternatives.

The last section of the book, Part V, contains chapters that, in one way or another, transcend the earlier sections. Chapter 11 provides an examination of the growth and applications of computers in assessment. Computer use has changed assessment dramatically and promises to continue to be an influence, particularly for the teacher in the classroom, where initial computer applications were designed almost exclusively for instructional purposes.

Although a formal discussion of ethical consideration does not emerge until Chapter 12, it is implicit in nearly every assessment issue that is covered. Having worked through the earlier chapters, readers will have a context for understanding the potential ethical problems discussed in Chapter 12. It is important to consider these issues now, during your preparation, before you find yourself in a situation that prompts you to compromise a principle that may result in harming a student or misrepresenting data.

There are some topics for which in-depth discussions are usually beyond the scope of an introductory assessment text, yet they are so closely related to topics that must be covered, they warrant at least an introduction. Chapter 13 presents many of these topics to enhance your understanding of this text.[2] If your author does his part, the material should whet the appetites of some to pursue these topics in greater detail.

SUMMARY

Education involves unique circumstances. Many of those engaged in it are scrutinized and sometimes criticized by people with no professional training in the field. Particularly in public education, everyone has the right to claim a voice, and some of the voices are acerbic. Bracey (1992) quoted a national columnist's assessment of "the bewildering failure of American education" (p. 5). It is a summary judgment offered by someone whose livelihood depends on his ability to attract a readership. However, educators can be forgiven for taking umbrage because there is a good deal of evidence (Bracey went on to cite some of it) that the charge is unfair and inaccurate. This book won't alter the fact that educational failures get more publicity than do educational successes, but it does provide educators with a series of lenses through which to view students' learning. You may not be able to correct all of the distorted perceptions, but you will be able to get a more accurate fix on the progress of the students in your classroom.

Although teachers *can* do a credible job of evaluating students' performances, there is evidence that they sometimes do not. Most of the emphasis in teacher preparation programs is directed at the instructional component. Assessment processes, techniques, and outcomes receive comparatively little attention, and there is ample room for improvement.

Besides a fundamental lack of emphasis, some of the blame for a comparatively weak assessment track record lies with the tendency to separate assessment from the balance of the educational program. When that happens, assessment loses its context. The assessment of the performance becomes dissociated from the factors that affect the performance. In fact, assessment should be viewed as an integral part of the process, with the potential to improve each of the other planning, preparation, and delivery components.

Norm- and criterion-references were introduced in this chapter because they help interpret assessment outcomes more accurately. Although some qualities transcend norm- and criterion-referenced assessment systems, each approach makes different assumptions about students and learning. One cannot hope to interpret the results accurately without recognizing those assumptions (Schilling and Schilling, 1998).

Although one cannot be arbitrary, there is no best way to organize an assessment textbook. Be reminded that Part I creates a context for assessment. Part II addresses criterion-referenced assessment and issues related to grading and standards. Although standardized testing has a great impact on individual classrooms, most of the assessments teachers conduct are probably according to criteria. Part III helps us develop items and construct tests for classroom application. Although technically the application might be either norm- or criterion-referenced, your author hopes to convince you that circumstances usually call for the latter. An assessment text must inevitably lead to an examination of standardized testing and its related issues. That is the focus of

Part IV, which is followed by issues dealing with computers in assessment, ethics in assessment, and other more advanced topics in Part V. As the man in the car commercial used to say, "Enjoy the ride."

ENDNOTES

1. Even so, note that we haven't established whether 7 points beyond the norm matters much or whether it is, to use a statistical term, "significant."
2. One of the author's very helpful reviewers suggested that not only was it risky to offer a Chapter 13 at all, but to load it with some of the more extended discussions was tantamount to a literary "death wish." Your author will leave that for you to decide. You can reach him at davidt@zimmer.csufresno.edu.

REFERENCES

Andrews, T. E., and Barnes, S. (1990). Assessment of teaching. In W. R. Houston (Ed.), *Handbook of research on teacher education* (pp. 569–598). New York: Macmillan.

Bracey, G. W. (1992). What assessment and research say about the condition of education. *Educational Measurement: Issues and Practice, 11*(4), 5–6, 41.

Bunderson, C. V., Inouye, D. K., and Olsen, J. B. (1989). The four generations of computerized educational measurement. In R. L. Linn (Ed.), *Educational measurement* (3rd ed., pp. 367–407). New York: Macmillan.

Glaser, R. (1963). Instructional technology and the measurement of learning outcomes: Some questions. *American Psychologist, 18,* 519–521.

Glaser, R. (1994). Instructional technology and the measurement of learning outcomes: Some questions. *Educational Measurement: Issues and Practice, 13*(4), 6–8.

Koelsch, N., Estrin, E. T., and Farr, B. (1995). *Guide to developing equitable performance assessments.* Washington, DC: Office of Educational Research and Development. (ERIC Document Reproduction Service No. ED 397 125)

Medley, D. (1985). Issues and problems in the validation of teaching and teacher professional behaviors. Paper presented at the annual meeting of the American Educational Research Association, Chicago.

Merriam-Webster's collegiate dictionary (10th ed.). (1994). Springfield, MA: Merriam-Webster.

Novak, J. D. (1998). *Learning, creating, and using knowledge.* Mahwah, NJ: Lawrence Erlbaum.

Principles and indicators for student assessment systems. (1995). Cambridge, MA: National Center for Fair and Open Testing. (ERIC Document Reproduction Service No. ED 400 334)

Schilling, K. M., and Schilling, K. L. (1998). Proclaiming and sustaining excellence: Assessment as a faculty role. *ASHE-ERIC Higher Education Reports, 26*(3). Washington, DC: The George Washington University Graduate School of Education and Human Development.

Stiggins, R. J. (1991). Relevant classroom assessment training for teachers. *Educational Measurement: Issues and Practice, 10*(1), 7–12.

Stodolsky, S. (1985). Teacher evaluation: The limits of looking. *Educational Researcher, 13*(9), 11–18.

Taylor, C. S., and Nolen, S. B. (1996). What does the psychometrician's classroom look like? Reframing assessment concepts in the context of learning. *Education Policy Analysis Archives, 14*(17), 1–18. [On-line]. Available: http://olam.ed.asu.edu/epaa/.

2

Using Assessment Data to Inform Instruction

■ *Readers will begin to view assessment as a mechanism for improving instruction.*

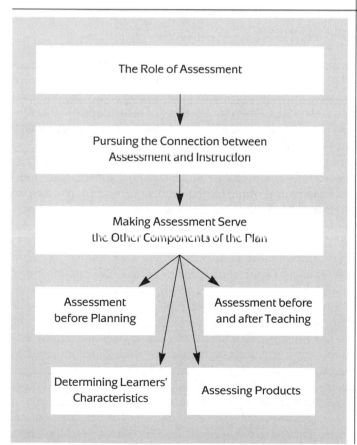

The Role of Assessment

↓

Pursuing the Connection between Assessment and Instruction

↓

Making Assessment Serve the Other Components of the Plan

Assessment before Planning

Assessment before and after Teaching

Determining Learners' Characteristics

Assessing Products

The rationale for the early part of this book rests heavily on our willingness to define assessment in a broader-than-usual context. When considering the larger picture, a logical and very important connection can be made between assessment and instructional quality, and that connection is the focus of this chapter. Your author's intent is to analyze the instructional program in terms of several individual components that can each be improved with assessment data. ■

Mr. Blumell looked closely at the letter grades listed opposite students' names in his grade book. It had not taken long for performance to settle into a pattern. One fairly stable group of learners usually scored well on each test, and another also quite predictable group usually did poorly. There were exceptions, however. On some tests, the entire continuum appeared to shift when the class as a whole exceeded his expectations, or when they struggled more with an assessment than he had anticipated. The student-to-student differences seemed easy enough to explain: Some students worked harder than others, and some certainly seemed brighter than others. But how was Mr. Blumell to explain shifts in the entire class's performance? Were they more motivated at some times than at others? When the entire class did poorly, could the responsibility safely be placed with the students? How else could changes in the performance of the group be explained? As he reviewed the grades, Mr. Blumell wondered whether the assessment data he gathered might reveal something more about the learning activities than merely how students performed. ■

THE ROLE OF ASSESSMENT

Mr. Blumell is not alone when he thinks of assessment primarily in terms of evaluating student achievement. His questions suggest promise, however. In broader terms, educational assessment provides the opportunity to move substantially beyond analyzing student performance and to begin to think in terms of other educational components. Assessment can reveal much about the quality of those components, as well as inform us about student performance.

There *is* a great deal of value in grading, of course. It is important as a performance indicator, and grades usually communicate much information about the individual student's standing. This is important to the students, to their parents, to educators, and sometimes even to the general public. Assessment has a broader purpose, however. It can be a mechanism for improving teaching, reviewing educational goals, and evaluating educational programs generally. If we restrict assessment to grading the students, we have missed most of its potential.

The broader view of assessment is not new. Some years ago, Bloom, Hastings, and Madaus (1971) suggested that when we view assessment as we ought to, it can serve these wider purposes. This possibility exists because student performance is one part of a complex enterprise. Student performance data can be the beginning, but the value of those performance data lies also in where they lead. It does not require any special intuition, for example, to know that student performance is connected to teaching quality. This means that when we begin to analyze achievement data and ask questions about why students perform as they do, one avenue leads us to inquire about instructional quality. In turn, instruction draws one to examine the curriculum that provides for the instructional activities, and so on. The elements of the instructional plan do not exist in isolation. Their interconnections lead us from one to the other, which makes assessment a much more ambitious task than just grading students. This idea represents the substance of this chapter.

Your author uses the term *assessment,* rather than **measurement** or **evaluation,** advisedly. Measurement and evaluation both tend to conjure up quite formal images of tests and testing. They are important elements of the business of gathering data (measurement) and making judgments about what the data reveal (evaluation). Both will be focal points at times, but they are too limited in scope to be applied to the broader purposes of improving teaching and learning generally.

You will recall from Chapter 1 that measurement is usually thought of as essentially a data-gathering activity. In formal definition, it is called the process of assigning numbers to data according to rules. This is an important component of assessment, but only the part that provides the raw material.

Evaluation involves judging the adequacy or the quality of some product. The risk is that one may focus *only* on the outcomes and ignore many of the earlier processes that can help teachers understand them. Perhaps students in two different classes of tenth-grade biology have the same textbook and spend the same amount of time with the material, but there are significantly different levels of achievement when final data are gathered. If the students from the higher performing class participated in a substantial lab component, and that was the only difference found, we should want to weigh that information, too. When one isolates the students' performances, one misses the opportunity to examine other factors that may help reveal why the learning occurred as it did. If reciting the multiplication tables has a greater positive impact on arithmetic test scores than more assigned calculation problems, it is important to interpret the student performance data in terms of that information.

> In order to be comprehensive, educational assessment activities ought to include all data-gathering and decision-making activities that affect teaching and learning outcomes

Educational **assessment** includes all of the data-gathering and evaluative processes that allow us to understand teaching and learning. Remember that the concept of assessment as *processes* is important because it helps us steer clear of treating it only as a culminating event (Lambdin and Forseth, 1996).

Clearly, your author is casting a wider assessment net than what classroom testing usually suggests. Armstrong (1994) maintained that the broader view of assessment involves several elements. At some point in educational assessment, one will wish to

1. measure how well students attain curricular and instructional goals,
2. determine what they know and need,
3. modify instruction on the basis of assessment data, and
4. define and, perhaps, compare students' performances.

Note that the traditional view of student assessment involves just the final component. Belk and Calais (1993) provide a summary of the discussion to this point:

> *Assessment should be an integral component of the curriculum. It should provide the teacher with a means of evaluating not only the child's progress, but also program goals and objectives as well as the extent to which methods of instruction are helping children accomplish these goals. (p. 3)*

There must be clarity on another point. People generally think of assessment data as a set of test scores, but assessment products may take on a variety of forms depending on what is assessed and what assessment purpose one has adopted. We will see, for example, that when one conducts an assessment to determine whether learners are ready for a particular lesson or whether they are making proper progress during a lesson, both approaches are different from how one tries to gauge students' performances after the instruction concludes. Even the data dealing with only student achievement suggest different procedures, depending on what is assessed and the students' levels of sophistication. The assessment data from a standardized reading test are different from the data derived from examining students' reading portfolios.

PURSUING THE CONNECTION BETWEEN ASSESSMENT AND INSTRUCTION

When one adopts the position that assessment ought to be a mechanism for improving teaching and learning (Bloom et al., 1971), educational planning, instruction, and assessment all become connected, and there is an implicit message that they ought to be approached as a coherent whole. Your author hinted at this connection in the introduction. Assessment might be viewed as the "glue" that holds the other components in the educational plan together, and when it is implemented properly, assessment offers the potential to make each part of the educational sequence more effective.

This issue arises because the consistency one hopes for among the various educational activities isn't always the order of the day. Too often, instruction and assessment are undertaken piecemeal, and sometimes efforts are simply misdirected. Maybe some examples will help in recognizing these problems.

The Risk of Disconnecting Assessment

Teachers of seventh-grade English students have a variety of goals for them during the term. Perhaps one is that the students will learn to enjoy reading more. What type of assessment is called for by such a goal? If the goal is accomplished, it is because, by the end of the semester, the students enjoy reading more than they did before. To say it a little differently, the goal is stated in relative terms, and the only way to evaluate it is to know how students felt about reading when the term began. Furthermore, reading enjoyment is connected to what we read (as engrossing as they are, you probably view reading textbooks differently than you view reading the newspaper or a novel). The teacher must know how well students read and what kinds of things they have read in the past. Those are questions that are answered, with any level of confidence, only after a thoughtful assessment, and perhaps after multiple assessments.

Aligning Assessment with Instruction

Sometimes the assessment, although it reflects a substantial time investment, fails to yield the information needed to make correct decisions. This can occur for many reasons, but it is particularly common if what is taught and what is assessed aren't aligned very well. If the instructional material illustrates how authors use a story's setting to help develop the theme, but the assessment centers on the characters, the data cannot reveal how well students understand the relationship between setting and theme. If this has been the focus of instruction, it must also be central to the assessment.

This sort of disconnection can also occur when instructors allow convenience to become the overriding factor in assessment. Sometimes the time crunch tempts one to select an "off-the-shelf" test. Perhaps it's the test the instructor used in a prior term or, worse yet, someone else's test. During the course of classroom instruction, we usually develop something tailored to the particular instruction. If we use something already developed, then we at least make modifications that reflect the particular learning activities; otherwise the assessment may miss the mark. When the test does not reflect what we taught, we have a problem in content validity. That issue will be pursued in some detail in Chapter 7 in connection with other test construction issues. For now, just note that it is another example of a potential discontinuity between the assessment and the instruction.

Do the Data Make a Difference?

When student assessment data are aggregated so that we are looking at classroom tendencies rather than an individual student's performance, they can provide very useful information regarding which elements of the instructional plan are working well and which are not. However, the data are helpful only if someone is willing to interpret them, and there is evidence that teachers can be quite selective in how they read achievement data. Some time ago, Ames (1982) reported a finding that Barros, Neto, and Barros (1989) replicated some years later. Although teachers believe that their own teaching behaviors are a factor in students' success, they are less eager to accept responsibility for students' academic failures. Since it is illogical that success, but not failure, is related to the teacher's performance (either both success and failure are connected to teaching behaviors or neither is), it seems we have a problem. When students are struggling, teachers appear to ignore data that could reveal a great deal about instructional planning and delivery.[1]

For Further Discussion

Having assessment data available is no guarantee that they will be used well. It's one thing to gather the information and draw conclusions, and sometimes quite another to see that the data are actually implemented in a way that improves the educational program. In fact, classroom instructors' willingness to make changes hinges on their answers to some questions:

Does student performance reflect teaching performance?

How closely are they related?

Is it fair to hold instructors responsible for students' performances?

The point is that, as logical as the relationship is between assessment and other educational activities, the coordination that ought to occur often is not the order of the day. In fact, none of the problems previously described are uncommon. There are probably many reasons. Ignorance, confusion, and the fragility of egos are among them, but one of the central difficulties is simply the way we often view assessment. If it is treated as a culminating activity rather than a process that can inform a number of elements, there is little incentive to make changes. We have effectively "shut the barn door after the horse is gone." The key is to begin to think of assessment as an integral element in each component of the educational process rather than a final procedure conducted so that students can be graded.

MAKING ASSESSMENT SERVE THE OTHER COMPONENTS OF THE PLAN

Thus far, the focus has been to build a case for an expanded role for assessment. Clearly, student performance is at least a partial reflection of the quality of the other elements in the educational plan, so it makes sense that assessment data ought to inform each of those other components. An instructional model by Armstrong, Denton, and Savage (1978) will help clarify the relationship between assessment and the other factors in classroom learning. It was originally developed to illustrate the fact that educational processes consist of several interconnected parts. The strength of the model (Figure 2.1) is that it suggests a consistent, logical progression from the early planning activities that precede instruction to the final assessment activities, *with assessment interwoven throughout.*

Note how thoroughly assessment is integrated with each of the other components. The several arrows suggest that, at each point in the plan's development, assessment data can provide the basis for the next set of decisions. Actually, the model suggests that we can look back at what has already occurred as well as forward. If it is designed carefully, the final assessment provides evaluative data that allow us to improve the earlier components of the plan before we use them again. Besides indicating student performance levels, the assessment data can reveal whether the objective was appropriate, whether our assumptions about students' knowledge were accurate, whether the instructional strategies were effective, and the like.

The model also suggests that, at least in this case, the assessment data are connected to the objectives that follow. Learning the multiplication tables, for example, opens the way for students to learn division. If learning the multiplication tables is the first objective, the assessment that follows the instruction can reveal a great deal about how prepared students are for the following objective.

Instructional objectives are not always incremental, with one leading logically to the next, but there is always some re-

> The goal-referenced model is an educational planning model. In it, everything in the plan stems from the initial goal, and assessment is connected to each component so that the assessment data reveal something about the performance of the students and the instructor and about the educational plan as a whole.

The Educational Goal

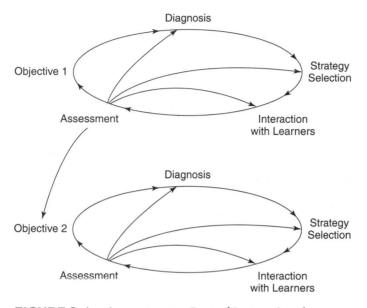

FIGURE 2.1 Assessment as Part of Instructional
Planning and Implementation

Source: From *Instructional Skills Handbook* (p. 14), by D. G. Armstrong,
J. J. Denton, and T. V. Savage, 1978, Englewood Cliffs, NJ: Educational
Technology Publications. Copyright 1978 by Educational Technology Pub-
lications. Adapted with permission.

lationship between them. At the least, the objectives emerge from a common discipline, and the skills and abilities that one develops in an instructional sequence can
be used in later activities.

In areas such as math and reading, the incremental relationship is particularly evident. In those subjects, one objective builds so squarely upon the next that the educator must be very attentive to assessment data. When we ignore the data other than
to assign a grade, we overlook information that will help us understand what students
must yet learn before they can successfully continue.

Assessment and Planning

Any instructional activity we plan involves assumptions about what learners already
know. Indeed, part of the value of the assessment we conduct after instruction is in the
opportunity it offers to verify the assumptions made when the unit was in the planning
stages. Sometimes the assumptions are so pivotal that one must verify them before proceeding. When United States History is a two-semester course, it is common to end the
first semester with the Civil War and begin the second with material on the postwar Reconstruction. Students can understand neither the Civil War nor Reconstruction very

well, however, unless they have read, discussed, and grasped the factors that contributed to the development of sectionalism in the country. Someone who is planning the second course must first determine how well students understand the growth of the sectional tendencies that competed with nationalism.

If students don't understand the concepts, it doesn't necessarily mean that the instructional plan is faulty, but it does mean that something is incomplete. Remedial instruction must usually precede the other planned activities. Assessing students' grasp of the issues is the key to making good decisions about whether to proceed with the instruction or to take time to offer remedial work first. There is no set form for the assessment, however. It might be a traditional paper and pencil test that the instructor administers before the new instructional unit begins. As an alternative, one might use a guided discussion that will allow the instructor to ask students questions about (in this example) sectionalism.

The questions are usually just a beginning place. The answers ought to be carefully probed to develop a clear understanding of what the students know. Simply asking the learners, "Do you remember studying sectionalism last term?" will probably not be very helpful; students usually do not want to admit that they do not remember, or that they do not understand.

Beyond content knowledge, the instructor must also know something about the students' skills. Their reading, writing, and analytical skills will matter in any academic discipline. The ability to appraise students' work accurately, particularly when the teacher is unfamiliar with the students, requires important prerequisite information in the planning process. Often a sample of work from some prior learning exercise is helpful. When work samples are not available, teachers can usually get the information they need with a seatwork or homework assignment, but it must be designed to call upon the skills and knowledge that are prerequisite to what students will do next.

Goals and Objectives

The point of all learning activities is to provide an opportunity for students to develop skills or knowledge that they do not have. Usually, statements of intent accompany the learning activities. Sometimes the statements are very formal and prominent, saying something like, "By the end of the grading period, each second-grade reading student will . . . ." Even when the intended outcomes are less apparent, we can usually find evidence for them in the instructional activities. A physical science unit on soil conservation prepared for secondary school students might list no formal objectives. Even so, a film that depicts the dust bowl conditions in the midwestern United States during the Great Depression provides its own clues. The pictures and narrative may suggest that students should come to recognize the cultivation methods and climate conditions that contributed to the wind erosion of the soil.

Identifying the author's intent is important because even if someone specifies the learning **objectives,** the person using the material must still determine what the intended outcomes were in order to pinpoint what to assess. Absent this information, there is no direct way to determine whether teachers and students were successful, nor can one evaluate the learning materials themselves.

> Goals and objectives are important because they specify educational purposes. They guide not just the instruction, but also the educational assessment activities.

By clarifying the purposes for the learning activities, the **goals** and objectives provide the framework for what will follow in the instructional setting. So in addition to general concerns about determining whether students and teachers were successful, goals and objectives help one determine what to preassess, as well, so that one can evaluate students' readiness. At the conclusion of the program, we must know whether the students learned what we had planned for them to learn. Defined objectives guide assessment, wherever it occurs, just as it guides the selection of instructional strategies.

Educational goals are usually defined as general statements of what the instructor intends to accomplish. We might want students to become better problem solvers, or participate more in class discussions, or perhaps become more physically fit. The related objectives are more specific. They are subordinate to the goal, and in more particular language, they indicate how the planners intend to realize the goal. In Figure 2.2 we can see the relationship between goals such as those we just mentioned and some related objectives.

FIGURE 2.2   Goals and Their Related Objectives

Goal: Students will become better problem solvers.

Objectives
- Sixth-grade students will solve four out of five story problems successfully.
- Presented with a historical dilemma, each senior history student will explain how diplomacy might have been used to avoid military conflict.
- Given the economic factors relevant to life in the Amazon Basin, physical science students will develop a plan that will allow greater prosperity for the residents *and* preservation of the rain forest.

Goal: Students will participate more in class discussions.

Objectives
- Every student will ask at least one question or volunteer at least one answer during the week.
- Twice each week, classroom activities will include small-group discussions.

Goal: Students will become more physically fit.

Objectives
- Each physical education student will jog one mile in 10 minutes or less.
- By the end of the semester, each student's resting heart rate will slow by 5 percent.
- Each student will participate in at least one intramural sport during the academic year.
- Each student will be required to take at least one physical education course that emphasizes a lifelong sport.

It used to be common for instructional designers and classroom teachers to write objectives according to a very rigid format, using language that allowed the assessor to verify by direct observation whether learners met the objective. Although it isn't nearly as common as it was in the days when behavioral psychology was more prominent, some educators still follow the practice. It has the effect of making assessment a good deal easier. The assessor usually needs to engage in very little interpretation to determine whether students met the objective.

In the language of assessment, when a behavior is obvious enough that it can be determined with little analysis, it is called a **low inference behavior.** The student's ability to spell particular words is an example of a low inference behavior. A simple spelling test allows the teacher to verify whether the student possesses the skill.

Problem-solving ability, on the other hand, is a relatively **high inference behavior.** It involves cognitive activities that are usually evident only with several inferences. Those who design the objectives try to simplify the task of assessing such behaviors by selecting activities that can be completed only by those students possessing the ability one is trying to teach, but the assessment may still require multiple inferences. Students may have several problems to solve and several activities to participate in before convincing the instructor that they are effective problem solvers.

> One way to gauge the behaviors we try to measure is in terms of how much inference the observer must draw to establish the behavior. Low inference behaviors (can the learner spell the word?) are easy to recognize. They require a brief observation or perhaps an item or two on an assessment. High inference behaviors (does the learner understand atomic weight?) require a number of indicators and perhaps several detailed items on an assessment before one has the assurance that students possess the behaviors.

When people use a format for objectives such that they carefully spell out the exact behaviors they expect to see, they often also specify who must perform the behavior, how well they must perform, and when the assessment will take place. Using this approach, we might have developed an objective for the goal at the beginning of the chapter that we could frame this way:

> On a chapter quiz, each teacher candidate will list 5 ways that assessment data can be used to improve the quality of instruction.

The "chapter quiz" defines when the assessment will take place. "Each teacher candidate" specifies the intended audience. Listing ways that assessment can improve instruction is the behavior we're interested in, and the "5" is the standard that will satisfy us that the objective was met.

Instructional Autonomy

Traditionally, goals and objectives—in fact, all facets of the educational plan—were the instructor's to formulate and develop. Classroom teachers had a good deal of latitude to respond to what they decided were the most compelling educational needs. Probably, some of the goals and objectives reflected the philosophy of the instructor as much as they reflected the interests of the public. Although a certain amount of instructional autonomy remains for elementary and secondary teachers, there is now much more oversight than was the case in the past. Prompted by disappointment in students' educational progress, government agencies have tried to legislate reforms by using states' departments of education to generate frameworks and curricula that are intended to provide more rigor and more uniformity. One of the reasons we are interested is that the new materials also usually include new performance standards that become the assessment criteria. Although there will surely be differences in emphasis from one classroom to the next, and instructors may continue to develop some of their own goals and objectives, all of this may exist within a framework that someone else has developed. A domain that was once the exclusive purview of the classroom teacher now receives much of its definition elsewhere.

These changes have important implications for assessment. It is sometimes disconcerting for classroom teachers to assess and accept accountability for outcomes that they did not define and toward which they feel little personal ownership. This issue will be examined with more care in Chapter 3.

There are other external influences in assessment activities. Sometimes specialists from beyond the classroom administer tests that the classroom teachers lack the expertise to handle. This has always been the case with intelligence testing in the schools, for example, but a related influence occurs when assessment data are collected at one location and affect the programs in others. This is what happens when a national sample indicates that students in a particular grade are weak in world geography, for example, and states respond by mandating changes to the social studies curriculum among students of that age to address the "deficit." The changes may be very helpful, but they reflect influences beyond the individual classroom teacher's control and so contribute to a loss of autonomy.

This can also occur at the school level when assessment data indicate that some fifth-grade students have average reading scores below grade level and administrators require all fifth-grade teachers to adjust their reading programs. The assessment data used in some planning activities may not be specific to the particular setting, but if conditions are similar enough to be useful, they may provide the impetus for changes.

Assessment for Developing Goals and Objectives

Educational goals and objectives don't emerge out of isolation. They exist because someone gathered assessment data at some point earlier in the process. Often the data gathering consists of the informal observations that teachers make about students' strengths and weaknesses, but in some instances the activities are quite formal. Someone who wishes to encourage more reading among students may review the research to determine the factors that are associated with reading for pleasure. The *Education Index,* the *Current Index to Journals in Education,* and other summaries of the published literature make it comparatively easy to compile research findings about what makes a difference and what may not. Computer databases and the availability of the Internet are also excellent data-gathering resources.

It is attractive (at least to your author) to think that occasionally teachers form objectives based on formal reviews of the scholarly literature, but that probably isn't very realistic. Besides (or perhaps because of) the fact that the time to conduct the research is usually in short supply, many instructors rely heavily on personal beliefs to form their goals and objectives. There is still an assessment involved, but it is the much less formal business of reviewing one's experiences in order to identify the factors that are related to reading for pleasure. Experience may suggest, for example, that students enjoy a short story most when they understand the story's plot, setting, and theme. This may prompt the instructor to try to boost reading pleasure—the goal—by constructing objectives that teach students how to identify the plot, the setting, and the theme of the short story and how to analyze the relationships among them.

The most general educational goals are frequently self-evident and comparatively stable. The goals for greater literacy, for more refined problem-solving abilities, or for a well-developed appreciation of the aesthetic are all examples of goals that remain relatively fixed over time, largely because they are so general. They are broad enough that probably any culture or civilization values them, which makes such things easy to agree upon, as long as they are kept abstract.

Their more specific nature makes objectives more concrete and sometimes also more objectionable. They are specific enough to be easy to assess, but they have an inherent instability. Any changes in the relevant conditions may affect the objective, even if the more general goal remains unaltered. The goal might be for students to appreciate good literature. Probably no one will take issue with it, and, without doubt, schools a hundred years ago had some similar goal. Consider a related objective, however. In the 1970s, the *Autobiography of Malcolm X* was part of a very popular literary genre in university and some secondary school courses. One rarely hears it mentioned in our own time, however. One of assessment's roles is to reveal the changing conditions that lead us to modify objectives. We can illustrate this situation with the example below.

> Goals are stated in quite general terms and tend to be stable over time. Objectives, however, are more specific and may change as relevant conditions are altered. Effective assessment will reveal the need to adjust objectives.

Changing Conditions and Changing Objectives

Many cultures try to foster students' problem-solving abilities by emphasizing mathematics performance. This is a goal that has been stable for hundreds of years in all advanced cultures. Basic calculation ability is generally emphasized, but usually as a means to more sophisticated problem-solving abilities. Historically, the Chinese used the abacus so that their complex math-related problems could be solved more quickly. Today we use calculators and electronic computers to serve the same purposes.

Prior to the 1970s, hand-held electronic calculators were unknown. For those who were obliged to perform a substantial amount of basic calculation, the slide rule was probably the most useful tool, but science and engineering people were the primary users. For most of the rest of the world, and particularly in the secondary school, mathematics objectives assumed that students would learn to work their way longhand through certain necessary mathematical functions. One's ability to calculate the square root of a number, for instance, was very important because a number of mathematical solutions require the use of square root products.

Today hand-held calculators, many of which have a square root function, are both common and inexpensive. Their ubiquitous nature has eliminated the need for most people to perform square root calculations, and probably no one but the occasional mathematics purist bothers with it. The concept of square root is still very important and has wide mathematical application, but calculators are so common that it is unlikely that very many people actually perform the calculations anymore, or even know how to perform them.

At some point, someone assessed current practice and, recognizing how the availability of hand calculators was changing conditions, decided that actually calculating square root was no longer necessary. Once the calculations no longer appeared as test questions, objectives devoted to the skill were likewise set aside. The skill may still have been taught initially, but more out of appreciation for the concept than for the utility of actually completing the calculation. Gradually, the objectives devoted to the task were eliminated entirely so that today they are absent, even though learners are still expected to perform a variety of other calculations that employ square root products. The business of assessing current practice in light of changing conditions continues—usually on a less dramatic scale.

> Occasionally, circumstances change enough that educational objectives change as well. Appropriate assessment allows one to recognize that the foundations for current practice have been sufficiently altered and that instructional practice must be modified.

In the square root example, an assessment of what students ought to be able to do in order to be skilled problem solvers altered the type of questions posed on tests, and objectives and instruction were adjusted accordingly. Note that the problem-solving goal has not changed. It remains something that every modern society emphasizes, and perhaps mathematical problem solving is more important now than ever. The assessment role in this instance had two parts: (a) to recognize that conditions had changed and that the way problem solving should be taught needed to change as well and (b) to modify assessment to emphasize the use of, rather than the calculation of, square root products.[2]

Preassessment

However logical the objective is in terms of what it was intended to help learners accomplish, it must be tempered with information about the current group of learners. To say it differently, the objective must not only further the goals we have adopted, but it must be appropriate for the students we are teaching at the time. Learning to appreciate good literature is a widely accepted educational goal. Studying Hamlet's relationship to the other characters in Shakespeare's play is an objective that may well further such a goal, but it isn't appropriate for second-grade students. It may not even be appropriate for high school seniors if they read substantially below grade level. The students must be prepared for the reading level (which is inadequate in both groups) and the nature of the content (which is probably too mature for seven- and eight-year-old children).

Preassessment, or what is more specifically pre-*instructional* assessment, ought to reveal any unusual needs learners may have. It also ought to suggest where we can best begin the instruction. Nitko (1989) noted that there are two kinds of decisions we make about students based on preassessment data—diagnostic decisions and placement decisions.

Diagnostic Decisions

In addition to the aptitude and achievement differences that distinguish learners generally, there are differences that make some learners' needs so dissimilar from most of their classmates' that we must make special provision for them. These "exceptional students" are those who have psychological, physical, or emotional conditions so serious that we must deal with them differently than we deal with others (Nitko, 1989).

Sometimes a debilitating condition is immediately apparent. Physical disabilities are sometimes immediately apparent, but some conditions are less obvious and may require quite sophisticated assessment procedures. At some point, anyone who makes a career as a classroom instructor will determine by either formal or informal assessment processes that a condition exists that impacts a student's performance and of which even the student may be unaware.

Before the middle 1970s, diagnosing a significant learning impairment usually meant that the student was excluded from regular school activities, but in the United States, the passage of Public Law 94-142 altered the traditional response permanently. Employing the "equal protection clause" of the Fourteenth Amendment to the Constitution as a legal base, Congress provided that all children in the United States are entitled to a free, public education in an appropriate environment. Increasingly, that environment is defined to mean that students with disabilities are included in conventional classrooms. The effect of those changes finds wide approval among educators, but the task of developing an educational plan that accommodates all students can substantially complicate the teacher's task.

Although educators are attentive to students' emotional/behavioral conditions as well as to their academic performance, it is often the latter that the typical classroom teacher relies upon for information about disabilities, particularly learning disabilities. Scoring differences between students are primarily an expression of aptitude, ability, and experience differences, but if there is a scoring difference that cannot be explained by those causes, it may reflect a disability. This can be a very complex problem because the instructor must be familiar enough to know when the student's performance and ability are so out of harmony that one must look to other factors for an explanation. Students who do not speak the primary language well, or (more difficult to detect) who have developed conversation skills but lack the academic language of the classroom, further complicate the issue. Responding to handicaps is primarily the purview of special education teachers, but it is often some other teacher who first recognizes a problem because of factors emerging from assessment data.

Placement Decisions

The way they are posed here, placement decisions are not the sort whereby we decide in which class to place the learner. Most classroom instructors have very little latitude about learner placement in that sense, but deciding the point in the curriculum at which to begin instruction is another kind of placement decision. It ought to reflect careful assessment.

Learning programs are always based upon assumptions about what the intended audience already knows and about what learning environment is most appropriate (Nitko, 1989). The required information may be gathered several ways. One approach is to use a pretest, which can:

- establish the learners' levels of skill,
- provide information about what content has already been taught,
- establish the learners' levels of interest in what is to be taught, and
- detect the presence of a handicap or other unusual condition that should affect how the instruction is presented.

The pretest data provide a baseline measure against which to gauge the students' future learning. Gathering baseline data is not unique to pretests since any test can perform the role of the pretest, but it is the pretest's particular function. Much of the assessment that follows can focus on improvement (Armstrong, 1994).

Most learning tasks involve several abilities rather than just one or two. Of course, when students lack some required skill or ability, their opportunity to benefit from the activity suffers. An activity developed to teach students to prepare book reports is not helpful to the child who cannot read any of the books from the selection list. One way to identify the prerequisites to a learning activity is to use **task analysis.**[3]

> Task analyses are assessment mechanisms that help us identify, in order, all of the skills and knowledge that are prerequisites to a particular learning product. One begins with the end product and works systematically backward, a level at a time, by asking what is immediately prerequisite to each subordinate accomplishment.

One conducts a task analysis by working from the final learning product backward, in order, through each of the activities that precede the final product until one has identified even the most elemental prerequisite abilities (Solity, 1991). At each level, one identifies the knowledge and abilities that the learner must possess to achieve the outcome. Before students can learn to write in a cursive style, for example, they must be able to print. Before they can print, they must have learned to read and to form letters. Before they learned to read, they learned the sounds letters make, and so on. At a time when task analysis was very popular, Gagne (1963) explained it this way:

> *When we consider a final performance to be learned, . . . we find that it can be analyzed into a number of subordinate topics which must first be mastered before the final task can be attained. These topics in turn depend upon the mastery of other subordinate topics. This kind of analysis, then, results in the identification of a hierarchy of subordinate knowledges. . . . Mastering the subordinate knowledge is considered to be essential to the attainment of a related higher-level topic; learning of the latter cannot occur without it. (p. 622)*

We can be more aware of what we are asking of learners when we develop an ordered list of all that a planned activity entails. The list also informs us of the areas most likely to be problematic. Although it isn't complete, Figure 2.3 is an example of the task analysis conducted before learners are assigned to write a book report.

Of course, task analysis also makes assumptions about the knowledge of the person who completes it. It requires that one be aware of all of the skills or abilities on which each learning product depends. In our example, a written book report has as a prerequisite the students' ability to read and write. In turn, reading and writing have their own prerequisites. Reading requires that the student be able to decode print, comprehend what is meant, and so on. As one identifies each of the immediate prerequisites, something like a map evolves. The destination is the end product, but the

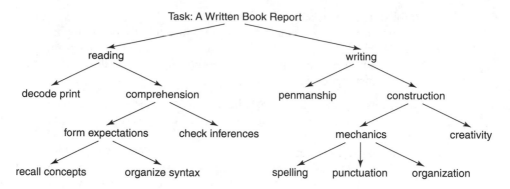

FIGURE 2.3   A Task Analysis for a Book Report

earlier portions should indicate, in order, each of the subordinate skills, abilities, or knowledge that allows one to reach the product. It is a good idea to conduct a task analysis while instructional planning is underway, because its detailed nature also provides the information needed for an informative pretest.

By the way, task analysis does not provide just one most accurate listing of the prerequisites to a learning product. Gagne's (1963, p. 622) question, "What must the learner know how to do in order to achieve this new performance?" can prompt different answers depending on the audience, the instructor's emphasis, and the circumstances under which one will proceed. Perhaps you don't care about writing mechanics until after learners have developed some confidence and creativity in their writing. In that case, spelling, punctuation, and the like may not even be listed on the task analysis.

Task analysis is just one procedure that allows one to identify what a new learning activity requires. There are alternatives, but whatever the approach, one must identify the prerequisites and develop a procedure that allows the educator to evaluate whether students are prepared to proceed. Do they read and write sufficiently well? Do they understand the concepts that we will use? Are their problem-solving skills adequate to the task? Can they work cooperatively with others as the task may require? Fundamentally, how interested are they in the learning activity?

When specific learner skills are the focus, there are a number of methods available. Reading ability can be evaluated by using simple tests such as a Fry's Readability Test (Fry, 1968), which measures the grade level at which a selection is written. Sometimes information about the grade level of a particular selection is not helpful because students' abilities vary so greatly. A Cloze procedure (Bormuth, 1968) will indicate whether a selection is appropriate for a particular group of students, given their reading level. Writing samples may be the best way to assess learners' writing abilities, and we can assess problem-solving ability by requiring learners to work a sample problem.

If we know how interested a learner is in completing an activity, then we have some sense of how great the motivational task will be. **Interest inventories** (Figure 2.4)

FIGURE 2.4   An Interest Inventory

Students: Please review the following activities and rank from 1 to 10 the one you prefer to do the **most** (1) to the one you prefer to do the **least** (10).

—— reading *National Geographic*   —— listening to music
—— playing sports   —— working in the science lab
—— performing in a play   —— reading a short story
—— solving math problems   —— playing board games
—— working on the computer   —— watching "The Learning Channel"

are used to assess students' preference for a series of tasks, in relative terms. The respondent typically ranks a list of activities from the most to the least preferred activity. It follows that we do not get much information about how much the student may enjoy solving math problems, for example, but only whether the student would rather solve math problems than read *National Geographic*. When the instructor and the learners are new to each other, an interest inventory can reveal a great deal about learners' priorities. If the choices are carefully selected, the learners' responses will indicate what the instructor and the subject are competing with for the learners' attention. The topic of interest inventories will appear again in Chapter 8.

The point of the interest inventory, and of all preassessment activities for that matter, is to gather the data one needs to properly prepare the instruction. This means that one must be willing to modify existing material or design new material in a way that makes it consistent with what the assessment reveals. Avoid the trap of relying too heavily on what students should have learned last term. In spite of what they were supposed to have done, requiring that students write a brief biographical sketch of Samuel Taylor Coleridge makes little sense if some of them do not know who Coleridge was, do not know what a biography is, or have not yet used library research resources. If the instruction is adjusted to accommodate such deficits, the learners can still profit from the learning exercises.

Besides revealing where the potential difficulties may be, an effective preassessment may also reveal that students have somehow already met the objective. This underscores the need to conduct assessments early, because if the information comes after the instruction has already been designed, sometimes we are tempted to proceed anyway rather than allowing the planning effort to go for naught. Although periodic reviews are an important component of good instruction, students ordinarily do not want to forge their way a second time through learning activities for skills and abilities they have already developed. Besides, it wastes valuable instructional time.

We want to gather assessment data that allow us to begin a new instructional sequence that neither repeats what was learned (except for intentional reviews) nor imposes what learners are unprepared to do. If the instructor assesses the current group of learners with some care, diagnostic data can provide a wealth of information regarding learners' skills, abilities, interests, and attitudes.

Speaking of Preassessment

What are the questions you should answer before you present a unit on short stories to a sixth-grade class? Would you wish to know which students are familiar with the structure of the short story, to whom the concepts of plot, setting, and theme are familiar? Would it be helpful to know who reads on grade level? How will you know whether the samples from the literature anthology are so demanding that you discourage, rather than encourage, further reading? If you know what students have read in the past, will that affect your selections? Will you want to know how many of your students read for pleasure?

Can you answer these questions by conducting an informal class discussion?
What are the risks involved in asking each student to read aloud in class without first pretesting their reading abilities?

Decisions about how much control the teacher must retain over student activity, including how large the groups should be, and how much variety to allow in learners' responses are also decisions that ought to be made during this preassessment period. These decisions are also directly related to the instructional strategies that will be selected. Instructional strategies, by the way, are frequently chosen on the basis of what has worked in the past. That determination itself is the result of an important assessment.

Preassessment and Elements of Cognitive Style

We spoke above of some of the disabilities that impede students' progress, but there are nonhandicapping conditions relating to the way students think and respond to stimuli that also affect learning. We may wish to consider them when we plan instruction. When students learn best from things they can see, for example, we call them visual learners. A preference for visual or auditory learning stimuli defines a **cognitive style** and suggests the form of instruction that will benefit particular learners. Students in a typical classroom will exhibit a mixture of cognitive styles, and careful preassessment will reveal what they are and allow one to prepare instruction that will accommodate each to some degree. Rather than employing formal instruments, one can usually assess the students' preferred style by observing them. Some students will respond best to the illustrations; others may ask, perhaps several times, for the teacher to explain the concept in words.

When your author was a fifth-grade student on the prairies of Western Canada, Mrs. Meldrum taught a lesson on British Columbia, the neighboring province. She taught the students about a commercial fishing industry that was completely foreign to children accustomed to dry farming and cattle ranching. On one particular day she brought pictures of commercial fishing boats, crab traps, and other visual stimuli, and as she spoke of commercial fishing (auditory stimuli), she distributed crackers and a small portion of crab meat for each student (stimuli involving the senses of taste, smell, feel). Forty years later, the lesson is still vivid for your author, but probably it is for all of the students because the presentation provided multiple stimuli and accommodated a variety of learning styles.

Some of the learning style differences are quite subtle. Beyond the preference for visual versus auditory presentations, for example, some students respond to one characteristic of the material the instructor presents, and others to some other feature. This is sometimes referred to as **perceptual style,** and it separates learners into those who are primarily **field dependent** from those who are **field independent** (Lu and Suen, 1995). Some students develop an overall sense of things, a global, or "big picture" view of a set of complex stimuli. These field dependent students generally recognize the theme in a presentation even though they are not very attentive to the details. Field independent learners, on the other hand, tend to be more focused on detail and more analytical. They are the learners who can explain the relevance of facts and concepts without paying too much attention to the context in which they are set. They are less aware of the larger perceptual field.

Now consider the implications this may have for assessment. The field dependent learner may respond accurately to a question about Crane's theme in *The Red Badge of Courage.* The same student may be unaware of all of the details that help establish the theme, however. The field independent reader, on the other hand, may be very adept at recalling details of the protagonist's experiences, but not relate them to the evolution of the character.

The important point is this: These different responses have little to do with whether the student read the book. For reasons unrelated to their levels of competency or their effort, different students sometimes respond to different elements of the content. The teacher who is aware of the differences may recognize the associated tendencies in students' responses and make adjustments that will give them a more complete grasp of the learning materials. One might emphasize the relevance of detail for the benefit of those who are field dependent and underscore more general themes or patterns to those who tend to be field independent.

The student's tendency to be **impulsive** or **reflective** defines another cognitive style. Entwisle and Hayduk (1981) found that impulsive students generally work quickly and make decisions on the spur of the moment. Those with a reflective style are much more deliberate in their actions. They take time to weigh decisions and choices. Your author once had a student in a statistics class who consistently trailed the others by a substantial margin whenever he worked a problem. Your author's suggestion (born of some frustration) appended to one of the student's tests was that he brush up on his algebra so that the problems could be completed with greater dispatch. The student's response was that his basic math skills were fine, and that he simply preferred to go slowly and work each problem several times. The student was reflective. The instructor happens to be more impulsive, a difference in style that might have been identified with more careful preassessment. It is probably a characteristic that will be revealed by direct questions such as the following:

- Do you prefer to finish an assignment quickly?
- Do you carefully recheck your answers on tests before handing them in?
- Do you ever offer a response that you are not sure of, but which seems right at the time?
- Do you prefer to hand in tests quickly upon completion and be done with them?

Cognitive style and perceptual style suggest that learners respond differently to learning materials, not because their levels of competency differ, but because they are responsive to different characteristics in the learning materials. When preassessment reveals these differences, the instructor is in a better position to understand students' responses and make needed adjustments in the instructional presentation.

We are not suggesting that one must adapt instructional materials to every conceivable difference among learners. To some degree, students need to do the accommodating and adjust to the way instructional materials are presented. No one has time to develop a different set of materials for each student in a large class, but careful preassessment holds the potential to reveal general trends that may exist among students that may improve the effect of an instructional plan.

Assessment before and after Implementation

Demonstrating a feel for the relationship between assessment and instruction, Lambdin and Forseth (1996) noted, "Teachers orchestrate a variety of classroom activities designed to help students learn, but even in the midst of this orchestration they must constantly gather information to make decisions about when to move on, stop, or change direction and when to question . . ." (p. 298).

Earlier (Figure 2.1) it was suggested that assessment should be common to all elements of instructional planning and implementation. It should be particularly evident throughout the implementation period, with alterations made whenever it becomes clear that learners aren't making the anticipated progress. When educators adjust educational programs after planning and during instruction, they do so on the basis of **formative assessment.** The focus in formative assessment is upon particular details of the instruction. This is in contrast to the **summative assessment** conducted after an instructional unit concludes, when a general judgment is made about the success of the plan.

Formative Assessment

Tessmer (1993) described four types of formative assessment. Each is connected to a different review process that can help one refine the instructional presentation. They are expert review, one-on-one assessment, small-group assessment, and field testing.

Expert review occurs when one solicits the feedback from others who have expertise in the discipline or the activity. This happens, for example, when an English teacher asks someone who also has a background in British literature to look over and critique the materials on Elizabethan sonnets prepared for the Honors English class.

One-on-one assessment is available when the instructor gathers information from learners, one at a time. Sometimes teachers have the opportunity to speak informally with former students who used similar materials. In a kind of debriefing session, we may ask students specific questions. Was the section on cell mitosis clear? Were the overheads helpful? Did the homework assignments make sense?

Often students can assist with the next unit based on their experience with the last. Are the homework assignments helping them to learn the material? How much time did the typical assignment require? Were the reading selections interesting? The content will change from unit to unit, but some of the structural elements will carry over, and it is helpful to know what worked well and what went wrong with other parts of the plan.

Small-group assessment occurs when the evaluator can test the instruction in a small trial group and then gather information from those participants. This is probably the type of assessment least accessible to most classroom teachers, but where it is available, it can be among the most helpful because circumstances tend to be quite consistent with conventional presentation.

Sometimes a teacher who has multiple sections of the same course will opt for a "test run"—or field test—of a new learning segment with one group of students and then modify the plan before proceeding with the other students. This is more feasible for secondary school teachers with their multiple sections of students than it usually is for teachers of primary school students.

Formative assessment allows us to fine-tune instruction before it begins for the bulk of the students. Figure 2.5 suggests the role these formative activities can play as we configure the instructional plan. It amplifies the relationship between assessment and,

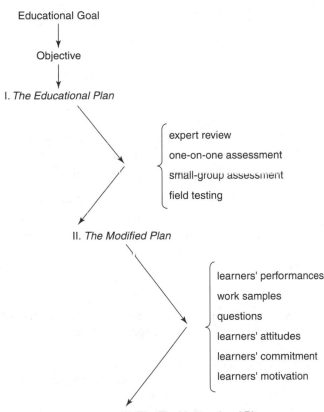

FIGURE 2.5 Formative Assessment and Decisions

in turn, diagnosis, strategy selection, and the interaction with learners that we presented earlier in Figure 2.1.

Once we begin to teach the material, formative assessment tends to be relatively informal. We rely on these sources of evidence:

- The teacher recognizes that repeated questions about a concept indicate confusion among the students and decides that the concept should be discussed more thoroughly, or perhaps approached differently, before proceeding.
- The homework assignments that most students have completed very quickly and correctly suggest that a related instructional component may not be necessary, or that less time will be required with it than was initially planned.
- A reading assignment that baffles students suggests that many lack the background necessary for the particular selection.
- After some initial enthusiasm, interest has waned in a class project, and getting students to meet established deadlines is difficult, which suggests to the teacher that motivation is low. Perhaps initial interest was misjudged, or activities that might have increased student interest have been ineffective.

Note that the general focus in these formative assessment activities is more toward adjustments to the instructor's performance than to the learners'.

Although much of the data is a record of the students' performance, it is primarily the instruction that we wish to make judgments about. There is little point in holding students responsible for inadequate instruction. "Pop quizzes" can probably be effective diagnostic and formative tools, but using them to grade learners makes little sense because they are typically administered when the students are still in the process of learning the material. At this point, student performance should be primarily a gauge of instructional performance. It is the planning, the plan, and the delivery that we are assessing. During the process of instruction, we still have a good opportunity to make the adjustments and corrections that can make the instruction more effective than it will be if we simply forge ahead, ignoring signs indicating that some of what we planned isn't very effective. There will probably be many times during your years in the classroom when instructional plans go badly. That happens to everyone. The greater difficulty occurs when teachers either ignore the signs or blame the students, without making any of the needed adjustments.[4]

> Even though students' scores are gathered in formative assessment, we're not yet interested in grading students. The task is to improve the educational experience for the learners, and their scores are data used to evaluate planning and instruction—not student achievement. Indeed, it is more the instructor's than the students' performance that is of interest.

Formative Assessment and Students' Differences

When we were speaking of preassessment, we made reference to differences in learners' skills and abilities. It may seem to be a statement of the obvious that the extent of students' knowledge affects their ability to perform in the content area (Sugrue, 1995), but there is an important point to be made here. Sometimes we begin instruction with the idea that, since everyone is going to hear and do the same things, everyone will respond similarly to the instruction. It is a convenient assumption with very little support in the realities of the classroom. Even if teachers have a very good feel for what a new learning task requires learners to do, differences in their abilities and experiences will still lead to marked performance variations. It is the task of formative assessment to document these variations, as Bloom et al. (1971) observed when they said, "the main purpose of formative observations is to determine the degree of mastery of a given learning task and to pinpoint the part of the task not mastered" (p. 61). If we know what adjustments to make early in the instruction, we can modify the program for those who are not making appropriate progress.

Assessing the Product

Usually, the product that people are most interested in is student performance. In this chapter, however, student performance data, and indeed the data from all sources, are sources of information about the instructional program. In the language of business, we are interested in quality control. The various assessment activities ought to help us improve the learning experience and validate what appears to be working successfully.

Sometimes we can improve quality with data from outside sources. Because the research literature has become quite comprehensive, a determined investigator can locate reports in the scholarly journals that will address the strengths and weaknesses of most common educational practices. If one is curious about the merits of grouping students according to past achievement, there is a wealth of literature to be consulted on ability grouping. Should one wish to know whether tangible rewards or intangible rewards are best when working with young students, the results are available. The same can be said of a host of other relevant topics ranging from cooperative learning techniques to holistic scoring. It is safe to say that there are very few tactics an instructor will adopt that someone else has not already tried, tested, and written about in one of the scholarly journals.

Noting that helpful information is available is not equivalent to saying that educators use it, however. There might be a variety of reasons for a gap between the theory associated with universities and the practical realities of the classroom. Whatever the explanation, there is evidence that educators sometimes ignore scientific data in favor of convenience, the strength of tradition, or even intuition. This can be illustrated with an example.

Retaining students in grade (the euphemism for requiring that they repeat the grade) for poor performance is very common, and the practice has staunch defenders among both educators and the interested public. The logic behind grade retention isn't difficult to follow. Clearly, those who spend a second year in a class will do better after a poor performance in the initial year. Because the practice of retention in grade is so common, one can be forgiven for thinking that the data support it as an effective quality-control mechanism. Or as an alternative, at least one ought to be able to be safe in assuming that that the logic is so compelling that no one has bothered to conduct a scientific assessment. In fact, neither is the case. There are several comprehensive studies available, and although the research findings are not absolutely uniform, generally, the

> The scholarly research journals provide data regarding most educational practices, but we have to be willing to ferret out and use the data if they are ever to make a difference in the classroom.

findings do not support the practice of grade retention (see Holmes and Matthews, 1984; Mantzicopoulos and Morrison, 1992; or Peterson, DeGracie, and Agabe, 1987 as examples). This means that assessment results are either ignored (Tomchin and Impara, 1992) or they are misinterpreted. This reminds us that, as with each contribution that assessment might make to quality control, there are no guarantees of improvement. Careful assessment offers only the *potential* for educational improvement.

Assessing Alternative Educational Practices

One element of assessing educational products is trying to determine which educational practices may hold the greatest promise. The educational literature and sometimes the popular press are frequently the forum in which the adoption of alternatives to existing educational practices is encouraged. Suggesting that one technique is an improvement is a simple enough statement to make, but the related assessment task can be very complicated. Often the "either/or" debates are conducted by proponents with a substantial professional and, perhaps, emotional investment in a particular outcome.

The "whole language versus phonics" approach to teaching reading is a serviceable example. The debate about which is the best practice has been contentious enough that it is difficult for individuals to make informed choices about which may serve their purposes better. Sometimes the problem is that the assessments lack objectivity; they are actually defenses of a particular practice.

Assessment *can* provide the answers about best practices, but it is most particularly effective when the questions are refined to ask—as they probably ought to be in this instance—not "Which is better?" but "Which is better for whom?" We may find that one practice is better for small groups of young learners who are new to English and that another is better for students in large-group instruction. Sometimes we need to frame the assessment issues so that, if benefits cannot be generalized, we can still detect them. The example of group size and student performance in mathematics is a case in point.

The virtues of small-group instruction are frequently extolled in educational discussions, and few people will argue the point. But according to Peterson, Janicki, and Swing, (1981), the value of small-group instruction depends upon the circumstances. Their study of geometry performance among fourth- and fifth-grade students revealed that high- and low-ability students appeared to flourish in small groups, but average-ability students did slightly better in large groups. The study illustrates the presence of what is called an interaction. In this instance it is an interaction of students' ability with the size of the instructional group. Assessment data are not very helpful when the question isn't framed carefully.[5]

Maintaining Assessment Relevance

During his graduate school days, your author learned of a principal with an interesting approach to assessing the teachers in his school. As an indicator of teaching quality, he glanced at the venetian blinds in each room. When they were straight and neat in appearance, he believed the teacher to be organized and in command of the classroom. Untidy blinds were (for him) an indicator of poor organization and sloppy classroom execution. The advantage of this approach, of course, is that one can evaluate many teachers very quickly. The principal didn't even need to enter the room in order to form a judgment about the instructor. The disadvantage is that the tidiness of the venetian blinds is probably **construct irrelevant,** which means that it has nothing to do with what we are trying to assess. Sacrificing validity for convenience, the principal selected an indicator that was probably not connected to any element of teaching quality that matters.

During preassessment, one of our tasks is to be attentive to differences in knowledge or skill among the learners we are planning to teach. To pursue the matter of relevance for a moment, the differences we are in interested in must be connected to what we will teach, and the same point ought to be made of all assessment. The discussion of validity appears in detail in Chapter 7, but it is important to emphasize that one of our most important tasks is to assess what we claim to be assessing.

By way of illustrating the difficulty, Breland, Danos, Kahn, Kubota, and Bonner (1994) noted that on several different kinds of standardized tests there are scoring differences related to gender. Sometimes the differences are relevant to the construct being measured, which of course is what is expected when the assessment is undertaken. Occasionally, however, what gets assessed is not relevant. Female students, the authors found, are more likely than males to be able to compensate for a lack of content knowledge with superior composition abilities when the assessment includes essay-type items. When this occurs, some portion of scoring differences may actually be penmanship differences, or differences in word choice, spelling ability, and the like.

Although those doing the assessment are more likely to respond to construct irrelevant differences on essay items than some other items, this is not to indict essays, which fill a vital assessment niche. Essay items are difficult to score objectively, however, and it is important to be attentive to only what is relevant to the construct we are trying to assess.

Summative Assessment as a Source of Feedback

By definition, the final assessment occurs after instruction has concluded. It is summative assessment and it actually occurs only after formal instruction has concluded. Although the formative assessment during instruction is an important data source because at that point instruction can still be modified, the final assessment is also an important source of feedback. Walberg's research (1986) demonstrated that one of the variables significantly correlated with student achievement is the teacher's practice of providing feedback. When it occurs during the formative period, feedback can help correct common errors the learners are making in new learning activities. Feedback coming from the final, summative assessment can reinforce key points, allow the teacher to make needed corrections, and provide a sense of how the current learning is related to other objectives. To be optimal, the feedback ought to occur as soon as possible after the summative assessment. It has minimal effect after learners are directed toward other objectives.

Much of the substance of learning is the business of connecting new ideas to prior learning. This is particularly evident in reading and math because their incremental nature is so clear, but to some degree it is true of all disciplines. The final assessment provides information about the learners' command of what they have just completed. The teacher can anticipate students' readiness for what will come next. Actually, when one instructional unit builds squarely upon the next, the summative assessment from a concluding unit can provide important preassessment data for the unit to come, which Figure 2.1 illustrated.

Data from a final assessment are helpful in improving instruction only when those who make the decisions are willing to modify their practice. That willingness isn't automatic.

For Further Discussion

Earlier we noted that, in some instances, teachers do not always relate student achievement back to the quality of their own planning and delivery. The evidence is in work by Ames (1982) and Barros et al. (1989), who found that teachers typically do not accept responsibility for student failure (although they are willing enough to claim a role in students' successes). Even casual observers assume some relationship between teaching quality and the level of learners' performances, but the teachers who are in the best position to capitalize on elements of the relationship do not always act. Your questions are these:

1. If instructors dissociate themselves from student failure, what motivation is there for teachers to adjust their presentations?

2. Educational accountability movements contain an element that attempts to hold teachers responsible for student outcomes. Weighing what you know of other factors in student performance, are such programs misguided?

> Even when formal instruction has concluded, the final assessment can provide an important source of feedback to students. Teachers should use the assessment data to review key points with students, make any needed corrections in the way students understand the material, and build connections between present instruction, past activities, and what is to come.

Of course, many of the variables associated with student performance *are* beyond the teacher's control. Whatever your conclusions in the preceding discussion, any enduring concept of formal education includes the idea that there is some connection between the quality of the environment that the teacher provides and the levels of the learners' accomplishments. Dissociating the two both denies that relationship and limits the effect that assessment data can have on future outcomes.

SUMMARY

There are many ways to view assessment. On one level, it is just a mechanism for grading students. On a much broader scale, student performance data can inform the other elements of the educational plan, even to the point of imposing an influence on a state's educational policy (Cooley, 1991). In a comment very reminiscent of the early 1990s, Armstrong (1994) noted that data from students' performance allow schools to be accountable to their communities. While that statement in isolation overly simplifies the relationship between student performance and the school variables, it does illustrate the tendency people now have to interpret student performance data differently than they once did.

Somewhere between extremes, your author took the position in this chapter that assessment data are an important source of information for planning, implementing, and evaluating the health of the instructional program. Noted Armstrong (1994), "Assessment should be an accepted, ongoing part of the instructional process. It looks for a cause-effect relationship between goals, instruction, and what students know and can do" (p. 15).

Little was said about grading the students because this topic will be taken up in Chapter 5, and by inference at several other points in the book. The purpose here was to see what we can learn from the students about some of the other variables in the learning equation.

A report by the National Council of Teachers of Mathematics (1991) noted, "Assessment of students and analysis of instruction are fundamentally interconnected" (p. 63). This interconnectedness is the heart of the matter. Lambdin and Forseth (1996) argue that we ought to view assessment and instruction as part of a common educational task. They observed, "Good teaching is seamless—assessment and instruction are often one and the same" (p. 298).

Stiggins (1987) found that it is not uncommon for many teachers to spend one third of their instructional time on assessment-related activities. This suggests that what is needed is probably not more assessment, but more organization and better application of the data that teachers may already possess.

We have outlined procedures for employing assessment activities throughout the educational sequence. Although most classroom teachers probably enjoy less academic freedom than their predecessors had in the classroom, they still have a good deal of autonomy in selecting goals, objectives, and classroom methods. Those decisions ought to be made on the basis of careful assessment. From time to time, assessment will dictate changes, often because the relevant conditions have changed.

Preassessment will tell us where students are in relation to what we wish to teach, what they need, and where we ought to begin. When there are conditions among particular students that should alter how we approach them—perhaps a disability or an unusual learning style—those findings will emerge with careful assessment. Formative assessment allows us to fine-tune the instruction as it is being delivered, and even the final assessment has a good deal to tell us about how well the learning program worked.

Often, in education, advocates of a particular alternative educational practice will tout its virtues. Sometimes the campaigning is long on enthusiasm and short on research support. An important dimension to the assessment task, and one that is frequently ignored, is the teacher's responsibility to review the empirical data to determine whether there is sufficient promise in a new practice to justify making fundamental changes to one's program. Remember that although there are many opportunities for assessment, all of the assessment activities spoken of in this chapter have a singular purpose—to improve the learning program for the students.

▮ Speaking of Assessment

Our discussion here has been one of creating a rationale for using various assessment procedures to give us information about not just student performance, but the other elements of a learning program as well. Although you will have a variety of options when you select assessments, not much has been said yet about which procedures you might choose. Note that assessment format is largely dictated by such questions as these: What information will you need in order to make the experience better for your students? When will the data from standardized tests be helpful? When should you set aside formal pencil and paper tests in lieu of some other measure of student performance? Do you have a clear view of what your students should be able to do, or will you gauge their performance in relative terms, with students compared to other students and groups of students to other groups? The answers to questions such as these will dictate your approach to assessment. Although much of the rest of the book is devoted to helping you formulate responses, it isn't too soon to begin developing tentative answers of your own.

ENDNOTES

1. The point, by the way, isn't that teachers are solely—or even primarily—responsible for student failure (or for student success, for that matter), but research demonstrates quite clearly that teaching effectiveness and student achievement *are* related, as Bloom et al. (1971) suggested (see Walberg, 1986, for example).
2. This is an example of what is called "measurement-driven instruction"—which is what occurs when the assessment, the test in this case, has the effect of altering the instruction that was intended to precede it.
3. As the context suggests, task analysis is referred to as a means of reducing a learning activity to its component parts so that the instructor is aware of what completing the task requires of the learners. For obvious reasons, this can be very important in instructional design. Traditionally, task analysis was a highly formalized procedure with a heavy behavioral emphasis. As examples, see Bower and Hilgard (1981, pp. 538–539), or Gagne (1963, p. 623). For a more current discussion of how task analysis might fit with current instructional programs, see Solity (1991).
4. Your author hesitates to mention this because the example is so negative, but a colleague early in his public school teaching career consistently planned poorly, and then when the plan went awry as it inevitably did, he would announce, "That's the dumbest class I have ever had!" He seemed to think that the announcement absolved him of any responsibility to adjust his instruction so that class work was more productive. You might consider the odds against each successive class being the "dumbest class," by the way.
5. Your author does not wish to belabor the point, but another example of assessment gone badly comes to mind regarding evaluating educational practice. Computer-aided instruction (CAI) represents another promising alternative educational practice in which assessment had an important role to play; but for a time at least, the opportunity was ignored. Beginning in the early 1980s after the advent of microcomputers, in spite of numerous instances of poor software, unsuitable hardware, or software mismatched with hardware, there was great pressure to implement CAI pro-

grams as broadly and as quickly as possible. It was (and is) considered an antiprogress heresy to be skeptical about the merits of using computers in education.

The appeal of using technologically sophisticated equipment on a broad scale allowed assessment activities to be pushed aside, and investigations that might have pinpointed what CAI can do well as well as the areas where it is not cost-effective were not conducted at all in the early days of microcomputers. There was some early research done at Stanford University and the University of Illinois in the early 1960s, and much of what was written later when microcomputers were becoming available assumed that conditions were the same as those that prevailed during the early work. The earlier assessment, however, was done with projects employing large, mainframe computers reading code written by experienced instructional designers for very tightly monitored reading programs. Those conditions are at variance with the early 1980s experience, where software quality was often suspect and CAI programs were poorly monitored, when there was any oversight at all. Very little assessment was conducted in the early 1980s at elementary and secondary classroom sites where microcomputers were being implemented on a large scale. An important element of quality control was not exercised and, in some instances, costly errors were made. Happily, that circumstance has begun to change and a healthy research body is accumulating, which helps to validate where CAI is helpful and where it may not be effective.

FOR FURTHER READING

The Lambdin and Forseth (1996) article cited in this chapter is a good introduction to many of the themes raised here. Although their focus is elementary school mathematics, one can easily generalize to other disciplines and age groups.

REFERENCES

Airasian, P. W. (1991). Perspectives in measurement instruction. *Educational Measurement: Issues and Practice, 10*(1), pp. 13 16, 26.

Ames, R. (1982). Teachers' attributions for their own teaching. In J. M. Levine and M. C. Wang (Eds.), *Teacher and student perceptions.* Hillsdale, NJ: Erlbaum.

Armstrong, C. L. (1994). *Designing assessment in art.* Reston, VA: National Art Education Association.

Armstrong, D. G., Denton, J. J., and Savage, T. V. (1978). *Instructional skills handbook,* Englewood Cliffs, NJ: Educational Technology Publications.

Barros, J. H., Neto, F., and Barros, A. M. (1989). *Socio-cognitive variables of teachers and their influence on teaching.* (ERIC Document Reproduction Service No. ED 346 032)

Belk, J. A., and Calais, G. J. (1993). Portfolio assessment in reading and writing: Linking assessment and instruction to learning. Paper presented at the annual meeting of Mid South Educational Research Association, New Orleans, November 10–12. (ERIC Document Reproduction Service No. ED 365 732)

Bloom, B. S., Hastings, J. T., and Madaus, G. F. (1971). *Handbook on formative and summative assessment of student learning.* New York: McGraw Hill.

Bormuth, J. R. (1968). The Cloze Readability Procedure. *Elementary English, 45,* 429–436.

Bower, G. H., and Hilgard, E. R. (1981). *Theories of learning* (5th ed.). Englewood Cliffs, NJ: Prentice-Hall.

Breland, H. M., Danos, D. O., Kahn, H. D., Kubota, M. Y., and Bonner, M. W. (1994). Performance versus objective testing and gender: An exploratory study of an advanced placement history examination. *Journal of Educational Measurement, 31,* 275–293.

Cooley, W. W. (1991). Testing and school improvement. Pittsburgh, PA: Pittsburgh University School of Education. (ERIC Document Reproduction Service No. ED 336 415)

Entwisle, D., and Hayduk, L. (1981). Academic expectations and the school achievement of young children. *Sociology of Education, 54,* 34–50.

Entwisle, N. (1981). *Styles of learning and teaching.* New York: Wiley.

Fry, E. (1968). A readability formula that saves time. *Journal of Reading, 11,* 513–516, 575–578.

Gagne, R. M. (1963). Learning and proficiency in mathematics. *The Mathematics Teacher, 56,* 620–626.

Holmes, C. T., and Matthews, K. M. (1984). The effects of nonpromotion on elementary and junior high school pupils: A meta-analysis. *Review of Educational Research, 54,* 225–236.

Lambdin, D. V., and Forseth, C. (1996). Seamless assessment/instruction = good teaching. *Teaching Children Mathematics, 2,* 294–299.

Lu, Chin-hsieh, and Suen, Hoi K. (1995). Assessment approaches and cognitive styles. *Journal of Educational Measurement, 32,* 1–7.

Mantzicopoulos, P., and Morrison, D. (1992). Kindergarten retention: Academic and behavioral outcomes through the end of the second grade. *American Educational Research Journal, 29,* 182–198.

National Council of Teachers of Mathematics. (1991). *Professional standards for teaching mathematics.* Reston, VA: The Council.

Nitko, A. J. (1989). Designing tests that are integrated with instruction. In R. L. Linn (Ed.), *Educational measurement* (3rd ed., pp. 447–474). New York: Macmillan.

Peterson, P. L., Janicki, T. C., and Swing, S. R. (1981). Ability X treatment interaction effects on children's learning in large-group and small-group approaches. *American Educational Research Journal, 18,* 453–473.

Peterson, S. E., DeGracie, J. S., and Agabe, C. R. (1987). A longitudinal study of the effects of retention/promotion on academic achievement. *American Educational Research Journal, 24,* 107–118.

Solity, J. (1991). An overview of behavioral approaches to teaching children with learning difficulties and the National Curriculum. *Educational Psychology: An International Journal of Experimental Psychology, 11*(2), 151–67.

Stiggins, R. J. (1987). Profiling classroom assessment environments. Paper presented at the annual meeting of the National Council on Measurement in Education, San Francisco.

Sugrue, B. (1995). A theory-based framework for assessing domain-specific problem-solving ability. *Educational Measurement: Issues and Practice, 14*(3), 29–35, 36.

Tessmer, M. (1993). *Planning and conducting formative evaluations: Improving the quality of education and training.* Philadelphia: Kogan & Page.

Tomchin, E. M., and Impara, J. C. (1992). Unraveling teachers' beliefs about grade retention. *American Educational Research Journal, 29,* 199–223.

Walberg, H. (1986). Synthesis of research on teaching. In M. C. Wittrock (Ed.), *Handbook of research on teaching* (pp. 214–229). New York: Macmillan.

PART II

Assessing Performance According to Criteria

Those who keep their finger on the pulse of education have noticed a growing distrust of standardized test data in recent years. There are many criticisms. Some detractors argue that what standardized tests measure is far less important than the emphasis they receive. What matters, the logic goes, is not how students compare, but what they can *do,* and to the degree that one can specify students' progress in terms of specific outcomes, both the student and the society are better served.

In fact, your author's experience has been that students often profit from knowing what they are to do in terms that are as specific as possible. In his introduction to Petraglia's (1998) book on authentic assessment, Bazerman observed, "People are more engaged (and thus learn more) the more real and meaningful they find tasks" (p. ix). The difficulty, however, is that in educational systems increasingly devoted to responding to students' uniqueness, it is very difficult to select criteria that are meaningful for all. Bazerman continued, "What people find real and engaging, nonetheless, may be of the greatest human artifice" (Petraglia, 1998). In spite of the difficulties, there are outcomes that reflect more or less general agreement. Chapter 3 will discuss the matter of selecting a criterion and then determining the point at which it is satisfied. It is more complicated than it seems at first.

Chapter 4 deals with a particular application of criterion-referenced assessment, authentic assessment. It was the difficulty of identifying outcomes that are authentic for different students to which Bazerman referred. Chapter 5 is devoted to the matter of grading students and grading the instruction. It is a logical extension of the position described in Chapter 1 when it was noted that assessment data ought to inform all elements of the educational plan.

3

Specifying the Standard and Focusing on the Outcome

■ *Readers will come to understand how assessment is connected to the goals, objectives, and standards that structure educational programs.*

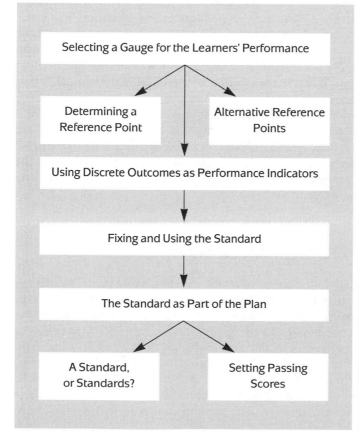

Selecting a Gauge for the Learners' Performance

Determining a Reference Point

Alternative Reference Points

Using Discrete Outcomes as Performance Indicators

Fixing and Using the Standard

The Standard as Part of the Plan

A Standard, or Standards?

Setting Passing Scores

Educational standards are not new, but disappointing student performance data have brought them new emphasis. Although standards can have different reference points and reflect a variety of different philosophical positions, the common element among them, and the source of much of their appeal, is the ready measure they provide of educational progress. Deciding how rigorous to make the standard and defending it once it is established are both quite complex processes. ■

Mr. Brown looked over the latest directive from the district office forwarded to him by his principal. The memo enumerated several English curriculum standards adopted for immediate implementation by the state's board of education. The principal's pencilled comment noted only, "we will have to find a way to fit these into your classes." The standards were particularly important to Mr. Brown, who, as the only English teacher in a small, rural high school, would be almost solely responsible for their implementation. The memo did not surprise him. He knew that declining scores on tests that measured students' verbal skills had prompted a great deal of discussion and that new standards were one of several possible outcomes. As he began the business of matching his content with the relevant standard, he wondered how these particular standards were chosen and whether they would have greater impact than the last batch of curricular reforms. ■

EDUCATIONAL REFORM

Reform movements in education are not unique to any particular historical period. There have been several efforts at change, driving educators and education first in one direction and then in another. Although educational reform movements tend to have a cyclical nature, each movement also has something unique. In the present reform effort, however, the difference is revealed less in the goals reformers adopted than in the process of goal setting itself and in the business of establishing the standards that give the goals their substance.

The standards are intended to serve as educational benchmarks. Whether the standards emerge from a state or national body, are imposed by district officials, or are established by the classroom teachers themselves, they raise issues that go to the heart of assessment. In fact, they suggest important questions about how to validate the standard as something worth working toward, and how to determine when learners' performances meet the standard.

THE CONCEPT OF A PERFORMANCE GAUGE

As friends do, a man exchanging pleasantries with the comedian Henny Youngman once asked him how a family member was faring. Youngman's response was, "Compared to what?" (Youngman, 1991). Flippancy aside, there is an important assessment principle implicit in the answer. Gauging performance requires that one have something to which the performance can be meaningfully compared. In education, this basis for comparison has increasingly been referred to as the standard, and in recent years, a good deal of attention has focused on establishing standards and validating the processes by which they are selected. This is necessary because, in an age of careful scrutiny and oversight, there is much more to an educational standard than simply declaring it. This chapter helps explain the issues involved in establishing and validating the educational standards that structure much of the most publicized educational assessment. We can approach that discussion by first reviewing the differences between norm- and criterion-references.

Referencing the Assessment

Alone, the measure of a student's performance on a learning task conveys no particular meaning. It is just an isolated fact. For example, noting that a student scored 57 on a problem-solving task really tells us nothing at all about how well the student did. We know the student's score, but we don't know what level of performance the score represents. In order to communicate meaning, we must reference the score, which means that we must compare it to something else. References allow us to use the score to make judgments. We can determine whether a learner understands the material, passed the test, or has demonstrated competency, or we can determine how the learner compares to others who took the test. These judgments relate to the norm- and criterion-references we first raised in Chapter 1.

Norm-references, you will recall, assign meaning to performance by comparing the student to others who completed the same assessment. We employ a norm-reference when we note that a student scored "in the top 10 percent," or falls into the "first quartile." These judgments reveal nothing about how much of the curriculum the student mastered. They indicate only how the student's performance compares to the others who are in the group.

With criterion-referenced assessment, on the other hand, meaning comes from comparing the student's performance to a set of external indicators. They are usually established with more that the immediate assessment in mind, and in theory at least, there is no implicit judgment about what proportion of those assessed will fall into a given category. Indicating that "answering 80 percent of the items correctly indicates mastery" or "one must satisfy six objectives in order to proceed to the next level" both reflect criteria.

Degrees of Accomplishment

Sometimes the criterion represents a dichotomy, a separation into two categories. This is the situation when the outcome is passing or failing a test and no further distinction among test takers is made. Sometimes, however, there are degrees of accomplishment. They are reflected in multiple descriptors such as "excellent," "good," "adequate," "barely adequate," or "unacceptable." They are also reflected in letter grades.

Logically, dichotomous assessments (pass/fail, credit/no credit) are the best choice when the issue is not how well one does something, but whether the person can perform at some minimal level. In this instance there is a discrete point separating those who can from those who cannot, and those who know from those who do not. It is often called a cut-off point, and those failing to reach it are judged to lack an ability or knowledge to the extent that they are considered not competent. This is the way most licensing exams are structured. There is a point on the test at which, should applicants miss another item or fail to execute some required maneuver, they are denied the license.

Dichotomous Scoring and Precision

One of the difficulties with dichotomous judgments is that they lack precision—not necessarily in the judgment itself, but within the two classified groups. Among those who meet the criterion and are judged competent, for example, there is no distinction between those who barely make the cut-off and those who score substantially above it. Someone who succeeds by a single point receives the same classification as someone who scores 100 percent. We can correct this deficiency if we indicate the *degree* of accomplishment.

> Dichotomous judgments of pass/fail and other such determinations draw no distinction within the two groups of those who pass and those who fail. One who succeeds by the tiniest of margins usually enjoys the same classification as one who performs perfectly. By the same token, one who fails to meet the criterion by a single question on a test, for example, may be judged to have performed similarly to another who misses every item on the test. One fails or passes, with no further distinction made.

Scoring Distributions

For any group of scores we can create a frequency distribution by arranging scores from the lowest to the highest and then indicating by a point above each score how frequently a particular score occurred. In very large groups, particularly when we are measuring mental characteristics, the points often take on a bell shape. The resulting frequency distribution is called a **normal distribution.**

Because normal distributions are so characteristic of large groups, we can often make beforehand (called *"a priori"*) predictions about how the scores will fall. Normal distributions will be discussed in a little more detail in Chapter 9, but note for now only that this is the symmetrical, bell-shaped curve so common in mental measurement discussions.

Speaking of Assessment

Although we may know beforehand how scores in a group are likely to be distributed, this refers only to the group as a whole rather than to individuals within the group. If we know, for example, what the distribution of fifth-grade students' reading scores looks like for students in the district, we can see whether the average score is rising or falling from year to year. Group characteristics reveal very little about individuals within the group, however. In fact, when we use group characteristics to define the individual, we employ a form of stereotyping.

Ordinarily, criterion-references are not based on any *a priori* judgment about how achievement measures will be distributed. It is technically possible for *everyone* to meet the criterion (and it is likewise possible for *no one* to meet the criterion). The outcomes are dictated by a number of factors related to the appropriateness of the curriculum, the instructor's effectiveness, the learners' motivation, and the like, but not a presupposition about how the students' performances will look in a frequency distribution.

The Heir to the Criterion

Although the language may seem unfamiliar today, criterion-referencing was prominent in the educational programs of the 1960s and 1970s. The concept is resurgent in current assessment discussions because the criterion still represents how well something must be done in order for a student to receive a particular evaluation. As such, it performs some of the same functions as a standard.

Although they both refer to a preselected measure, one arrives at standards and criteria quite differently. Frequently, an individual classroom instructor can define performance criteria. Standards, on the other hand, are usually the product of a group of people, some of them perhaps noneducators, with a variety of different backgrounds.

Although they both refer to a required level of performance, there are also important differences between criteria and standards. Individual instructors acting independently often set the criteria that are the measures for learning in the classroom. Standards, on the other hand, generally involve a broader consulting group. Those who help establish standards often represent several different constituencies, all of whom are involved in a formative discussion about what learners ought to accomplish.

Because of the level of participation, standards reflect something of a consensus forged regarding society's educational priorities. This window on priorities provides a changing view, however. Some of the most pertinent educational issues, and the standards that help to give them expression, are dynamic, not static. They change from time to time as conditions in society change and also as different constituencies involved in forming the standards gain primacy. Labaree (1997) observed:

> *Schools, it seems, occupy an awkward position at the intersection between what we hope society will become and what we think it really is, between political ideals and economic realities. This in turn leads to some crucial questions: Should schools present themselves as a model of our best hopes for our society and a mechanism for remaking that society in the image of those hopes? Should schools focus on adapting students to the needs of society as currently constructed? Or should they focus primarily on serving the individual hopes and ambitions of their students? (p. 41)*

If you review some of the arguments you have heard about what schools should accomplish, the implications for standard setting should become quite apparent. Members of one segment of society may see the schools as the means for producing an enlightened citizenry. They may clamor for a standard providing that each student will learn a second language. Others may see the schools as the mechanism for making young people employable and adopt a standard that advances vocational training. Still others may propose standards that will advance the nation's scientific, technological, or economic interests. They may advocate a college preparation curriculum for all students.

Goals, Objectives, and Standards

Although there is always some tension among champions of various philosophies, the ascendancy of one or the other brings the educational program into focus, even if it

> Remember that goals are statements of general intent. Objectives are not only more specific than goals, but they also often provide some detail regarding how the goal will be realized. They often specify the particular behavior we wish learners to adopt.

is a temporary focus. Statements defining new educational ends signify that a change has occurred. In his historic analysis of how school curricula are derived and implemented, Tyler (1949) noted that the first step in curriculum planning is to determine the educational purposes, or goals, that the school intends to pursue.

Goals, you will recall from our discussion in Chapter 2, are general statements. "Encouraging analytical thinking" and "learning to appreciate literature" are examples of educational goals. Note that such phrases offer nothing regarding how the goal is to be accomplished or when it will be addressed, or even how one can know when the goal is satisfied. They are simply stated aspirations for a group of students.

Objectives are subordinate to and differ from goals in two respects. Besides having a more restricted scope, they often are written to specify "what," "where," and "how" the designer plans to reach the objective.

When an objective specifies how well a learner must perform, it resembles the educational **standard.** Figure 3.1 illustrates the relationships among goals, objectives, and standards.

We might be inclined to view any performance criterion as a standard. Like the standard, it is a reference point for student performance, but remember that educational standards have a different origin. Although individual instructors often select the criteria for instructional objectives, as previously discussed, it isn't unusual for noneducators to be involved in the discussions that result in educational standards. As a consequence, standards often suggest more pressing political and social considerations than conventional classroom goals and objectives reflect.

Standards and Educational Reform

Goals and objectives are both student-centered, and student learning is the end to which they are formed. Educational standards certainly reference student learning,

FIGURE 3.1   Educational Goals, Objectives, and Standards

Indicator	Level of Specificity	Author	Intended Audience
Goal	Very general	Ranges from individual classroom teachers to national groups	May be relevant from the classroom to the national level
Objective	Classroom-specific	Usually the classroom teacher	Usually the students in a particular classroom
Standard	Very specific	Often national groups, including noneducators	Usually those who fall within a particular grade/age designation

but the individual student's accomplishment is often a means to furthering some national or societal accomplishment. In fact, standards are often identified directly with educational reform efforts. Koelsch, Estrin, and Farr (1995) captured the role that standards are expected to play when they observed:

> *Current educational reforms in the United States have converged around one theme: It is not acceptable for just a small percentage of students to achieve at a high level; we must raise our expectations for learning for all students. Acting on these beliefs, educators at national, state, and local levels have developed standards—goal statements describing what students should know and be able to do—within and across subject areas. Indeed, a plethora of standards is available from national professional organizations . . . State departments of education have developed curriculum frameworks that detail content standards for learning as well. And, districts and schools have also set local standards for student learning and achievement. (p. 6)*

Because of the connection between standards and educational reform, standards include an assessment element, which is why the discussion is raised here. The connection is logical. Those who are interested in establishing educational standards are also interested in progress toward them.

A Word about Origins

Although all goals, objectives, and standards serve as benchmarks in education, standards and objectives are different from goals in that they include an assessment component. In the case of the objective, the assessment relates to what was once called the "behavioral objective." In order to respond to circumstances in which learning objects were so ill-defined that it was difficult to determine whether anyone actually accomplished them, behavioral objectives specified what should occur in very specific, observable terms. One may not be able to judge with certainty whether the student can reason in mathematics, but one can at least detect whether the student can solve eight of ten long division problems correctly.

Fundamental Assessment Problems

At first glance, writing learning outcomes in behavioral terms probably seems to be a solution to many educational assessment problems, and it is—of sorts. It certainly makes assessment tasks more objective, but it is also quite restrictive. Some of the outcomes we prize are not directly observable, and we cannot always express them in terms that will not require some level of inference by the assessor. Creativity, analytical ability, comprehension, and problem-solving ability are all characteristics that we wish students to develop, but describing the manifestation of those traits in terms of a particular observable outcome can be difficult. Many advocates of the format recognize the limitations but pursue it because they prefer an approach that makes both the learning and the assessment task more objective. The built-in assessment component suits the educator's need to be able to document learning, which is much of the accountability movement's substance.

The alternative is to settle on a less direct approach to assessment. When one cannot observe the learning directly, one must develop assessment tasks that represent the underlying ability, and then infer learning from the students' performance on those tasks. Demonstrating the connection between an assessment activity and the characteristic it is supposed to represent introduces us to some of the validity issues that will be raised in Chapter 7.

> Goals, objectives, and standards all suggest educational purposes. There are differences in the breadth of the discussion that precedes them, and also in their specificity. They all have the potential to affect the curriculum, but as the indicators become increasingly specific, as objectives tend to be, they can also trivialize the curriculum by compelling the focus to become too narrow.

Setting validity aside for now, consider another problem that may emerge when we focus closely on defined outcomes. Although standards tend to deal with general learning outcomes, objectives are quite specific. If the easiest-to-assess behaviors dictate instruction without regard to whether they are the most educationally valuable outcomes, there is a great potential to trivialize the curriculum.

The standard and the objective both imply an assessment component, but their respective constructions differ. Objectives are usually written for a particular class. The standard has a more general character. It is often prepared for a regional, or even a nationwide, student population. Standards may have a level of abstraction or complexity that makes them difficult to assess by a simple observation. Although it is not necessarily so, determining whether the students have met the standard may require extensive measurement and analysis.

FOCUSING ON THE OUTCOME

One of the reasons for the current interest in educational standards is that they provide an opportunity to focus on educational shortfalls. When students can't locate Zaire on a map, or they are unable to solve a particular kind of word problem, reformers may target such concerns in the new standards they construct for education. In turn, they affect the school curricula and instructional procedures that educators must modify in order to bring them into harmony with the outcomes. In these instances, the new standards may actually be the dominant influence in the educational plan that preceded it. It may seem to be a case of getting things backward, but that type of **measurement-driven instruction** (Airasian, 1988) was very characteristic of reform efforts in the 1980s and 1990s.

The interest in educational standards is not just a contemporary discussion. It surfaces whenever critics are restless about what they perceive to be a lack of educational progress. Much of the current interest in what is called **outcomes-based education** (Spady, 1988) can be explained this way.

Outcomes-Based Education

As the name suggests, outcomes-based education (OBE) makes the focal point for classroom instruction an accomplishment that students must demonstrate when they exit (Glatthorn, 1993). Rather than the grade level competencies that have been common in the past, exit outcomes represent culminating demonstrations of learning, although in the classroom they are often approached as discrete learning elements. They represent what adults, some of them noneducators, consider relevant, and they often extend beyond the bounds of a particular academic discipline. Figure 3.2 lists the exit outcomes developed for a school district in Illinois.

Although the outcomes often extend beyond a single discipline, the form of OBE is similar to what educators once called "mastery learning." Both mastery learning and OBE require that the learner demonstrate a prescribed level of competency for each outcome before moving on. They also both require frequent assessment so that one can monitor students' progress as well as their achievement. Although an important body of literature is beginning to accumulate on outcomes models (Marzano, 1994), it isn't our task to critically evaluate it here.[1] Your author raises it because of the assessment element.

Although determining which outcomes to pursue is a question for curriculum specialists, it is an assessment task to determine whether the learner's performance demonstrates the outcome and when the student may begin working on the next outcome. Outcomes-based education leads logically to outcomes-based assessment.

Assessing Outcomes

The supporters of outcomes-based assessment tout its advantages over multiple-choice tests.[2] They argue that there are several advantages over more conventional assessment. Figure 3.3 is a list of the claims.

In Chapter 4 we will speak of **authentic assessment,** which also emphasizes that assessment should reflect (authentic) conditions beyond the classroom. For now, think of outcomes-based assessment as a particular kind of authentic assessment. Its supporters claim important advantages.

FIGURE 3.2   A School District's Exit Outcomes

- The ability to communicate in reading, writing, speaking and listening, and mathematically
- Facility in social interactions
- Analytic capabilities
- Problem-solving skills
- Skill in making value judgments and decisions
- Skill in creative expression and in responding to the creative work of others
- Civic responsibility
- Responsible participation in a global environment
- Skill in developing and maintaining wellness
- Skill in using technology as a tool for learning
- Skill in life and career planning

Source: Adapted from Glatthorn (1993).

FIGURE 3.3   **Advantages Claimed for Performance Assessment as Opposed to Conventional Assessment Practices**

- Offers clear guidelines to students about what the teacher expects
- Requires tasks that will be meaningful beyond the classroom
- More directly involves the classroom teacher in making the judgments
- Can be made to more easily accommodate student differences
- Offers a higher level of intrinsic appeal than alternative approaches to assessment

Source: Adapted from Marzano (1994).

Clarity

Because outcomes assessment tends to be task-specific, it is often easier to be precise about what the learner must do in order to meet the standard. This is particularly the case compared to norm-referenced assessment. It represents the difference between saying to the learner, "you must explain the structure of Elizabethan sonnets" and, "you must score beyond the 70th percentile to be admitted." Both objectives are reasonably specific, but it is much easier to define the learning that will satisfy the first objective than to explain what will accomplish the second.

Authenticity

When the assessment is authentic, it has meaning beyond the assessment setting. It should not be conducted only for data-gathering purposes, but must be a learning experience that will help prepare learners to succeed beyond the classroom. For a student who is preparing to teach literature, explaining the structure of a sonnet has more authentic learning value than a requirement to score better than a specified proportion of other students on a test about Elizabethan literature.

Use of Teacher Judgment

This approach to assessment attempts to capitalize on the teacher's ability to judge students' progress, using more than just a test score in the process. It allows the teacher to exercise the very subjectivity that standardized tests were developed to avoid, but sometimes perhaps one ought to consider more than a score. Particularly with younger students, one may wish to include such factors as effort and improvement in an evaluation. Fundamentally, those who know the students may be in a far better position to make the decisions about their progress than the people who developed the test or defined the standard.

Allowing for Differences

Implicit in outcomes assessment, and its alternative forms, is the idea that educators ought to have the latitude to alter learning activities from student to student according to the differences in students' levels of preparation, motivation, interests, and the like. Of course, assessment must vary correspondingly. Perhaps students are working on a world history unit that deals with civil conflict and conflict resolution. In order to encourage student motivation, teachers may prepare several options that will each satisfy the course demands and then allow students to select their own. Some students may work cooperatively in a group attempting to determine why the League of Nations was unable to resolve some of the conflicts that preceded the Second World War. Others may choose to study the newspaper, looking for parallels between United Nations efforts to resolve the fighting in the former Yugoslavia and the problems the British faced because of the strife in Northern Ireland.

Perhaps the best way to assess the learners in the cooperative group is to require a research paper. The other students might present a panel discussion, with individual participants representing the primary issues facing the various groups embroiled in the former Yugoslavia, as well as those in Northern Ireland. When students have such a wide range of choices available, there is no opportunity to assess everyone with a common instrument.

More Engaging Assessment

Advocates of outcomes-based education often use their criticism of standardized tests as a sort of rallying point (see Darling-Hammond, Ancess, and Falk, 1995, p. 5, for example). They contend that the assessment activity ought to be provocative as well as informative. It should, they maintain, be an extension of the learning process for the students. Indeed, among proponents of outcomes-based programs, the validity of an assessment activity has less to do with its technical merits than with how well it promotes further learning and better teaching.

A Caveat or Two for Programs That Focus Exclusively on Discrete Outcomes

Outcomes-based approaches are intuitively appealing. At least in the abstract, it is difficult to find fault with an educational plan that clarifies precisely what learners must do and defines those products in terms of knowledge or abilities that have value beyond the classroom. At some point, however, every educator has a responsibility to seek verifiable evidence that the program does what it is supposed to do. Outcomes-based advocates maintain that because they tailor their assessments to particular circumstances, they yield more usable information. In turn, better information brings about improvements in teaching and learning.

As logical as this is, Shepard, Flexer, Hiebert, Marion, Mayfield, and Weston (1996) found that there is still some uncertainty about the approach. After a year of the new assessment called for by an outcomes-based program in one school district, the investigators concluded that the program failed to bring about any significant changes in student performance. The learners who had the outcomes-based assessments may have grasped the structure of the material better than students who had conventional assessment procedures, but these effects were minor.

Outcomes-based education also assumes that people agree about the outcomes. This is certainly not difficult if they are not too closely defined. There is general agreement that students should be "literate" and "responsible," for example. It can be a much greater problem to nail down the specific outcomes that demonstrate literacy and responsibility, and then determine how to assess them.

The next chapter will suggest that even when we turn to the less conventional assessment methods, some of the technical characteristics that we associate with traditional testing still matter. These include reliability and validity, attributes that define the

Outcomes-based programs have substantial appeal among educational critics. It is particularly attractive to those who hold that educational programs generally lack a clear sense of purpose and direction, and that students emerge having failed to acquire the knowledge and abilities they need. Advocates of OBE see it as an opportunity to protect the public, advance educational policy, and hold educators accountable for their product (Cizek, 1996). The research base on OBE is still not sufficient to allow any definitive judgment regarding the impact that outcomes programs have on student performance, however.

consistency of the assessment data as well as the accuracy with which they measure what they are supposed to measure.

Part of the appeal that outcomes-based assessments have for some educators resides in the way they minimize the technical characteristics of assessment. In truth, one will find little mention of reliability and validity in performance assessment discussions, but the fact that they do not occur does not mean that outcomes assessment renders them unimportant. Outcomes models frequently call upon different learners to perform different tasks in order to satisfy the outcome. With little consistency in the students' tasks, it is doubly difficult for the teacher who must evaluate multiple tasks even though each is supposed to meet the same standard (Yen, 1997). One may maintain that traditional reliability does not matter with outcomes assessment, but there remains the need to evaluate each student's work with consistency, and that, as will be demonstrated later in the book, is very much a reliability issue.

Outcomes advocates typically reject objective scoring formats, and certainly some multiple-choice assessments do a poor job of revealing what students have learned. One of their strengths, however, is that they minimize scoring subjectivity. Allowing the teacher the latitude to weigh the various conditions that affect students' performance into an assessment may strengthen it, as we noted above. On the other hand, instructors also have the opportunity to allow irrelevant factors to creep in and affect their judgment.

A final issue is perhaps mostly a philosophical concern. Outcomes systems have their greatest appeal to those who view educational activities as the products of a series of discrete activities that are designed to meet specified standards. Although disappointing educational performance helped make outcomes programs popular, not everyone agrees that students' progress ought to be viewed as a set of specified activities that result in an educated individual. An alternative view is that education is better thought of as a process, perhaps lifelong, that involves experiences and pursuits that do not always lend themselves to precise specification. Many of the more rewarding activities, as one gains ability and understanding, may be difficult to anticipate and thus defy enumeration as outcomes. Assessment is required in either case, but it will be different in situations in which the standards and experiences are established from the outset.

THE DIMENSIONS OF THE EDUCATIONAL STANDARD

Standards can define more than what students ought to be able to do. By implication, they also define what the content will be and how instruction ought to proceed. Figure 3.4 outlines this broader view of the standard.

FIGURE 3.4   **An Overview of Educational Standards**

Domain	Content	Instruction	Student Performance
Focus	What is to be taught?	How is it to be taught?	What must students learn?
Issue	What is the basis for selecting content?	What is the standard for instructional quality?	What is the minimal level of acceptable performance?

The standards for student performance receive most of the attention (Cizek, 1996). We do not understand them very well, however, when we isolate them from the curriculum and instruction standards that provide the context for student performance.[3]

Standard Setting

Besides including more people than goals and objectives usually involve, standard setting is also a comparatively formal process. At the local level it is usually a matter of aligning standards with what has already occurred at the state and national levels. It is, therefore, a characteristically "top-down" process with classroom teachers and local school officials taking their cues from what has occurred elsewhere. Koelsch, Estrin, and Farr (1995) described the process, and it is outlined in Figure 3.5.

As straightforward as the steps appear, it can be very difficult to forge a consensus among disparate members of a standards committee. For example, some members might be very committed to a history curriculum for which the standards emphasize a proper chronology of the most significant events. For others, it may be more important to analyze the national experience from the standpoint of the changing characteristics of the population. The heart of the matter is in step 6, where the

FIGURE 3.5   **Setting Local Standards That Conform with National Expectations**

1. Those involved constitute a standards committee. They review state and national standards as well as any state and district curriculum frameworks available.
2. Using an outline of state and national expectations as a rubric, the committee reviews local instructional practices to see how well they align with expectations beyond that level.
3. As a result of the review process, the committee identifies the strengths and weaknesses in the local program.
4. The committee comes to a consensus about what will be expected of students.
5. Content standards determine what should be taught.
6. Performance standards that identify what is exemplary and what is adequate emerge from a review of students' work.

committee must identify what is exemplary and what is adequate. This step begs an important question: "How 'good' is good enough?" (House, 1997).

Since the standard often implies the type of assessment teachers will need, it might be thought of as the first step in developing an assessment system (Koelsch et al., 1995), but standards can influence much more that just the assessment system. There is so much attention focused on the outcomes specified by standards that instead of being just a component in the educational plan, assessment sometimes appears to drive it. In the vernacular, the assessment tail may sometimes wag the curriculum and instruction dog.

Standards are imposed from beyond the classroom. Since classroom teachers are often judged by how successful their students are in meeting the standards, they often modify their practices to address the standards more directly. We noted earlier that when teachers tailor content and strategies to improve learning outcomes, the assessment drives the instruction.

Measurement-driven instruction has a virtue in that content and instruction are aligned very carefully with assessment and there is less ambiguity in educational plans. The difficulty is that people pay very little attention to objectives that are beyond what will be assessed. Even very worthy learning outcomes will probably be set aside if the standards do not acknowledge them.

Determining Whether Students Have Met the Standard

Although the standard is a factor in several different elements of the educational plan, remember what it defines. The standard specifies a minimal level of acceptable performance. It allows one to discriminate between those who have satisfied the standard and those who have not. Sometimes standards are expressed as a list of qualities, such as one expects students to demonstrate when they write a well-developed essay. Some standards are expressed as numbers. This is what occurs when we say that students must read a particular passage within 15 minutes and answer the related questions with 80 percent comprehension.

Cut-Scores

When an assessment yields a range of scores, the standard identifies the lowest acceptable score, called a **cut-score**. It distinguishes between those who satisfied some requirement and those who did not.

Think of the cut-score as a point on a continuum that stretches from the lowest possible score, where the expected learning is completely absent, to the other extreme, where students perform the learning perfectly. When students perform near either end of the continuum, making correct judgments about them is easy. If 15-year-old students cannot read anything, we know exactly how to classify them in relation to a reading standard. Likewise, 15-year-olds who read Chaucer in their spare time are generally easy to judge. The problem occurs among those who fall somewhere in the middle of the continuum.

The first part of the problem is the location of the cut-score. Whether the test is a nationally administered assessment of teaching competency or the unit test in geography, we must develop reasonable answers to two important questions related to the cut-score: (1) How did we decide where to locate it? (2) Does the cut-score consistently allow us to distinguish between those who met the standard and those who did not?

In a simpler world, identifying a population of students who have met a standard also indicates, by inference, those who have not. However, it is quite possible to identify a group who have met the standard and to find that because of assessment errors some of those in the group judged to have failed actually have the necessary learning. This possibility becomes more important when we realize that there is often a great deal at stake for the students. When they satisfy a cut-score, they are permitted to continue, to graduate, or to do something else valuable. These rewards are denied to those who fall short. The procedures we use to establish minimum standards must bear scrutiny because they will certainly be challenged if they appear arbitrary or misplaced.

We can illustrate some of the problems with a simple example. We might establish a standard that, in order to proceed to the seventh grade, sixth-grade students must read a particular passage within 15 minutes and with 80 percent comprehension. Stipulating the cut-scores is relatively easy to do, but there must be something meaningful about (in this example) both the level of comprehension and the time requirement. It must represent something relevant beyond just accomplishing it. One must be able to demonstrate that there is an important relationship between meeting the standard and succeeding in the seventh grade, for example.

Those who reach the standard must be able to perform, and we ought to be able to demonstrate that those who fall below the cut-score lack the ability. It is easier to demonstrate either classification independently than both at the same time. One might require that the first-grade students read a book written on a first-grade reading level with 100 percent comprehension, and one might have every assurance that those who meet this standard can read well enough to proceed. The problem is that some of those who fail to reach the standard (what of someone who reads with 99 percent comprehension, for example?) may also be able to read well enough to continue.

> Ideally, cut-scores satisfy two judgments. Not only must those reaching the criterion possess the quality or ability the test is intended to identify, but also the quality should be absent among those who fail to reach the criterion.

At the other extreme, the admissions officer at a university might establish 220 as the minimum Scholastic Assessment Test (SAT) verbal score for entering students and know that those who fall below that score lack the literacy skills that they need to flourish at the university. Since the minimum SAT score is 200, with scores ranging from 200 to 800, the judgment would be correct virtually every time. Unfortunately, some of those who exceed the minimum standard will probably also lack the literacy skills they need as beginning university students. The difficulty in setting cut-scores is being able to place them where they have a reasonable chance of satisfying *both* judgments.

Cut-scores mean that some members of a group will be excluded from some activity. That, of course, is the cut-score's purpose. Because the stakes are so high in some instances, the processes for determining cut-scores are very closely scrutinized. The costs associated with not being allowed to graduate, being excluded from a profession, or not being permitted to register for the next class in the sequence can be substantial. For these reasons, the related assessments are **high-stakes tests.** When the consequences are comparatively unimportant, we speak of **low-stakes tests** (Woolfolk, 1995).

Indirect Assessment and Decision Errors

Assessing human performance is difficult under the best of circumstances because it is so complicated. We rely on multiple variables to help us understand why people perform academic tasks as they do. By definition, variables change from situation to situation. To further complicate matters, we must assess much in the classroom inferentially. There is no direct way, for example, to determine how well the student understands photosynthesis. Understanding photosynthesis is not like running a race. It cannot be measured with a stopwatch. Instead, the assessor must select tasks or test items that can be completed successfully only by one who has the learning one is trying to assess. The difficulty is that when one relies on indirect rather than direct information, the potential for making a mistake about what the student has learned is compounded. When the mistakes result in errors about whether the student has met a standard or a criterion, they are called **decision errors.**

For Further Discussion

A certain amount of decision error is inevitable because educators are primarily involved in assessing characteristics that they cannot directly measure. In which kinds of educational decisions are errors least important? When do they matter most? What kinds of decision errors are preferable—those in which students who are competent are judged incompetent, or those in which the incompetent are judged competent? Does the answer to these questions depend upon who is asked?

Decision errors occur in large part because assessment errors occur, and, as we noted, assessment errors are most common when we must rely on some level of inference. Errors are probably less common when we assess a kindergarten child's ability to name the colors than when assessing a student's critical-thinking ability. In either case there is a risk (both students can make a series of lucky guesses, for example), but the inferences we must make to determine critical thinking invite the greater potential for error.

The Relationship between the Different Types of Error

Although our discussion suggests that cut-scores should provide some assurance that those who meet the score have the ability and those who miss the score do not, this is more of an ideal than a reality. Because of the problems associated with indirect assessment and other concerns that will be elaborated later, some amount of error is probably unavoidable. Usually, it is more realistic to think in terms of minimizing, rather than eliminating, error. Assessors *can* exercise a measure of control. The level of one type of error is affected by how much of the other one is willing to accept. This is important because, in some cases, one type is clearly preferable to the other.

Consider a program that trains airline pilots, for example. Some of the variables that contribute to safe and efficient flying will be difficult to assess directly, which suggests a potential for error variance in the scores. Some candidates will score higher than they ought to, given their abilities, and others' scores will be erroneously low. Which poses the greater risk, trainees who are **false positives** (their scores suggest they are competent when they are not), or those who are **false negatives** (competent fliers whose scores indicate that they lack competency)? Actually, the answers may depend to some degree on who is answering the questions. The pilot trainee may be more concerned about a false negative error, but potential passengers and regulatory agencies are going to be most concerned about false positives.

We observed earlier that those who have extreme scores in either direction are those about whom it is easiest to make error-free judgments. To turn that statement around, decision errors are most common among scores that fall in the middle of the distribution. Since one type of error is preferable to the other in some circumstances, we often find it appropriate to manipulate outcomes accordingly. We can do this by adjusting the cut-off score. If we move the cut-off score lower, we reduce the number of false negatives because more candidates whose scores may be low because of assessment errors are judged competent. However, some of those whose scores fall into this area have accurate scores, and some have erroneously high scores. The effect of minimizing false negatives will also be to increase the number of false positives, which means that more candidates who lack the competencies will be judged competent.

Speaking of Assessment

The way the different kinds of decision errors interact can place the educator in a difficult position. Think of a math test administered to fifth-grade students, some of whom do not speak English at home. Ordinarily math probably minimizes these problems because much of it employs symbols and numbers that help transcend the language differences. In this instance, however, there are many word problems, which are necessary because of a state mathematics framework that calls for fifth-grade students to be able to solve such problems.

If you are allowed to set your own cut-off score, you have a dilemma. If you set the cut-score relatively low, you will be able to adjust for some students whose scores are lower only because of language differences. On the other hand, some of the low scores will reflect a poor grasp of the mathematics concepts, and the result will be a false positive classification: Students who lack competency will be judged competent. If you move the cut-score high enough, at some point you will eliminate all the false positive classifications, but with the handicap of also making false negative classifications: Some who actually have the math competencies will be judged not to have them.

Which is the safer course for the student?
Which suits the needs of the society?
Which course will the ninth-grade math teacher prefer?

If you were the math teacher, would it be feasible to gather all those students whose scores fell into a specified band around the cut-score and use some other method to assess them further? Would it help you to make accurate judgments about the students in this questionable area to select some of the problems that they missed and ask the students one at a time to explain to you what was asked and how the problem can be solved?

The decision error is not just an artifact of contemporary education. We can make either kind of error in judgment in almost any assessment situation, particularly when the learning cannot be directly observed. What makes the issue particularly important today is the prominence of educational standards. When standards are the criteria for evaluating educational progress, the decisions about who has satisfied them (and who has not) take on a new importance. This translates into a higher profile for decision errors.

THE STANDARD AND THE EDUCATIONAL PLAN

Besides indicating what learners must do, the standard should also direct the instructor because student data can reveal a great deal about what the students must yet do and how the instructor can adjust the plan to assist them. The discussion of decision errors should underscore the fact that we have to be careful when we set standards. Although we can never escape decision errors entirely, we can minimize them. When the standard is haphazard or arbitrary, errors are more common and the resulting damage increases. Allowing an incompetent driver to possess a license poses a risk to everyone else on the road. On the other hand, it is also unfair to require a student to repeat a course if he or she may have accomplished the course objectives generally, but made some uncharacteristic mistakes on the test.

Discussing decision errors seems to imply that one can identify a discrete point separating those who are competent from those who are not. In reality it is rarely that simple. As Jaeger (1976) noted, "All standard-setting is judgmental. No amount of data-collection, data analysis and model building can replace the ultimate judgmental act of deciding which performances are meritorious or acceptable and which are unacceptable or inadequate" (p. 2). There has not yet been discussion of precisely how one identifies the cut-score. Later in the chapter we will consider what is called **standard setting,** and then leave the balance of the discussion to Chapter 13. Another comment or two here will be useful.

Are Standards Always Necessary?

There may be certain circumstances when a discrete standard for performance is unnecessary. In a certification or licensing situation, the need for a standard is easy enough to establish, even if locating it is difficult, but elsewhere the standard may not make a great deal of sense. Millman and Greene (1989) noted that unless test scores are used to determine particular outcomes, such as when one is granting a certificate of graduation or awarding a license, there may be no point in establishing a standard. It may not be helpful, for example, for the Honors Biology teacher to try to establish a standard for those wishing to take the class the coming year. Maybe it is more practical to rank candidates according to some relevant measure, such as final exam scores from the prior year, and then fill the class by selecting the highest ranked performer, the second highest, and so on until the class is filled.

Standards also have more appeal when there are substantial risks involved. Perhaps the Industrial Arts instructor has several assessments in a repertoire of tests. The first is an assessment of learners' familiarity with the safety procedures for operating the shop's power tools. The second instrument is an assessment of students' familiarity with the different types of hardwood and softwood available to them for their projects. We probably have no argument with a safety standard requiring students to receive further instruction if they fail to recognize the need for safety goggles or the need to avoid loose-fitting clothing around machinery. The second assessment, however, involves no comparable risk. The issue for the instructor is to determine how well students know the different woods, and a minimal level of required performance is, at the least, arbitrary. There must be a compelling reason to have the test (the cost involved in using the wrong type of wood for a project might be one, by the way), and also some sound reason for adopting a particular minimal level of performance.

When passing scores are needed, there are a number of important operational and procedural concerns that should be addressed in planning. If there are multiple areas tested, one must determine whether there should be a minimal level of performance required for each area, or whether the different areas tested are so related that higher levels of performance in one area can logically compensate for lower performances in another. If we have an English assessment with sections on spelling and punctuation, we might argue that strength in one area should be allowed to compensate for weakness in another. This is the decision when the standard is based on an aggregated score rather than on individual subtest scores.

Alternatively, one might require learners to respond correctly to 15 of the 20 items on each of the punctuation and spelling sections in order to meet the standard. This approach is safer when there are distinct abilities or knowledge domains being assessed.

Millman and Greene (1989) observed, "Setting passing scores is both psychologically and psychometrically difficult, and it is often further complicated by external political considerations" (p. 345). Although the political considerations are rarely explicit, one can usually recognize them. See if you can see evidence of politics in the accompanying *Speaking of Assessment* box.

Speaking of Assessment

The competency exam administered to teacher candidates in California is an interesting case study. The assessment includes separate subtests of reading, writing, and math. The procedures the state's regulatory agency adopted allow performance beyond the minimum on any one of the tests to compensate, to a point, for lower scores in another area. High reading scores can compensate for low math scores, and so forth. Since reading, writing, and math represent quite separate skills and disciplines, the practice of allowing scores to compensate in this manner suggests what?

Might one conclude that decision makers lack confidence in the standards?

Can one make a convincing argument that teachers don't need to be competent in all three areas?

Which do teacher licensing officials appear to be more concerned about, false positive classifications or false negative classifications?

What are the implications of a false positive classification, or of a false negative? Which type of error will most concern the parents of the prospective students? Which type of error is most important to the candidate? What other factors might influence such a decision?

Sometimes passing scores do appear arbitrary. Hopkins and Stanley (1981) related the following:

> *One large federally funded ($350,000 per year) experimental education program with which the authors are familiar set a prespecified criterion performance standard of 80% correct on a . . . [test] to denote the point at which the curricular objectives would be said to have been achieved. After year 1, when most pupils failed to achieve the desired criterion, it was "readjusted" to 60%; thus after year 2 it was concluded that 83% of the students achieved the curricular objectives of the project. . . . Such meaningless "bootstrapping" . . . illustrate[s] the problem of an arbitrary criterion. (p. 185)*

Unfortunately, sometimes the business of setting passing scores has less to do with sound assessment practices than it ought.

The Standard as a Particular Score versus Levels of Competency

Earlier in the chapter there was a discussion of whether there are sometimes degrees of accomplishment, rather than a "did" or "did not" judgment. That discussion is very much an element when we consider standards. As Jaeger (1989) observed, "state models assume that competence is binary, an examinee either has it or doesn't" (p. 492). Besides the problems we have already noted, judging competency is complicated by the fact that we often think in relative terms, rather than the absolute terms suggested in a cut-score. Jaeger's contention is that, in many instances, there are degrees of competency. Without getting into a discussion of the different kinds of assessment data we deal with—which will be taken up in Chapter 9—this means we have choices in addition to viewing learners in a competent/not competent dichotomy. Sometimes it is more accurate to recognize that there are greater or lesser degrees of competency, and in some instances distinct, definable levels of competency.

The concept of degrees of competency is common in traditional educational practices. Conventional letter grading, for example, represents multiple levels of acceptable performance. Even though the letters A, B, C, and D represent different levels of performance, the first three, and sometimes even D grades, may indicate that a learner has adequately met a standard. In this instance, there are different degrees of competency, each reflecting a particular standard (although the instructor might be hard-pressed to specify the differences clearly).

Setting Passing Scores

Even in those situations in which it is most accurate to consider degrees of competency, there is some point in separating students who demonstrate the various levels of competency from those who are incompetent. Usually it falls to classroom teachers to identify the passing score, and although they operate independently and less formally, they perform essentially the same task as a committee that sets a standard. Unfortunately, the individual teacher's procedures are probably more difficult to defend. It is common, for example, to select a percentage point as a passing score. However well entrenched the practice is, it is also arbitrary. As alternatives, we will very briefly review some of the standard-setting practices that your author will elaborate in Chapter 13.

There are different ways to determine the standard's location. One approach is to use a procedure called **parameter estimation** (Cizek, 1996). In statistical jargon, a parameter is a characteristic of an entire, defined group called a population. "All seventh-grade mathematics students" defines a population, as does "All female teacher candidates at Idaho State University." In parameter estimation, the characteristics of the group are determined not by consulting every member of the population, but by using inferential statistical methods to draw conclusions based on what occurs in representative samples.[4] The population's characteristics, or parameters, are inferred from a representative sample. Those characteristics become the standard for gauging individual learners' performances.

This occurs in the classroom as well. In that setting, there is usually no need for inferential procedures, however, because teachers are generally concerned only with the students in their classes. Their students represent their entire population.

As a standard-setting procedure, parameter estimation is often criticized because it is arbitrary. A national parameter for fifth-grade English achievement is not sensitive to what may be very different conditions for fifth-grade students in Bangor, Maine, and another group in Bakersfield, California. Perhaps the fifth grade in Bakersfield has large numbers of children from immigrant families. English may not be their primary language. Whether the standard should be sensitive to these differences is hotly debated, but the fact is that national standards generally do not reflect differences in region or situation when they are based on population parameters.

Fundamentally, educators often have difficulty, for philosophical reasons, using parameters in individual classrooms. The procedure often relies on a normative reference that many educators find distasteful. If one uses the characteristics of one's students to determine who will pass and who will not, students are competing against one another, something the research on cooperative learning advises against (see Johnson and Johnson, 1999, for example).

Other Approaches to Setting the Standard

Parameter estimation approaches are now often supplanted by alternative standard-setting procedures that focus on establishing standards tailored to particular groups. One approach is to determine the standard based on the difficulty of the assessment items. More difficult items prompt one to lower the standard for performance, and those with a lower difficulty level result in a higher standard. If multiple-choice items are written well, for example, usually those with the most choices are the more difficult. Using this logic, the standard for 5-choice items will be lower than for 4-choice items.

In another standard-setting variation, sometimes we base the standard on the ability of the students. More particularly, one may attempt to determine the performance of the minimally competent person (how well would the student who just barely has

Standards can be established by determining the characteristics of the entire population, called parameter estimation. When used at the national level, parameter estimation is not sensitive to regional or local differences. When used in individual classrooms, parameters as standards have the effect of pitting students against each other for positive evaluations. Alternatively, one may base standards and passing scores on test difficulty or upon a judgment of how well the minimally competent person in a particular group might perform.

the quality perform?), and then use that as a standard for judging everyone's performance. If one has developed a history test with 30 points possible and concludes that the student who has just barely met the standard will score at least 22 points, that score may become the standard for all students.

When we use a combination approach, we use data regarding both item difficulty and student ability in order to place the standard. Clearly there remains a subjective element in these procedures, but they are at least less arbitrary than picking a specified percentage correct and maintaining that number across different assessments and assignments of different levels of difficulty.

The Standard-Setting Track Record

The commentary on standard setting represents a confluence of several discussions. When confidence in student progress is flagging, standards have great appeal because they offer gauges for students' (and educators') performances at a time when educational accountability movements clamor for them. If the literature on standard setting is conclusive on any point, however, it is the difficulty of setting defensible standards on competency tests. There is no agreement on a best method, although some procedures are more popular than others.

The lack of consensus extends to whether performance standards should be employed at all. Several learned groups and individuals have suggested that they not be used (Glass, 1978). Critics argue that in spite of the public's interest in a measuring stick, standards, as they are presently determined, still have an arbitrary character and an instability that makes them unreliable. They have the potential to create new problems even as they are used to resolve existing difficulties. In something far short of a vote of confidence, Glass (1978) concluded a discussion of standard setting by observing, "To my knowledge, every attempt to derive a criterion score is either blatantly arbitrary or derives from a set of arbitrary premises" (p. 258).

SUMMARY

Historically, students' performances were assessed either by comparing them to their peers or by gauging them against some set of specifications describing what the students should learn. Both options can be thought of as a standard, whether it is for students to occupy a particular ranking among their peers or to perform a specified task. Current discussions of educational progress place a good deal of emphasis on both. One often hears critics raise the need for national standards within the context of norm-referenced discussions about how students of one country compare to those of another. At the same time, we continue to speak in terms of the objective outcomes specified by students' command of "the three Rs."

The latter emphasis is uniquely important to assessment and to education as a whole because, to a great degree, assessment and effective education are both dependent upon our ability to articulate what we wish students to learn. Although standard setting takes these issues up, we should not confuse the desirability of identifying specific standards or instructional outcomes with the ease of doing so. It can be a difficult process.

In spite of the complexities that are inherent in standard setting, however, there is a great impetus for pursuing educational processes that hinge on fixed outcomes. They appear to offer the security of a result more tangible than norm-referenced testing offers, but with the specificity come costs. When the focus is on specified outcomes, the assessment has a tendency to shape the instruction that precedes it. If the specified outcomes are the only things we care about, there is no problem, but this is rarely the case. There are usually other outcomes that are also important, even though they are not specified. They also have value, but instruction that is driven by assessment can become so narrow that one cannot safely generalize student performance beyond the specified assessment tasks. In practical terms, we may adopt a writing standard that calls for students to be able to (a) paraphrase a passage that is read to them and then (b) describe the author's intent. If teaching students to complete these tasks is the only focus, one may not be able to generalize the results to the students' ability to spell, use punctuation, recognize imagery, explain parts of speech, and the like. This is a solvable problem, but it is wise to at least be sensitive to the difficulty since one of the strengths of traditional standardized testing is one's ability to extrapolate the learner's performance beyond the particular test items.

There is no point in worrying about an optimal method of assessment for something that one has not yet clearly defined. However the standard is established, the procedure must be obvious, even if it arouses some controversy. Those who may wish to review the standard-setting procedures must find them to be accessible and understandable. The classroom teacher's circumstances are unique in this regard. The public is sometimes involved to the point that the instructor receives oversight from noneducators. These conditions require teachers to document standard-setting processes carefully and to provide a rationale for whatever they use to define the standard (Cizek, 1996).

Implementation issues and problems aside, it appears that standards will be a fixture in elementary and secondary school settings for some time. Government agencies may encourage schools to adopt content and performance standards by tying funding to compliance. Clearly, this will have important implications for assessment. In particular, it will introduce the complexities associated with the large-scale assessment necessary when one must evaluate all students falling within a particular category according to a common standard (Phillips, 1996).

ENDNOTES

1. OBE has been examined elsewhere, however. The reader may wish to consult Glatthorn (1993) or McKernan (1993) for very readable reviews of this approach to classroom teaching.
2. As we shall see in discussions to come up in later chapters, the charge doesn't necessarily have veracity, but it is a frequently heard argument and helps explain the popularity of outcomes-based assessment and other forms of nontraditional assessment.

3. The evidence suggests that student performance is not understood very well when it is separated from what the instructor is doing. There is an extensive literature, often referred to as the teacher effectiveness research, that deals with the relationship between variables that teachers control, such as the use of positive reinforcement and the willingness to provide cues and feedback, and the level of students' performances.

4. In a statistical sense, a population is a universe of all who fit into a particular classification. All fifth-grade students, or all teachers, for example, describe particular populations. The sample is some subset of the population. Populations, particularly in areas related to mental measurement, are assumed to have predictable shapes and characteristics, one of which is normality. The normal distribution has substantial importance in statistics generally and in mental measurement in particular. We'll consider it more carefully in Part IV of the book.

FOR FURTHER READING

Although it was written several decades ago, Glaser's (1963) discussion of criterion references is very instructive, in light of the current interest in educational standards. Glass's (1978) article would make excellent follow-up reading.

A review of the pertinent issues involved in outcomes-based education (OBE) is contained in articles by Glatthorn (1993) and McKernan (1993).

The critique of traditional assessment that alternative-assessment advocates frequently offer is represented in Darling-Hammond et al. (1995), Chapter 1.

The business of generalizing from a specified outcome to the larger content area is an important issue. Marzano (1994) discusses it in a very readable article in *Educational Leadership*.

Galluzo (1993) has written an accessible and helpful article on educational standards, particularly as they relate to teaching.

REFERENCES

Airasian, P. W. (1988). Measurement driven instruction: A closer look. *Educational Measurement: Issues and Practice, 7*(4), 6–11.

Cizek, G. J. (1996). Standard-setting guidelines. *Educational Measurement: Issues and Practice, 15*(1), 13–21, 12.

Darling-Hammond, L., Ancess, J., and Falk, B. (1995). *Authentic assessment in action: Studies of schools and students at work.* New York: Teachers College Press.

Galluzzo, G. R. (1993). The standards are coming! The standards are coming! In *Essays on emerging assessment issues.* Washington, DC: American Association of Colleges for Teacher Education.

Glaser, R. (1963). Instructional technology and the measurement of learning outcomes: Some questions. *American Psychologist, 18*, 519–521.

Glaser, R. (1994). Instructional technology and the measurement of learning outcomes: Some questions. *Educational Measurement: Issues and Practice, 13*(4), 6–8.

Glass, G. V. (1978). Standards and criteria. *Journal of Educational Measurement, 15*, 237–261.

Glatthorn, A. A. (1993). Outcome-based education: Reform and the curriculum process. *Journal of Curriculum and Supervision, 8*(4), 354–363.

Hambleton, R. K., and Eignor, D. R. (1980). Competency test development, validation, and standard setting. In R. M. Jaeger and C. K. Tittle (Eds.), *Minimum competence achievement testing: Motives, models, measures, and consequences* (pp. 367–396). Berkeley, CA: McCutchan.

Hopkins, K. D., and Stanley, J. C. (1981). *Educational and psychological measurement* (6th ed.). Englewood Cliffs, NJ: Prentice-Hall.

House, N. G. (1997). How 'good' is good enough? *SEF News, 11*(2), a publication of the Southern Education Foundation, Inc.

Jaeger, R. M. (1976). Measurement consequences of selected standard-setting models. *Florida Journal of Educational Research, 18,* 22–27.

Jaeger, R. M. (1989). Certification of student competence. In R. L. Linn, *Educational measurement* (3rd ed.). New York: Macmillan.

Johnson, D. W., and Johnson, R. T. (1999). *Learning together and alone: Cooperative, competitive, and individualistic learning* (5th ed.). Boston: Allyn & Bacon.

Koelsch, N., Estrin, E. T., and Farr, B. (1995). Guide to developing equitable performance assessments. Washington, DC: Office of Educational Research and Development. (ERIC Document Reproduction Service No. ED 397 125).

Labaree, D. F. (1997). Public goods, private goods: The American struggle over educational goals. *American Educational Research Journal, 34,* 39–81.

Marzano, R. J. (1994). Lesson from the field about outcome-based performance assessments. *Educational Leadership, 51* (March), 44–50.

McKernan, J. (1993). Some limitations of outcome-based education. *The Journal of Curriculum and Supervision, 8*(4), 343–353.

Millman, J., and Greene, J. (1989). The specification and development of tests of achievement and ability. In R. L. Linn, *Educational measurement* (3rd ed.). New York: Macmillan.

Petersen, N. S., Kolen, M. J., and Hoover, H. D. (1989). Scaling, norming, and equating. In R. L. Linn, *Educational measurement* (3rd ed.). New York: Macmillan.

Petraglia, J. (1998). *Reality by design: The rhetoric and technology of authenticity in education.* Mahweh, NJ: Lawrence Erlbaum.

Phillips, S. E. (1996). Legal defensibility of standards: Issues and policy perspectives. *Educational Measurement: Issues and Practice, 15*(2), 5–13, 19.

Shepard, L. A., Flexer, R. J., Hiebert, E. H., Marion, S. F., Mayfield, V., and Weston, T. J. (1996). Effects of introducing classroom performance assessments on student learning. *Educational Measurement: Issues and Practice, 15*(3), 7–18.

Skinner, B. F. (1987). *Upon further reflection.* Englewood Cliffs, NJ: Prentice Hall.

Spady, W. G. (1988). Organizing for results: The basis of authentic restructuring and reform. *Educational Leadership, 46,* 4–8.

Tyler, R. W. (1949). *Basic principles of curriculum and instruction.* Chicago: University of Chicago Press.

Whitney, D. R. (1989). Educational admissions and placement. In R. L. Linn, *Educational measurement* (3rd ed.). New York: Macmillan.

Woolfolk, A. E. (1995). *Educational psychology* (6th ed.). Boston: Allyn & Bacon.

Yen, W. M. (1997). The technical quality of performance assessments: Standard errors of percents of pupils reaching standards. *Educational Measurement: Issues and Practice, 16*(3), 5–15.

Youngman, H. (1991). *Take my life, please!* New York: Morrow.

4

Employing Authentic Assessment

■ *The reader will learn to analyze assessment approaches focusing on student activities that will still be relevant after formal schooling concludes.*

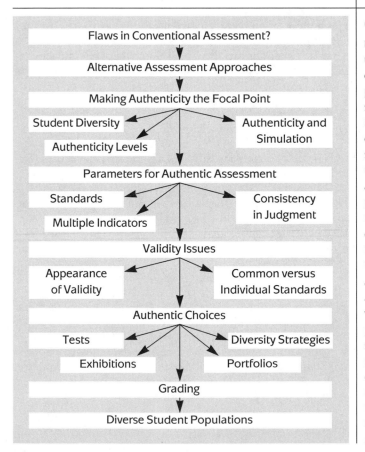

Flaws in Conventional Assessment?

↓

Alternative Assessment Approaches

↓

Making Authenticity the Focal Point

Student Diversity   Authenticity and Simulation

Authenticity Levels

↓

Parameters for Authentic Assessment

Standards   Consistency in Judgment

Multiple Indicators

↓

Validity Issues

Appearance of Validity   Common versus Individual Standards

↓

Authentic Choices

Tests   Diversity Strategies

Exhibitions   Portfolios

↓

Grading

↓

Diverse Student Populations

Often the most convenient way to assess groups of students is to use one instrument with multiple-choice test items and standardized procedures for administering and scoring the test. The difficulty is that some of the abilities that students develop in order to demonstrate their knowledge and skill are unique to the testing setting. The authentic assessment movement proposes to use assessment techniques that require students to demonstrate their learning in a way that will have value in the world beyond the classroom. Although authentic assessment has been associated with some disciplines virtually from their beginnings, the present movement can be understood best as a reaction to the present heavy reliance on standardized testing. Predictably, authentic assessment does not solve the problems associated with traditional testing without creating new challenges in their place. ■

Mr. Dow glanced at the pile of test booklets on his desk. Administering this particular achievement test was a yearly ritual the school district required, and he did his part by reminding the students to get a good night's rest, eat a good breakfast, and come prepared on the morrow with a sharpened #2 pencil. It was his estimation that this test—in fact most standardized tests—added little to the quality of the learning experience, however. He made instructional decisions based on what he thought would be most helpful to his students, and he found that the content of the test sometimes offered a poor match for what he had decided to do in the classroom. Besides, bubbling in circles on a machine-scored answer sheet seemed like a poor substitute for the assessment setting he preferred, one in which he could probe a partial answer and guide the learners' responses by offering feedback. Fundamentally, the published tests seemed a weak and sterile substitute for the kind of assessment he thought was most helpful to the students and most informative to him. ■

THE CASE FOR CHANGES IN ASSESSMENT

The 1983 publication of *A Nation at Risk,* by the National Commission on Excellence in Education, helped to crystallize a general sense that fundamental changes were needed in American elementary and secondary school education. Whatever the veracity of the charges made of a "rising tide of mediocrity" and other attendant ills, the call to reform has continued to be a dominant theme in both the United States and the United Kingdom. One expression is the call for changes in the way that we evaluate student performance. Noted Darling-Hammond, Ancess, and Falk (1995):

> *Increasingly, local schools, school districts, and states are experimenting with . . . alternatives to standardized testing for assessing student learning and performance. Persuaded that traditional standardized tests fail to measure many of the important aspects of learning, and that they do not support many of the most useful strategies for teaching, practitioners are introducing alternative approaches to assessment into the classroom—approaches that help teachers look more carefully and closely at students, their learning, and their work. (p. 4)*

A few years ago, Resnick (1987) complained that many of the tests used in education are not responsive to what she called the "thinking" curriculum. That is, they often do not assess higher levels of students' cognitive processing, and they are not sensitive to students' ability to apply skills and knowledge to real-world problems. In fact, a close examination of the tests that teachers administer suggests that they sometimes offer poor content coverage, emphasize a narrow range of cognitive skills, and can be substantially removed from the experiences for which students need to be prepared. Kamphaus (1991) reported, for example, that as little as two thirds of the material in a typical mathematics textbook appears on most survey achievement tests.

There has been an earnest search for new approaches to assessing student learning in recent years. It has broadened the field of study and given rise to a developing body of literature that is the basis for this chapter.

ALTERNATIVE APPROACHES TO ASSESSMENT

Advocates for alternative assessment express two points of view. The more moderate position is that current assessment techniques have become misdirected. These critics argue that most classroom assessment relies too heavily on multiple-choice format and aims disproportionately at recall abilities rather than more prized learning outcomes such as higher level analysis and problem-solving skills. Furthermore, the setting for the assessment is frequently so sterile and artificial that the data reveal little of how learners will perform later when they are beyond the school's boundaries.

A more extreme attitude is reflected in this broadside: "What counts for success in school is often considered trivial, meaningless, and contrived—by students and adults alike" (Newmann and Archbald, 1992, p. 71). The earlier position suggests that we must change the way we assess student learning. The second implies that a full-scale overhaul of elementary and secondary school curriculum and instruction is necessary so that what is assessed is relevant. This is not a text on curriculum or school reform, and it is, therefore, confined mostly to the more moderate position.

AUTHENTIC ASSESSMENT

There are a number of terms associated with alternative assessment approaches. One of the more serviceable is authentic assessment, discussed in Chapter 3. *Authentic assessment* is an assessment system designed to provide a greater transfer of learning from the setting in which the learning occurs to the world beyond. Rather than learning so that one can pass a test, the idea is to assess performance in a fashion that will be worthwhile and meaningful after formal schooling ends, as well as in the classroom. *Performance assessment* is an alternative term. The approach in both authentic and performance assessment is to construct assessment activities that are less abstract than usual. The terms refer to assessing students' actual demonstrations of the learning rather than just their ability to answer questions about it. The result will be students who can function effectively even when conditions differ fairly dramatically from those in which the original learning occurred. This is not ordinarily the case. Students are often stymied when the conditions that prevailed in the classroom are altered. According to Gardner (1991), traditional students often lack sufficient mastery of a discipline to apply what they know to novel situations.

This concept of assessment is not new. Physical education, art, music, and many vocational education classes have a lengthy tradition of assessing authentic work samples. The approach is much less common, although certainly not unknown, in traditional academic subjects. It has come to the fore as a component part of many education reform efforts. Authentic assessment in the academic areas is part of the

> Authentic assessment refers to the assessment of specific academic accomplishments that have meaning and value beyond the classroom. It is intended to foster a transfer of learning from the setting in which the learning occurred to all of the situations in which it will have application by making the assessment setting as similar as possible to the setting for which the learner is being prepared.

larger movement that places the educational focus on educational outcomes rather than processes (Elliott, 1991).

Authentic assessment practices are related to the standard-setting and the outcomes-based education described in the last chapter. Advocates of each movement show great interest in carefully defined educational products that are specific and practical. The use of authentic assessment, by its nature, requires a discrete product. It is not helpful when the outcomes are general or vaguely defined. "The ability to write a paragraph" is a good deal easier to assess than "verbal ability," for example. The focus on the specific is also very consistent with the more general educational reform movement. Although there continues to be an increasing emphasis on statewide and nationwide testing, those assessments are frequently structured around specific outcomes selected because they have an authentic relationship to what society expects students to be able to do once their schooling ends.

It stands to reason, therefore, that the similarity between the assessment and life beyond the classroom is a critical element in authentic assessment. This is what makes the transfer of learning possible. Critics of conventional testing argue that that relationship is not typical in assessment. In particular, standardized testing prompts students to learn test-taking skills that will have little value once school ends. Authentic assessment, say its supporters, prepares one to do much more than just pass a test. Consider the two problems posed in Figure 4.1.

Both problems involve the same mathematics. In either case the learner should multiply 9,000 by .12 and arrive at 1,080, but the multiplication problem has relatively little meaning unless it is connected to some authentic situation. From learners' solutions of the problem as it is first posed, we don't know, for example, whether they can transfer the multiplication solution to a setting where they must determine how much interest one will pay on a $9,000 loan for one year when the interest rate is 12 percent. Solving problem (a) successfully is no guarantee that students will understand how to solve (b), and that is very much the issue for authentic assessment advocates. As satisfying as it may be for some to work a multiplication problem "just for the fun of it," authentic assessment efforts oblige us to focus on situations where the skill or understanding will likely be used.

Traditional tests pose symbolic problems to the learner (.12 × 9,000), and the responses the learner generates are also symbolic (1,080). Although test items are always connected to a real-world set of circumstances, the level of symbolism is often

---

FIGURE 4.1   Two Similar Problems?

(a)   9,000

     ×   .12

     _____

(b) You have determined that tuition and living expenses for each year at college will be $9,000. Your parents have offered to lend you the money if you will work each summer to pay them at least the interest on the loan. Prepare a work sheet that indicates how much interest you will owe on a $9,000 loan at the end of one year if the interest rate is 12 percent.

---

great enough that students may miss the connection. To them the problem may be purely an abstraction.

Speaking of Authentic Assessment

Have you ever heard students complain, "Who cares if I can't solve an algebraic equation?" or "Why does it matter if we don't know the difference between the definite and the indefinite article?" Implicit in such questions is this reality: The students do not understand the authentic purpose of the related learning. This is very much the point for advocates of authentic assessment.

Sometimes traditional test results are poor predictors of student performance beyond the school, a problem that has not been recognized only recently. Some time before contemporary reformers made authentic assessment a rallying point, Fitzpatrick and Morrison (1971) offered a harbinger of the movement:

> One reason to teach children arithmetic is so that they can carry out transactions with money in stores, banks, etc. But arithmetic tests are seldom designed to simulate concretely either the stimuli or the responses involved in, say, making change for a purchase of $2.89 out of a $5 bill. Rather the test is an abstract representation of only those stimuli and responses that are considered to constitute subtraction. Efficiency thereby is served since it would be difficult to test each student in actual financial transactions, not to mention the various other contexts in which subtraction is used. However, this efficiency often may be achieved at the price of applicability. It is a common failing of educational endeavors that the student cannot, or at any rate does not, apply what he has learned when it is appropriate. He may be able to subtract accurately on a paper-and-pencil test but commits errors in making change in the store. (p. 237)

Authentic Assessment and Student Diversity

Very few people will take issue with the need for student performance to serve everyday purposes. The task is more complicated than one of merely making assessment more practical, however. Reformers expect that the educational plan, including the assessment, must help *all* students do better, not just most of the students, and not just the most able. The level of student heterogeneity makes the issue a particularly knotty one. Any educational reform movement that ignores students' ethnic, cultural, and linguistic differences is incomplete, because those characteristics have a demonstrable relationship to students' educational progress.

Developing instructional materials and assessment procedures that respond to learners' differences can be a problem because teachers and curriculum specialists tend to concentrate on the content, rather than the learner. If mathematics performance is the issue, for example, the usual approach is for educators to identify the concepts that are causing the most difficulty, and then select the procedures that appear most likely to provide the remedy.

Although student diversity is a very common discussion, many classroom teachers have not yet begun to evaluate learning tasks from the point of view of their language demands or of the interplay between instructional approach and culture (Koelsch, Estrin, and Farr, 1995, p. 3). This is important in the face of evidence that using language to show what one has learned varies greatly by culture. Among Native American groups, for example, students often prefer quiet, self-guided practice, rather than the heavily verbal explicit instruction that instructors often employ. Instead of demonstrating on demand, the children prefer to determine when they are ready to show what they have learned (Koelsch, et al., 1995, p. 16).

Teachers with students from diverse backgrounds are hardly in a position to provide a different program of instruction and assessment for each. However, with awareness of how linguistic and cultural differences may affect what occurs in the classroom, the instructor can provide multiple ways for students to demonstrate what they have learned.

This is part of the rationale for authentic assessment. Besides advancing the transferability of learning, it also encourages teachers to use multiple assessment options so that each student can demonstrate learning in the fashion that is personally most appropriate. The assessment is supposed to accommodate the student and the learning, in contrast to traditional testing, which requires that the learner adjust to the assessment circumstances. Relying on only one form of assessment can lead to a very limited, and perhaps a not very valid, understanding of students. It constrains them to a setting that may not mesh very well with their optimal performance.

A Solution, or Part of the Problem?

As we have noted, authentic assessment is supposed to neutralize some of the disadvantages that some students, including children who are minorities culturally or with respect to language, must shoulder. From one point of view, however, authentic assessment compounds, rather than alleviates, the problems. Authentic mathematics assessments commonly require that students elaborate their solutions by explaining how they solved a problem and why they used a particular approach. Such elaboration can provide important insight regarding the students' grasp of the content, but it also taxes their language ability in a fashion not characteristic of traditional assessment. Koelsch et al. (1995) have noted:

> The level of language that students are expected to process and produce in the course of completing performance assessments is nearly always more complex than the language of traditional standardized tests. Students who are still learning English and those who have not grown up in households where language forms and uses parallel those of the classroom are likely to be at an even greater disadvantage with performance assessments than they were with multiple-choice and short answer tests. (p. 15)

Levels of Authenticity

Rather than an authentic/not authentic characterization, authenticity is better considered in relative terms. A multiplication problem posed as the amount of interest

> Rather than viewing authenticity as an "is" or "is not" dichotomy, it is more helpful to view the different assessment tasks arrayed along a continuum ranging from completely authentic to completely contrived.

on a loan probably provides a more authentic setting for predicting how the learner will perform away from the school setting than will a test item presented simply as a multiplication problem. It is still less authentic, however, than if the student were sitting at a loan officer's desk making a decision about a car loan of $9,000 at 12 percent interest.

Actually, assessment tasks usually involve degrees of authenticity. In a teacher-preparation course where candidates must develop the materials for an instructional plan, participants might be asked to complete any of the tasks in Figure 4.2.

Although each of the tasks is logically related to preparing instructional units, each has a different level of authenticity. The language may suggest otherwise, but it should be clear that authentic assessment does not exist as half of a dichotomy with traditional, paper and pencil, test-type assessment representing the (not authentic) other half.

A more helpful way to view authenticity is in terms of what we might call a "fidelity continuum" in which assessment tasks range from those that are completely authentic to those that are completely contrived. When settings are authentic, assessment takes place in circumstances indistinguishable from those that will prevail once formal education ends. The other extreme involves using assessment technology and circumstances that may bear little resemblance to that for which the learner is being prepared.

It is important that we not make assumptions about authenticity based only on the physical structure of the materials. Portfolio assessment is a frequently touted alternative form of assessment, but some portfolio entries are no more authentic than the paper and pencil assessments they replace. Perhaps a teacher-preparation program calls for candidates to include a copy of one of their instructional units in their professional portfolios. The ability to produce an instructional unit is certainly important for preparing teachers, and in an exercise intended to teach candidates instructional planning skills, it has great authenticity. On the other hand, if the portfolio is used to judge the candidate's ability to deal with disruptive behavior in the classroom, it is not at all authentic.

Note that sometimes paper and pencil tests are *not* artificial, because many of the things we have to do once school ends legitimately involve paper and pencil and checking boxes on machine-scored sheets (filling out income tax returns comes to mind).

FIGURE 4.2   Educational Tasks with Varying Degrees of Authenticity

1. Complete a multiple-choice quiz with items based on what is good and what is poor practice in preparing instructional units.
2. Write an essay on the "do's" and "don'ts" of preparing instructional units.
3. Develop an outline for an instructional unit that meets the criteria associated with effective units.
4. Complete a critique of an instructional unit.
5. Prepare an instructional unit.
6. Prepare and field-test an instructional unit.

Remember that what makes an assessment authentic is its resemblance to what learners must do when they are functioning independent of school, not its dissimilarity from conventional assessment procedures.

By their nature, however, most traditional tests do appear substantially removed from the setting in which the learning will ultimately be used. Years before authentic assessment became descriptive of real-word settings, Fitzpatrick and Morrison (1971) spoke of the **criterion situation.** Authentic assessment tries to emulate the criterion situation for both the learning and the assessment activities in order to produce "a genuine rather than a contrived learning experience that provides both the teacher and student with opportunities to learn what the students can do" (Darling-Hammond et al., 1995, pp. 3–4).

In many situations, authentic assessment offers the evaluator a clearer view of students' abilities and learning than conventional assessment can provide. Because the setting is consistent with real-world conditions, as an additional benefit, often the assessment itself is a learning exercise for the student. This final element makes the approach particularly appealing to those who tire of preparing students to "take the test," when there appears to be little involved in the activity that has more lasting value.

Simulation

The key to authenticity, of course, is the educator's ability to provide an authentic simulation of the setting in which the learning will be required. Often, however, complete fidelity with the criterion situation is not possible. Sometimes it isn't even desirable because of the expense or the safety considerations involved. For example, rather than run the inherent risks, driver education programs sometimes employ driving simulators, which offer elements of driving realism without releasing inexperienced students to drive on public roads in cars they do not yet know how to operate safely.

To counter the risks and costs, we often rely on some level of simulation rather than a complete replication of all the relevant conditions. Accurate simulation allows us to create assessment circumstances that are similar enough to be realistic, but which still allow a level of control that may be impossible in the actual setting. Computer modeling can allow the budding chemist to mix elements and compounds without the danger of actually doing so in a real laboratory. A model United Nations allows students the benefit of at least some elements of international collaboration and diplomacy without the costs and organizational problems involved in a trip to New York.

Even simulation is not free, however, and often one must temper the desire for fidelity with a realistic assessment of the associated costs. Happily, not all aspects of the stimulus situation must be replicated in order to achieve an appropriate level of fidelity between the assessment setting and the criterion setting. Recreating the Globe Theater for Shakespeare students would be a fascinating and very informative exercise. Some less authentic setting might serve well enough to teach students something about how Shakespeare's plays were presented in his own time, however. Perhaps a small table-top model, built to scale, will do.

This suggests that there is a subjective component to the judgments about what one must include in order to make an exercise authentic. One must separate the essential from the nonessential and recognize a point of diminishing returns. Some elements contribute so little to fidelity that they are not worth the associated costs (Fitzpatrick and Morrison, 1971).

PRINCIPLES OF AUTHENTIC ASSESSMENT

Authentic assessment is part of a system that includes more than an authentic setting. Newmann and Archbald (1992) identified three characteristics that are essential to an authentic assessment program. In order to be effective, the authentic assessment system must include

- criterion-based standards
- multiple indicators of quality
- judgment reliability

Criterion-Based Standards

Criterion-based standards provide the yardstick one uses to evaluate the learners' performances by providing descriptions of the different levels of performance one might expect. Although most of the attention is toward the acceptable performances, by implication at least, the standards also define what is unacceptable.

Sometimes the standards are quite simple. Standards for a writing assignment required of 8-year-olds might be as basic as "complete," "partially complete," "not attempted."

Circumstances often call for more detailed information about the student's performance, however. Criteria might specify the student's level of creativity ("creative" or "lacks creativity"), the student's effort ("superior effort," "average effort," "little effort"), and mechanical correctness of the product ("no misspellings," "minor misspellings," "numerous misspellings"). Besides suggesting differences, each level must have descriptors that explain what is meant by "creative," for example. To illustrate, perhaps the instructor has just presented a demonstration on probability to sixth-grade math students using dice. After the teacher's presentation, the students are assigned to groups to develop their own demonstrations of probability. One might determine that students have demonstrated creativity when they can explain probability with something other than the dice the instructor used. Perhaps they will use random number tables, a card deck, or a coin toss. The level of effort can be gauged by the amount of time spent on a research project. A "superior effort" may reflect more than two hours, based on the entries in fourth grade students' journals, "average effort," one to two hours, and "little effort," less than one hour.

Although some might be inclined to use the different criteria to rank learners, ranking is contrary to the spirit of authentic assessment. The educator's interest is in describing and classifying the performance of the learners, not in comparing them to each other.

Gauging students' performance with a set of evaluative criteria actually suggests a link between authentic assessment and the criterion-referenced assessment that belonged to another period of educational reform, the 1960s.[1] To some degree, both movements reacted to a predominant norm-referencing in education. The latter movement, however, places greater emphasis on variety in students' responses. Because students often select different approaches to demonstrate their command of the material, assessment systems must be flexible enough to accommodate a variety of different projects. Figure 4.3 provides the standards for a seventh-grade science project after students have studied the Earth's geology for several weeks. Students have the option to produce any one of several different projects. Note that however different the projects may be, all will be evaluated according to the standards reflected in the scoring criteria.

Assessment data might indicate that several students satisfied the criteria for "excellent" projects. Does that mean that each excellent project reflects the same level of quality? In the discussion of **scoring reliability** that follows, the needed consistency turns out to be quite elusive. Sometimes the instructor's judgments change from project to project, and sometimes multiple scorers who are assessing the same project do not agree on the quality of the effort.

Multiple Indicators of Quality

The need for multiple indicators of quality stems from the fact that most academic tasks involve more than one skill or ability. Although we traditionally sum up a learner's performance in a letter grade or a brief verbal comment ("pass," or "credit"), those final descriptors nearly always represent a generalization about several discrete skills and abilities. In effect, they are *aggregated* indicators and may communicate little regarding the several individual components that contribute to the learner's performance.

FIGURE 4.3   Criteria for Assessing a Science Project

Scoring Protocol

Very good	18–20
Good	15–17
Fair	12–14
Unacceptable	<12

Assessment Criteria

A. Degree to which project reflects geologic concepts _____
B. Level of creativity _____
C. Clarity _____
D. Visual appeal of the project _____
E. Level of effort _____

Total _____

Interpretation

The project is acceptable if the score for A is equal to or greater than 14, the total score is at least 70 points, and there are no individual scores lower than 12. Should any of these conditions not prevail, the project is unacceptable and must be resubmitted after appropriate corrections are made.

A unit of history instruction dealing with the Great Depression would certainly involve recall ability. It probably also involves a grasp of basic economics principles and the skills of listening, reading, and writing. It could conceivably require research and critical analysis, as well as the ability to synthesize previously unrelated bits of information. If the learner receives a C on the unit and we accept "average" as the operational definition of that letter grade, what does it tell us of the learner's several abilities? In which of those activities is the learner "average," and what does "average writing ability"—to take one example—mean?

Sometimes single indicators are not misleading or inappropriate. There are certainly settings in which "holistic scoring" is appropriate. University applicants are probably not particularly interested in how the admissions people viewed their strengths and weakness. What they wish to know is whether they were admitted. In the academic setting, however, such situations are the exception and generally contrary to principles of authentic assessment. Even ordinary learning activities usually call for something more communicative than a single, summary evaluation.

In addition to the multiple quality indicators, authentic assessment advocates note that there should be multiple products to assess. Newmann and Archbald (1992) wrote:

> In much of our assessment, we use aggregated grades. Such grades are one summary comment that may actually represent the student's performance in several component areas. Those who employ authentic assessment champion the use of both multiple grading criteria and multiple products to assess.

> *In making overall assessments about individuals' accomplishments, it is usually necessary to consider not just one performance (even if it is judged by multiple criteria), but instead to characterize a variety of performances over time. Just as it becomes more informative to examine a full portfolio of work, an athlete's record over a whole season, or several tunes in a musician's repertoire, the assessment of students will be more authentic if it permits observation of patterns of strengths and weakness over a sustained period. (p. 81)*

The writing assessment should reflect several writing samples; the music grade should be based on several performances, and so on.

Judgment Reliability

Reliability and validity are concepts ordinarily associated with traditional assessment, and particularly with standardized testing. However, they actually have a very general application and are appropriately a part of any assessment discussion. In traditional settings, test reliability refers to the degree to which students' scores remain consistent over multiple assessments when the relevant conditions do not change. If we assess third-grade students' spelling ability several times, and their spelling ability does not increase or diminish (an unlikely scenario for sure, but bear with your author while he makes the point), the consistency in the students' scores reflects the reliability of the spelling data. If scores change substantially even though students' abilities have not, reliability is poor.

The historical approach to minimizing reliability problems in standardized testing and, in fact, in much of traditional testing is to limit the human element. The student's response to test items is either right or wrong. There is no middle ground, no "degree" of correctness with which the assessor need be concerned. These conditions minimize subjectivity and maximize the potential for achieving consistent (reliable) scoring results.

Environmental conditions can contribute to low reliability as well, so standardized testing procedures require assessment circumstances that are as consistent as possible from application to application. Everyone receives the same tasks to complete, all are allotted the same amount of time, they use the same implements, and so forth.

Because teachers want to accommodate differences in students' backgrounds and motivation, those using an authentic assessment system intend for environmental conditions to vary. Students are encouraged to express their learning in different ways. The ideal is to develop a learning activity that is authentic for each student, which means that there may be no common assessment exercise and no common setting for the assessment. In fact, Fitzpatrick and Morrison (1971) claim that if teachers control the learning and assessment circumstances so that students' performances are comparable, they probably sacrifice authenticity in the process.

In a Contemporary Problems class, perhaps students are asked to analyze public opinion on an upcoming school bond issue. One student may make a study of the political cartoons and editorials published in the local newspaper. Another student in the same class may decide to develop a questionnaire and sample opinion. The multiple assessment criteria must be relevant to all students' projects, and the teacher must find a way to interpret them such that if the assessment were to occur again under similar circumstances, the teacher would draw the same conclusion.

Perhaps the criteria for the assignment are:

the clarity with which the student defined the issue: 0–3 points
the level of scholarship reflected in the research: 0–5 points
the aesthetic appeal of the final product: 0–2 points

The teacher must then explain how the points are assigned. For the first criterion, for example, one might rely on the following as a guide:

3—The student clearly explained the bond issue in an introductory paragraph.

2—The student explained the bond issue in the introductory paragraph, but elements of the explanation lacked clarity.

1—The student mentioned the bond issue in the introductory paragraph but made no effort to explain.

0—The student did not mention the bond issue in the introductory paragraph.

These criteria are probably broad enough to accommodate a variety of different projects. The criteria alone are no guarantee that teachers' judgments will be consistent, but it is almost certain that they will be variable without the criteria.

Other Dimensions of Performance Variability

Besides allowing students to satisfy classroom objectives in a variety of different ways, authentic assessment proponents oppose tasks that offer only one answer. Since life's problems usually allow more than one solution, it seems logical to develop classroom activities that reflect the same options. All of these characteristics seriously complicate the assessment task, however.

Interrater Reliability

As we noted, judgment reliability occurs when a response that is adequate or correct for one test taker is judged equally adequate or correct for any other learner. In authentic assessment situations, however, there is another dimension to reliability—whether multiple judges assessing the same performance draw the same conclusion. This is called **interrater reliability,** and, as one might imagine, it is more difficult to achieve when each learner produces something unique. Not only must the judges' expectations be consistent from learner to learner, but also the judges must agree among themselves about the quality of a variety of different work samples.

In spite of the difficulties, Koelsch et al. (1995) recognize multiple scorers as the only solution to assessment tasks that encourage different students to tackle different problems. They suggest that teachers refine their own understanding by holding "professional discussions" that will help them develop a closer consensus on scoring issues as well as providing some other benefits. The discussions will probably help teachers both increase their own understanding of the content and garner new ideas about how to deliver the curriculum in the future.

Developing a consensus about how to score students' work doesn't occur spontaneously. There are at least three requirements:

1. The judges select "anchor" or "benchmark" student performances that serve as examples of how points ought to be assigned.
2. The judges score training papers for practice in scoring the range of performances possible.
3. The judges hold discussions about the performance standards that guide the scoring (Koelsch et al., 1995).

The anchor papers or samples illustrate the characteristics of each possible score. Once judges understand the samples, it is easier for them to score the training papers and then later the students' papers. It is important for the scorers to hold continued discussions about the scoring and about students' performances. This has the effect of reaffirming the scoring standards that are associated with each score.

Even with guidelines, developing acceptable interrater reliability places a premium on the judgment skills of the evaluators (Mehrens, 1992), and the training sessions are often quite lengthy and involved. Although there are guidelines for what level of reliability is acceptable (see Koelsch et al., 1995, for example), this is largely a subjective determination. Suffice it to say that when there is substantial disagreement, one begins to wonder which score is the most accurate. The issue becomes increasingly important as the stakes for the student (and perhaps the instructor) increase.

Unfortunately, performance measures of learners' projects have traditionally suffered from quite low interrater reliability, and achieving even moderate levels can be difficult and expensive (Reckase, 1995). It can be done, however. Reckase examined portfolio assessment specifically. He found that interrater reliability reaches acceptable levels if the assessor scores the components of the portfolio individually and then aggregates them to a composite score. A common alternative is holistic scoring, mentioned above, which produces just one score for the complete project. However, holistic scoring and the practice of scoring the individual components of the project without aggregating them both characteristically exhibit a great deal of scoring inconsistency.

In addition to better reliability, scoring individual components and then aggregating the scores serves another purpose. The aggregated score is often what the students are interested in, and it may also serve the administration's need for a single, summary judgment of the student's performance. The individual components, on the other hand, can provide detailed feedback about the learner's performance that can be very helpful to a classroom teacher interested in identifying ways to improve the instruction as well as the areas where students may still need help.

Speaking of Authentic Assessment

Like those involved in traditional assessment, authentic assessment advocates ought to be concerned about assessment reliability. Although the object of reliability changes from a standardized test score to a project or performance evaluation, the question remains the same: Will the judgment of the student's performance be consistent as long as the relevant conditions do not change? When it is not feasible for multiple judges to assess the same materials, the classroom teacher can assess the same performance multiple times.

Traditional assessment minimizes scoring reliability problems by employing objectively scored test items that limit the judgments one must make. That option is typically unavailable to advocates of authentic assessment who avoid most of the traditional testing practices. To achieve scoring consistency in an authentic assessment setting, one must adopt clearly established scoring standards and take the time to train in their use and application. This is particularly important where students are engaged in a variety of different kinds of projects.

VALIDITY IN AUTHENTIC ASSESSMENT

The discussion of validity, too, is more associated with traditional standardized testing than with authentic assessment. Indeed, authentic assessment advocates often fail even to speak of it, but on some level, validity is important to any assessment activity.

Assessment Relevance and Consequential Validity

Remember that a driving force behind authentic assessment is the criticism that many learning products—test scores in particular—have little to do with what the learner should be able to do beyond school. Correspondingly, the justification for the criterion-based performance standards is that they are more relevant indicators of the desired outcomes. In traditional assessment discussions, **content validity, criterion-related validity,** and **construct validity** define assessment quality. The different dimensions of validity are discussed at some length in Chapter 8, but for now note that results have content validity when the test items accurately represent the related discipline. Criterion-related validity reflects how well the data from one measure correspond with some other measure of the same skill or learning. Construct validity indicates how well a test gauges some theoretical construct or trait (Messick, 1989). All of these aspects of assessment validity can be quantified (represented as a number).

In authentic assessment discussions, the validity issues are raised a little differently. **Assessment relevance** deals with the degree to which the assessment is related to what the learner is being prepared to do beyond the particular assessment setting. For many people, assessment relevance is synonymous with authentic assessment. Note that although the circumstances and language may be a little different, assessment relevance is quite similar to criterion-related validity. Both deal with how closely connected classroom results are to some other measure—another assessment or the student's performance in the world of work.

The other assessment standard is **consequential validity.** It is "the consequence for students and for schools of using a particular form of assessment" (Darling-Hammond et al., 1995, p. 64). The argument is that if teaching and learning improve because of the particular assessment, then it is valid; in the negative, assessment activities that have no impact lack consequential validity.

There is also an important institutional context. Procedures that have consequential validity will reflect the learning and assessment activities most valued by the school community (Darling-Hammond et al., 1995). They elevate the skills and abilities that educators are trying to foster and minimize those that appear to have lesser value.

Consider a situation in which a learner develops an exhibit of labeled rocks for a physical science unit based on the geology of the region. A collection of rocks certainly appears to be a more authentic product than a score from a paper and pencil test of how well the learner can differentiate among igneous, sedimentary, and metamorphic rocks. The validity question, however, is whether the students' development of the exhibit represents their grasp of the area's geology better than test scores. The supplementary question is whether the learning project fosters the most valued learning activities.

These are not easy questions to answer. Consequential validity can be analyzed only by comparing the kind of teaching and learning that resulted in the rock collection to what would have occurred in a more conventional setting. Simply setting aside procedures that rely heavily on conventional testing is no guarantee that a nontesting substitute provides greater validity, in spite of what appears to be a more authentic product and a more authentic setting.

Authentic Assessment and the Appearance of Validity

As you are continually reminded, the hallmark of authentic assessment practices is the appeal they make to real-world circumstances. Actually, we are talking largely about appearances, and this appearance factor is very much akin to what was traditionally called **face validity** in assessment. By definition, face validity is not a formal aspect of validity at all, but rather the appearance of validity. It is ironic that this least substantive of the dimensions of validity would become a central tenet to the authentic assessment philosophy.

Employing Common versus Individual Standards

A central theme in this book is that educational planning should include attention to both instruction and assessment. There are a number of benefits from this (e.g., there is harmony between what students learn and what they demonstrate). On a general level, authentic assessment and traditional testing are in agreement here. Classroom instruction in problem solving should include a plan for assessment activities that allow one to evaluate the students' progress and achievement in problem solving. Remember that authentic assessment advocates argue, however, that the assessment should not obligate all students to the same problem-solving activity when they demonstrate what they have learned. Berlak (1992) explained the position when he noted that one of the problems with traditional testing is the very idea that the desired behavior can be generalized to all learners.

> The assumption that there can be a meaningful nation-wide, statewide, district-wide, or even school-wide consensus on the goals of schooling and on what students should learn and how they should learn is untenable . . . In a multicultural society which values difference, consensus is undesirable. (p. 14)

So although probably no one argues against determining what must be accomplished to demonstrate learning, Berlak's logic embraces potentially a different accomplishment for each state, district, school, and—perhaps by extension—for each learner.

This is an important point of departure for advocates of authentic assessment. Traditional assessment techniques sustain a set of quite specific goals and objectives intended for all students who fall within a particular age or grade classification. Often goals and objectives are established with little concern for differences between individuals, classrooms, schools, and so forth. Authentic assessment advocates champion the need for standards that are nonspecific enough that one can adapt them to a variety of circumstances. In fact, instructional activities often ask each learner to construct what is for them an original response (Mehrens, 1992), a practice that accommodates student diversity.

> The quality of traditional assessment procedures is often defined in terms of whether the assessment looks like it is supposed to look (face validity), represents the discipline well (content validity), agrees with other measures of the same learning (criterion-related validity), and measures the trait it claims to measure (construct validity). Of these, authentic assessment advocates care for only face validity, content validity, and what is called consequential validity—the degree to which teaching and learning improve because of the assessment procedures.

VARIATIONS ON THE THEME: AUTHENTIC ASSESSMENT CHOICES

Having discussed some of the theoretical and conceptual issues involved in authentic assessment, we can examine some of the authentic assessment products. Archbald and Newmann (1992) have identified three classifications. **Tests of discrete competencies** provide a fairly simple summary of learners' performances in a reasonably well-defined content area. **Exhibitions** are learning demonstrations that may take learners beyond the boundaries of their schools. They involve a public demonstration of what the learner has accomplished, and the project is one for which the learner takes the major responsibility. **Portfolios** are collections of work samples. They are multiple indicators of learning that provide a profile of some important element of student performance examined from several authentic vantages.

Tests of Discrete Competencies

We noted that one criticism of conventional testing is a suspicion about the real-world value of some of the traits or characteristics that standardized tests measure. However, even the most ardent critics recognize the need for the capability to measure reading, writing, analytical ability, problem-solving ability, reasoning ability, and the like.

Conventional reading comprehension tests have a quite predictable format. They ordinarily include a passage that learners must read before they respond to several related multiple-choice items. An alternative—and many would argue a far more authentic—approach is to require that the learner explain a text passage to a listener. This is probably a better demonstration of reading comprehension, but it is also a more difficult work sample to score reliably. We can address that problem with a scoring guide or protocol such as the one in Figure 4.4. The protocol indicates what the listener must look for and suggests how to determine the quality of the reader's explanation.

A scoring protocol must outline what the desired behaviors are and describe the relevant differences in the learners' performances. It must be detailed enough that one who is familiar with it can consistently employ the same standards for different learners. If the judge's assessment indicates that several learners have "a general grasp of the issues" (Figure 4.4, no. 3), they all ought to have very similar levels of reading comprehension. Besides consistency from learner to learner, multiple assessors of one learner ought to draw similar conclusions about the quality of a particular learner's responses (the interrater reliability previously mentioned), something that often requires some practice.

FIGURE 4.4   Assessing Reading Comprehension

Questions

How is the setting related to the theme in this particular story?

Which of the characters does the author develop most thoroughly?

Does the plot unfold in a way that appears reasonable to you?

Scoring Indicator

5—The learner is able to respond with examples to support the position taken; response reflects a thorough understanding of the passage.

4—The learner is able to respond to the question and defend the position taken.

3—The learner has a general grasp of the issues but lacks specific support for the response.

2—The learner's understanding of the related concepts is vague and without any particular insight.

1—The learner's response reflects little understanding.

0—The learner did not respond.

Exhibitions

Some learning experiences result in the sort of tangible product that learners can demonstrate in a presentation, and which can be very revealing. Among authentic assessment options, exhibitions are among the most used and frequently discussed (Elliott, 1991). They are popular because they usually require that learners integrate a variety of skills and abilities that are valuable beyond the exhibition. They are also appealing because the learner has the major responsibility for organizing and presenting the exhibition.

As we noted earlier, the exhibition approach to assessment is not new to some disciplines. It has been the norm for musicians and athletes, for example, and it has been a long-standing requirement for teacher candidates during the student teaching experience. Authentic assessment advocates claim that exhibition should be common in more conventional learning activities as well.

Elliott (1991) explained that the exhibition setting is optimal for "a recital, a debate, a play, a game, an oral report in front of a class, or any event where a student can be observed using acquired knowledge or skills" (p. 275). Part of the traditional history experience is to help learners develop a chronology of important historical events and then to encourage them to grasp some of the issues that helped define each historical period. As an alternative, students might be better served with the exhibition assignment in Figure 4.5.

Before the presentation can begin, learners must do enough research that they can determine which characteristics are relevant to each historical period and decide who can represent them most effectively. These tasks require familiarity with research resources as well as a substantial time commitment in order to organize the materials and the profiles of the individuals featured in the case studies. Students must also write well enough to maintain common themes across the different individuals in the written text. They also need some sense of the artistic to prepare the final exhibit. Those same skills and abilities must be the focus in the assessment as well, with each element reflecting an appropriate scoring emphasis.

Concern over the competencies, particularly among high school graduates, has prompted many schools to develop comprehensive exit exams as a final screening device. Authentic assessment proposes a final exhibit analogous to a "rite of passage"

FIGURE 4.5 **A History Exhibition**

Instructions: Prepare a poster display that presents case studies of a series of individuals, one selected from each century of the American experience from the time the Spanish discovered the continent to the present day. Demonstrate that each of the featured individuals is representative of the century from which she or he is drawn, but develop themes that transcend the centuries, such as:

- How did these people earn their livings?
- What was likely the level of their education?
- What were the pressing political concerns of their age?
- What was America's place in the world during their time?
- How was their age most different from our own?

for graduates as an alternative. These culminating presentations are reminiscent of the projects that adolescents in some cultures undertake to demonstrate their readiness for adulthood.

Learners who successfully navigate this terminal experience do so by making an involved presentation to a board of examiners. It is a synthesis of several areas of knowledge and competence integrated in such a way that the learner can demonstrate each of the required outcomes. Board members who review the presentation ask questions about the details and significance of the learner's work, and students field the questions as an important element of their eligibility to "pass" (Archbald and Newmann, 1992).

Elliott (1991) described one application of this rite of passage experience. It is an exhibition comprehensive enough that it involves tests of discrete competencies and the organization of a portfolio. For the formal presentation:

> Exhibitions can take a variety of forms—from a simple lab exercise to a major multidisciplinary academic presentation. In each instance, however, exhibitions give the students a large measure of control. Students are in a position to demonstrate what they have learned by making and then defending a presentation. This can be very revealing to assessors.

> *All seniors must demonstrate mastery in fifteen areas of knowledge and competence by completing a portfolio, a project, and six other presentations before a . . . committee consisting of staff members (including the student's home room teacher), a student from the grade below, and an adult from the community. Nine of the presentations are based on the materials in the portfolio and the project, the remaining six presentations are developed especially for the presentation process. . . . The student must field questions during the presentation given during the 2nd semester [of the] senior year. (p. 276)*

Portfolios

For many people, portfolio assessment *is* authentic assessment, perhaps because it has such a lengthy tradition in the academic setting. In particular, those involved with teaching language and communication skills have a history of using portfolios as the mechanism for evaluating students' progress in their written work. Strictly speaking, "A portfolio is a file or folder containing a variety of information that provides a record of students' experiences and accomplishments" (Archbald and Newmann, 1992, p. 169). The record may document the learner's work experiences in a brief instructional unit or in an entire course. It may even reflect the learner's work in a discipline over several years.

The decision about which work samples to include should rest primarily with the instructor, although students may have some input. The materials document what the learner can do. They also provide the substance for evaluating how well the learner can perform (Elliott, 1991). Because these accomplishments usually connect to a prescribed curriculum, it is important that the entries relate to specific learning objectives, not just to the students' best work samples. If the portfolio is to be an accurate reflection of how well students have completed the important learning activities, the quite common practice of allowing students to select portfolio entries ought to be tempered. Besides the possibility of a portfolio that does not include the most important entries, it is very difficult to score portfolios reliably when each contains different entries.

While a portfolio might conceivably have as many individual items to score as a conventional test, usually this is not the case. The tasks are usually fewer, more comprehensive, and more directly related to the skill or ability the learner is developing. Not all entries are equally important, so portfolios may require scoring methods that allow one to weight the elements differentially.

Presume for a moment that all of your seventh-grade history students have been assigned to develop portfolios containing materials from their study of their families' histories and roots. Two of those entries are (a) a card indicating the place and date of their parents' births and (b) a transcript of an extended interview they've conducted with a grandparent regarding the grandparent's childhood experiences. Both entries are relevant to the task, but the interview will likely be more difficult to conduct, and it will provide more information about the family's history than just a statement of date of birth. The two entries ought to be weighted accordingly.

Portfolio entries may include a variety of materials. Writing samples, homework assignments, audio or video records, minutes of a student government meeting in which the learner was a participant, and even a judge's sheets from one of the learner's debate tournaments may be appropriate. Nearly anything that can serve as an indicator of the student's skills and abilities is potentially helpful. However, the portfolio should not be a file folder indiscriminately filled with everything related to the student's experiences. The entries, and each entry's relative weight, ought to be established beforehand. There must be standards for scoring each sample and procedures developed that will help the assessor(s) maintain judgment reliability.

Assume that you teach a fifth-grade class and you have decided to assign your students a portfolio as part of a unit you will teach in the autumn titled "Getting Ready for Winter." Figure 4.6 suggests how you might meet each of the authentic assessment standards for portfolios.

Portfolios can be very helpful beyond the normal bounds of assessing student learning. Someone selecting students for an eleventh-grade Honors English class might ask applicants to complete a portfolio, for example, with entries such as these:

- a writing sample of 200 words or more from the tenth grade.
- a written recommendation from an English teacher.
- a copy of the learner's English grade from the prior year.
- the author and title of the last book the student read for pleasure.

The irony of this particular use of the portfolio, by the way, is that it would probably serve as a mechanism for ranking applicants.

Note that the final element in Figure 4.6 addresses the problem of achieving reliable portfolio scores. The approach in that example is for the individual teacher to score the students' work twice or three times. A safer, but for obvious reasons less practical, practice is to have multiple scorers. If another fifth-grade teacher is willing to score the portfolios, there are generally three factors that affect the way scorers view a student's work. These questions reflect them:

1. Do scorers understand the objectives?
2. Do the scorers have previous experience with the work in the portfolio?
3. Are scorers familiar with the scoring procedures?

FIGURE 4.6   Requirements for a Fifth-Grade Portfolio: "Getting Ready for Winter"

Standards

There are to be five separate photo, drawing, or sample entries, each of which illustrates how an animal or plant changes as a result of the onset of fall and winter. A brief written narrative will explain each entry's significance.

Quality Indicators

Each entry will be assessed according to the following criteria. Acceptable portfolios include a score of at least 5 on instructiveness and 4 on the narrative.

Assessment Criteria	Points
Degree to which portfolio is instructive	1–10
Completeness and accuracy of narrative	1–7
Aesthetic appeal	1–4
Apparent level of effort	1–4
Originality	1–3
Neatness	1–3

Scoring Protocol

Very well done	28–31
Good	23–27
Adequate	17–22
Inadequate (requires learner to resubmit with corrections)	<17

Assessment

The teacher will score each portfolio twice using a "blind" procedure. The average of the two total scores will be the learner's score. In those instances in which the learner's total score varies more than 5 points, the teacher will score the portfolio a third time and average all three scores.

Until everyone involved can answer the questions in the affirmative, they probably should not proceed. Reckase (1995) has explained how to proceed with multiple scorers in order to achieve maximum interrater reliability:

- Each item in the portfolio must be assessed separately by two people who are trained in the specific assessment task.
- If evaluators disagree on a score, the portfolio must be submitted to a third evaluator.
- Individual item scores are aggregated to form a total score.

As you have probably noticed, this is likely a very time-intensive and, therefore, costly procedure. The University of Miami currently requires a portfolio of each applicant to the university. Reckase (1995) reported that the cost of scoring the portfolios in 1995 was approximately $17.50 for each candidate. Where the stakes are as high as they are in university admissions decisions, however, the procedure is likely to be more deliberate and time-consuming (costly) than it will be for the classroom teacher scoring a few portfolios.

Although reliability is best when a portfolio finally yields one score, remember that the score used to calculate reliability is actually an aggregated one, a product of multiple portfolio components. The temptation to provide only a holistic score for the portfolio does not reflect sound assessment practice, particularly as the number of entries in the portfolio increases. Besides reliability problems, a holistic score suggests only a single skill or ability in the portfolio. Although the portfolio may have a central objective and the student's success with it may be prominent in the aggregated score, there are nearly always multiple objectives.

There is a rather delicate balance here. We need multiple scores because a total performance has several component parts, each of which we wish to measure, particularly when they are relatively independent. Neatness is unrelated to the accuracy of the narrative in the portfolio assignment in Figure 4.6, but both are important enough to assess, and each can be very revealing. The composite score, however, must primarily reflect the central objective. In the prior assignment, the objective is for learners to demonstrate how well they understand the concept of the changes that occur in plants and animals in the autumn. For this reason the "instructiveness" and "quality of the narrative" criteria that are most directly related to the learner's grasp of the concept are more heavily weighted than the other categories. We have also protected against the possibility of an acceptable portfolio that contains an unacceptable level of either instructiveness or narrative quality by establishing minimum allowable scores in those two areas.

> Portfolios almost always have multiple objectives. There is usually a central purpose for completing the portfolio, however, and the student's performance in terms of that primary objective ought to reflect a major portion of the aggregated portfolio grade.

Strategies for Diverse Groups

The need for clear criteria, multiple indicators of performance quality, and judgment reliability spell out the technical qualities that an effective program of authentic assessment contains. As discussed, students' performances may take the form of a competency test, an exhibition, or a portfolio. Beyond the technical characteristics and structure, however, other qualities allow this form of assessment to be responsive to particularly diverse groups of learners. The criteria deal primarily with design:

- The different responses the instructor allows should accommodate the students' backgrounds.
- The assessments should be meaningful learning experiences in themselves.
- When there is reliable evidence of culturally based cognitive styles and modes of representation, the assessment should accommodate them.

Figure 4.7 is a list of assessment strategies that may be effective with diverse groups of learners. Although the suggestions might be helpful in any assessment setting, they are particularly useful in situations in which learners may have cultural or linguistic backgrounds that may place them at a disadvantage.

The strategies certainly are not a panacea. Although a translation can reflect a superficial familiarity, sometimes the substance of an educational task does not lend itself very well to translation because concepts common to one language or culture

FIGURE 4.7   **Assessment Strategies for Diverse Groups of Learners**

1. Translate an existing assessment into students' primary languages.
2. Make the names and relevant information in an existing assessment consistent with the learners' background and language.
3. Require exhibitions that allow some element of the learner's perspectives and experiences.
4. Develop class projects that allow learners to connect what they have learned in the classroom to what exists outside, with particular sensitivity to local language and culture.
5. Develop assessment tasks that are sensitive to students' cognitive styles and to multiple ways (oral, visual, behavioral) of knowing and demonstrating knowledge.

Source: Adapted from Koelsch, Estrin, and Farr (1995).

are foreign to another. This means that translation may compromise the validity of the assessment. Finally, in some instances, adaptation is no substitute for a new assessment (Koelsch et al., 1995).

AUTHENTIC ASSESSMENT AND GRADING

Elliott (1991) outlined the position authentic assessment advocates often take regarding grades when he noted:

> *Grading is unnecessary, if not inconsistent in an authentic assessment system. Instead students' progress toward mastery of the agreed upon learning outcomes is evaluated by comparing their work to the terminal learning objectives for any given subject or school year. Students' work and accomplishments are compared to a standard of performance, as opposed to other students. (p. 277)*

The last sentence suggests that Elliott is equating grading with a normative ranking of students. There are, of course, other approaches to grading. Earlier a logical relationship was established between authentic assessment and the criterion-referenced assessment that emerged in the 1960s. In either system, one evaluates students' progress by comparing their work to an established standard rather than by comparing them to each other. Although authentic assessment has probably fostered greater latitude for students than criterion-referenced approaches, disciples of both argue for a standard not connected to students' rankings among their peers.

In both traditions, the classroom teacher and/or other experts determine the objectives before instruction begins. In criterion-referenced approaches, the objective's criterion and the degree to which learners must demonstrate their command of the material are both specified. Authentic assessment is less well defined in this regard so that it may accommodate different approaches. The related evaluative schemes are often called "profiles" (Elliott, 1991), and "grading" is a matter of deter-

> Advocates of alternative assessment often oppose traditional grading. The element they are most opposed to, however, is ranking the students against each other. Inasmuch as the grade represents some summary statement of the learner's performance, there is always a need for some sort of determination, but it need not compare learners to each other.

mining how learners measure up to a profile. A subjective evaluation by the instructor often replaces the letter grade. Clearly, authentic assessment places much emphasis on the instructor's judgment, a characteristic reflected in all of the procedures called for in Figures 4.3 through 4.6. This is a fundamental distinction between authentic assessment and traditional, test-based assessment wherein the human element and attendant subjectivity are both quite limited.

For Further Discussion

We just noted that traditional, multiple-choice tests attempt to limit the amount of subjectivity in assessment. The reasoning is that subjectivity contributes to error in the measurement. Those in favor of alternative assessment methods turn this argument almost completely around. They claim that because no one knows the students better than the classroom teachers know them, teachers should have a certain amount of latitude as they evaluate student performance. This permits them to moderate their judgments based on characteristics that might affect evaluations such as past performance, linguistic skill, cultural background, and the like. In light of these contrary positions, consider the following questions:

- How would you prefer to be judged, by a completely objective standard, or by someone who is willing to make allowances for specific, performance-related variables?
- What is fairest to your future students?
- In what instances is an assessment with a subjective element fairest?
- When is objectivity the safest course?

SUMMARY

Sometimes movements are defined by what they are not, which may be the case with authentic assessment. Archbald (1991) noted that it "appears to describe just about any alternative to a standardized multiple-choice test" (pp. 279–280). The educational reform movement, which began in the early 1980s, called for improvements in student achievement and school quality. Increased testing did not alter the state of things in the schools, and for at least some critics, standardized testing appeared to be part of the problem. An element of the reform movement expanded to reflect a distrust of tests.

Traditional tests were an easy target. Kamphaus (1991) reported tests' sampling of content domains in some instances to be "nothing short of appalling" (p. 301), but content coverage was not the only issue. There were also concerns about the level of thinking that students must manifest, since traditional school assessment procedures sometimes address nothing beyond the level of recall. Fundamentally, critics argued, standardized tests have only a tenuous link to teaching practice, which means that they offer little to the educator looking for ways to improve curriculum and instruction (Kamphaus, 1991). Archbald (1991) noted:

> Used properly, standardized tests are a quick way to spot academic weaknesses among pupils. If a test is used to supplement a teacher's knowledge of individual

students and the teacher teaches effectively, then it can be a tool of academic improvement. But it cannot (and is not designed to) implement substantial changes in how teachers teach and define achievement. (p. 286)

Having noted some of the criticisms that have prompted the rise of authentic assessment, we need to note that the optimism for this approach does not necessarily reflect a substantial research base. Authentic assessment is a movement in process, and educators are still defining both its role and its relationship to standardized testing. Archbald's (1991) position is that the role of standardized testing, as the previous quotation suggests, is primarily in the area of individual student diagnosis. Interestingly, Mehrens (1992) assigned that role to authentic assessment.

Although some of the language has changed, many of the concepts associated with authentic assessment are not new. Elliott (1991) recognized that the methods employed in authentic assessment clearly relate to what was "applied behavior analysis" 30 years ago. That movement spawned criterion-referenced testing, which in many ways is a precursor to authentic assessment in spite of the fact that there is very little effort to cross-reference current procedures with the earlier work. Beyond that theoretical link, the idea of placing assessment in the most authentic setting possible has long been a fixture in some disciplines. The effect of the current movement is to expand the concept into disciplines in which it is new.

Authentic assessment reflects more than an approach to student evaluation. It presumes that students will produce something that reflects not a compartmentalized, narrow repetition of what was presented to them, but an integrated scholarship that connects their learning to learning housed in other disciplines. It should also occur in a setting consistent with that in which the learning is likely to be most useful in the future. Those objectives are difficult to argue with and, indeed, reflect outcomes that are highly regarded by all educators, whether or not they advocate authentic assessment.

One of the limitations in standardized testing situations is the tendency educators have to coach students in order to prepare them to score as high as possible on high-stakes tests. Problems such as these are not automatically resolved simply because someone changes the assessment, however. As Shepard (1995) has noted, "even authentic measures are corruptible and, when practiced for, can distort curriculum and undermine professional autonomy" (p. 38).

As stated in Chapter 2, besides evaluating learners' progress, assessment should inform instruction. The multiple indicators of multiple performances called for by authentic assessment offer the potential to inform instruction more effectively than test scores can. By doing so, they provide the promise of better instructional decisions. Mehrens (1992) suggested that part of authentic assessment's strength is the greater ease with which it can be integrated into instruction and become part of the larger educational picture. Perhaps any kind of assessment drives the associated instruction to some degree, but authentic assessment's focus on a wide range of skills and abilities probably provides a basis for instructional decision making that is sounder than many of the alternatives. This was Christenson's (1991) theme when she noted:

Authentic assessment models good instruction. The concept of authentic assessment is reified by thinking of our knowledge base on instructional effectiveness. By determining how to assess students' performance on meaningful tasks, the probability that instruction will be modified is high. In this way, authentic assessment may be the stimulus for implementing the instructional effectiveness guidelines more systematically. (p. 297)

Authentic assessment has much to offer, but it does not come without drawbacks. Christenson (1991) noted that it is time- and cost-intensive. It requires that educators identify the essential learning competencies by grade level and discipline, and in some cases across disciplines, so that the synthesis that advocates prize can occur.

Authentic assessment advocates eschew much of the reliability and validity discussion associated with more traditional testing. Although content validity is a highlight, other technical characteristics of an assessment should also matter. There needs to be some assurance, for example, beyond calling the assessment "authentic," that the students' performances predict the behaviors for which they are being prepared. Perhaps the greatest promise will be to those who refuse to make authentic assessment an either-or proposition and find ways to integrate elements of authentic and traditional assessment in their educational plans. An appropriate closing comment is offered by Kamphaus (1991), who noted, "authentic assessment is . . . not a technological breakthrough, it's a complementary . . . tradition aimed, with others, at improving educational assessment practice" (p. 302).

ENDNOTE

1. The earlier movement had its origins in behavioral psychology, which lauded the safety inherent in the kinds of learner activities that could be observed directly and which required very few conclusions that had to be based on inference. Although most advocates of authentic assessment do not recognize that relationship with behavioral psychology and what was called "criterion-referenced testing," the use of an objective set of performance criteria is common to both movements.

FOR FURTHER READING

Christenson's (1991) paper listed in the references is one of the more evenhanded treatments of the promise and difficulties posed by authentic assessment.

Estrin (1993) has written a very readable paper dealing with some of the complexities of language and culture in assessment, and O'Connor's (1989) chapter raises important issues connected with differential performance in minority groups.

The early chapters in Gardner's (1991) book are very helpful. He has developed a framework for distinguishing between students who can respond properly to problems when they occur as they were taught and those who can respond even if circumstances change. Although not an argument for authentic assessment, the framework is consistent with much of the authentic assessment literature.

REFERENCES

Anastasi, A. (1977). *Psychological testing* (4th ed.). New York: Macmillan.
Archbald, D. A. (1991). Authentic assessment: Principles, practices, and issues. *School Psychology Quarterly, 6,* 279–293.

Archbald, D. A., and Newmann, F. M. (1992). "Approaches to assessing academic achievement." In H. Berlak, F. M. Newmann, E. Adams, D. A. Archbald, T. Burgess, J. Raven, and T. A. Romberg (Eds.), *Toward a new science of educational testing and assessment* (pp. 139–180). New York: State University of New York Press.

Berlak, H. (1992). "The need for a new science of assessment." In H. Berlak, F. M. Newmann, E. Adams, D. A. Archbald, T. Burgess, J. Raven, and T. A. Romberg (Eds.), *Toward a new science of educational testing and assessment* (pp. 1–21). New York: State University of New York Press.

Christenson, S. L. (1991). Authentic assessment: Straw man or prescription for progress? *School Psychology Quarterly, 6,* 294–299.

Darling-Hammond, L., Ancess, J., and Falk, B. (1995). *Authentic assessment in action: Studies of schools and students at work.* National center for restructuring education, schools, and teaching. New York: Teachers College, Columbia University.

Elliott, S. N. (1991). Authentic assessment: An introduction to a neobehavioral approach to classroom assessment. *School Psychology Quarterly, 6,* 273–278.

Estrin, E. T. (1993). Alternative assessment: Issues in language, culture, and equity. (Brief #11). San Francisco: Far West Laboratory.

Fitzpatrick, R., and Morrison, E. J. (1971). Performance and product evaluation. In E. L. Thorndike (Ed.), *Educational measurement* (2nd ed., pp. 237–270). Washington DC: American Council on Education.

Gardner, H. (1991). *The unschooled mind.* New York: Basic Books.

Kamphaus, R. W. (1991). Authentic assessment and content validity. *School Psychology Quarterly, 6,* 300–304.

Koelsch, N., Estrin, E. T., and Farr, B. (1995). *Guide to developing equitable performance assessments.* Washington, DC: Office of Educational Research and Development. (ERIC Document Reproduction Service No. ED 397 125)

Mehrens, W. A. (1992). Using performance assessment for accountability purposes. *Educational Measurement: Issues and Practice, 11*(1), 3–9, 20.

Messick, S. (1989). Validity. In R. L. Linn (Ed.), *Educational measurement* (3rd ed.). New York: Macmillan.

National Commission on Excellence in Education. (1983). *A nation at risk.* Washington, DC: U.S. Department of Education.

Newmann, F. M., and Archbald, D. A. (1992). "The nature of authentic academic achievement." In H. Berlak, F. M. Newmann, E. Adams, D. A. Archbald, T. Burgess, J. Raven, and T. A. Romberg (Eds.), *Toward a new science of educational testing and assessment* (pp. 71–83). New York: State University of New York Press.

O'Connor, M. C. (1989). Aspects of differential performance by minorities on standardized tests: Linguistic and sociocultural factors. In B. Gifford (Ed.), *Test policy and test performance: Education, language and culture.* Boston: Kluwer Academic Publishers.

Reckase, M. D. (1995). Portfolio assessment: A theoretical estimate of score reliability. *Educational Measurement: Issues and Practice, 14*(1), 12–14, 31.

Resnick, L. B. (1987). *Education and learning to think.* Washington, DC: National Academy Press.

Shepard, L. A. (1995). Using assessment to improve learning. *Educational Leadership, 54*(5), 38–43.

5

Grading Students and Evaluating Instruction

■ *The reader will develop procedures for grading students and also for evaluating the quality of the teacher's performance.*

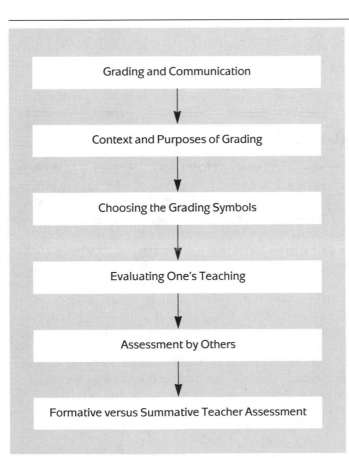

Grading and Communication

↓

Context and Purposes of Grading

↓

Choosing the Grading Symbols

↓

Evaluating One's Teaching

↓

Assessment by Others

↓

Formative versus Summative Teacher Assessment

Different audiences have different expectations for grades. The common element is that grades must be as objective as possible and as precise as conditions allow. Different situations will call for different grading symbols, but in each instance grading procedures must reflect careful planning. Furthermore, one must explain the grades to those who will be affected by them. Because student performance is affected by teaching performance, we also have an interest in grading the teacher. The primary source of data is self-assessment, but evaluation by others is also important, particularly when those procedures are related to the conditions of the teacher's employment. ■

Mrs. Sabey thought about her second-grade students with fondness. They were children from families with very diverse backgrounds. Their homes were in a mix of rural and suburban locations, and their circumstances ranged from upper-middle to lower class. Some of the children's parents were high school dropouts, and others were professionals with advanced degrees. Mrs. Sabey was aware of the differences, but she refused to allow them to affect they way she treated the students, since they were variables that neither she nor the children could control. Her greatest interest was in providing each child with an even chance to succeed in school. To that end, she worried a good deal about her grading procedures. Were it not for the pressure she felt from parents, school officials, and the children themselves, she would probably have elected not to grade the children at all, leaving such evaluation for some later grade.

Her colleagues generally based grades on how well students met criteria established by the district's curriculum office, which Mrs. Sabey found to be discouraging for the slower learners. Should she grade the students for their effort? In some ways, at least, that seemed the most equitable approach. Perhaps progress was the best measure. If she could focus on how much the students' skills and knowledge improved, she could reward those who made progress, even if they remained behind the more aggressive learners. It struck Mrs. Sabey that developing a grading plan offered more questions than answers. ■

GRADING AND COMMUNICATION

Grading is a culmination activity, and it might be helpful to review some of the terms connected with activities that precede it. One is measurement, which is essentially a data-gathering activity. It is based on observations that lead us to assign numbers to particular elements of performance. For example, a score of 12 on a spelling quiz represents a measurement. Measurement should be as objective as possible so that it occurs according to specified rules.

Evaluation follows measurement. It involves making a judgment about the quality of a performance, giving it a subjective element, which measurement lacks. One evaluates a performance by determining that 12 on the spelling test is "acceptable" or "good." We will pursue the topic only briefly here, but it is important to recognize that evaluations do not emerge from a vacuum. They have a social or political context that, when understood, helps explain how we come to particular decisions (Andrews and Barnes, 1990). The teacher's decision that 12 is acceptable performance rather than very good performance, for example, may reflect the fact that the instructor's superiors have asked for more rigor in evaluation. They in turn may be reacting to a report from the state department of education indicating that the district has lost ground on achievement tests relative to the performance of the neighboring school districts.

Measurement and evaluation lead logically to grading. In simple terms, grading is the evaluation in abbreviated form. Its brevity suggests its function, which is primarily communication. We say "primarily" because there may be other purposes served as well. To students who have high levels of achievement motivation, sometimes grades are perceived as rewards, for example.

Although grades and grading are prominent in the flow of classroom events, grading is not a necessary part of the learning process at all. Although it is usually interpreted as a representation of learning, grading is actually quite incidental (Frisbie and Waltman, 1992). All of the various teaching and learning activities can occur quite effectively without grading, but from time to time there are particular audiences who request some type of performance indicator. Learners need to know something about their levels of accomplishment, as do their teachers and interested others. When learners are young, grades may be directed more toward their parents than to the learners themselves. Removed as they are from the classroom, parents often wish to have some evaluative reference point for the child's progress.

> *Measurement* is a data-gathering activity. When we use the data to make a judgment, we have made an *evaluation*. If we represent performance symbolically, we are *grading* the student's performance.

Later in one's academic career, grades communicate past performance to others to whom the student may be unfamiliar. Admissions officers, program administrators, and prospective employers rely on grades to indicate past academic performance and to predict what they can expect. Grades are a brief, symbolic representation of the quality of one's performance—but what performance? Back to Mrs. Sabey's quandary in the prologue, we could grade achievement, improvement, effort, appearance, or a variety of other characteristics. The decision about what to grade is reflected in the discussion to follow.

GRADING IN CONTEXT

In Chapter 2 we made a point of distinguishing between the different purposes of assessment. Recall that one of the rationales offered for studying assessment is the potential it offers to inform the other parts of the educational process from the earliest planning to the final, finished performance. Too often, we make assessment synonymous with grading. When we focus only on the culminating activity, we minimize the other elements of measurement and evaluation. Although grading is represented in assessment, it is only one segment.

Mrs. Sabey's thoughts about grading ought to suggest that some of the decisions that shape one's plans are really philosophical. The question is often not of the correct or the incorrect procedure, but rather of what one values in education and therefore wishes to see represented in the grade. Answers to those questions are important because they shape grading procedures. Although all educators operate within parameters imposed by district, school, or department grading policies, the traditional pattern has been to leave the instructor a good deal of latitude in most of the grading decisions.

GRADING PURPOSES AND PROCEDURES

As has been noted, grades serve more than a communication function. They also have an incentive value to many students. Grades serve as gatekeepers, as well, and sometimes take on their greatest import in that context.

For Further Discussion

In his first year as a public school teacher, your author told the senior students in the advanced placement course he was assigned to teach, "Focus your attention on the learning. Learn as much as you can, and the grade will take care of itself." Your author was convinced that if students would stop thinking in terms of 'What must I do for an A?' and if they focused instead on developing a command of the subject, they would make better progress. While that may be true, it is at least naïve. Your author had not yet recognized how important grades were for many of his students. Grades often have an incentive value. Your author does not know why he expected that their experiences should be substantially different from those of many other students, but he was treating grades as a distraction. For many of the students, the grades were their reason for being. However much one may wish to diminish grades, the truth is that they matter a great deal for several reasons—not the least of which is their impact as rewards. Consider the following question:

In your experience, have grades been an impediment or an inducement to learning?

Grades as Gatekeepers

Before universal literacy became every modern nation's goal, schooling beyond the most rudimentary levels was uncommon. As industrialization grew, so did the demand for an educated workforce, however, and this demand is magnified in postindustrial societies. When most jobs were relatively simple and easy to learn, evaluating a candidate's aptitude for them was also simple, but populations have increased, society is more complex, and making judgments about people by person-to-person interaction is increasingly problematic. As a result, decision makers turn to secondary indicators for information about an individual's qualifications, and grades provide that service. They are often used to determine whether one may enter a program, graduate from a school, receive a license, be hired to a new position, be admitted to university, and so on. Grades help determine opportunity. By extension, they determine the financial rewards related to a course of action. The importance of the consequences involved (the "stakes") obliges us to be very careful.

The Grading Plan

Fundamentally, we must be able to defend the procedures that determine grades. Frisbie and Waltman (1992) maintain that the safest approach is to develop a personal grading plan. They recommend the following:

1. Determine whether the district has a grading policy. When a policy exists, implement those elements that apply to one's circumstances.
2. When they are not set down by district or school policy, develop descriptive criteria that explain the meaning of each grade.
3. Align the grading procedures with the instruction.
4. Determine the grading variables.
5. Determine whether grades should conform to a particular distribution.
6. Determine the number and nature of the graded components.
7. Develop a plan for appropriately weighting the components of the final grade.

Implementing Grading Policy

Compared to other elements such as the curriculum, school districts usually prescribe comparatively little about grading procedures beyond the need to have them. If there are specific requirements, instructors are obligated to implement them, however. The district may require everyone in the district to use the same grading symbols and descriptors, but rather than an attempt to manage individual teachers, this is usually an effort to have consistency throughout the district. It also allows one to compare a student's performance in different subject areas or across multiple years of study.

Grading Criteria

If administrative guidelines do not explain how to define each grade, the instructor must develop the rationale. It is not uncommon to be queried about grades, and the questions may come from a variety of different audiences, so it is important to make the explanations simple and direct.

> A grading plan specifies what the criteria are for the particular grades. It also indicates how to weight the individual projects and assignments that will contribute to the grade.

Remember that judging a student's progress requires a reference point. Chapter 1 described norm-references, systems that compare students to each other, and criterion-references, whereby we gauge students with a set of performance criteria. Without reviewing the merits of each, note that criterion-references are more common in elementary and secondary education. Before instruction begins, teachers usually establish what the student must "do" to receive an A, a B, and so forth. A complete grading plan allows one to determine the level of performance for any particular grade.

Often, the best place to explain grading procedures is in a brief document called a syllabus. Syllabi (the plural) usually explain the content of the course, the course objectives, and the instructor's expectations. They also explain how the instructor will determine students' grades. This sort of information is very important to students, of course, and although syllabi are more common in secondary than elementary school classrooms, they can serve an important function in all classes.

The component of the syllabus that explains the grading can be quite simple. The syllabus in Figure 5.1 might be used for English and Reading in a sixth-grade classroom.

Internal Grading Consistency

One of the persistent (tiresome?) themes in this book is that all of the elements of the educational plan ought to fit together in a coherent fashion. Specifically, assessment

FIGURE 5.1   Grading Criteria from a Course Syllabus

Course Requirements		Possible Points
1 oral presentation		30
1 written book report		20
7 biweekly tests at 5 points each		35
homework		20
1 final		30
	Total	135

Grade	Total Points	Percentage
A	>121	(90% and above)
B	108–120	(80–89%)
C	94–107	(70–79%)
D	81–93	(60–69%)
F	<81	

should not be isolated from the balance of the classroom program. This is particularly important with a grading policy that must be in harmony with the balance of the instructional program. Cooperative learning, for example, emphasizes collaborative work among the students. The learning activities are usually designed so that students who work well together receive the highest grades. One often assigns an individual grade, but there is greater emphasis on the common grade awarded to all the students in the group. Under those circumstances, a grading plan that ignores a common grade and awards the highest performing student an A, the second most productive a B, and so on, makes very little sense. In fact, it works against the instructional plan. Achievement motivation might quickly overwhelm any sense of cooperation among group members as they compete for the top grade.

Speaking of Assessment

Mastery learning presents another example of how important it is to develop grading and instructional plans that complement each other. Those who advocate mastery learning maintain that differences in various students' performances are really differences in how much time each student needs to learn the material. It follows that if the teacher allows the instructional time to vary according to each student's requirements, everyone can master the content. Although it is quite common to do so, holding rigidly to deadlines and basing the students' grades on how much work they complete violates a central mastery learning tenet. Determining students' grades by comparing their performances to their classmates' is likewise contrary to the approach. Indeed, for someone who develops mastery learning to its logical conclusion, there may be no grading in a conventional sense at all, just a record of what the learners have completed and what they have yet to do.

Interpreting the Grade

Frequently we are grading more than one characteristic. It is common for younger students' report cards, for example, to contain grades for achievement, perhaps for effort, and commonly for some sort of social deportment variable often called citizenship. When there is only one grade on the grading record, it must be clear to the observer which characteristic is at issue.

Although it may be useful to adopt grades, such as "pass" or "credit"—which represent a final judgment of student performance—we usually take a different approach with individual learning activities because we can be more precise about what the student has accomplished. Even letter grades may not be very helpful in evaluating some assignments.

Perhaps the students have prepared a lab report on the growth of bacteria in a petri dish. If a B grade is given, for example, and the definition of B is "work of a quality significantly beyond the minimum required, but which lacks some essential element," what exactly does the B mean on this particular assignment? Is it how well the student demonstrated the required principles, the quality of the writing, the level of collaboration among lab partners, the neatness of the report, the art in the drawings, the effort? All of these are probably worth grading, and a single grade does not tell us much about them. If the grade reflects multiple criteria, then whenever possible, a single grade should be accompanied by multiple descriptors. We can supplement the B on the lab report with such comments as "well-written," "good cooperative effort," "some elements of the drawing are not as neat as they might have been," and the like. This approach is very important when we are trying to provide feedback to the learner.

> By necessity, letter grades are aggregated representations. They reflect the student's performance over several, sometimes dissimilar, areas. When one wishes to comment on something more than a general performance, the letter grade is supplemented with verbal descriptions of how the student is performing in specific areas.

If the grade primarily reflects the student's achievement, other factors we may wish to comment on should be separate, or we compromise the validity of the grade. For example, if one deducts points because the student's assignments are late, is the grade still a good achievement indicator? The same point can be made concerning the learners' attitudes, their attendance in class, and numerous other variables. The point is not that these other factors are unimportant, but rather that there must be consistency between how one determines and how one interprets the grade. Once the variables that will constitute the basis for grading are set, it takes some vigilance to maintain their centrality and their validity in the grading process.

Consistency with an Expected Distribution of Grades

There are many reasons that we might expect a certain distribution of grades. Perhaps there is a new resource available that prompts grades to improve. If a computer lab opens to sixth-grade math students and they can use effective tutorial software, we might expect their grades to improve compared to prior classes, for example. On the other hand, if the new third-grade class has a higher than ordinary number of students who speak English as a second language, we might expect their reading grades to be lower than usual.

For Further Discussion

A. When the author scored the first assessment he gave to his students in a community college history class, the supervising instructor (the author was the equivalent of a student teacher) asked just one question: "Do grades reflect a bell-shaped curve?" The instructor had a particular distribution of grades in mind, and the fact that these grades (as it turned out) did not conform to a normal distribution troubled him. They were not consistent with his grading plan, although it probably existed only as an expectation he held rather than anything more formal.

In a class of 30 or so students, is it wise to assume that *anything* will be normally distributed?
Is it reasonable to assume that the present group's performance will mirror that of earlier groups?
If so, what have we also assumed about instruction and the other environmental conditions that affect learning?

B. A principal in the high school where the author taught announced to the faculty that students received too many failing grades. Clearly he had expected a different grade distribution than what we had produced.

What does the principal's statement imply?
What adjustments might one wish to make?

The issues in the accompanying box illustrate a point. Educational leaders do not often specify grading procedures, or grading distributions in any kind of detail, but they may have expectations nevertheless. Classroom teachers usually make their own decisions about how much they will alter their activities in order to conform to the expectation.

Determining Which Components to Grade

Many of us learned from grim college experiences that a sure way to raise anxiety levels is to base the grade for an entire term on one or two assignments. Besides the stress this engenders, one or two graded activities probably do not provide a very accurate measure of student achievement if the course has any length at all. It is not possible to generalize across different learning conditions about the minimum number of tests or assignments, but remember that grades provide information. As the number of graded components diminishes, one's ability to represent an accurate measure of various students' performances similarly declines.

On the other hand, although more information is usually an asset, one should be selective. Often instructors are tempted to evaluate every learning activity and to make every assessment part of the grading record. One must be careful here. Some work samples are assessed only to determine students' progress, a point made in Chapter 2. There are also times when our only grading interest is in the quality of the instruction. Neither of those necessarily constitutes a grade book entry; both are examples of formative assessment. They allow one to determine whether the instructional planning and activities mesh well with the students' circumstances and, of course, they also provide information about students' progress. There is little point in assigning a grade for a learning activity *until the opportunity to learn is complete.* Neither is there any point in holding students responsible for mistaken assumptions about what they knew when the instruction began, or for learning activities that are ineffective or disconnected from the learning objectives. Formative assessment, which we conduct to evaluate progress, should be distinct from the summative assessment activities that legitimately produce students' grades.

Distinguishing between what is fair to judge and what is not comes into particular focus when students have limited English proficiency (LEP). When instruction is in English, one must be careful not to represent LEP students' command of the language rather than their competency with the discipline. When there are language problems, we ought to be able to discover them during preassessment, or during the formative assessment that occurs from time to time during the presentation.

Weighting the Graded Components

At the end of the grading period, and in the absence of a grading plan, one might be tempted simply to add up students' scores and divide the totals by the maximum possible to arrive at a final grade. However, this is usually a poor procedure. It assumes a direct relationship between the number of points the assignment carries and its importance to the total grade. Does a 24-point quiz cover 20 percent more content that a 20-point quiz? If one assignment deals with a unique part of the course and the other assignment covers content that will also be assessed on the final exam, should not the score weights reflect this? There are several guidelines that will help us weight individual assignments in a coherent fashion. They reflect some overlapping, but they each also address a particular problem.

1. The individual components ought to be weighted according to the proportion of the material they cover (Frisbie and Waltman, 1992).
2. The most important tasks should be weighted most heavily.
3. When a learning activity deals with material that no other activity will cover, the grade ought to be more heavily weighted.
4. Aggregate the scores in a fashion that reflects the relative importance of the activities.

Probably the most common difficulty occurs when the number of points for an activity seems almost randomly assigned. A quiz has 26 points because it happened to have 26 items, rather than because it carried 26 percent of the weight of a 100-point assignment by design. A better approach is to use the grading plan to guide one to the relative importance of each graded activity. In the elementary school curriculum, although they are all necessary parts of one's language, reading and writing usually deserve more attention than spelling. If the instructor uses two weeks in a term of 16 weeks to develop a particular set of concepts, assessments that deal with those concepts should probably reflect one eighth of the point total for the term.

Speaking of Assessment

Sometimes we unwittingly assign the greatest grading weight to what is most apparent, whether it is most important. When the author was in the second grade, Mrs. Sabey (you will recognize her name from earlier in the chapter) assigned each child to bring an example of some important, locally grown crop. (The most important crops were wheat, barley, oats, alfalfa, and sugar beets.) Since the author lived in town rather than on a farm and everyone in those days cultivated a vegetable garden, he brought a squash and received the highest grade. He suspects that the grade had more to do with the size of the vegetable and the teacher's appreciation for the difficulty she knew the child experienced in getting it to class than with the squash's importance. Grain and livestock generate cash in southern Alberta, not squash.

Also, relatively heavier emphasis should be provided for learning activities that will not be evaluated elsewhere. Comprehensive final tests provide a good picture of the learners' knowledge and abilities, but they probably also repeat elements that were assessed earlier. If the topics are equally important, those that were not assessed earlier should carry more weight on the final than repeated topics.

There are elaborate procedures for equating and weighting grades, but in the typical classroom the process need not be complicated. If the grading plan prescribes the particular weight that individual assessment activities are to have, one can allow them to take on any number of points that is convenient at the time of the assessment and simply adjust them before the final grade is calculated. This is particularly easy

FIGURE 5.2   **Balancing Component Grades to Make Them Consistent with the Grading Plan**

Grading Plan for an Educational Psychology Course

Topics	Percentage of Grade (totals 100)	Score Totals	Weighting Factors (? = student's score)
Learning Theory	20%	37	?/37 x 20 =
Motivation and Self-Esteem	10%	28	?/28 x 10 =
Development	15%	32	?/32 x 15 =
Dealing with Group and Individual Differences	10%	43	?/43 x 10 =
Assessment	20%	40	?/40 x 20 =
Instruction	10%	28	?/28 x 10 =
Classroom Management	15%	36	?/36 x 15 =

Grade	Total Weighted Score
A	>90
B	80–89
C	70–79
D	60–69
F	<60

However many points a particular assignment or activity may carry initially, it is important to adjust the totals so that the activity reflects the proper weight relative to the other assignments and projects.

when one uses a computer and electronic spreadsheet software to tally grades. In Figure 5.2 we have an example of manipulating point totals that were not originally consistent with the grading plan.

Besides using procedures for equating grades, one can purchase computer software designed for the purpose. However, computer spreadsheets have become very common, and they can be adapted with ease to provide a very efficient and flexible grading record. Using the computer to maintain grade records and for other educational applications is the subject of discussion in Chapter 11.

CHOOSING THE SYMBOLS

Although they are designed to be brief, grades cannot be cryptic. One must be careful to develop the descriptive criteria that define them because different grading systems involve different assumptions. Some of the differences have more to do with the educator's philosophy than with the strengths and weaknesses of each type of grade, however.

Letter Grades

In one form or another, letter grades probably constitute the most common approach to grading. The A-to-F pattern is familiar, but certainly not exclusive. In the elementary and secondary schools of the author's experience, the highest grade was "H" (it stood for "honorable"), and there are certainly other alternatives to the A, B, C, D, and F grades.

Although they are very common, letter grades do not offer a great deal of flexibility. In fact, they impose a certain amount of imprecision and may even offer a distorted view of the student's performance. The achievement difference between a high B and a low A, for example, is nearly always less than the difference between a high B and a low B. Examine Figure 5.3 for a moment.

FIGURE 5.3 A Lack of Precision in A to F Letter Grades

Assume that the grading plan calls for the use of letter grades A through F. The total number of points possible is 70, and letter grades are determined according to the following grading schedule.

A	63–70
B	56–62
C	49–55
D	42–48
F	<42

Situation 1: One student accumulates 42 points, and another 41.

Situation 2: One student accumulates 62 points, a second 63, and a third student scores a perfect 70.

In the first scenario, just one point separates the two students, but that single point has a great symbolic difference. By the narrowest of margins, one student will probably receive a passing grade, and the other will not. Although a D carries its own stigma, the fact that it is the lowest of Ds is not apparent to someone who sees only the letter grade.

The second scenario poses a related problem. Because of the grading plan, the students who score 63 and 70 both receive the same grade in spite of the 7-point differential. The student whose score is just one point below the 63 will receive a different grade, however, and that grade usually involves a different set of perceptions about the student's performance/ability. Although these particular circumstances are unique to this grading plan, the problems are common to most. The B grade prompts a quite different perception than an A grade. The grades alone may be deceptive because one might overemphasize the difference between the A student and the B student.

Letter grades are more precise when the plus/minus system is used. If A– is added to the A grade (A+ grades are in less common use) and each of B, C, and D grades is supplemented with + and – grades, this effectively allows for 12 gradations rather than five. (Since the F is interpreted usually to mean "failed" or "failing," there is little point to F+ and F– grades.)

Numerical Grades

Many of the problems connected to letter grades relate to their lack of precision. A number scale allows as many gradations as there are numbers and therefore rectifies at least the lack of precision. If the instructor elects to grade students along a 100-point scale, the whole numbers alone provide (with 0) 101 separate possible grades. In this instance, however, an opposite problem emerges. The message in 101 distinct grades is that there are 101 meaningful distinctions. Is it safe to assume that the achievement difference between a learner who scores 74 and another scoring 75 is significant?

As an extension of the precision problem, a 100-point scale suggests that the whole numbers that constitute the grades have equal intervals. If that is the case, the difference between a student who scores 82 and another who scores 87 is precisely the same as any other 5-point differential on the scale. This would probably be difficult to validate. We might raise the same issue for letter grades and ask whether the difference between an A– and B+ performance is the same as that from C– to D+. However, people are probably more inclined to view letter grades as rankings than as the expression of equal achievement intervals.

Still, 100-point scales have substantial appeal. They represent a range of scores that even noneducators are familiar with and which, in appearance at least, are easy to interpret.

Pass/Fail and Credit/No Credit Grades

Pass/fail and credit/no credit grades gained currency during the 1970s. The philosophy behind them suggested that letter grading often impeded—rather than motivated—student achievement. The actual impact that pass/fail grades have on student achievement is unclear since comparatively little research has been done in this area (Stiggins,

Frisbie, and Griswold, 1989). Pass/fail grades remain, but they are not prominent in elementary and secondary schools, primarily because they lack precision.

Pass/fail and credit/no credit systems are examples of dichotomous grades. They are effective when the problem is to determine only whether some necessary characteristic is present. Can the student driver perform well enough to receive a license? Has the student met the writing requirement? Should the applicant be admitted to the jazz ensemble?

The sensitive among us may blanch at the use of "fail" as a descriptor of students' performances, particularly where younger children are involved. It sounds abrupt and unfeeling, which is why many prefer a more palatable designation such as "no credit."

Grading via the Checklist

Sometimes the best way to represent a student's performance is to list the class requirements and indicate which have been accomplished. Actually, this is a variation on dichotomous grading of the credit/no credit type, with several "met" or "not met" judgments the focus, rather than just one. We have an example of a checklist for a history course in Figure 5.4.

FIGURE 5.4   **Grading Checklist for a History Course**

Criteria	Accomplished
I. Completed the chapter reading	_____
A. Read on grade level	_____
B. Understood the academic language	_____
II. Completed the chapter questions	_____
A. Submitted on time	_____
B. Understood the chronology	_____
C. Recognized the key historical figures	_____
III. Completed the research paper	_____
A. Used the required amount of source material	_____
B. Posed relevant research question	_____
C. Exhibited adequate writing mechanics	_____
D. Showed sufficient evidence of analytical thought	_____
IV. Read one supplementary book on a historical figure	_____
A. Submitted a written report	_____
B. Indicated a thorough grasp of the content in report	_____

Interpretation

Each of the Roman numeral items is required for credit in the course. The other (lettered) requirements are supplementary and define whether the learner's performance is *excellent* (10 of the 11 supplementary categories are met), *very good* (8–9 of the categories are met), *good* (6–7 of the categories), *fair* (4–5), or *poor* (1–3).

Although scoring for the individual items is yes/no, collectively, the items on the checklist allow one to make a more comprehensive judgment about the learner's performance. There are as many criteria included as the instructor needs, and one can make judgments about very dissimilar elements of the content. One summary grade obscures variable performance on the different components of the discipline, but grading via the checklist offers the option not to combine "apples and oranges."

For Further Discussion

Each grading choice has advantages and drawbacks. Letter grades are easy to understand, but they lack precision. Numerical grades correct the precision problem, but they may suggest greater accuracy than is actually the case. Pass/fail grades are appropriate only when the judgment about performance is dichotomous (one did, or did not). Checklists can communicate performance for a number of disparate activities, but they are difficult to summarize.

In a conventional classroom, under what circumstances might one rely upon each approach?

EVALUATING THE TEACHING

One of the most basic themes in this book is that assessment activities should be an integral part of every component of the educational plan. The goal-referenced model in Chapter 2 illustrates the centrality of assessment. You will recall that it was connected to each of the other components in the plan.

Teacher evaluation has lagged behind the other elements of educational evaluation. Webster (1994) noted that, for a good deal of the time in the 1960s and 1970s, teacher evaluation "was deliberately ignored as too politically volatile to be linked to the still developing field of educational evaluation" (p. 93). To the degree that teacher evaluation *was* developed, it took a different direction than school, program, and student evaluation. Teacher evaluation efforts were directed at the processes of teaching, rather than the outcomes. In other words, teacher evaluation focused on how the teachers performed their job rather than on whether they achieved specified objectives (Webster, 1994).

Webster (1994) maintains that much of the program development work of earlier decades, his own included, assumed that educational programs could be designed to be teacher-proof. He and others assumed that, by improving the curricula and resources, they could overwhelm any differences in the quality of instruction. In 1994, he concluded with remarkable candor, "Teacher-proof programs cannot be designed. Competent teachers can make almost anything work, while incompetent ones can ruin even the most brilliant instructional design" (p. 94).

Webster's (1994) work indicates that the quality of the instruction and the level of students' performances are inherently related. So even if our only focus were student achievement, we would still have an interest in assessing teaching effectiveness. Accordingly, the data about teaching quality will be assessed based on three sources: the information instructors accumulate about their own performances, the feedback that students provide, and, in the section "Other Views of Teacher Assessment,"the data available from one's colleagues and supervisors.

Self-Assessment

As fundamental as it seems to good teaching, self-assessment has not been examined very carefully, and there is comparatively little research available on the topic. It is certainly the source of information most immediate to instructors, but there are problems. It is difficult to be objective, as Good and Brophy (1987) discovered. In their study, they found that instructors are generally poor judges of their own performances. Carroll (1981) reported that the correlation between instructors' self-evaluations and those of either their colleagues or their students is quite low, in the .2 to .3 range (1.0 indicates perfect agreement and 0 reflects no agreement).

Still, self-assessment is worth pursuing. There is some evidence that when there is a discrepancy between the instructor's self-evaluation and data from the students, instructors adjust what they do (Carroll, 1981). Perhaps this is because self-assessment is comparatively nonthreatening. When teachers assess their own performances they control access to the data. When someone else collects the information, it may become part of a decision about whether a teacher is retained or terminated. There are times when the teacher's performance ought to be the basis for a personnel decision, and there are other times when the teacher must have the assurance that the data are only to help improve his or her performance.

Formative and Summative Teacher Assessment

We differentiated between examining the students' performance while instruction is in process and measuring their performance once it has concluded. There is a parallel for teacher assessment. Sometimes we are interested in checking progress. This is formative assessment that includes self-assessment. Sometimes assessors want a summative measure of the teacher's performance in order to make personnel decisions about who will continue in the position.

Objectivity

When we evaluate our own performance, sometimes we confuse our efforts and our intentions with actual outcomes. It can be very difficult to be detached enough to recognize that the unit on punctuation was not very effective and the students bear no fault. The amount of work that goes into preparing the material and probably the fragility of our own egos make it difficult to acknowledge responsibility.

Another problem for those involved in self-assessment is the very complex nature of human activity. Whether we are watching students or other teachers or attempting to evaluate our own performance, people are very difficult to research. Classroom dynamics are particularly complicated, and it can be taxing even to a trained observer to separate what is relevant from what is not.

High and Low Inference Behaviors

One of the problems associated with assessing teaching behaviors, or any behavior for that matter, is the level of inference required to establish whether the behavior occurred.

Low inference behaviors are easy to verify. They include actions such as whether a student responds to a question. Such behaviors require very little inference on the part of the assessor.

High inference behaviors are much more difficult. They include such tasks as determining whether teachers communicate high expectations to students. High inference behaviors may require several observations and a good deal of interpretation by the observer. As one example, research makes it easy to agree on the value of communicating positive expectations to students (see Good and Brophy, 1987, for example). Agreeing on whether the teacher does so in a particular situation is a different matter. There are many communications between teachers and students. Some of them convey performance expectations and some do not, and some are intentional and some are not. The type of questions we ask, the amount of time we allow for students to respond to the questions, our comments about past performances, and even our body language may affect the learners' expectations. These complications are what make communicating positive expectations a high inference behavior.

For Further Discussion

Intentional communications can be difficult enough to analyze, but some communications are unintentional.

If the teacher calls on some students more frequently than others, does that communicate an expectation?

Is the sophistication of the question asked of a particular student significant?

Does it matter that the instructor tends to spend more time in certain parts of the room than in others?

High inference behaviors require interpretation. Students tend to do better in classrooms in which the atmosphere can be defined as academic but relaxed (Walberg, 1984), but sometimes it is difficult to determine whether a student is relaxed or bored. Is the fact that students are "on task" evidence of a proper academic atmosphere? Is the room quiet because students wish to work, or because they fear punishment? Some of the behaviors we must interpret when we assess our performance are high inference. They are an integral part of what the teacher does, but recognize that assessing them complicates an already complex task.

Assessment systems that rely on low inference indicators are objective. Systems that include high inference behaviors are more subjective. Although any self-assessment model will require both measurement and evaluation, one can understand the appeal of teacher assessment systems that rely on low inference behaviors. They emphasize measurement and minimize the evaluation component with its related subjectivity. That position is not universal. Others prefer a greater level of subjectivity, although the judgment must be the product of careful training among multiple observers (Andrews and Barnes, 1990).

Because most of the instructional assessment we receive is self-assessment, it is probably safest to rely on low inference behaviors as the primary performance indicators. Of course, they must have a demonstrated relationship to student performance and they must be variables that the instructor controls. Figure 5.5 is an example of a checklist made up of variables that can serve as the basis for a self-assessment instrument with these criteria.

This particular list comes from research Bloom (1984) compiled.[1] He relied on an extensive review of the teacher effectiveness research to identify variables that correlate with student achievement. By using procedures that measure their individual effect sizes,[2] Bloom quantified the impact those variables have on student achievement. The list in Figure 5.5 represents some of the findings. In terms of their impact, they are in descending order. Consistent reinforcement, for example, can improve the average student's performance 1.2 standard deviations on a typical achievement measure. At the lower end of the list, using advance organizers can have an effect of .2 standard deviations.[3] You may have little context for the language Bloom uses, but note that a 1 standard deviation improvement will boost a student scoring at the 50th percentile to the 84th percentile, a substantial improvement.

Each variable meets the criteria established earlier for a self-assessment instrument. The research is clear regarding their connections to student achievement.

FIGURE 5.5   Instructor-Controlled Variables Related to Student Achievement

Reinforcement is the practice of imposing a stimulus after a relevant behavior that has the effect of strengthening that behavior. Verbal praise and supportive written comments on students' assignments are among the most common.

Feedback and correctives involve providing information that indicates to the learner why a response is correct and how responses can be improved.

Cues and explanations guide students' responses such that they understand what is asked of them.

Time on task refers primarily to the planning, preparation, and management activities that allow learners to begin their learning tasks with minimal instruction and to remain engaged with the learning task throughout the instructional period.

Cooperative learning activities are those that require learners to collaborate with one another, and which provide the impetus for prompting students to help one another accomplish the objective.

Graded homework overlaps, to some degree, with feedback and correctives. Homework that is graded provides information to students regarding the quality of their work.

Higher order questions, whether oral or written, require the learner to process each question and develop a response beyond the level of rote.

High teacher expectations communicate to students the instructor's confidence that learners have the ability to succeed at something beyond the minimal level.

Advance organizers introduce learners to the structure of information before it is actually presented. They allow learners to focus on the content without worrying about the organization of the material.

Source: Adapted from Bloom (1984).

Although self-assessment provides the most accessible data source for teacher assessment, it is difficult for teachers to be accurate and objective about their own performances. One way to improve the quality of the information is to focus on low inference behaviors that have a positive relationship to student achievement. Low inference behaviors are easy to observe and require very little interpretation on the part of the observer, even when it is oneself.

They require relatively little inference by an observer, even if it is oneself. They each are variables the instructor can control.

The variables from Bloom's list have other attractions. Besides a solid research base, none of the variables are unique to a particular grade level, to a specific discipline, or—with some allowance—to one theory of instruction more than some other. Whatever the setting in which one teaches and with little concern that including the variable might corrupt the technique one has invested in, interested teachers can find a way to build all of the variables into their instructional plans. The assessment task is to determine whether the activities that relate to each variable actually occur. When they do, we can expect that student performance will be better than when they are absent, and that is at least one basis for instructional assessment, and for self-assessment.

Reexamining Student Achievement as a Basis for Teacher Assessment

If we use the variables from Bloom's (1984) list, we assume that student achievement is a reasonable basis for evaluating teaching performance. We need to analyze that assumption more carefully, and perhaps qualify it a little. In truth, employing student achievement is partly a matter of convenience. We gather student data anyway, and if we can use them for evaluating teaching as well as students' learning, so much the better. Students' attitudes and social behaviors are also important, and society expects the classroom experience to affect them. Some of those data are not immediately available, however, and those that are may represent the more elusive high inference behaviors that we find problematic.

If we proceed with student achievement variables, we need to be clear about the assumptions we are making. Millman (1981) maintains that the connection between student achievement and teacher assessment involves four "propositions:"

1. The teacher's primary role is to encourage and enhance student learning.
2. The teacher's influence is not the only variable that explains student achievement.
3. In order to define teaching competence in terms of student performance, one must make some allowance for students' differences.
4. Student achievement data can be used to make improvements in the educational plan, as well as to evaluate teaching.

The proposition that the teacher's role is to encourage student learning might seem self-evident, but sometimes other responsibilities take precedence, even if they are not formally acknowledged. If a building principal evaluates teachers by determining how orderly their classrooms are, then managing students' behavior becomes the teacher's primary task. As a further illustration, your author has had colleagues for whom a winning record with the athletic team they coached was more important than their students' performance on standardized achievement tests, or any other cognitive assessment. In those instances, the won/lost record *was* the relevant assessment criterion. They could teach poorly and remain, but they had no such assurance if the team did poorly. If student achievement data are the criterion for teacher assessment, students' learning must be the instructor's primary role.

Even should students' academic performance be the focus, assessors must acknowledge that the teacher's behavior is just one of many variables that have an influence. The environmental determinism of John Watson's[4] day has passed, and everyone recognizes that, even if the teacher controls much of the student's environment (an implausible scenario at best), still some elements of their progress are explained by other factors. Assessment procedures may establish teacher performance as an important—perhaps even a critical—variable, but it cannot be the sole variable. Sometimes students do poorly despite the best efforts of a capable teacher. Happily, they also sometimes succeed in spite of poor teaching.

> Student achievement data can be used for grading students or for evaluating their progress toward a defined goal. It is the same for teachers. We may gather information to use in providing constructive feedback, or we may wish to provide a summary judgment of the teacher's performance. Although there is usually more interest in the latter, a comprehensive teacher assessment model should allow for both.

The third proposition maintains that one must consider not only influences beyond the classroom but also the variability in students' responses. Different students respond differently to the classroom experience, and even the same students respond differently when conditions change. Bloom (1984) noted that reinforcement has a great impact on student performance, but that represents a generalization, even if it is widely supported. What is reinforcing for one student may not have the same effect on another. Good assessment procedure will involve procedures that acknowledge differences from student to student rather than imposing a common set of activities on all teachers in all situations.

The fourth proposition will be developed in the section on formative versus summative assessment. The substance of the proposition is that student achievement information may be the data source for evaluating teaching and for making modifications to the educational plan. Although the data source is common to both, one must recognize that the two tasks are distinct.

OTHER VIEWS OF TEACHER ASSESSMENT

It is an inescapable conclusion that for many who analyze educational progress, students' achievement on standardized tests is a very important indicator of the teacher's effectiveness (Andrews and Barnes, 1990). It is not the only option, however. As an alternative, or perhaps as a supplement, one might make the teachers' instructional materials the object of assessment. One might also survey the students to get their impressions of teaching quality. Perhaps one might interview colleagues who have observed the instructor, and who have enough experience to make informed judgments about instructional quality. The following sections discuss some of the alternative approaches to teacher assessment.

Examining States' Teacher Assessment Procedures

Since the early 1980s, educational reform movements have placed a considerable amount of emphasis on teacher accountability, and several states within the United States have sponsored efforts to develop evaluation instruments. One of the leaders was Georgia, where the Department of Education contracted with the University of Georgia to develop a process for teacher appraisal that ultimately included the Teacher Performance Appraisal Instrument (TPAI). This approach is important because many other states followed Georgia's lead and constructed similar assessment approaches (Andrews and Barnes, 1990).

In revised form, the TPAI contains eight competencies that teachers must meet. The competencies have several indicators, each of which has multiple descriptors. Figure 5.6 lists the competencies and indicators for the 1985 version of the TPAI. For the sake of simplicity, the descriptors that relate to each indicator are not listed.

The first three competencies refer primarily to planning activities, and they involve examining the instructor's lesson materials (Andrews and Barnes, 1990). For the balance of the indicators, one must observe the instructor's classroom performance.

The Georgia approach is clearly a good deal more involved than the self-assessment we proposed in Figure 5.5. Because it was to be employed to make decisions about teachers' advancement, a situation with very high stakes, the developers were obliged to keep an eye on potential legal challenges. Our earlier effort provided only the framework for a self-assessment exercise, a factor that minimizes at least the legal entanglements.

Grading the Assessment

Because teacher assessment can be an important element in educational progress, it, too, should be the subject of evaluation. In Chapter 4, in the examination of authentic assessment, we looked at several characteristics related to assessment quality. With minor alterations, they can be adapted to help us evaluate the quality of teacher assessment data.

1. The behaviors observed during the assessment exercise should be authentic. They should be characteristic of the teacher's in-class behavior.
2. Judgments about the teacher's work quality must reflect criteria that are established before the performance data are gathered.
3. There must be judgment reliability. Various judges with similar backgrounds ought to come to the same conclusions about the teacher's performance.
4. The judgments must be based on multiple work samples.

These criteria, each representing topics we discussed earlier in the book, offer a framework for examining teacher assessment data. They are helpful guidelines when one must make judgments about behaviors and activities that do not lend themselves to a simple paper and pencil checklist.

FIGURE 5.6 **Assessment Categories in the Teacher Performance Assessment Instrument (TPAI)**

I. Plans instruction to achieve selected objectives
   A. Specifies or selects learner objectives for lessons
   B. Specifies or selects learning activities
   C. Specifies or selects materials and/or media
   D. Plans activities and/or assignments that accommodate learner differences

II. Obtains information about needs and progress of learners
   A. Specifies or selects procedures or materials for assessing learning performance on objectives
   B. Uses systematic procedures to assess all learners
   C. Assesses learner progress during the lesson observed

III. Demonstrates acceptable written and oral expression and knowledge of subject
   A. Uses acceptable written expression
   B. Uses acceptable written expression with learners
   C. Uses acceptable oral expression
   D. Demonstrates command of school subject being taught

IV. Organizes time, space, materials, and equipment for instruction
   A. Attends to routine tasks
   B. Uses instructional time efficiently
   C. Provides a physical environment conducive to learning

V. Communicates with learners
   A. Gives explanations related to lesson content
   B. Clarifies explanations when learners misunderstand lesson content
   C. Uses learner responses or questions regarding lesson content
   D. Provides information to learners about their progress throughout lesson

VI. Demonstrates appropriate instructional methods
   A. Uses instructional methods acceptably
   B. Matches instruction to learners
   C. Uses instructional aids and materials during lesson observed
   D. Implements activities in a logical sequence

VII. Maintains positive learning environment
   A. Communicates personal enthusiasm
   B. Stimulates learner interest
   C. Demonstrates warmth and friendliness
   D. Helps learners develop positive self-concepts

VIII. Maintains appropriate classroom behavior
   A. Maintains learner involvement in instruction
   B. Redirects learners who are off task
   C. Communicates clear expectations about behavior
   D. Manages disruptive behavior

Source: Adapted from Andrews and Barnes (1990).

When the assessment *is* more objective, perhaps like the approach we took in Figure 5.5, we rely on different criteria to indicate the assessment's quality. The following are more appropriate in this instance:

1. The assessment data must be stable enough that a second assessment will yield similar conclusions.
2. As a whole, the assessment items ought to cover the content area.
3. Scoring differences from teacher to teacher or from setting to setting must reflect actual differences in the characteristic measured.
4. The assessment data ought to predict other, independent measures of the teacher's performance.

The concepts represented in these four statements will be developed more thoroughly in Chapter 7, but a brief comment is appropriate here as well. If the data are not consistent, the lack of reliability suggests a problem in either the item being assessed or the experience of those who are doing the assessment. If the item is not clear, or if the assessor lacks experience evaluating teaching behaviors, it is difficult for the data to be reliable.

Not only must the test represent the content fairly, the individual categories must be sampled in appropriate proportion. Logically, major categories must reflect greater emphasis (more comprehensive items, or just more test items) than minor categories. Teachers' instructional competence deserves more attention that their attendance-keeping skills.

We must have some assurance that, when scores change, it is because what one is assessing has changed. If someone evaluates the teacher's ability to deal with students' misbehavior, and then does so again in six months, different scores must indicate a change in performance. This issue is related to the reliability alluded to in the first point. If score changes are an artifact of the assessment instrument, or of the person completing the assessment, assessors cannot be measuring what they claim.

If two different assessments both evaluate the sophistication of the same questions the teacher asks, the data from one must agree with those from the other. When a teacher who has performed well on one assessment does poorly on some other assessment intended to measure the same qualities, one or the other—or both—is flawed.

The assessment instrument itself is part of the larger educational program. It is important to evaluate it just as one would any other component of the plan. The items mentioned are certainly not an exhaustive list of all the important elements, but they represent at least some of the necessary elements.

Assessment Data from Peers and Supervisors

Often the person in the best position to make a judgment about teaching quality is the colleague who shares a similar academic background and who probably understands the teaching conditions better than most others. There are some important potential problems, however. Just as we tend to be poor judges of our own teaching behaviors, it can be quite difficult to be objective about a colleague's performance (Good and Brophy, 1987). Figure 5.7 lists several factors that can interfere with accurate assessment when one teacher observes another.

FIGURE 5.7   **Sources of Error When Evaluating Instructors**

Error	Explanation of Error
Primacy	Initial events in an observation have a tendency to distort everything that follows.
Recency	The final event during an observation sequence may be given an emphasis that exaggerates the event's importance when the performance is recounted.
Bias	An observer may inject personal expectations for the instructor's performance that are separate from the required behaviors.
Generalization	A behavior that is actually unique to the situation may be generalized to all teaching situations.
Poor Instrumentation	There can be a variety of problems with observation instruments that cause them to provide data lacking consistency and validity.
Observer Naiveté	The observer may lack the experience necessary to observe the particular instructional setting, or the observer may lack sufficient training with the relevant observation instruments.

Source: Adapted from Good and Brophy (1987).

Although these problems are persistent, none of them is insurmountable. Training and dependable assessment instruments are usually the keys.

A primacy effect occurs when the first thing one observes colors everything that follows. Perhaps one's first impression is of a disorganized teacher. A primacy effect prompts one to interpret everything that follows in light of that impression, even if other behaviors do not support it.

When a recency effect is dominant, the last thing one sees affects one the most. For example, the instructor may ask several higher level questions, but if the last is a memory level question, this is how the observer influenced by recency will describe the teacher's questioning technique.

Primacy and recency effects represent distortions, of course, and the distortions are greatest when the observer's visits are brief or irregular. Unfortunately, this is the norm because peer evaluation is usually not a part of the teacher's job description. Fellow teachers may view peer evaluation as a time-consuming and thankless chore. By formal assignment, the task usually falls to school administrators rather than to one's teacher colleagues. Some administrators treat teacher evaluation very seriously; others place it low on their list of priorities and give it only cursory attention.[5]

In spite of the fact that observation data have an uneven quality, a supervisor's feedback can be helpful. Glickman and Bey (1990) reported that this is most likely when

1. the supervisor is available,
2. the supervisor recognizes the teacher's expertise,
3. information provided to the instructor is immediate and nonpunitive,
4. the supervisor discusses the performance in descriptive terms, minimizing judgment and listening to the instructor's explanations, and
5. the focus is on cooperation between the parties and on problem solving.

These findings can be summarized to suggest that observations are most helpful when supervisor and teacher work together with an attitude of mutual respect, and when the emphasis is on description more than judgment.

When we ask a colleague to evaluate our performance, we ask for formative, rather than summative, assessment, but the task should still have a level of formality. McHaney and Impey (1992) suggested a four-stage process for instructional supervision that defines an observation procedure. It is outlined in Figure 5.8.

There are many different kinds of clinical supervision models. This one is helpful because it integrates what the instructor is trying to accomplish with the observer's objectives.

Reducing Teacher Assessment to Its Necessary Elements

Not all supervision models appear as formal as that in Figure 5.8, but there are two components that are common to each—development and implementation. In the development phase, one selects (or develops) the necessary instruments and establishes the procedures. This opens the way for the implementation phase, in which the actual observation occurs. Stronge (1997) described the step-by-step process this way:

Developmental Phase
1. Identify the goals.
2. Define the teacher's role in connection with the goals.
3. Establish standards for the teacher's performance.

FIGURE 5.8   Stages Model for Instructional Supervision

Stage One	The following must occur before the observation begins:
	(a) establish rapport between observer and instructor
	(b) explain the observer's objectives
	(c) discuss the lesson that will be presented
	(d) discuss the class and the students, including any uniqueness
Stage Two	The following occur during the observation:
	(a) record what occurs during the lesson presentation
	(b) complete any instrument that may be used in the observation
Stage Three	The analysis of the observation data should include the following:
	(a) review what was intended (stage one), and what occurred
	(b) examine data for significant patterns and important incidents
	(c) select the most relevant findings
	(d) prepare feedback that will assist the instructor
Stage Four	The postobservation conference should include the following:
	(a) communicate the instructor's strengths and weaknesses
	(b) evaluate the instructor's overall level of performance

Source: Adapted from McHaney and Impey (1992).

Implementation Phase

4. Document the teacher's performance.
5. Assess the performance.

Note that Stronge (1997) did not define the goals. They will depend upon the circumstances. For the individual teacher developing a procedure for self-assessment, a goal might be to help students develop greater ability with mathematical problem solving. An institutional goal, on the other hand, might be to improve students' standardized test scores, or to improve the school's ranking among similar schools in the county.

FORMATIVE VERSUS SUMMATIVE TEACHER ASSESSMENT

The assessor's *intent* has much to do with the type of assessment. The procedures in Figure 5.8 include a question about the observer's objective. The answer will reveal much about whether the assessment is primarily a diagnostic procedure designed to provide feedback to the teacher, or whether there is something more final intended.

Summative instructional assessment involves making decisions about the instructor's standing. New classroom teachers have a probationary period (three years is typical), after which supervisors decide whether to award them tenure or to terminate them. During the probationary period, formative assessment should provide the information that will help one become a better teacher. At the end of the probation, shaping performance is no longer the objective. The focus is on summative assessment, which allows supervisors to judge what the teacher's future standing with the institution should be.

For obvious reasons, instructors have a more benign view of formative assessment than of summative assessment. Sometimes it is difficult to convince a teacher that *any* assessment truly has a formative purpose. The problem is not unique to instructors, of course. It may also be difficult to convince students that test scores help the instructor to modify the instruction and are not destined for the grade book.

For Further Discussion

The way topics have been treated here begs questions about whether formative and summative procedures are entirely separate. Can evaluators use a single assessment approach to satisfy both formative and summative assessment purposes? Are there different questions you want answered when someone is (a) evaluating your progress as opposed to (b) determining your teaching competency?

Is it different for a student in your seventh-grade history class, or can you use an assessment exercise to both grade and provide feedback to the student?

Students' Evaluations of Their Instructors

Student evaluation data are not a common source of information to teachers in the elementary and secondary schools, although Scriven (1977) maintained that this is more a result of practice or custom than because of any real deterrent. At the college and university level, however, such data have a lengthy history, and the research in that setting is comparatively deep. Indeed, at the postsecondary level, student evaluations are often the major—and sometimes the sole—source of data regarding teaching quality. Although instructors tend to be quite critical of them, there are indications that data from students can be quite helpful. Some of the college-level findings may generalize at least to the secondary school. Aleamoni (1981) reported the following:

1. Although there are certainly exceptions, students' judgments tend to be quite stable.
2. Students can distinguish between the personality characteristics that make instructors popular and the teaching characteristics that make the instruction effective.
3. Generally, the level of students' learning bears a positive correlation with students' ratings of their instructors.
4. The relationship between class size and instructors' ratings is unclear. The relationship may be curvilinear.
5. The relationship is unclear between the grades the students expect to receive and the ratings they give their instructors.
6. Whether instructors implement the data from students' evaluations is unclear.

Each of these research findings responds to a criticism of student evaluations. One complaint is that students' judgments of the same teacher are not consistent, that even if conditions are similar, a second assessment may yield substantially different conclusions. If this is accurate, there is little point in placing confidence in students' evaluations, but the research data suggest that this generally is not the case. In measurement terms, student evaluations tend to have substantial reliability. This assumes, of course, that they use dependable questionnaires, an issue that follows.

College and university students, at least, are apparently not seduced into giving laudatory marks for instruction simply because they like their instructors. Whether this is true for younger students is not clear and needs investigation. In something of an extension of the second finding, students tend to evaluate instructors most favorably when they feel their learning has been substantial. Clearly, having a positive learning experience is not the same as expecting a good grade. Whether those who expect high

> Instructors harbor some distrust of student evaluations, but past experience indicates that student data can provide a good deal of insight regarding instructor performance. Unfortunately, there is very little research regarding the reliability or validity of students' evaluations of elementary and secondary school teachers.

grades rate instructors more highly than those who expect low grades (the fifth point) is unclear.

Conventional wisdom has it that students dislike large class sizes, and that instructional quality and learning both suffer when students' numbers increase beyond minimal levels. The picture the research provides is not so straightforward. Aleamoni (1981) suggests that sometimes there is no relationship. Some of the lack of clarity may reflect the fact that teachers may not adjust their teaching behaviors even when class size changes. If one's class size falls from 40 to 20, but one uses the same methods, the opportunity to spend more time with individual students is lost, as is the chance to affect student performance.

Finally, providing information to instructors about their classroom performances does not assume that they will change what they do. It seems that they are most likely to adjust when conferences are held, and the procedures McHaney and Impey (1992) outlined in Figure 5.8 suggest that conferences both before and after the classroom presentation are helpful.

A Questionnaire for Students

When they assess instruction, students must distinguish between the teacher and the teaching, something that may be particularly difficult for younger students. For good or ill, students of all ages tend to be very attentive to the instructor's personality. A questionnaire that focuses on the teacher's personality probably directs attention toward characteristics that are unrelated to teaching performance and relatively fixed, in any case. In fact, none of the teacher's clothing, grooming, or personality tendencies are likely to change to any degree, even when they know students are critical of them. Teaching characteristics, on the other hand, can be modified. We can alter the level of question we ask, or the frequency with which we reinforce desired behaviors.

A colleague or supervisor may gather student data for either formative or summative purposes. When we gather information from our own students about the instructor's performance, however, it is always for the value of the feedback. To protect the integrity of the process, we try to collect the data in a way that assures students of anonymity.

When we wish to gather data from our students, it is probably wisest to collaborate with our colleagues and develop instruments that are fairly general in tone so that they can work in a variety of settings. Perhaps the most common form is a Likert-type format, where the items are statements to which one can express the degree of agreement or disagreement. The sample questionnaire in Figure 5.9 uses this format.

This list certainly does not exhaust the questions one might ask of one's students, but the items are at least representative. Note that responses to item 9 must be interpreted differently than other responses because students who strongly agree, or agree, with the statement are indicating that there is a problem with assignments.

FIGURE 5.9   A Questionnaire for Students

Indicate the choice for each item that represents your level of agreement or disagreement with the corresponding statement.

SA = strongly agree
 A = agree
 N = neither agree nor disagree
 D = disagree
SD = strongly disagree

A. General class content

1. I found this subject to be worth my time.
    SA__   A__   N__   D__   SD__
2. I found this subject to be interesting.
    SA__   A__   N__   D__   SD__
3. I understand the connection between this subject and other subjects.
    SA__   A__   N__   D__   SD__

B. Class procedures

4. The teacher was well organized each day.
    SA__   A__   N__   D__   SD__
5. Class discussion was always focused on the subject at hand.
    SA__   A__   N__   D__   SD__
6. The instructional objective was clear to me.
    SA__   A__   N__   D__   SD__

C. Out-of-class work

7. I always understood what I was to do for homework.
    SA__   A__   N__   D__   SD__
8. The assignments required too much work.
    SA__   A__   N__   D__   SD__
9. Assignments that required I work with other students were a burden.
    SA__   A__   N__   D__   SD__

D. Assessment

10. The teacher understands how much work I do.
    SA__   A__   N__   D__   SD__
11. I feel that I am being graded fairly.
    SA__   A__   N__   D__   SD__

SUMMARY

The problems Mrs. Sabey mused over in the beginning of the chapter are quite common. Classrooms are made of students with very different kinds of abilities and background experiences and, somehow, the grading system has to be as accurate and coherent as it can be for all of them.

Remember that people have different views of grades. Although most believe that grades are important, people tend to approach them with different expectations. Students, parents, and teachers may view grades as an objective to strive for, a reinforcer, or perhaps a gatekeeper that defines who will have particular opportunities and who will not.

The gatekeeper function, particularly, brings grades under close scrutiny. They will surely be questioned if they appear arbitrary or unclear, so it is important for teachers to be able to defend grading procedures. An important first step is to provide a straightforward explanation of how grades are determined and what they mean.

Letters are probably the most common grades, but they are relatively imprecise as performance indicators. In some instances the difference in performance between two letter grades is actually smaller than the range of differences within a grade. Numerical grades offer more precision, particularly when they range from 1 to 100, and those numbers communicate quite readily to most people. They may also overstate the precision case, however, suggesting greater measurement accuracy than the grade actually reflects. Pass/fail and credit/no credit grades are effective when the issue is whether the student has accomplished some specific learning outcome. Otherwise, they often leave the students and others clamoring for more information than such grades provide.

Because we know that teaching performance is related to student achievement, we are also interested in evaluating teaching. The most accessible information about teaching quality may be the data we can collect about ourselves. Those data are not particularly helpful, however, unless we develop procedures, such as checklists, that provide some control for the inherent lack of objectivity that characterizes evaluation of our own performance.

One way to evaluate teaching performance is in terms of student achievement. It is not a novel idea. Webster (1994) noted that it dates at least to fifteenth-century Italy, where a teaching master's salary was directly dependent upon the performance of his students. Even for the present day, he maintains, "Student achievement data seem to provide the most direct evidence of teacher effect. While classroom observations and ratings by principals, teachers, and students measure a teacher's behavior on the job, student achievement data relate directly to the outcomes of that behavior" (p. 109).

However, because of the controversy in using student achievement data to evaluate teachers, the data are used primarily for incentive programs such as merit pay programs. Student achievement data are rarely used in teachers' tenure and dismissal decisions.

There is another dimension to teacher assessment. Even those who are new to teaching are drawn into the discussion of whether teaching is a profession. However the issue is decided, one of the characteristics of professions is that they judge their own members' performances. Kilbourn (1991) noted, "Among the various views about professions is the observation that those occupations that have undeniable professional status set their own standards of performance and have their own professional bodies to adjudicate transgressions. They monitor themselves" (p. 722). At its most fundamental level, this means that professionals review their own performance. Kilbourn calls it "the personal supervision of one's own practice" (1991).

Whether one is evaluating teaching performance, student achievement, the quality of an instructional plan, or some other educational element, grading represents that point at which we have gathered enough information that we can communicate an informed judgment about something's quality. The communication element is common to each grading situation and, indeed, is why grading is undertaken. This chapter has considered the procedures we can adopt to make the communication as precise and informative as possible. Although little additional time will be spent on grading as such, you will notice the concepts related to judgment accuracy and quality occurring repeatedly throughout the balance of the book.

ENDNOTES

1. Bloom's work capitalized on Walberg's (1984) research. Rather than focus on instructional technique as the key to student achievement, Walberg analyzed the students' progress and the instructional setting by identifying key variables. He focused on those variables that are present in classrooms where students consistently score well on standardized achievement tests. They do not all spring from a common theory, but all have a substantial research base, indicating their importance and relationship to student performance. Your author's approach here, of course, assumes that the variables that relate to student performance on standardized tests are reasonable criteria for a teacher assessment instrument. There are, no doubt, those who will disagree.
2. The process is called meta-analysis, and although there are differences from researcher to researcher, the technique involves pooling the results from many independent studies in order to arrive at a common and more robust set of conclusions regarding the impact of some variable or procedure.
3. The effect sizes are not simply additive, by the way. Using both reinforcement, which has an average effect size of 1.2 standard deviations, and advance organizers (.2 std. dev.) is unlikely to boost the average student's performance 1.4 standard deviations. Some of the improvement represented in one variable is also common to the other.
4. It was Watson's contention that, if he were given healthy infants and allowed to rear them in a controlled environment, he could make them into anything he pleased, from doctors and lawyers to beggars and thieves. His pronouncement, "Give me a dozen infants well-formed, . . ." reflects the behaviorist's rejection of heredity's role in explaining human behavior. Contemporary theory allows that both heredity and experience are important in understanding behavior, although there is argument about how much each matters.
5. During the three years before your author was awarded tenure, the assistant principal evaluated his instruction once—during the first year. Thereafter, he simply sent your author the blank forms to be completed at his leisure, after which your author returned them to him for the administrator's signature. (Your author did *very* well.) To your author's knowledge, the forms were never altered after completion.

FOR FURTHER READING

Susan Brookhart (1999) has written a very helpful article dealing with the matter of communicating grades. She has dealt with conventional grading systems, as well as with authentic assessment, and she has approached grading within the larger context of a grading plan.

REFERENCES

Aleamoni, L. M. (1981). Student ratings of instruction. In J. Millman (Ed.), *Handbook of teacher evaluation* (pp. 110–145). Beverly Hills, CA: Sage Publications and the National Council on Measurement in Education.

Ames, R. (1982). Teachers' attributions for their own teaching. In J. M. Levine and M. C. Wang (Eds.), *Teacher and student perceptions*. Hillsdale, NJ: Erlbaum.

Andrews, T. E., and Barnes, S. (1990). Assessment of teaching. In W. R. Houston (Ed.), *Handbook of research on teacher education*. New York: Macmillan.

Bloom, B. S. (1984). The 2 sigma problem: The search for methods of group instruction as effective as one-to-one tutoring. *Educational Researcher, 13*(6), 4–16.

Brookhart, S. (1999). Teaching about communicating assessment results and grading. *Educational Measurement: Issues and Practice, 18*(1), 5–13.

Cangelosi, J. (1991). *Evaluating classroom instruction.* New York: Longman.

Carroll, J. G. (1981). Faculty self-evaluation. In J. Millman (Ed.), *Handbook of teacher evaluation* (pp. 180–200). Beverly Hills, CA: Sage Publications and the National Council on Measurement in Education.

Frisbie, D. A., and Waltman, K. K. (1992). Developing a personal grading plan. *Educational Measurement: Issues and Practice, 11*(3), 35–42.

Glickman, C. D., and Bey, T. M. (1990). Supervision. In W. R. Houston (Ed.), *Handbook of research on teacher education*. New York: Macmillan.

Good, T. (1987). Teacher expectations. In D. Berliner and B. Rosenshine (Eds.), *Talks to teachers* (pp. 159–200). New York: Random House.

Good, T. L., and Brophy, J. E. (1987). *Looking in classrooms* (4th ed.). New York: Harper & Row.

Kilbourn, B. (1991). Self-monitoring in teaching. *American Educational Research Journal, 28,* 721–736.

McHaney, J. H., and Impey, W. D. (1992). Strategies for analyzing and evaluating teaching effectiveness using a clinical supervision model. Paper presented at the annual meeting of the Mid-South Educational Research Association, Knoxville, Tennessee.

Millman, J. (1981). Student achievement as a measure of teacher competence. In J. Millman (Ed.), *Handbook of teacher evaluation* (pp. 146–166). Beverly Hills, CA: Sage Publications and the National Council on Measurement in Education.

Scriven, M. (1977). The evaluation of teachers and teaching. In G. D. Borich and K. S. Fenton, *The appraisal of teaching: Concepts and process* (pp. 186–193). Reading, MA: Addison-Wesley.

Stiggins, R. J., Frisbie, D. A., and Griswold, P. A. (1989). Inside high school grading practices: Building a research agenda. *Educational Measurement: Issues and Practices, 8*(2), 5–14.

Stronge, J. H. (1997). *Evaluating teaching: A guide to current thinking and best practice.* Thousand Oaks, CA: Corwin Press.

Walberg, H. J. (1984). Improving the productivity of America's schools. *Educational Leadership, 41*(8), 19–27.

Webster, W. J. (1994). The connection between personnel evaluation and school evaluation. In A. McConney (Ed.), *Toward a unified model: The foundations of educational personnel evaluation*. Western Michigan University: The Center for Research on Educational Accountability and Teacher Evaluation.

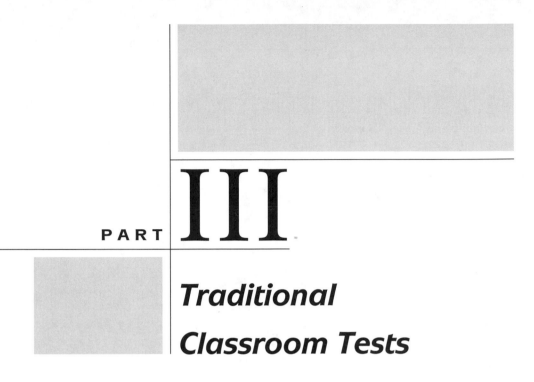

PART **III**

Traditional Classroom Tests

Even the most ardent supporters of standardized testing acknowledge that the classroom instructor must develop much of the assessment. Sometimes it will be a variation on the authentic assessment techniques developed in Chapter 4, but it is also the more conventional business of constructing and administering paper and pencil test items. With few exceptions, we will find that each type of item has its niche. Successful assessment is often a matter of identifying what the different items can measure, and then working toward the strengths that each possesses.

Chapter 7 takes up the matter of constructing an instrument and evaluating its quality. We will find that a careful analysis of student performance data can yield a great deal of information about (a) how well the students performed and (b) how well the assessment instrument did its job. It is the second part of this process that is often overlooked. It represents an untapped data source since test analysis can yield a wealth of information about how ordinary classroom assessment procedures might be improved.

6

Test Items and Item Construction

■ *The reader will learn to design a variety of test items and to analyze each in terms of what it can contribute to educational assessment.*

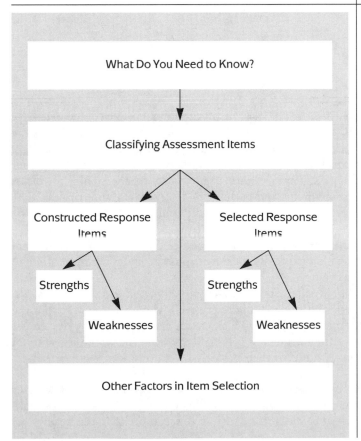

Generally speaking, there are not good or bad test items so much as there are items that are well-suited or ill-suited to particular tasks and to particular populations of learners. In constructing assessments, we must recognize that test items are tools, and like any other type of tool, they have strengths and weaknesses. With perhaps one exception, each of the items discussed has a place in classroom assessment. Sometimes we are hesitant to construct a test when something published is available, but no one is in a better position than the classroom teacher to determine what to ask of students and which items to use in order to conduct the assessment. The task is to recognize the limitations of specific items and then to construct the assessment carefully enough that it can provide the information one seeks. ■

Mr. Wheeler is new to the classroom, but he is optimistic about the way the Introductory Chemistry class is beginning. If the level of the students' in-class discussion and their general participation in the labs are any gauge, they are responding well to "his" science, and some of the trepidation he felt has been replaced with assurance. He has yet to conduct any formal evaluation of what they have learned, however, and although he came to the classroom with a number of sample lesson plans, he is less well prepared to assess student performance. He has several options: The book publisher has provided a collection of test items based on the text material, and since his beginning unit covered roughly the first chapter and a half, perhaps it makes good sense to just use the prepared items from those chapters. Mr. Wheeler knows from his brief review of them that they are primarily in multiple-choice format, with fill-in-the-blank items employed to test learners' grasp of definitions. There are also a few essay items directed toward the major topics. He feels some hesitancy. Multiple-choice items are often criticized for measuring only the learners' ability to memorize, and he's not sure he has the background necessary to score the essay items properly. Perhaps the fill-in items are the best choice. At least with them, he reasoned, he can measure specific elements of learning that he knows are important. ■

DIFFICULT BEGINNINGS

There is a tendency for first-year teachers to be unsettled by how prepared everyone else appears to be to teach. The veterans always seem to have something tucked away that will be perfect for teaching this concept or that one. The problem is particularly acute in assessment, perhaps because it is often an area of lesser emphasis in teacher preparation programs (Stiggins, 1991). Although most new teachers enter the classroom with some sample lesson plans and perhaps an instructional unit or two, they often have much less experience with the assessment component. Authentic assessment was considered in Chapter 4, but there will be times when authentic assessment, with all that is implicit in that approach, is not the choice. Sometimes a conventional paper and pencil test we develop expressly for the purpose provides the most efficient avenue to the information we need.

Recall that your author went to some lengths in Chapter 2 to note that assessment can be neither understood nor executed very well when it's isolated from the other components of the educational plan. This extends also to preparing the assessment. One must undertake the business of physically writing the test items with an eye to the intended audience and what their performance levels and past experiences have been.

As the chapter beginning suggests, people often begin by asking, "Which kind of test is best?" However, that question really ought to be preceded by another, more fundamental one: What do I need to measure? As we shall see, more than the business of choosing good test items and avoiding bad ones, the task is to determine what to measure, and then to decide which item is most appropriate to the task. What we wish to know should dictate the kind of items we select and the type of test we will construct as a consequence. Those issues provide the focus for most of the chapter.

WHAT ARE WE ASSESSING?

Depending upon circumstances, sometimes conventional paper and pencil testing is the best assessment tool. All tests are not created equal, however, because even if assessment instruments are prepared with equal care, they often have different functions. Different assessment instruments often help us measure different skills and abilities. Some test items require only rote memory of the learner, whereas others call for sophisticated problem-solving activities; so to maintain some order, we need a system for classifying items by what they measure.

There are a number of systems available for ordering thinking tasks, as well as the test items that are appropriate for each. Baxter and Glaser (1998) recently proposed classifying science tasks in terms of how much science content the task requires of the student and how many different skills the students may use to complete the task. Perhaps the most widely used classification system, however, is that proposed by Bloom (1956). In *Taxonomy of Educational Objectives: Handbook I: Cognitive Domain,* the author proposed the organizational approach represented in Figure 6.1.

A *taxonomy* is a classification of objects according to their characteristics. In this instance, the authors classified cognitive (thinking) activities in a hierarchy from their simplest (knowledge) to their most complex (evaluation). The hierarchy is also cumulative, which means that each successive level includes the characteristics of the less sophisticated levels that precede it. To illustrate, the authors maintained not only that comprehension is more demanding than knowledge (the hierarchical element), but also that, in order to comprehend, one must have a command of the relevant

FIGURE 6.1 The Bloom Taxonomy

Evaluation	The ability to develop a rationale for either position in a conflict that can be described as a moral dilemma.
Synthesis	The ability to draw information from several sources in order to develop a solution to a problem that, for the particular learner, is novel.
Analysis	The ability to determine the relevant component elements in any problem or scenario.
Application	The ability to perform a skill or demonstrate an ability in a setting dissimilar from the one in which it was learned.
Comprehension	The ability to explain a concept or define something in one's own words.
Knowledge	Rote memory. It is the recall of information in the form in which it was originally learned.

Source: Adapted from Bloom (1956).

knowledge (the cumulative characteristic). This makes sense when we consider that to define something (comprehension), we must first be able to recall the words and meaning (knowledge) that allow us to construct the definition.

All levels of the taxonomy are cumulative, with each level requiring thinking that is more complex and more comprehensive than the thought in the preceding levels. In order to perform an evaluation, the individual must be able to engage in all of the prior levels, plus recognize what is unique to the last.

Classifying Test Items

Taxonomies are relevant to our discussion because they also provide a system for classifying test items in terms of the level of thought they help us measure. To say it a little differently, all test items do not allow one to sample all levels of thought with equal facility. Indeed, some items are completely inappropriate to measuring some levels of thought. If we determine the thinking a particular task requires, then we can select an item that is effective at the particular level.

It should be noted that there is not a complete consensus, even among Bloom's coauthors, about the ordering in the taxonomy. In a paper published well after the book appeared, one of the original coauthors (Furst, 1981) suggested that synthesis-level functioning may be more demanding than evaluation. If Furst is correct, the first problem below, which calls for synthesis, requires more sophisticated thought than the second, an evaluation problem:

1. Write an essay explaining the degree to which Jefferson and Madison relied on Locke's *Second Treatise on Civil Government* in their preparation of the Declaration of Independence.
2. Write an essay in which you explain whether the Continental Congress made the best choice when it decided to declare independence.

The first item asks one to draw on information from multiple sources (at least the Declaration and Locke's book) in order to respond. That is the hallmark of synthesis. The second item requires that one take a position on an issue for which there might legitimately be differences of opinion. With evaluation tasks, the position taken is less important that the quality of the evidence and of one's logic in defending the position.

If one must design test items that sample learners' thinking at all six levels, the difference of opinion about which is more demanding might be troublesome, but ordinarily one need not be quite so precise. In fact, it is a common practice to divide the different levels of thinking into "lower order," and "higher order." It depends on the operational definition one uses, but often knowledge and comprehension are lumped into the lower category and the other four levels represent higher level thought. Although reordering six levels into two sacrifices some precision, it is quite serviceable for most classroom activities and it is usually more practical than worrying about the point, for example, at which an analysis problem becomes a synthesis problem.

It is also worthy of note that the taxonomy suggests that thinking tasks have just one dimension. The Baxter and Glaser (1998) approach we mentioned above involves two (the type of content and the students' skills). In the Bloom taxonomy all that matters is how much the learner must manipulate the information in order to complete the task. Solomon (1970) suggested that this might actually oversimplify cognitive tasks. He noted that Bloom (1956) assumed that, as thinking becomes more complex, it also necessarily becomes more abstract, although there is evidence that this is not necessarily so (Tanner, 1988). However, perhaps the (over)simplicity of the taxonomy helps explain its popularity. In spite of some imprecision and perhaps even some ambiguity, it remains the most commonly used system educators use to classify thinking tasks.

As a final comment on the Bloom taxonomy, and this is particularly important in assessment discussions, we need to remember that a task's cognitive level has everything to do with the student's experience with the task. What was a synthesis-level question yesterday, because the item required that the learner combine information from multiple sources, is just a knowledge-level question today if the same question is asked again. In the second instance, all that is required is recall. The repetition may or may not diminish the importance of the content; indeed, repetition can have great value, but it should at least alter the way we interpret the response.

Our early question was "What do you want to assess?" If we are going to tailor our assessments so that they match the testing requirements, we must be able to classify test items according to what they will allow us to evaluate. This is the point of the taxonomy. If the instructional plan calls for students to explain how Newton's Laws of Motion affect their daily activities, assessment items must be consistent with that outcome. It is pointless, for example, to develop an assessment instrument using items that are restricted to helping us measure the students' ability to recall and define vocabulary words. The students may engage in very sophisticated thinking before they respond to the item, but an item written at the knowledge or comprehension levels leaves us no way to verify thought beyond those levels. At a time when educators are very attentive to specified, higher level learning outcomes, verification is very important.

> The Bloom taxonomy offers a classification system for thinking tasks. Because test items are developed to reflect different kinds of thinking, the system also allows us to classify test items. The classification must reflect changes in students' experiences, however. Yesterday's analysis item may be today's knowledge item

Remember, however, that a very restricted assessment range for a particular item shouldn't be considered a weakness so much as it is simply one of the item's characteristics. All test items and all educational tasks have limitations. We want to determine what insight they offer regarding students' learning or abilities so we know when a particular item is appropriate.

Other Item Classification Considerations

The highest level of thinking that a particular type of item will allow one to assess is an important characteristic. Related to it is the range of thinking to which the item will respond. We will see, for example, that essay items have the greatest assessment range. They can be constructed so that they assess any level of thinking from the simplest to the most complex. There are important reasons not to use essays for recall tasks, but potentially, at least, essays can be constructed to elicit any level of cognitive functioning from a test taker.

All assessment items allow one to assess recall ability. In order to classify items, we must know how effective a particular type of item is with more sophisticated thinking.

Most items have a far more restricted range than essays. Fill-in items, for example, allow one to validate only recall ability. As one considers item flexibility, it is important not to confuse what learners *might* have thought with the level of thinking one can verify from their responses. One may address a variety of levels of thought even with the simplest of items. The problem comes in verifying the higher levels of cognitive activity because instructional plans often call for students to perform at a specified level. This is the case when objectives call for students to "analyze a story problem and determine which information is relevant," for example, or "define the part of speech *adjective*."

As previously noted, items that work well for higher level thought also work for tasks that are less demanding, which is the cumulative nature of the taxonomy. An item's *range* is an expression of the number of different levels of thought it will assess. Some items have a very restricted range, and others offer a great deal of assessment flexibility. That characteristic, along with the following, helps us classify test items: (1) construction difficulty, (2) scoring difficulty, (3) scoring reliability, and (4) response type.

Item Convenience

Some of these characteristics reflect convenience, and the convenience that the item offers to the teacher is also an important consideration. Convenience reflects the amount of effort consumed in preparing the items and then scoring them after students have completed the assessment. Teachers are often pressed for time, which makes both the construction difficulty of the item and the time required for scoring it criteria for item selection. Those who know they will have little time to score a final exam before they must submit grades may elect not to use essay items, for example. Students may enjoy items based on a crossword puzzle format, but they are complicated to create, and someone who must generate several test items in comparatively little time probably uses something else. Note that we have said nothing about what either item measures, nor whether either item is otherwise appropriate. We are referring only to whether a particular item is convenient to use under particular circumstances.

Ordinarily, convenience should be subordinate to the type of information one needs, but it can become an overriding factor. If Mr. Wheeler selects fill-in-the-blank items because they are relatively easy to develop, he'll probably save some time preparing the assessment—fill-in items don't take long to construct, or to score—but he'll probably sacrifice much of the information he needs. The learner's ability to memorize and retrieve is about all one can verify from a fill-in response.

Another characteristic of item convenience is the ability required of the person doing the scoring, because some test items necessitate a more knowledgeable and experienced scorer than others. Essay items, for example, are particularly demanding. Besides the time and content knowledge they require, essays usually have a more complex structure than other items, since part of their purpose is to allow the learner to explain something or to develop a logical argument. Essays also introduce the possibility that the scorer might be influenced by several other characteristics. The student's word choice, spelling ability, legibility, punctuation, analysis, and comprehensiveness all could conceivably become factors in the score for an essay. When there are many factors contributing to the score, it is easy for multiple people scoring the item to disagree about the quality of the response.

True/false, matching, and multiple-choice items are called "objectively scored" items. Several different people can score them with perfect objectivity as long as they have a scoring key to follow. The content expertise of the person scoring the tests is incidental with objectively scored items because the correct answers are not logically connected to the content at all. They are a list of symbols that anyone can follow whether or not they know the material the symbol represents. In a test on learning theory, for example, the person scoring the test need not know whether the conditioned stimulus in Pavlov's experiments was a bell, nor even what a conditioned stimulus is. The only judgment the person who scores the test must make is whether the student selected the same symbol or number that the scoring key provided.

Scoring Reliability

When one cannot score assessment items objectively, one risks poor scoring reliability. High scoring reliability occurs when multiple scorings yield the same result. Two circumstances illustrate a lack of scoring reliability. In one instance an individual who scores the same response several times finds that the multiple scores vary even though they all relate to the same work sample. In a second instance, multiple people scoring the same item fail to agree on the quality of the response. While they both reflect poor reliability, in the latter instance, we speak of poor interrater reliability.

> Scoring reliability occurs when we have multiple scores for the same work sample that essentially agree. Either several people draw the same conclusion about the quality of the work, or one person who scores the same work sample repeatedly makes the same decision each time about the "correctness" of the response.

When scoring reliability is poor, either the individual is responding to different elements of the response each time, or the multiple scorers have different views of what is important. In either case, the scoring rubrics or protocols discussed in Chapter 3 can help us achieve greater scoring consistency. Without something to generate consensus and provide guidance, people can change their minds about what to look for, or have different opinions from others about what to look for in the response.

Classifying Items by the Type of Response

As noted above, item flexibility, construction difficulty, scoring difficulty, and the reliability of the assessment scores are all characteristics that help us classify test items. Most of them also reflect the type of response required by the item, which leads us to a final classification element. When students must create or develop the answer to the item, we have **constructed response items.** With **selected response items,** the students choose the best answer from those provided.

The distinction between these kinds of items is not just a matter of classification convenience. Constructing a response usually involves a different kind of thinking than recognizing the best choice from among alternatives, since the choices themselves cannot be retrieval cues. However, be careful about assuming that selected response items elicit only lower level thinking. Although one may be able to document only recall ability for some selected response items, we shall see that others can require very sophisticated thought.

Constructed Response Items

Constructed response items often allow us a better view of the learners' thinking and skills than selected responses offer. One way to think of the difference is that constructed response items require that learners *produce* what they know. Selected responses require that learners *recognize* the best response among alternatives or eliminate incorrect choices.

Within the parameters imposed by the item and the testing conditions, sometimes students not only construct a response but also elaborate it, which allows one an even more complete view of what the student has learned. The common forms of constructed response items are (1) fill-in-the blank, (2) short-answer, and (3) essay.

As an operational definition, we are treating any response that the student develops in complete, written sentences as an essay item. Short-answer items require a single word, a phrase, or perhaps a list of related concepts. Fill-in-the-blank items may also require a single word or a phrase, but they usually have the form of an incomplete sentence, which the respondent completes by providing the "correct" word(s). We need to investigate each item type more completely, but first some comments on the strengths and weaknesses of constructed response items as a group.

Strengths and Weaknesses

Generally, constructed response items are relatively easy for the instructor to develop.

> Constructed response items are relatively easy to develop. They require that the student produce, rather than just recognize, a correct response. The essay item allows one to probe learning more deeply than any other pencil and paper item allows, but the time it takes the student to answer limits the breadth of learning the instructor can sample. Both responding and scoring are very time-consuming, and scoring reliability can become a problem with essay items, as with all constructed response items.

As we noted, they require that the respondent produce, or create, rather than just recognize an appropriate response. Unique among the different types of items, the essay allows the student to develop an explanation and so allows the teacher to follow the student's line of logic or argument. If the teacher constructs the essay item well, students' responses will provide an effective window from which to view their ability to grasp and explain.

Constructed response items bring a certain number of disadvantages as well. Although the items generally take very little time to construct, they require more time for learner response than selected response items. Consequently, one trade-off when one uses constructed response items that there is time for fewer items during a typical testing period, and less opportunity to probe the content. Particularly with essay items, we can examine an area in depth, but we give up breadth of coverage.

Constructed response items can also be very time-consuming to score. This is particularly true of the essay item because there are usually several different things to look for. Indeed, the opportunity to examine multiple facets of the students' learning is a primary reason one elects to use essays.

Beyond the time it takes to score constructed response items, they tend to be quite difficult to score in a way that eliminates the effect of the assessor's subjectivity. Constructed response items bring with them a great potential for the scoring reliability difficulties that we considered earlier.

The Fill-in-the-Blank Item

Fill-in items are pervasive in testing from the elementary school room to the university classroom. They are popular because they are easy to construct and they lend themselves to assessing the students' command of concepts and definitions, circumstances very common in most school situations. They have a very restricted assessment range, probably nothing above recall ability, and they present the same scoring reliability problems characteristic of constructed response items generally. There are certainly times when what we want to assess is how well students recall basic information. It is basic to their grasp of concepts, definitions, rules, facts, and so forth—which are the elements of higher thinking. When we conduct an assessment with fill-in items, however, the cost may outweigh the benefits. Consider the item in Figure 6.2:

Debates about whether Columbus actually discovered America aside, the item is problematic. There are several responses to the question that, although not what the instructor may have anticipated, are still technically not incorrect. It can be quite difficult to judge such responses from student to student consistently, in which case there is likely to be a scoring reliability problem. The unanticipated response places the assessor in the position of making decisions about how much latitude to give respondents. It also places the instructor at odds with the students when one rules out one unanticipated response but allows another. Recognizing that Columbus made his discovery on his first transoceanic voyage (Figure 6.2) has at least some value. It is difficult not to sound arbitrary when one rules some of the unanticipated responses acceptable and some unacceptable.

Part of the difficulty in the sample item can be corrected by asking the item this way: "Columbus discovered America in the year _____." Even that approach isn't fail-safe, however. Occasionally students may respond with "1942," and argue truthfully that they knew the correct answer but inadvertently transposed the 4 and the 9. Is such a response worth the full point, half a point, or no points? Do you really want to make such decisions?

Their restriction to recall ability and the ever present scoring reliability difficulties make fill-in items among the least flexible, and, from your author's point of view

---

FIGURE 6.2   Fill-in-the-Blank Items and
                  Scoring Reliability

Christopher Columbus discovered America in _____ .

A list of "correct" responses might include:

1492	the morning
October	the fall of the year
the Santa Maria	his attempt to find India
a boat	his first transoceanic voyage

anyway, among the least attractive, of the items we will review. Many educators never use them. If you need to measure lower level thought (from time to time every educator must), there are alternatives to fill-in items that provide the information one needs without some of the difficulties. Short-answer, true/false, and matching are all possible candidates. The alternatives require fewer on-the-spot decisions by the scorer about response correctness. With fill-in items, often one must make decisions on a case-by-case basis. The scorer has to determine the acceptability of misspelled words, and of synonyms for the word one intended. In most instances, test constructors are better advised to use items that are easier to score reliably.

If you are determined to use fill-in items, at least take precautions against some of the more common problems. Note the following item:

_____ authorized wartime use of the first atomic bomb.

Asking an item in this form invites a broad range of nouns that might technically fit the item. It would be better to word the item as follows:

The last name of the only U.S. president to authorize the use of an atomic bomb on a foreign city is _____ .

As with all assessment items, be as clear as you can be about what you are asking.

Another problem emerges when we attempt to make several items out of one statement by inserting too many blanks. For example, the following item on Chinook winds gives a clear indication of what is wanted, even if one knows little of the subject.

A warm wind common to northern Montana and southern Alberta that can quickly melt the snow in the winter is called a _____ .

But the same concept becomes unintelligible when too many words are left out.

A warm wind common to northern Montana and southern Alberta that can quickly _____ the snow in the _____ is called a _____ .

Ordinarily, one blank per item is best, and there will be less confusion for the student if the blank occurs at the end of the sentence. Your author maintains, however, that fill-in items offer few advantages besides their ease of construction and breadth of coverage.

Short-Answer Items

Sometimes a list of concepts is so fundamental to one's grasp of a content area that we want to be satisfied that learners can retrieve them from memory without the cue that a provided choice offers. There is a difference between asking, "What are the primary colors?" and asking, "Which of the following are the primary colors?" followed by a list of several combinations of colors. At other times we need to know that learners can retrieve information in a particular order ("Conjugate the French verb which means 'to be,'" or "What are the days of the week?"). Short-answer items help us assess these abilities, although the level of cognitive processing is quite low (knowledge or comprehension on the Bloom taxonomy).

Remember that the scoring reliability concerns that we associated with fill-in items occur to some degree in all constructed response items. The person scoring these items must decide before administering the test how much latitude to allow students. Should one deduct for spelling errors? If one asks for names, is a last name (or a first) sufficient? If one asks for a list and the learner omits part of the list, will there be partial credit? One must make such decisions early and communicate them to the learners before administering the assessment. Figure 6.3 lists a few of the more common types of short-answer items.

Note that we have some latitude in terms of the kinds of things we can ask with short-answer items. In each case the requested response ought to be clearly outlined, and there should be enough direction that the most common variations are eliminated, if they are deemed unacceptable.

Essay Items

A well-constructed essay item can require a response at any level from the most simple to the most complex. This makes the essay the most flexible of items. One of the more sophisticated tasks we require of learners is to draw information from multiple sources and then synthesize a coherent response to a question. This is the essence of problem solving. Although such syntheses are the strength of the essay, those who construct the items do not always allow them to reach their potential. In fact, sometimes essays become elaborate recall items. It is unlikely that anyone sets out to construct a rote-memory-level essay item, but it can happen inadvertently. Consider the following:

> Write an essay describing the levels of the Bloom taxonomy in their proper order.

FIGURE 6.3 Sample Short-Answer Items

Retrieval of a Definition	What is the name for words that look alike but have different pronunciations and different meanings?
	Explain "indentured servant."
Retrieval of a Series	List all of the planets in our solar system in order, beginning nearest the Sun.
Requiring a Name	Provide the last name of the primary author of the Declaration of Independence.
	Who was the main character in the story?
	Who was telling the story?
Providing an Association	Name two plants that develop seeds with "wings" that help them scatter.
	In 1914, what nations made up the Triple Entente?

When the item requires very detailed information without any opportunity to make an application or to analyze a situation, it becomes a recall task. It would be more consistent with the item's potential to ask:

> What did Bloom mean when he spoke of the taxonomy as a "cumulative hierarchy?"

Knowledge-level items certainly have their place, but it takes too much time and effort to use essays this way. There are alternative item choices—easier than essays to score—that will also measure lower level thought.

By definition, the essay calls for an extended response. Longer responses increase the probability that the scorer will respond to subjective elements they contain. For this reason, there are usually multiple scorers evaluating responses on standardized tests. Besides the safety of second opinions, these scorers usually receive training intended to guide them so that they all look for the same elements and try to weigh them uniformly. There is usually a significant time investment in the training, and the costs required for maintaining high interrater reliability levels sometimes make the training impractical. This is particularly true in the classroom, for which school districts usually do not have the resources to train people to score constructed responses (Braun, Bennett, Frye, and Soloway, 1990). Sometimes one can rely on a colleague to score at least a sample of the responses a second time to provide a cross-check of one's scores, but other teachers usually have their own time restrictions.

Scoring reliability can be strengthened by using a scoring key for constructed response items, sometimes called a **scoring protocol,** or a **rubric.** Scoring protocols serve two purposes. They indicate what the scorer should look for in the response by indicating what is most relevant, and, by implication, also what ought to be ignored. In addition, protocols help the person scoring the response to determine how much emphasis the various elements of the response should receive. Their use can result in essay scores that are much more reliable, even when only one person scores them. In Figure 6.4 we have an example of a scoring protocol for an essay item dealing with the Great Depression.

Even the best scoring protocol devised cannot help one salvage items that are poorly constructed, nor can it compensate for unclear or incomplete instructions. Asking fourth-grade science students to "Write a paragraph about traveling seeds" deals with an important concept, but the point of the exercise is ill-defined. Better to ask students to "Write a paragraph about the different ways plant seeds arrive at new locations." Consider the following three essay items developed for secondary school literature students:

1. Describe the setting for Hawthorne's novel *The Scarlet Letter.*

2. Explain how the setting contributes to the theme in *The Scarlet Letter.*

3. Discuss the minister in *The Scarlet Letter.*

The setting for the novel is an important aspect, but item 1 is likely to become a recall item. It invites students to list details of the setting with no apparent purpose

FIGURE 6.4   **Essay Item Scoring Protocol**

Item: Write an essay with an introduction, a supporting body, and a conclusion that explains how the Great Depression differed from other, prior economic downturns experienced in the United States. Make reference to social and political, as well as economic, differences.

Scoring Protocol

I. Content/Examples	*Scoring Range*
Unemployment	0–5
Climactic conditions	0–5
Stock market reverses	0–5
Bank failures	0–5
Political "lunatic fringe"	0–10
Government intervention (New Deal)	0–10

II. Mechanics	*Scoring Range*
Organization	0–10
Clarity	0–10
Grammar and punctuation	0–5

Scoring Indicator

Scoring Range 0–5		*Scoring Range 0–10*	
5	indicates excellence	9–10	indicates excellence
4	indicates better than average	7–8	indicates better than average
3	indicates average	5–6	indicates average
2	indicates less than average	3–4	indicates less than average
1	indicates very poor	1–2	indicates very poor
0	indicates a substantial amount of remediation is needed	0	indicates a substantial amount of remediation is needed

other than simple description. Hawthorne's setting for the novel makes an important contribution to the theme. If one wishes students to elaborate that relationship, it is better to rewrite item 1 as it appears in item 2.

In order to respond well to item 2, one must synthesize information about both the setting and the theme of the novel. Although this item is brief, it contains enough information that students who have read the novel can demonstrate their grasp of the relationship in their responses. Note that the synthesis called for by this item represents a level of thought that is peculiar to the essay among constructed response items.

Item 3 is too vague to be very useful. The minister is a central figure in the novel, but there isn't any guidance regarding characteristics of the minister that the learner ought to discuss. Should his morality be analyzed? Should his physical characteristics be described, or his involvement with the other characters? Should he be contrasted to Hester's husband? The ambiguity makes it very difficult because the instructor will probably end up scoring a variety of responses, each one prepared by a student with a different interpretation of what the instructor asked. Such items change the learners' task from using their abilities to demonstrate their command of the material to the business of trying to figure out what will satisfy the instructor. It will be more helpful to the student who will construct the response and the teacher who must score it to ask students:

> Who demonstrates the greater morality, Hester Prynne or the Reverend Dimmesdale?

Although responses will still vary because some students will take one position and some another, at least the nature of the task is more clear.

The most common problems associated with constructing essay items can be avoided if some ground rules are followed.

1. **Make the essay consistent with established goals and objectives.** Ordinarily, the need for essay items emerges when we write objectives and plan instruction.
2. **Clarify the instructions.** Provide enough information that students know what they are expected to do. If the essay's length and mechanics (spelling, punctuation, and so forth) are going to be factors in the scoring, this should be evident in the instructions.
3. **Avoid making the item an elaborate recall item.** Consider the level of processing that the item requires. If one expects the students to retrieve a great deal of factual information, the response is probably restricted to knowledge or comprehension. In such situations, select an alternative item type.
4. **Prepare a scoring protocol before administering the item.** With sensitivity to what students generally know and are able to do, specify what the scorer will look for and determine how heavily the different components will be weighted.
5. **Require all respondents to answer the same items.** Scoring reliability is difficult under the best of circumstances. The problem is compounded when learners aren't responding to the same items. One way to control this problem is to select two or three essay items that each allow one to gauge the relevant learning, and then permit students to choose which among the three they will answer. In that instance there is still choice, but there are likely to be multiple responses to each item.

For Further Discussion

We have noted that constructed response items all introduce scoring reliability problems. Whenever responses vary, we have to make scoring decisions on a case-by-case basis. Under what circumstances do the advantages of constructed response items outweigh the problems they create?

Selected Response Items

Assessments based on selected response items have attracted a good deal of criticism over the years. Their association with standardized testing, coupled with the disappointing results from those measures, have made them an easy target. Evidence indicates, however, that the difficulties lie mostly not with using, but with misusing, selected response items.

There are certainly variations on the theme, but the most common types of selected response items are true/false, matching, and multiple-choice. Of course, selected response means that learners choose the correct, or the best, response. As was the case with the constructed response items, true/false, matching, and multiple-choice items all have characteristics in common. The advantages explain their popularity, and their drawbacks help indicate why people criticize them so often.

Strengths and Weaknesses

When we write them carefully, selected response items offer high scoring reliability. This is possible because the person who scores the item usually has nothing to interpret. One need not determine, for example, whether the learner has some underlying knowledge or ability (although one may ask such questions when developing the items), but only whether the learner selected the correct response. With such a direct judgment to make, it is easy for multiple scorers to come to the same conclusion, or for one scorer to draw the same conclusion when scoring an instrument multiple times.

> Selected response items require no content expertise of the person who scores them. Indeed, they are often machine-scored. Because respondents can deal with larger numbers of items in a discrete period of time, they also allow one to sample more content than constructed response items allow. They are time-consuming to construct, however, and often, they are written to address only the lower levels of thought, something for which they are widely criticized. The potential for guessing correctly is high, particularly with true/false items, and the opportunity to skew results with a few lucky guesses is significant when the test is brief.

Ideally, of course, selecting the correct response indicates that the learner has the related learning. The item was constructed for such a purpose. But the person doing the scoring does not have to make that determination. The result is that there is very little in the scoring process that can diminish scoring reliability.

Because learners select, rather than develop, correct responses, administering the assessment takes much less time than an assessment made up of constructed response items. The relative time efficiency allows one to sample more of the content than would otherwise be possible. Therefore, when breadth of coverage is important, selected response items will generally be a better choice than constructed responses.

However, there are drawbacks to using selected response items, even when we design them carefully and use them appropriately. Although we save time during administration and scoring, developing selected response items, particularly in multiple-choice format, takes a great deal of time. Even experienced item writers cannot write multiple-choice items both quickly and well.

Because the learner has all of the choices of responses to the item, there is always a potential for guessing. As the opportunity to guess the correct response increases, so does the potential to make an incorrect judgment about what students know. If the test happens to be brief, one or two chance correct guesses can have a substantial impact on the score. For this reason, there is safety in longer rather than shorter tests, as long as fatigue does not become a factor, as it can with younger students.

What one gains in breadth, because selected response items require comparatively little response time, one may sacrifice in depth. Although the multiple-choice item can represent an exception, even several items can often provide only a superficial look at the depth of the students' understanding.

Finally, two of the three item types (true/false and matching items) are similar to the short-answer and fill-in items discussed earlier, in that they sample thinking at the lower levels of cognitive functioning. They allow one to assess mostly rote memory and so restrict the test developer to questions about facts.

True/False Items

True/false items often get negative press, but when the instructor writes them carefully and does not presume them to assess higher level thinking, they can work very well. They are easier to construct than other forms of selected response items and, because students can deal with each item fairly quickly, they allow the test developer to sample comparatively large portions of the content. Note that in order for one to have content validity, the instrument as a whole must accurately represent the content from which the items are drawn—something that gets increasingly difficult as the number of assessment items diminishes.

The problems we associate with selected response items generally tend to be particularly evident with true/false items, especially with regard to the potential for guessing. Because there are only two responses possible, the probability that one may guess correctly on any item and know nothing of the related content is, of course, 50 percent, or .5. This means that if an assessment instrument is based exclusively on true/false items, there should be some concern about how accurate and also how stable the individual's score will be. Although scoring reliability is probably very high, test reliability (the degree to which the score would remain the same if we tested a second time under similar conditions) can be very difficult to achieve when the tendency to guess is high and there are comparatively few items. We can make adjustments, however, in how we construct the items, and how we use them. The following guidelines will be helpful:

1. Avoid the use of absolutes.
2. Avoid the use of double negatives.
3. If questions refer to any subjective opinion, attribute the opinion to someone before asking whether the statement is true or false.
4. Keep the items brief so that each item refers to only one concept.

Examples of the problems that occur and the adjustments one ought to make are illustrated in Figure 6.5.

Often, we can ameliorate the effect of guessing by supplementing true/false items with items of some other construction. Students are probably less likely to guess at the answers of any other type of item. Besides, rarely will we wish to measure only lower level thought, so we usually include other types of items anyway.

Another adjustment takes us back to the length of the test. Brief tests compound the impact of guessing correctly. Lengthening the test to correct these problems is help-

FIGURE 6.5   Strengthening True/False Items

Problem	The use of absolutes.
Example	T/F All plant seeds are scattered by the wind.
Principle	An item containing "all" or "never" will nearly always be false.

Problem	The use of double negatives.
Example	T/F It isn't inconsistent with the desert environment for there to be intense heat.
Principle	Even when they are grammatically correct, items employing double negatives are confusing to students.

Problem	Asking whether an inconclusive opinion or finding is true or false.
Example	T/F The environment explains human behavior.
Principle	If a question refers to a subjective opinion, or something that is controversial, provide attribution before asking whether it's true or false.
Improved Example	T/F According to John Watson, the environment explains human behavior.

Problem	Inadvertently asking more than one question.
Example	T/F Multiple-choice items are frequently used in effective classroom assessment programs.
Principle	Brevity and conciseness are both virtues in true/false item construction. Note that we've really asked two questions: *Are multiple-choice items used frequently?* and *Are they effective?* If both are legitimate questions, they deserve separate items.

ful only to a point, however. A longer test means that we also increase the potential for fatigue, especially among students in the primary grades who may be unaccustomed to lengthy instruments.

We can also limit the impact of scoring with what is sometimes called a correction for guessing. The correction (a procedure more accurately called **formula scoring**) modifies test scores to neutralize the inflating effect of guessing correctly. Chapter 13 outlines some of the more widely used procedures for formula scoring.

Speaking of Assessment

Your author had a fifth-grade teacher who discouraged students from guessing by calculating the final scores as follows: One subtracts the number incorrect from the number correct. For scoring purposes, the instructor ignores the items not attempted. If a student correctly scores 15 of 20 items, misses three, and leaves two blank, the final score is 12. If instead of leaving the two items blank, the student guesses the answers incorrectly, the final score becomes 10.

Does this procedure seem a little draconian to you?

Consider whether such an adjustment is likely to have the same effect on very cautious and very impulsive students.

Matching Items

Matching items are convenient tools for measuring learners' knowledge and comprehension when the task involves lists of related data. The items also tend to be popular as a change of pace. The usual format is to employ two lists, arranged vertically. Frequently, one consists of concepts or names. The other is a list of explanations or identifying descriptions that the learner associates with the concepts/names. The items aren't difficult to construct as long as a few conventions are followed:

1. Restrict the matching item to one concept or theme.
2. Present the lengthier list on the left, the briefer on the right.
3. Ordinarily, there ought to be a different number of names, concepts, and so forth than there are definitions and descriptions.
4. Employ whatever natural order (chronology, for example) the list provides.
5. Take great care with the instructions.

If the task is to match names with descriptions, use only the names of those who actually belong to the group. Avoid developing an item that mixes the names of political figures with important scientific inventions, for example. If both are important, it is better to design two separate items to accommodate them.

Often, the matching item involves a brief list of concepts or names, with a more lengthy definition or description to which the name is matched. Convention suggests that the lengthier portion—usually the definition or description—be numbered on the left side of the item. The briefer list is usually presented on the right and designated with letters. This is really just to help the student who ordinarily reads the first item on the left and then scans the other list for an appropriate match. When they are not sure, students read up and down the right side of the item several times before making a choice. If the lengthier portion is on the right, the item becomes more time-consuming to complete for all students, but particularly for those who may not read well.

Classroom testing has become so common that students have learned to look for short-cuts, and of course one of the simplest tricks with matching items is to use elimination for the last answer. Ordinarily, the matching item should be structured so that determining the correct responses for five list entries on an item with six choices does not automatically reveal the sixth.

If there is a natural order to the concepts/names, it is better to reflect it in the list. There is usually little point in mixing up the order with a random presentation.

Although all of these are important issues, the problems in matching items probably arise less from construction problems than from instructions that are unclear. Good instructions for matching items address three questions:

- Must all the choices be used?
- May a choice be used more than once?
- Must all correct choices be listed?

If there are only as many choices as there are list entries, and each entry has only one choice, the first question is moot, but we usually design more choices than entries so that elimination cannot be a strategy. In that event, one ought to indicate whether some choices may be left unused.

Indicating whether all correct choices must be listed is the alternative to listing any correct choice, or the requirement that only the best choice be listed. To the degree that these questions are answered properly in the directions, at least some elements of guessing are more limited and data reliability may increase. Figure 6.6 is an example of a matching question that makes use of these guidelines.

Multiple-Choice Items

Among selected response items, multiple-choice are probably the most frequently used, and with good reason. The advantages we noted for selected response items exist for multiple-choice (M/C) items in particular. In addition, an experienced test developer can write M/C items so that they require processing at very sophisticated levels (Armstrong, 1993). Nunnally (1978) observed, "Time and again it has been shown that [scores from] a test composed of good multiple-choice items correlates with an essay test of the same topic almost as highly as the reliability of the latter will permit" (p. 259). That is, data from multiple-choice tests will correlate with data from essay tests on the same topic almost as well as the essay data will correlate with a second set of essay scores gathered under the same circumstances. In addition to the range of lower-to-higher levels of assessment that they allow, multiple-choice items can provide the same sharp curricular focus that all selected response item tests can provide. In many instances, items can be constructed to sample a great number of very specific content areas.

On the other hand, it has been noted that multiple-choice items cannot be written both quickly and well, particularly when they are designed for the more complex levels of thought. When M/C items are not constructed well, the problems associated with guessing and with the accompanying instability in the students' scores are magnified. Rather than compensating for weak items by lengthening the instrument—although there may be other reasons for a longer test—the safer course is to develop better items.

As a final comment on potential difficulties, note that one of the problems associated with all test items is particularly evident when using multiple-choice. Too often, classroom teachers develop a series of test items less because the material deserves the

---

FIGURE 6.6　Matching Item for "Traveling Seeds"

Directions: Column A is a list of several different ways seeds are scattered. Column B is a list of different kinds of seeds. Match the seed with how it is scattered. List all seeds that fit the description. A seed may be used with more than one description.

A	**B**
_____ 1. A seed with wings	a. cocklebur
_____ 2. A seed a squirrel is likely to scatter	b. dandelion
_____ 3. A seed that often gets stuck in animals' coats	c. maple
_____ 4. A seed that can be seen rolling across the road	d. elm
_____ 5. A seed that "pops" from a pod	e. tumbleweed
_____ 6. A seed that floats like a parachute in the wind	f. cattail
	g. acorn

attention than because the content lends itself to asking questions. The multiple alternative choices that the items involve make it tempting to use them with concepts that offer several ready-made options. It would not be difficult, for example, to design several items on the correct ordering of the planets in our solar system (Which of the following planets is between Mercury and Earth?, for example). One must ask, however, whether several items on such an issue are worthwhile, particularly since items of that type primarily test rote memory.

In terms of their structure, multiple-choice items have a **stem** in which the problem or issue is presented, followed by several **choices.** The choices include both the correct answer(s) and incorrect choices, called **distracters.** The stem should be a complete sentence, which allows students to know what is asked before they read the choices. Students can read the stem, attempt to predict what the best response will be, and then look for a match among the choices. In one of the sample items below, the problem is defined in the stem, and the learner knows that the task is to identify the mammal among the choices. Although one will not know what the choices will be, the task is clear. In the other item, the task is not as well defined. All that the learner knows is that one option will make the stem become a true statement.

Which of the following animals is a mammal?
a. a duck-billed platypus
b. a cattle egret
c. a bull snake
d. a tiger shark

The duck-billed platypus is actually
a. a member of the bird family.
b. a member of the reptile family.
c. a member of the amphibian family.
d. a member of the mammal family.

Because it is often difficult to write four reasonable distracters plus a correct choice, probably the most frequent pattern is three distracters, as in the examples above. With fewer than three choices, the items lose some of their technical advantage over alternative types, such as true/false (Willson, 1982).

The Discriminating Function of Multiple-Choice Items

It is important to keep in mind why we use test items in the first place. When they function well, test items allow us to discriminate. In achievement testing, the task is to separate those who have reached a particular level of achievement from those who have not. In order for multiple-choice items to serve that purpose, all of the choices, including the distracters, ought to be plausible to someone who has not learned the related materials. An obviously wrong choice contributes nothing to the assessment. The first of our items above might have listed "reptile" as choice "e," but it isn't going to be plausible to someone even vaguely familiar with the subject and so lends little to the discrimination the test developer is trying to achieve. Sometimes a throw-away choice is added for humor. It may be justified from the standpoint of helping test takers relax, but note that it doesn't add anything to the quality of the data.

> Multiple-choice items consist of a stem, where the problem is presented, and choices. The stem should be a complete sentence. Among the choices are a correct choice and distracters. In order for the item to help one discriminate between those who know and those who do not know the material, the distracters must be plausible to someone who does not know.

In some standardized testing, there is another dimension to discrimination. Ordinarily, standardized test data are norm-referenced. The task is not to determine who has reached a requisite level of achievement and who has not, but to establish an ordering, or a ranking representing more or less of a specific ability among the students (Ackerman, 1992). When the task is discriminating among people with similar levels of an ability, item difficulty is very important. This matter will be taken up in Part IV of the book, but for now note that difficulty plays a role in creating a broad scoring distribution. Items that everyone either scores correctly (low difficulty items) or misses (high difficulty items) do not help one discriminate *within* the group of test takers. On the other hand, items on which everyone (or no one) scores successfully can be quite helpful to the classroom teacher—who must know which concepts students have mastered and which they do not understand at all.

Manipulating the Difficulty of Multiple-Choice Items

If nearly everyone scores an item correctly, it may not indicate that everyone knows the material, however. Perhaps a little probing on the teacher's part suggests that students responded correctly because the item was too easy. In a multiple-choice item this means that the correct choice is so dissimilar from the distracters that even students who are unfamiliar with the content can determine the best answer. When the distracter is more like the correct choice, students must discriminate more precisely. Perhaps it sounds perverse to make the distracters more like the correct choice to fine-tune item difficulty, but sometimes it is appropriate to "raise the bar" a little when the original item does not separate those who know from those who do not. If the first item below is too easy, one can strengthen it by making the adjustments represented in the second.

1. Words that look alike but are pronounced differently and have different meanings describes which of the following?
   (a) nouns
   (b) homographs
   (c) figures of speech
   (d) comparatives

2. Words that look alike but are pronounced differently and have different meanings describes which of the following?
   (a) synonyms
   (b) homographs
   (c) homonyms
   (d) similes

The same principle applies to an item that no one scores correctly. If careful examination suggests that students actually do grasp the material, one can make the item more effective by rewriting the distracters so that they are less similar to the correct choice.

There are other options. Willson (1982) demonstrated that item difficulty is also related to allowing the number of correct choices to vary from item to item. The reliability of the data also improves when the learner must determine whether there are none, one, or more than one correct choice. Although the technical merits of this approach appeal to test developers, students usually do not care for it. They prefer the security of knowing that they must identify just one best choice.

Beyond these issues that relate primarily to the way the item is formatted, Carter (1986) documented some of the more common errors we commit when we construct multiple-choice items. Figure 6.7 is a summary of her findings.

Although multiple-choice items are often written at the recall level, they need not be. As Mehrens (1992) observed, "The notion that multiple-choice items cannot measure higher order thinking skills is unfortunate and incorrect" (p. 4). The items may be more difficult to construct at the higher levels, but the tendency to write multiple-choice items to sample lower level thinking reflects habit and convenience, not a limitation in the item. One approach to writing more demanding items is to give learners something they must interpret in order to respond. Consider the contrived data and the accompanying items in Figure 6.8.

Besides interpreting the graph, the learners must draw on what they know about supply and demand in order to answer the questions correctly. This format works well for a variety of different types of content. One might present a political cartoon, a news headline, a photograph, or something else relevant to the content, and then ask a series of interpretive questions about the related issues. When they are thoughtfully prepared, these items can all be excellent for those functioning at a higher cognitive level.

Some Final Considerations in Item Selection

As one reviews the different strengths and weaknesses that each item type has, one should remember to decide which item to use well before testing time. Often the instructional objective, which is prepared early during the planning period, dictates the type of item used in the assessment.

The discussion of choices began by noting that the item we select depends upon what we wish to measure. This means that we have to select an item that will reveal what students have learned. Learning that is intended to reflect the students' ability to analyze literary essays cannot be assessed very well with items that focus on retrieval, although that may be part of what we wish to know. We ought to use the lower level items to assess fundamental facts and information—the "boilerplate" kind of knowledge that all learning activities require—and then use essay and multiple-choice items to assess higher level thought.

Besides revealing complex thinking activities, the strength of the essay is that it allows one to probe a concept or an issue in depth. Alternatively, the multiple-choice item offers breadth of coverage in addition to the opportunity to sample higher level thought. One basis for deciding between the two, therefore, is whether depth or breadth is required. Another distinction is the opportunity the essay grants the respondent to develop a logical argument. There is no occasion to be persuasive with selected response items, even when they are developed to sample problem-solving activities.

FIGURE 6.7 **Errors Common to Constructing Multiple-Choice Items**

Problem "C" is keyed the correct choice more often than random chance would suggest.

Problem The desire to be unambiguous prompts the correct choice to be longer than distracters.

Example For which of the following reasons does the computer use binary code?
  (a) it was an arbitrary choice by programmers
  (b) the computer recognizes just two states, off and on, which are analogous to 0, 1
  (c) computers can only count to 2
  (d) it is more convenient for programmers than base-10

Problem The use of parallel language in the stem of the item and one of the choices can indicate a correct choice to a student who may not otherwise know the answer. The correct choice for this item *is* (d), but parallel language could just as easily cue the student to an incorrect choice.

Example Which of the following mountain ranges is the eastern boundary of the Great Basin?
  (a) the Sierra Nevada Mountains
  (b) the Appalachian Mountains
  (c) the Laurentian Mountains
  (d) the Rocky Mountain range

Problem Grammatical cues in the stem can cue a particular choice.

Example In the sentence "The night was very black," how is the word "black" used? It is an
  (a) noun
  (b) adjective
  (c) verb
  (d) conjunction

  The use of "an" will tip the test-wise student to the choice that begins with a vowel. Perhaps he may not even know why, except that the other choices "didn't sound right."

Problem One choice that is inconsistent with others will often serve as a cue.

Example In Hawthorne's short story "The Devil and Tom Walker," the fate of Tom's wife does which of the following?
  (a) has no bearing on the balance of the story
  (b) offers no particular insight to her character
  (c) tells nothing of what she values
  (d) offers a foreboding of Tom's fate

  The problem with this item is that all choices but "d" are worded negatively. This often serves as a cue, whether or not "d" is the correct choice.

Source: Adapted from Carter (1986).

There are other distinctions between the item types, of course. Recall that selected response items are far less time-sensitive, both in administration and in scoring, although they often take more time to develop initially. When the time for administering the test is very limited, selected responses are usually the better choice. Historically, a major problem with essay items has been scoring reliability, but that problem may

FIGURE 6.8 Constructing Higher Level Multiple-Choice Items

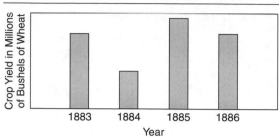

Study the graph before responding to the next three items.

1. If all other relevant conditions were similar, in which year would you expect prices for grain to have been the lowest?
   (a) 1883
   (b) 1884
   (c) 1885
   (d) 1886

2. In which year does it seem most likely that there was a drought?
   (a) 1883
   (b) 1884
   (c) 1885
   (d) 1886

3. In which year would you expect demand for grain to be highest?
   (a) 1883
   (b) 1884
   (c) 1885
   (d) 1886

be less a factor in the future, at least on standardized tests. Work by Braun and others (1990) indicates that "expert systems" can be devised that allow constructed responses to be reliably and accurately scored by computers. Although the technology will probably remain beyond the reach of classroom teachers for the foreseeable future, expert systems will be discussed in Chapter 11, on computer applications.

Item Quality

Two final thoughts on item choice: First, Nunnally (1978) reminds us that "a test can be no better than the items of which it is composed" (p. 259). His related warning is that, as test items are constructed, educators have a tendency toward ambiguity and triviality. Whereas someone who lacks the learning *should* be unsure of the proper response, an ambiguous item leaves even the informed student without needed direction. Earlier we offered the caveat that the fact that something is easy to ask questions about does not necessarily mean that it is important enough to warrant several items, or sometimes even a single item. These are problems we can detect in a review of the assessment, and it is an excellent practice to ask an experienced colleague to look tests over before they are administered (and students are held accountable for the results).

The Assessment Context and Item Bias

The second reminder is to note that the decision regarding which item is best for a particular assessment application has much to do with what learners have done in the past. The questions and tasks we use during instruction should prepare students for the types of items that will appear on the test. If that is not the case, the validity of the results is probably suspect, even when we take great care to match the particular item with the assessment task.

Related to this issue is the problem of item bias, an issue that will be taken up in some detail in Chapter 12, on ethics, but it should be mentioned here. If assessment items employ content more familiar to some students than to others, content unrelated to the learning we really wish to measure, the unfamiliar students are at a disadvantage. Read the following item as an example.

> An outfielder for the Florida Marlins has 13 hits in 43 at-bats. What is his batting average?

If we use the concept of batting averages in baseball to teach division or proportion, those unfamiliar with the sport may have more difficulty than baseball fans—not because of the arithmetic, but because of the context. As groups of learners are more linguistically or culturally diverse, the potential for using a concept or an example that some students do not understand becomes a more pressing problem and may contribute to item bias. Educators must consider the learners' background experiences carefully when preparing instructional materials and test items.

For Further Discussion

Suppose you have a class of students who are linguistically or culturally diverse. If test results correlate with students' group membership, does this mean the items are biased? How will you know whether students do not know what you taught, or whether they are struggling with the form of the item or with the words you have elected to use?

SUMMARY

The chapter began with Mr. Wheeler's problem of item choice for his science assessment. There is something reassuring about a published assessment. It may even seem presumptuous for the classroom teacher to develop assessment items when published items are already available. However, much of what makes an instrument appropriate is knowledge of the setting and a grasp of how the educator will use the assessment. No one has a better context for the students and what they have learned than the classroom teacher. Not even those who designed the curriculum will know exactly how the teacher implemented it in the classroom, and these are factors that ought to affect the items we construct and the way we assess our students. There is nothing wrong with deferring to someone's superior expertise in item construction and assessment, but classroom teachers can accumulate most of the information they need to conduct effective assessments. The teacher's insight can help make the difference between an instrument designed for an abstraction (the typical fifth-grade class) and an instrument developed specifically for the circumstances (*your* fifth-grade class).

We know now that some types of items are ill-suited to particular assessment tasks. The fill-in items that Mr. Wheeler favored are probably not a good choice. They introduce too many scoring reliability problems and, under the best of circumstances, allow us to assess only lower level thought. Although what he has heard of multiple-choice items is true—that they *are* generally written at the lower levels—it need not be. In fact, they may provide the best option for him, given his particular circumstances. He can use multiple-choice items to test his students in a wide range of content areas and on several different levels of cognitive complexity. It will take time to construct the items, but he can score them quickly and reliably. Although they will not allow him to view higher level thought, matching and especially true/false items also provide some breadth-of-coverage advantages. They are similarly easy to score and easier to construct than are multiple-choice items.

If the student's depth of understanding is more important than breadth of coverage, one may wish to use essay items. They are relatively easy to develop, but teachers must allow a good deal of time for scoring. A rubric will help minimize the scoring reliability problems; it will also offer a more systematic way to evaluate the extent of the most relevant information students know, and what they do not.

Science classes, especially introductory classes, are often heavily laden with new terms. Short-answer items are an effective way to test the students' ability to retrieve or define relevant concepts. We must deal with the scoring problems associated with misspellings and synonyms, but the items call for students to construct their responses from memory rather than merely to recognize correct answers, and they allow students to demonstrate their understanding of the ordering in a list when that is relevant.

The lesson in test construction is that when we understand the strengths and limitations that all items have, we can tailor assessment to fit most of the circumstances a classroom teacher encounters. Difficulties arise when we make decisions out of convenience, or out of ignorance, rather than with an eye to the role that the different items can fill in classroom assessment.

Good items take time to construct. In fact, there is a good deal of skill involved in item writing, which means that it is the kind of ability we can develop with practice. Even under the best of circumstances, however, it is easier to revise than to create. Once you have developed effective test items, and the determination of item quality will be pursued in the next chapter, it makes good sense to retain the items for future use. Your author does not suggest that it is a good idea to repeat a test, but individual items are too important to use once and then discard. Just as one may improve the quality of multiple-choice items by manipulating the distracters, the principle of fine-tuning test items carries over to all types of items. It will allow us to continue to improve the quality of the information we receive, not just about students, but about all elements of the educational plan. The care we take to prepare an assessment should be consistent with the potential that assessment data offer to improve the other educational elements.

FOR FURTHER READING

The National Council on Measurement in Education often publishes an NCME "Instructional Module" in the journal *Educational Measurement: Issues and Practice.* "Design and development of performance instruments," in the Fall 1987 issue (pp. 33–42), provides a systematic and quite sophisticated guide to developing performance instruments.

Kathy Carter's findings in her (1986) article, "Test-wiseness for teachers and students," *Educational Measurement: Issues and Practice* 5(4), pp. 20–23, have important implications for the way multiple-choice items should be written.

REFERENCES

Ackerman, T. A. (1992). A didactic explanation of item bias, item impact, and item validity from a multidimensional perspective. *Journal of Educational Measurement, 29,* 67–91.

Allen, M. J., and Yen, W. M. (1979). *Introduction to measurement theory.* Monterey, CA: Brooks/Cole.

Armstrong, A-M. (1993). Cognitive-style difference in testing situations. *Educational Measurement: Issues and Practice, 12*(3), 17–22.

Armstrong, D. G., and Savage, T. V. (1983). *Secondary education: An introduction.* New York: Macmillan.

Baxter, G. P., and Glaser, R. (1998). Investigating the cognitive complexity of science assessments. *Educational Measurement: Issues and Practice, 17*(3), 37–45.

Bennett, R. E., Rock, D. A., and Wang, M. (1991). Equivalence of free-response and multiple-choice items. *Journal of Educational Measurement, 28,* 77–92.

Bloom, B. S. (Ed.). (1956). *Taxonomy of educational objectives, Handbook I: Cognitive domain.* New York: David McKay.

Braun, H. I., Bennett, R. E., Frye, D., and Soloway, E. (1990). Scoring constructed responses using expert systems. *Journal of Educational Measurement, 27,* 93–108.

Carter, K. (1986). Test-wiseness for teachers and students. *Educational Measurement: Issues and Practice, 5*(4), 20–23.

Furst, E. J. (1981). Bloom's taxonomy of educational objectives for the cognitive domain: Philosophical and educational issues. *Review of Educational Research, 51,* 441–453.

Kubiszyn, T., and Borich, G. (1987). *Educational testing and measurement: Classroom application and practice* (2nd ed.). Glenview, IL: Scott, Foresman and Company.

Mehrens, W. A. (1992). Using performance assessment for accountability purposes. *Educational Measurement: Issues and Practice, 11*(1), 3–9.

Nunnally, J. C. (1978). *Psychometric theory* (2nd ed.). New York: McGraw-Hill.

Solomon, G. (1970). The analysis of concrete to abstract classroom instructional patterns utilizing TIP profile. *Journal of Research and Development in Education, 4* , 52–61.

Stiggins, R. J. (1991). Relevant classroom assessment training for teachers. *Educational Measurement: Issues and Practice, 10*(1), 7–12.

Tanner, D. E. (1988). Achievement as a function of abstractness and cognitive level. *Joural of Research and Development in Education, 21*(2), 16–21.

Willson, V. L. (1982). Maximizing reliability in multiple-choice questions. *Educational and Psychological Measurement, 42,* 69–72.

CHAPTER 7

Constructing Tests and Analyzing Test Data

■ *Readers will learn to evaluate an assessment instrument according to traditional measurement principles and to use assessment data to improve both teaching and assessment.*

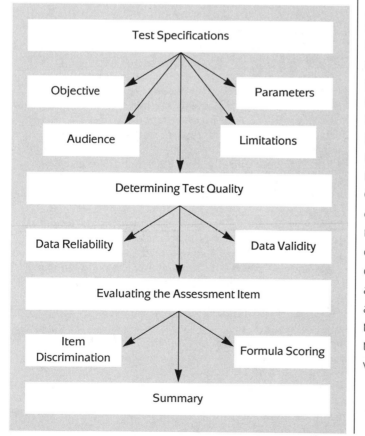

Test Specifications

Objective

Parameters

Audience

Limitations

Determining Test Quality

Data Reliability

Data Validity

Evaluating the Assessment Item

Item Discrimination

Formula Scoring

Summary

Professional test developers usually begin by outlining test specifications. The bother of preparing them may seem to be overkill for classroom teachers, but specifications serve an important classroom purpose, too. They provide a sense of focus for test development. Once the assessment exists, its quality is the fidelity with which the test measures what the user claims, a judgment based upon data reliability and the different aspects of validity. Once we administer the test, we improve the individual items by reviewing their performance one at a time via item analysis. ■

Mrs. Bondy thoroughly enjoys teaching the seventh grade. She teaches a variety of academic disciplines in a a small school, a situation that she finds renewing and interesting. Although she feels that she's a competent teacher, she has a good deal of insecurity about testing, particularly when she must conduct assessments in a variety of academic areas. She has many friends in her school, and over the years she has made it a practice to collect samples of the instruments they use. Those materials and the tests that her textbook publishers make available result in a substantial file, but the tests never seem to fit her teaching exactly. Either she must tailor her teaching to the tests, or she must adapt the materials to make them fit her students and her instructional plan. In the past Mrs. Bondy has often taken components of the existing tests and reassembled them, but she is never sure that the result is an improvement. She needs to be able to evaluate the test data so that she can make informed judgments about how well the assessments are working and how she might improve them. ■

TEACHER-CONSTRUCTED ASSESSMENTS AND PUBLISHED ASSESSMENTS

The classroom teacher's responsibilities are remarkable for their range and also for their complexity. Perhaps because even the title ("teacher") directs attention to the instructional side of things, the assessment tasks that provide information about students' progress and are so central to reform efforts receive comparatively little emphasis. Standardized testing is prominent in contemporary education, and that area may receive some attention, but the teachers' role in developing assessments is generally not a focal point either during their preparation or in the general discussion of the state of education. Stiggins (1991) noted that "the vast majority of teacher training institutions require no [classroom assessment] training, and many do not even offer an option of assessment training" (p. 7). Consequently, it isn't too difficult to understand that when given an option, teachers often defer assessment tasks to others. Probably every textbook you will use in your college study or your classroom teaching, including this one, has a "teacher's supplement" that contains a variety of assistance for the instructor, including sample test items and other assessment materials. Time demands and perhaps a little assessment insecurity prompt instructors to demand such help, and book publishers comply.

May we assume that, because materials are published for fourth-grade students, they are appropriate for *your* fourth-grade students? Not necessarily; even if they have been prepared with great care, we usually do not know whether anyone has actually used them to assess learners. May we at least assume that the materials that accompany a textbook are appropriate for a specified class or grade level? Probably, but this is a difficult question to answer with finality in light of the diversity that some classrooms reflect. By necessity, those for whom the published assessment is intended are a generic group of students. They are expected to be typical of the grade or level,

161

Most academic texts have a supplement intended, among other things, to help the instructor with student assessment. As carefully as published assessment materials might be prepared, it is difficult to compensate for the fact that the author, by necessity, prepares for a generic group. Such supplements may not serve you very well if your students have atypical needs.

but an assessment prepared for an "average" group cannot possibly reflect all of the differences that might occur in a particular class. Remember that no one will understand the conditions in your classroom as well as you do, and this gives you a great advantage—not just when you are preparing instruction, but also when you are planning the assessment activities.

The point of this chapter is to equip you with the techniques and skills you will need to construct in-class assessments and evaluate assessment materials. In Chapter 4 these tasks were approached with an eye to authentic and performance-based assessments. Here our interest is in more conventional assessments. We will extend the Chapter 6 discussion of item types and item construction to the development of complete instruments and the interpretation of test data.

Recall that one of the themes of this book has been that all components of the educational plan are interconnected, and assessment data should help us improve each. This includes the assessments we use. If we have procedures for evaluating the instruments, we can more easily judge the quality of the data that we gather. A teacher who can improve the history test has a better view of how well students understand history. In turn, this helps one understand which components of the instruction worked well and which need more work. It also reveals where pre-assessment detected relevant differences among students and where those conditions might have been missed. Better assessment data allow us to make more informed judgments—not just about student performance, but also about the quality of the planning and the instruction that preceded the assessment.

TEST SPECIFICATIONS

At least on a superficial level, assessment is not a particularly difficult task. Anyone can assess a group of students. The difficulty comes in having enough confidence in the results that we are willing to base important decisions on them. The planning model introduced in Chapter 2 suggests that assessment should be ongoing and assessment data should impact every other part of the educational plan. The need for this approach is more apparent when we recognize that the educational process requires that teachers make continual judgments about what students have learned, what they should learn, what they are prepared to learn, and how one should proceed with teaching them. Those four issues lie at the heart of education, and our responses to the related questions are incoherent and misdirected unless we take the time to conduct the appropriate assessments.

Educational programs revolve around four questions: What do learners already know? What should they know? What are they prepared to learn? and How can one best proceed with the teaching? The only way to have accurate answers is to conduct the relevant assessments.

Assessments are most effective when the developer takes the time to construct a set of test specifications that defines

Although assessment data often help one answer a number of different questions about the quality of the learning and teaching, the assessment should be developed with quite specific purposes in mind. They are defined by test specifications defining why the assessment was constructed, for whom, how it is to be used, and what limitations the developer assumed.

both the purposes and the context for the assessment before it is actually developed. Although the process for establishing test specifications can be very detailed (see Millman and Greene, 1989, pp. 338–339, for example), the specifications for the typical classroom can probably be established by answering the following questions:

1. What is the objective of the assessment?
2. For whom is the assessment intended?
3. Under what conditions will one administer the assessment?
4. What are the parameters within which the test developer and administrator must operate?

The Assessment Objective

Think of the assessment objective in terms of the type of information one might need. An achievement test, for example, is supposed to reveal the learner's command of a skill or of a body of knowledge. An effective test allows the instructor to make informed judgments about students' progress.

The purpose of the placement test, on the other hand, is to guide the instructor regarding where to begin instruction and how to proceed. When students lack a prerequisite, the data from a placement test should reveal what it is. This makes a good placement test an effective guide to the content that must be taught and to the cognitive processes that ought to be emphasized in a learning plan. Note that any emphasis on the different cognitive processes (analysis, problem solving, memorization) has implications for the types of items we can use in the assessment.

Besides specifying the structure of the assessment, sometimes the objective also indicates the intended setting. Demonstrating specific skills may require the type of setting that is only possible in a laboratory, for example. The assessment will be most informative when we have a clear picture of its purposes, or objectives, before we begin to create the test.

The Audience

The test developer must have some grasp of who will be assessed. This includes some knowledge of students' cognitive skills and abilities, and such related characteristics as their attentiveness, their level of maturity, and their experience with formal assessment. Older students tolerate longer assessments better than younger students. With older students, one also has the latitude of employing skills, such as writing ability, that younger students may not yet possess. A science assessment in which students present oral reports on the possible effects of greenhouse gases on world climate is probably appropriate for most 14-year-olds. This isn't the case, however, if some have not given oral reports before, are not yet comfortable in the primary language, or have a disability that would make it awkward or embarrassing for them to stand in front of their classmates.

Although one should be sensitive to what students have done, past experience is not always the dominant factor in future assessment—or we would never introduce them to anything new. Whether students have dealt very much with the sort of abstract content that algebra problems require, for example, a good placement test may suggest that they are ready.

What Are the Environmental Limitations for the Assessment?

Every test imposes certain environmental limitations. How much time will students have to complete the test? Must they work independently? Are hand calculators, dictionaries, and laptop computers allowed? On selected response items, are students encouraged to guess? Is there an adjustment in scores for guessing? Is a sheet with a list of formulae allowed for the math test? Not only should students know what the limitations are, but in some instances they must know well ahead of the test, since some limitations affect their preparations.

One of the more important assessment limitations is the length of the test. It is difficult to have a complete picture of student performance with brief assessments, but the time we can allot to assessment is finite, particularly for younger students. Because the need for brevity conspires against assessment precision (Millman and Greene, 1989), there is a constant tension between the number of items that time and student maturity allow, and what we wish to know. Permitting or banning the use of hand calculators in a math assessment also has implications for time. Allowing them eliminates some of the time-consuming basic calculations and lets students respond to more questions.[1]

What Are the Parameters for the Test Developer?

The students' limitations reflect the parameters experienced by test developers. Even if it might allow one a better view of the student's command of the subject, it makes little sense to prepare an instrument that includes 50 multiple-choice items and three essays if it must be completed in 30 minutes. The length of the test reflects the decision the instructor makes about what one can reasonably expect within the available time.

Some of the decisions are products of more subtle considerations. Computer use is becoming increasingly common, even in elementary and secondary school classrooms, but there is a question about whether computer use materially alters the assessment. If some students have computers and some do not, is it possible that those who have them will receive more positive evaluations for reasons unrelated to their command of the subject? Virtually all word processing programs can help the user correct the common spelling and grammatical mistakes. If those characteristics are not the focus of the assessment, they should not alter the outcome, but it can be quite difficult not to react to repeated errors, even when they are not relevant to what we wish to measure.

If circumstances allow us to administer the assessment to one student at a time, it will be different than if it is intended as a group test. Individual testing permits the instructor to probe and the learner to elaborate. For obvious reasons, group testing usually provides for neither. In fact, the group assessment may require little of the test administrator beyond distributing the assessments, reading the directions, and proctoring the test. This places a different burden on those who develop the assessment, however. Group-administered assessments must include either written or oral instructions that are clear enough that learners can work independently.

For Further Discussion

There is a trade-off between what we may wish to know about students' understanding and what circumstances allow. Besides their writing (in)ability, what are the factors that might impact the assessment of eight-year-old students?

DETERMINING THE QUALITY OF THE ASSESSMENT DATA

As noted earlier, anyone can assess a group of students, but all assessment data are not created equal, and what instructors need is sufficient technical understanding to make informed judgments about the quality of the information we gather. The material in this chapter can't resolve the time difficulties that every committed educator struggles with, but there are some guidelines that will help one make good decisions. The risks that accompany poor assessment practices are substantial. In a nutshell, if our procedures are flawed, the data we gather will be, at best, inaccurate, and perhaps even deceptive; and the decisions based upon them can have only limited effect.

The traditional gauges for assessment quality are the data's **reliability** and **validity**.[2] Both concepts were discussed earlier in Chapter 4, on authentic assessment, but they will be taken up again here, prefaced with this comment: At least in the abstract, reliability and validity are important, whatever type of assessment one uses. However, we must adapt the principles to the particular application. Recall that reliability refers to the assessment data's consistency. In the context of authentic assessment, it refers primarily to what is called interrater reliability. It is the degree to which separate assessors agree on the quality of a learner's performance or, as an alternative, the level of agreement between one assessor's multiple, independent assessments of the same performance. The argument is that as long as the relevant conditions do not change (the learner's grasp of and experience with the materials, the environmental characteristics of the assessment), multiple assessments of the performance ought to also remain consistent. The issue is stability and, at least on a general level, stability is also the issue in more traditional reliability discussions.

Validity in traditional assessment is a little more complex. For purposes of authentic assessment, the concerns are whether the assessment bears a resemblance to real-world conditions (face validity), and whether the assessment itself has a positive effect on the quality of teaching and learning (consequential validity). There is some discussion of face validity in traditional assessment as well, but the issue is less the assessment's consistency with conditions beyond the classroom than it is the consistency

Although they are construed differently depending upon the task, the importance of data reliability and validity transcends the type of assessment involved.

between appearance and function. The assessment must look as if it does what it is supposed to do. Face validity is actually one of the lesser issues in traditional assessment, however. There are other validity issues not yet raised; each of them relates to this central question: "Are we measuring what we claim?"

The Relationship between Reliability and Validity

Of the two concepts, reliability is perhaps a little easier to understand, but there are other reasons to consider it first. Reliability is a prerequisite to validity. If assessment results are not consistent, how can we claim to measure what we wish? If you administer the same reading comprehension test to your fifth-grade students twice in the same day and find that the class average is substantially beyond grade level the first time and very near grade level the second, how would you explain the change? It is obvious that we have unstable data, but there is also a validity problem. Although both scores represent assessments of reading ability, in at least one case, and perhaps in both, the data are flawed. An individual student's performance is unlikely to change significantly during the day, particularly in the negative direction. An entire class is even less likely to fluctuate this way. The class is unlikely to be both on grade level and beyond in the same day. Whatever else occurs, the assessment data must at least be consistent.

Suppose we have stable data. Is that fact sufficient to establish assessment validity? Do stable data indicate that we are assessing what we claim? Some of the early work on intelligence suggested that reaction time might be an indicator of intelligence. Suppose we devise a test in which we gauge intelligence by how quickly subjects can move their hands from point A to point B when prompted by a signal. With some training and a decent stopwatch, we could probably get quite consistent results, but validity requires some evidence that what we are assessing is actually intelligence. Do those with the greatest physical quickness also demonstrate the greatest intelligence? However attractive the test may be for someone with quick hands, we have no evidence that reaction time predicts intelligence. When Binet, who is recognized as the father of intelligence measures, tested the reaction time hypothesis, he found it invalid. Reliability is certainly necessary, but it is not sufficient for validity.

When what we are trying to assess is an abstraction—and intelligence is a good example of an abstract ability—establishing validity is particularly difficult. When the level of abstraction is low, validity is almost as easy to satisfy as reliability. Physical weight is very concrete, and if you were gathering weight data for a health and nutrition exercise, the only inference necessary is whether the bathroom scale is accurate, something that can be established by comparing the reading on one scale to that on another. One could establish reliability by checking one individual multiple times during a short period to note whether the scale registers the same weight each time. When we have these assurances, we can be quite certain that two people who register 110 pounds actually do weigh the same, and we can assume that someone who registers 109 actually weighs less than someone who registers 110, and so forth.

Even with our confidence in scales and weighing, if we were conducting an experiment on subjects' weight that was to last several weeks, we would observe certain controls. We would weigh our subjects on the same day each week, and probably at the same time of the day, but absent damage to the scale, we probably wouldn't worry too much about the reliability or the validity of the data.

When we are measuring physical properties (How much does that weigh? How tall is he? How many are there?), validity is almost as easy to verify as reliability. In the academic disciplines, however, what we assess is rarely so concrete. Instead, we contend with concepts such as students' comprehension and their analytical ability, characteristics that cannot be measured directly. Rather than employing a bathroom scale or a yardstick to collect data, we must develop test items and construct assessments in order to determine the degree to which a trait or characteristic is present. As the characteristic becomes more abstract, so do the problems related to demonstrating the reliability and the validity of the data.

Reliability and validity topics rarely receive equal billing in teacher-preparation programs with such matters as lesson planning and objective writing (Frisbie, 1988). It shouldn't be any surprise that veteran classroom teachers often gloss over reliability and validity as well, or even ignore them altogether. It is an unfortunate consequence that the technical quality of teacher-made assessments is generally quite poor (Frisbie, 1988).

Reliability and Assessment Error

It has been noted that data are reliable when one can administer a test repeatedly and derive the same scores each time, as long as conditions among the students do not change. This must seem a little far-fetched because, at least in the classroom, no one gives tests repeatedly and conditions never remain constant. However, the concept is important, so bear with your author a little. Although scoring consistency defines reliability, it also illustrates the relationship between reliability and validity because an assessment that really measures what it is supposed to measure (that is, it is valid) also will provide the same data each time, if conditions do not change.

If some part of students' scores reflects something other than what they have learned, then scores may vary even when learning remains constant. The culprit in this variation is error, and it is almost inescapable because we are concentrating on areas of academic learning that are rarely easy to measure. It is not immediately apparent, for example, how much of the student's score reflects the ability to spell, and how much of it reflects the ability to guess which words will be on the test. Be careful about equating error in this sense with a mistake or with sloppy procedure, although those can contribute to error. Error is any component of the score that is unrelated to skill or knowledge we set out to measure.

Even with great care, we might never get perfect measures, but we can, at least, work toward minimizing error. Part of good assessment is to determine how much of the student's score reflects the intended ability and how much reflects other factors.

Error can have a variety of origins. Perhaps some learners are test-wise. They recognize that the more lengthy response on multiple-choice items is frequently the best choice, so they respond to the longer answers when they are unsure. Or maybe environmental conditions affect some students more than others. If a crew is busy jack-hammering the sidewalk outside during the assessment and some students are more distracted than others, the accuracy of their scores may likewise vary. A flu epidemic might make some learners feel listless and distracted. It seems clear that often error is less a mistake than an influence on the score that is unrelated to how well students actually know or can do what we are trying to measure. Lucky guessing gives an inaccurately high measure of how well the learner grasps the material and, by the same token, ambiguous test items can prompt a score that is too low. The object of the assessment is to produce data that are as representative as possible of the learner's true grasp of the content. We want to know the learner's **true score,** which is what the assessment would yield if the data were completely free of such contaminating influences.

Students' academic achievement is nearly always the central focus of classroom assessment. We noted, however, that it is not the kind of thing that one can assess by the pound, or by the inch. Because of the level of abstraction, we can never be completely certain we have established the students' true levels of achievement, their true scores. Nevertheless, true scores are important as theoretical concepts. They remind us that there is a value that represents how well the learner actually knows, or can do, something, even if circumstances and environmental conditions obscure it. The true score is the score we would have if we (a) administered the same assessment an infinite number of times to the same student, (b) held testing conditions constant, and (c) averaged the scores from all of the assessments.

Although this clarifies the concept, it also seems to place the true score out of reach, since the conditions for deriving it are completely unrealistic. As it turns out, however, we can use the scores the students receive on their one assessment as an estimate of the true score. This is most feasible when we observe certain conventions as we prepare and administer the test. As our skill increases and we take greater care in the process, we can have greater confidence in the connection between the observed score and the true score.

This fidelity between observed score and true score is the object—whether we develop our own assessment or we select something from another source. In terms of what is called classical test theory,[3] the relationship is expressed symbolically this way:

$x = t + e$
where x = the score from the assessment, the observed score
t = the true measure of the trait or ability, the true score
e = random variations from the true score, error

The equation indicates what we have stated, that the observed score (x) has two components, the true score (t) and then some portion of the observed score called error (e). Error represents the effect of all factors that separate the observed score from the true score. The error can be random or systematic, and its influence can make the observed score higher or lower than it ought to be as an accurate estimate of the true score.

As the "random" in random error suggests, it is unpredictable. Perhaps it affects only one student, as when someone becomes sick during the assessment and is unable to respond. On the other hand, interruptions during the testing period may disrupt everyone and depress the performance of the entire group.

By contrast, **systematic errors** are reflected in such effects as test-wiseness, which allows some students to consistently score higher than their true level of achievement warrants. This is what may occur when students attend seminars in "How to Pass the _____ Test" and learn techniques that may boost their scores without teaching them the content that the scores are supposed to reflect.

For Further Discussion

For classroom teachers, there is a natural tension in academic testing that we ought to acknowledge. On one hand, we wish our students to do well; on the other, we must have accurate measures of their performance if we are to know how to proceed with them. If helping them do well is the primary interest, we do what we can to boost their scores by, for example, teaching them how to take tests well.

When are you willing to allow the desire (yours or theirs) for a high score to override the need for a precise measure?

Is there an ethical consideration here?

As the effects of error on the assessment data are eliminated, the data become more consistent. Because data that are not reliable cannot be valid, anything that dilutes reliability must diminish validity as well, so be aware of the logical connection between the two.

A myriad of things can contribute to measurement error. In a most obvious case, incorrectly counting the number of correct responses on a student's test represents assessment error. But usually, error is reflected in more subtle problems. We may be able to verify with exactness (that is, without error) that a learner scored 22 of 25 items correctly on a geography assessment. However, it does not necessarily follow that the learner has a command of 22/25ths of the content represented on the assessment, although that assumption is often implicit in the way we treat the score.

Some of the reasons scores might vary if the test were repeated are related to changes in the learner, others reflect circumstances in the assessment setting, and still others stem from the assessment itself. We expect scores to change if the learners' understanding changes. We exercise a measure of control over environmental conditions by making sure that students have the same amount of time, the same access to resources, and the like, but changes connected to the assessment itself are worrisome.

Assessment error is inversely related to reliability. Whether random or systematic, error diminishes the quality of the assessment data.

When items mean different things to different learners even when they have a common understanding of the subject, the scoring variability represents error. Often this stems from language that students do not understand, or language that some interpret one way and some another. Good assessment minimizes any scoring variability that is unrelated to what one wishes to assess.

It has been noted that the observed score serves as an estimate of the true score. Actually, the assumption is that the true score falls within a band created by the observed score, plus or minus a margin of error called **the standard error of measurement (SEM)**. If the student scores 62 on an achievement test and the standard error of measurement is 4.5, one could argue with a specified level of probability that the true score resides somewhere between 57.5 and 66.5. The discussion of how the SEM is calculated appears in Chapter 9. For now, note that since error diminishes reliability, reliability by extension provides an estimate of error. This means that assessment data with high reliability come from procedures in which we have neutralized most of the unrelated factors.

Test–Retest and Alternate Forms Approaches to Reliability

The classic approach to reliability, and the approach that is implied in most discussions of reliability, is called test–retest. Under test–retest conditions, reliability is determined by the similarity in scores derived from two independent administrations of an assessment to the same group, with a minimal interval between administrations.

Even if environmental conditions are held constant, which means that the test is administered the same time of day, in the same room, by the same person who reads the same instructions, and so forth, a number of other factors can interfere. Someone who has been administered the assessment may respond differently the second time because he or she has thought about the test items during the interim. Perhaps additional learning occurred between administrations, or maybe there is sufficient ambiguity in the wording of an assessment item that some learners adopt different interpretations each time they read the item. These situations can pose problems even if great efforts are expended to hold constant the other environmental conditions under which the learners perform.

To some degree, the problems with test–retest can be resolved by developing a second, equivalent assessment that has a distinct form. Although we avoid the problem of those who are taking the test having seen it before, we must be concerned about the equivalence of the two forms. Consider two fourth-grade math assessments developed from the same curricular materials, for example. If "form A" presents each of the items in numerical format, and "form B" uses some word format, can the two forms be equivalent? We might argue that the tests measure traits that are different enough (computation ability versus computation and reading/analysis) to undermine equivalence, even if both come from the same learning materials.

Test designers can solve the equivalence problem by constructing alternate forms of a test side by side. They design the test items in pairs so that, although they are not exactly the same, the items are similar in construction and they address the same characteristic.

Motivation, intelligence, and self-concept are mental traits that tend to be quite stable in an individual, which means that they change very little as a result of experience. If the test items are clear and unambiguous, a second administration of a test designed to assess any of those characteristics will probably prompt the same responses as the initial exposure, since the trait will not have changed. As a consequence, the reliability of data can ordinarily be checked using a test–retest procedure. But academic achievement is not stable. Because what a student knows or can do at a particular time tends to be quite fluid, establishing reliability for classroom applications often calls for different procedures.

Internal Consistency Reliability Measures

Even if the conditions could be held constant and the equivalence problem resolved, the need for at least two testing periods makes test–retest, as well as alternate forms procedures, cumbersome and inconvenient. When the assessment has multiple items, there is an alternative to administering the test twice called **internal consistency reliability,** which requires only one administration of the instrument.

Perhaps a simple way to visualize internal consistency is in terms of **split-half reliability.** In this instance, the effect is to turn one assessment into two by comparing the responses on one half of the assessment to those on the other. This presumes that the entire test assesses the same characteristic, by the way. There is little value in a reliability estimate based on a comparison of the half that deals with punctuation to the half that deals with rhyme and meter in poetry. It is also wise to avoid comparing the first half of the items to the last half, since the difficulty tends to increase as the assessment proceeds.

There are several other variations on the internal consistency reliability theme. Kuder and Richardson (Ebel and Frisbie, 1986) developed several reliability formulae, including one that we will calculate here. They each focus on interitem consistency rather than the consistency between halves of the instrument. The Kuder and Richardson formulae are easy to recognize because of their K-R prefix.

From a conceptual point of view, remember that reliability represents the consistency in item scoring. This is the case whether test–retest, alternate forms, or internal consistency reliability procedures are used. Reliability can be thought of as the correlation between sets of scores. Indeed both correlation and reliability are designated by the same notation, a lowercase *r*. Although correlation values can range from $r = -1$ (a perfect negative correlation; as the value of one variable decreases, the value of the other increases correspondingly) to $r = 1$ (a perfect positive correlation; the value increases or decreases in exact correspondence with the other), reliability statistics have only positive values. They range from $r = 0$ to $r = 1$.

A reliability statistic of $r = 0$ means there is no relationship between the two sets of scores. The first set does not predict a second set. Reliability of $r = 1$, on the other hand, indicates perfect consistency. Administering the test a second time would yield the same scores, if conditions were controlled.

As a practical matter, we usually rely on computers to deliver reliability statistics since the calculations are rather involved and software for the purpose is widely available. However, some of the formulae are simple enough to calculate by hand. One can calculate some of the internal consistency formulae that Kuder and Richardson developed quite readily with a hand calculator. One Kuder and Richardson formula, for example, requires only a measure of the test mean, which is the average of all scores, the number of items on the assessment, and the **variance** of the test scores. If *variance* is unfamiliar to you, just note that, as the name suggests, it is one gauge of how much individual students' scores vary from the class average. An example of the procedure for calculating internal consistency reliability with a revised form of Kuder and Richardson's formula 21 (K-R 21', Frisbie, 1988) is shown in Figure 7.1.

Interpreting Reliability Data

In our (contrived) example we found the reliability of the data $r = .69$, which might be considered a fairly high measure compared to teacher assessments generally. In

FIGURE 7.1   Calculating Test Reliability

Assume that on a 30-item test we have the following scores for 15 learners:

22	22	20
19	23	15
16	24	28
27	17	23
26	18	19

Procedure: Step 1. Calculate the mean

Step 2. Calculate the variance

Step 3. Calculate internal consistency reliability

Step 1. The Mean $M = \dfrac{\Sigma X}{N}$

Sum of all scores divided by number of scores

ΣX = summation of all scores

N = number of scores

$\dfrac{\Sigma X}{N} = \dfrac{319}{15} = 21.27$

Step 2. The Variance $S^2 = \dfrac{\Sigma X}{N} - M^2$

Sum of squares of each individual score ($22^2 + 19^2 + \cdots 19^2$), divided by the number of scores ($\frac{319}{15}$), and subtracted from the result—the square of the mean

$S^2 = \dfrac{7007}{15} - 452.41 = 14.72$

Step 3. Internal Consistency Reliability

$K\text{-}R\,21' = 1 - \dfrac{(.8)\,(\text{mean})\,(\text{number of items} - \text{mean})}{(\text{number of items})\,(\text{test variance})}$

$= 1 - \dfrac{(.8)\,(21.27)\,(30 - 21.27)}{(30)\,(15.92)}$

$= 1 - .31 = .69$

truth, however, making such a judgment is at least partly subjective. We know that the data from teacher-made tests generally average a reliability of about $r = .50$ (Frisbie, 1988). Published standardized tests, on the other hand, have reliability figures that range from .85 to .95. Deciding what is adequate depends very much on how we will use the data, as the following indicates:

> *Experts in educational measurement have agreed informally that the reliability coefficient should be at least .85 if the scores will be used to make decisions about individuals and if the scores are the only available useful information. (This ought to be a very rare circumstance.) However, if the decision is about a group of individuals, the generally accepted minimum standard is .65. (Frisbie, 1988, p. 29)*

In the classroom, we use assessment data to make decisions about individual students, but test scores should never be the only information we use, even if data reliability is very good. When we include nontest data (homework, projects, and so forth) to make judgments, we almost certainly base the decision on a wider range of the students' abilities than the test alone represents. In the case of a weak test, we can ameliorate the impact of assessment data that might have low reliability.

It won't surprise you to know that most classroom teachers have almost no experience calculating or interpreting reliability statistics; nevertheless, they are important indicators of test quality. Your author's hope is that readers will become convinced that determining data reliability is an essential part of evaluating students' progress.

Enhancing Reliability Estimates

Reliability is affected by a number of factors. Some, such as the physical or emotional state of the learners, are generally beyond the control of the person administering the assessment, but educators can manage many of the others. Some of the factors emerge during development of the instrument, some occur during administration, and others when the data are scored. The person who constructs and administers the instrument often has some control over the following:

the length of the test
the type of item used
the quality of the item
the difficulty of the item
academic language
the conditions under which the assessment is administered
the size of the group
the group's characteristics

Test Length and Reliability

Other things equal, reliability increases with the number of assessment items. The "other things" means that the type of item used and the quality of their construction must remain even if new items are added. It also means that problems such as the fatigue that might be a problem for any student, but is most particularly so for primary grade children, must not be a factor. The relationship between the length of the assessment and the data's reliability is quite logical. In order to represent the content fairly, we usually need multiple items, and the number of items we need increases with the size of the content area. When we use brief assessments, we limit our ability to sample the content and proportionately increase the impact that a learner's guesses may have on the outcome.

Although we know we can increase reliability by adding more test items, *the magnitude of the increase* depends on how long the instrument is to begin with and how many items we add. We can predict the change with the **Spearman–Brown formula.** The example in Figure 7.2 estimates the impact on assessment reliability of doubling the length of the instrument we examined in Figure 7.1. Note that Spearman–Brown is accurate only if conditions other than the number of items remain constant.

FIGURE 7.2   The Spearman–Brown Prophecy Formula

Assume we have doubled the length of the 30-item instrument featured in Figure 7.1. Using the Spearman–Brown formula, we can predict the effect on reliability of altering the length of our assessment.

$$r_{adj} = \frac{n'}{1 + (n - 1)r'}$$

where r_{adj} = the predicted reliability coefficient after making the change in instrument length
n = the magnitude of the change in test length
r' = the reliability coefficient of the existing instrument

The adjusted reliability coefficient is calculated as follows: The number of times the test is to be lengthened (n) times the original reliability coefficient (r'), divided by 1 plus the number of times the test is to be lengthened minus 1 ($n - 1$) times the original reliability coefficient (r').

Recall that the calculations in Figure 7.1 resulted in a reliability coefficient of .69. Therefore, we can determine the adjusted reliability coefficient as follows:

$$r_{adj} = \frac{2 \times .69}{1 + (2 - 1).69}$$
$$= \frac{1.38}{1.69}$$
$$= .82$$

As you can see, the calculations aren't particularly difficult. It is just a matter of determining by what factor test length will change and then inserting the appropriate numbers in the formula. We can make the estimation whether we are lengthening or abbreviating the test. If you decide the test is too long for the time you have to administer it, you may wish to know how reliability will be affected by reducing test length. If you reduce the assessment from 30 to 20 items, test length becomes two thirds of its present length. In decimal form, two thirds is .67. Halving the test length to 15 items makes n = .5, and so on.

It is important to recognize that the relationship between the length of the assessment and the gain in reliability diminishes as test length grows. The original 30-item instrument yielded r = .69. Doubling the instrument with another 30 items nets an increase of .13 in reliability, and if one takes the time to continue this process, another 30 items would yield a yet smaller increase in reliability. Although it is something of a judgment call, we often quickly arrive at a point at which the increase in reliability does not justify the added work involved in constructing more items.

As an aside, remember that in a split-half reliability estimate, one derives a reliability coefficient by halving the test and then comparing the two halves for consistency. This procedure actually produces an underestimate because it treats one test as two. Rather than a 38-item instrument, for example, one has two tests of 19 items. Using the Spearman–Brown formula, one can compensate for the effect of halving the instrument by making n = 2.

Item Type

It is no coincidence that selected response items dominate on standardized tests. For all of the reasons noted in Chapter 6, multiple-choice assessments, particularly, yield much more reliable data than instruments requiring constructed responses. There are two primary reasons for this. The first was alluded to earlier when it was noted that it is very difficult to sample a content area of any breadth with essay items. They can provide great insight regarding the learner's analytical ability and clarity of thought, but the time it takes to develop an essay makes them quite limiting when it comes to coverage. Learners can respond to far more multiple-choice items than essay items in a finite period. Very simply, selected response items allow us to ask more questions.

The other reason for increased reliability with selected response items has to do with scoring. As noted earlier, even when one has a protocol that defines the scoring procedure, some subjectivity often creeps in when scoring constructed response items. It is very difficult for the scorer not to react, or not to overreact, to such things as spelling, word choice, grammar, the length of the response, and even the legibility of the handwriting. To the degree that ancillary variables become reflected in the scores, reliability suffers because different scorers have variable reactions to these characteristics.

By contrast, selected response items can be scored with almost perfect precision by anyone possessing a scoring key, regardless of whether the scorer has any background in the content area. Items that offer little opportunity for subjectivity yield higher reliability than the alternatives. More numerous items offer both better content coverage and higher reliability than fewer items.

Remember that all of this assumes that all of the items on a test address a common theme. Otherwise, reliability estimates don't make much sense. The concept of stability in scoring quickly loses its meaning when there is no unifying topic measured. This issue is actually connected to a grading problem that was considered earlier in the book. If the instrument samples several different concepts or characteristics, how would one interpret the score? For example, if one wishes to assess students' grasp of atomic structure and the periodic table of elements, and also must assess learners' understanding of correct procedures in the chemistry lab, it is better to construct two separate assessments—one devoted to each area. We can then be clearer about the meaning of both the students' scores and the data reliability estimates.

As a footnote, concession should be made to some of the other assessment circumstances. In large classes, particularly where the instructor does not enjoy the luxury of a teacher's aide or assistant who can assist with scoring, there is often no alternative to selected response items. In Nunnally's (1978) words, a careful grading of the 100 or so essay examinations one might have with multiple sections of the same class is a "monstrous job." On the other hand, when there are 15 or so students in a class, the time required for constructing multiple-choice instruments actually makes it more time-efficient to construct and score an essay test. As a decision rule, Nunnally offers the following:

> When there are as many as 30 students, the practical advantage is on the side of the multiple-choice examination. When the class contains between 15 and 30 students, there is no strong practical advantage for either type of test, and consequently the decision between them should be made on other grounds. If instructors feel more comfortable in constructing one type of test than the other, they should probably follow their own intuitions in that regard. (p. 260)

Item Quality and Difficulty

Think of item quality as a function of how well the item allows one to discriminate between those learners who know the content, or have developed the skill, and those who lack the learning. Moreover, an item that doesn't discriminate well contributes little to assessment reliability and may even detract from it. We have two issues here: One relates to item clarity, the other to item difficulty.

Different learners understand ambiguous items to mean different things. This lack of clarity is an artifact not of different levels of learning, which is probably what we want to evaluate, but of errors committed in item construction. Consider a true/false item such as the following:

> T/F   Pavlov's contributions were most important in the area of
> learning theory.

In his own time, Pavlov was most important for his work in physiology. In fact, he received a Nobel Prize in connection with work in which he measured salivary secretions in dogs. The answer to the question depends at least upon the time context, and when that is left undefined, the item is ambiguous.

Academic Language

When the vocabulary in the item is unfamiliar, it interferes with learners' ability to respond correctly. This is a particular problem if the language used in school is not the students' primary language. Sometimes students are unacquainted with what is termed "academic language." Aside from the particular discipline, which is often riddled with terms and concepts unique to the subject, there is a language of the classroom that is also different from ordinary speaking. This general academic language tends to be more formal than day-to-day usage, and it appears to particularly affect those who are already at greatest risk of failure in the academic setting (Wright and Kuehn, 1998). When the author began taking courses in teacher preparation, he wondered about the "units" that others were working on and that everyone else seemed to understand. The concept was not novel, but because he lacked formal teacher training, the word itself was new to him. When items are being constructed, we need to be attentive to the degree to which the item "loads" on some trait or ability other than what we intend to assess.

Note that items that either everyone, or no one, can answer correctly contribute nothing to reliability. Items that everyone scores correctly may boost the student's ego, and good items will let us know when everyone has mastered a concept. Such items contribute nothing to how consistently we can determine who "knows," or can perform, some behavior, however, and who cannot. Items that no one can score correctly may be helpful to the degree that they indicate areas of the curriculum that need some remedial help, but they do not strengthen reliability.[4]

> The student's inexperience with the language used in the classroom can pose multiple impediments at assessment time. There may be problems because the student's primary language is something other than English, or because the words and concepts used in the classroom represent an academic language the student is not yet comfortable with. In either case, there is a risk that, when an assessment relies more heavily than necessary on abilities other than those that one wishes to measure, the score may not reflect the relevant learning.

The Assessment Conditions

As anyone who has tried to work amid distractions knows, environmental conditions can impact assessment results. We want to have a physical setting for the activity that is not intrusive. Some environmental conditions cannot be controlled, but one can usually neutralize factors such as room temperature, some of the extraneous noise, and perhaps some of the visual stimuli that may interfere with the learners' performances.

Sometimes we seem to work at cross-purposes. Exciting bulletin board displays are designed to attract the students' attention. Exotic cars and sports or movie stars are certainly entertaining, and they probably communicate that the instructor understands students' interests, but distractions are counterproductive—both to learning and to measuring performance.

Ordinarily, classroom assessment involves only the most general time limitations: The students must conclude the assessment when the period ends. But the time allotted to complete an assessment can play a role in reliability. As it turns out, reliability increases when the difference among students' scores (scoring variability) also increases. Using the logic that standardized testing employs, we can increase variability by imposing time limits that are stringent enough that some students may not finish. Although this makes reliability coefficients higher, they are unrealistically high whenever the scoring variability is an element of the time limitation rather than of differences in the levels of learning. In classroom assessment, we generally try to minimize the impact that the allotted time has on students' performance differences.

Some tests are legitimately timed (speeded). They usually have a low level of difficulty, and performance is gauged by how much the learners complete. Although there are certainly advantages to being able to finish a task quickly and accurately, in the classroom we are generally more interested in what the learners can do. The typical classroom assessment should not be speeded.

> Reliability is a factor in assessment quality, but it is not the sole factor. If it were, the difficulty of the items and our ability to maximally discriminate among students would be the overriding factors in test construction. However, we often elect not to use some of the mechanisms that increase reliability because we are interested in uncovering something else that might be obscured. A case in point is imposing stringent time limitations for a test. When scoring variability increases, reliability does as well; but strictly timed tests may provide us with a better view of how quickly the students work than whether they understand the concepts underlying the problems. As it is, we pursue data reliability when we can do so without obscuring other relevant elements of student performance.

Group Characteristics and Size

Other conditions equal, reliability estimates are highest when scores reflect different levels of accomplishment among the students. It is more difficult to have stable scores when the characteristic we are measuring is much the same from student to student. Think of this in terms of testing and then retesting. When group members are very similar, small changes in their responses may reflect substantial changes in their rank ordering from the first test to the retest. This characteristic carries over to the discussion of group size. In small groups, comparatively small changes in scoring have a magnified impact on the group pattern. Reliability estimates increase with group size because there is a greater potential for more variety in level of accomplishment, and small variations in scoring have less impact on the outcome.

With the amount of standardized testing that occurs in some school settings, many students have developed "test-wiseness." They have learned to determine the correct response even though they lack a grasp of the underlying concept or ability. This becomes a particular problem when test-wiseness is unevenly distributed among those being assessed (Frisbie, 1988). Test-wise learners appear to perform at an inaccurately high level, which may be gratifying to both teacher and student; however, any increase in scores due to test-wiseness is nothing more than measurement error. Sometimes teachers attempt to "level the playing field" by coaching all students in elements of test-wiseness. If only certain students recognize that "C" choices and longer choices are most often the correct choices (Carter, 1986), those students have an advantage on multiple-choice tests that has nothing to do with their grasp of the content.

Note that for performance to be optimal, learners must be motivated, and the student's level of motivation is connected to the assessment's consequences (Frisbie, 1988). A learner who is determined to attend college will approach an entrance examination more carefully than one who is indifferent to the possibilities. Explaining why the assessment is relevant is an element in encouraging learners to perform at their highest level.

Assessment Validity

Because validity will be looked at carefully in the next chapter, there is no need to go too deeply into it here, but some basic concepts will be helpful. In general terms, remember that validity is reflected in the degree to which one assesses what one claims to have assessed. A measure of problem-solving ability ought to reflect how well learners can solve problems, not how well they guess correct answers. Next, although great emphasis will be placed on the way assessment instruments are constructed, note that, like reliability, validity is a characteristic of the data, not of the instrument. If the data do not reveal what the educator must know, it will make no difference how much time was taken preparing the instrument. Nor will it matter whether the instrument was prepared by the classroom teacher or by someone entirely removed from the students.

Face Validity

Face validity is the appearance of validity, not validity in a formal sense at all. We want students to take our tests seriously, so they must look as though they will do what we claim. Although there is a formal approach to establishing face validity (Secolsky, 1987), those who prepare tests are nearly always familiar enough with what passes for a test that they do not bother with the procedures. Problems with face validity usually emerge when the assessment is very unconventional. Those who read the poetry of John Keats may be brighter than the general populace, but a screening device for an academic honors program that includes a question about whether the individual has ever read "Ode on a Grecian Urn" might not be very effective. It lacks face validity.

Content Validity

Content validity goes awry when the assessment instrument does not represent the content accurately. A test can never duplicate every detail of a discipline, but we can usually sample the subject with a reasonable level of fidelity. However, even if the assessment represents the content fairly, the instructor can still distort the discipline and diminish validity by emphasizing minor points and ignoring central themes during instruction. Sometimes the teaching is fine but the assessment deals too much with minor elements of the content. A punctuation test that deals almost exclusively with comma use lacks content validity. District curriculum guidelines and state frameworks can help minimize the problems, but occasionally there is an important discontinuity.

Speaking of Assessment

Perhaps an eighth-grade health teacher really has very little passion for health but a burning interest in politics. If the discussion throughout the term is of government and of parliamentary procedure, what should the assessment cover? The instructor can do justice to the discipline by constructing a good, balanced test of health concepts, but it will be unfair to the students. The students will think it more equitable to evaluate their grasp of parliamentary procedure, but their scores will not be valid indicators of their grasp of health.

Does the example seem far-fetched? Your author learned more than he wanted to know of parliamentary procedure in an eighth-grade health class. (Some may be inclined to relate his argumentative nature to that formative experience as a member of "the loyal opposition.")

Typically, the mistakes are less egregious than the example in the box. Content validity problems usually occur because a topic is inadvertently omitted, or because what ought to be assessed is confused with what is convenient to assess, and in the process one elevates minor topics to a major emphasis. The order of the planets rotating around the Sun in our solar system is a natural subject for factual test items prepared for younger students who are studying astronomy for the first time. One might easily design several questions dealing with how well students know which planet is between Mercury and Earth, what planet is the largest, which is associated with rings of dust, which was discovered last, and so forth. Probably each of these facts is important, but whether they are important enough to warrant as many items as one might be able to construct is another matter.

Consider another aspect of content validity. Perhaps students read *To Kill a Mockingbird* and analyze the novel for what it reveals of race relations in the American South during the Great Depression. If the assessment consists exclusively of recall-type items, is there a content validity problem? With class discussion centered on analysis, and an assessment centered on recall, most would agree that there is.

Many of the content validity problems can be resolved with a chart for classifying test items called a **table of specifications** (see Figure 7.3). The table allows one to create item categories based on the topic the item addresses and usually one other characteristic, such as the item type (true/false, short answer, and so forth). Usually the topics are listed with some indicator of their relative importance, allowing one to know at a glance whether the number of items is consistent with each topic's importance.

The level of thought that assessment items require of learners has become a very important issue. With that in mind, one might arrange the table of specifications so

FIGURE 7.3 Table of Specifications for Basic Geometry Test

				Topic			
Type of Test Item	*1*	*2*	*3*	*4*	*5*	*6*	*7*
Problem-solving	*	*	* *	* *	*	*	*
Application	*	*	*	*	*	*	
Definition	* *	* *	*	*	* *	* *	*
Fact	*	*		*	*		

Key to Topics

1 = Angles	5 = Radius
2 = Triangles	6 = Diameter
3 = Perimeter	7 = Rectangles
4 = Area	

that one dimension reflects the topic and the other reflects the complexity of thought the item requires. Figure 7.3 is a table of specifications for a basic geometry assessment. Its dimensions are the topic and the level of response the item solicits.

> The table of specifications is a tool used to establish content validity. Preparing and then referring to the table allows instructors to determine whether they have addressed all of the relevant content areas, and whether the number and type of test items represent an appropriate balance.

It is also common to use the levels of Bloom taxonomy (Bloom, 1956) to classify items. The descriptors here are a little simpler than Bloom's six levels, but if you review the Chapter 6 discussion of the taxonomy, you will see the connection. Remember that classifying the complexity of educational tasks always involves some risk because, in order to be accurate, one must also make quite precise judgments about what the learners already know and have already done.[5]

Nunnally (1978) observed that it is best to see to content validity before we actually construct the test. The table of specifications is an important help, but content validity cannot be any better than the individual assessment items. Two items we construct to address the same element of content may not perform equally well. Consider, for example, the following constructed response items that both deal with content validity:

(a) Define content validity.

(b) Explain the relationship between item quality and content validity.

Certainly, there are instances in which either item might be useful and both might be categorized on a table of specifications as items appropriate for a test on that particular content, but they are not equivalent items. The first item is constructed to require recall of the learner. One can memorize well and respond to it perfectly. The second item requires a deeper understanding. They both respond to a similar element of content, but they offer quite different levels of coverage.

Criterion-Related Validity

Criterion-related validity has two facets, **concurrent validity** and **predictive validity.** The difference between them is largely the time frame. Predictive validity indicates the degree to which data from one assessment predict data from a later assessment. Concurrent validity indicates the consistency—or the correlation—between two independent measures of the same characteristic taken near the same time. Teachers can demonstrate that a vocabulary test has concurrent validity when their results agree with the data from a standardized vocabulary test administered at about the same time.

The intent is not to determine whether the scores from two separate measures match. Scoring ranges and scales that are unique to each test usually make that impossible. The issue is whether the scores of those assessed reflect similar rank ordering on both tests, whether those assessed occupy similar positions relative to the others on both measures. If there is concurrent validity, those who score low on one measure relative to others in the group will also score low on the other, and so on.

EVALUATING THE ASSESSMENT ITEM

However reliability and validity are defined, and it has already been noted that advocates of traditional assessment and authentic assessment take different approaches, remember that they represent some of the more important gauges of assessment quality. The quality of the assessment must ultimately rest on the quality of the individual test items, which brings us to their evaluation.

There are two optimal opportunities to evaluate assessment items. The first occurs when the test items are either being constructed, or selected from an existing item bank. Many of those issues were raised in Chapter 6. The second good opportunity occurs after we administer the assessment and can analyze the responses. As Figure 7.4 indicates, certain criteria are anticipated at each juncture.

The scrutiny that occurs during the construction of the assessment is largely in terms of the format and the content of the item. Those are the issues related to accuracy, clarity, importance, and relevance to the curriculum, which were addressed earlier. Later,

FIGURE 7.4 Elements of Item Evaluation

Focus of Evaluation	Criteria
A. Item Content	Accuracy
	Clarity
	Importance
	Fairness
	Relevance to the curriculum
B. Item Response	Difficulty
	Discrimination

Source: Adapted from Millman and Greene (1989).

in Chapter 12, dealing with ethics in assessment, fairness issues will be discussed in the context of test bias, which must also be a construction consideration.

Sometimes we misjudge how difficult an item turns out to be for the students. As careful as we try when constructing items and administering tests, sometimes the item is too difficult. Sometimes it is unclear. We ought to take note when several students ask for clarification of certain points, or they ask for definition of a word one thought they understood. Be careful not to blame the messenger. This kind of subjective information helps you know when you might have made an error with the way you constructed an item, or in terms of your evaluation of the learners.

There is a more objective procedure for reviewing items, called item analysis, that can be very helpful. Although the concept is not new, classroom teachers are relatively unacquainted with the approach, which provides a systematic, mathematical procedure for analyzing responses to determine which items served the assessment purposes most closely. Examine Figure 7.4 for a moment, and you will see that **item discrimination** and **item difficulty** are at the heart of the item analysis.

Item Discrimination

Beyond the correctness of the responses, item analysis focuses on what the response patterns reveal. The assumption is that, besides higher scores, those who do well on the assessment as a whole have different response patterns from those who do poorly. Although the principle applies to any type of item, we can illustrate it most easily with selected response items and with multiple-choice items in particular.

Perhaps the most important measure of item quality is the degree to which the item helps us discriminate among the different levels of learning that learners have. A single multiple-choice item cannot accomplish this because one item cannot assess enough of the content, so we use multiple items. If the items are effective as a group, the students' scores allow us to determine how well they understand the different concepts and principles that make up a subject area.

Assume that you have developed a measure of how well your third-grade students understand the characteristics that make some animals amphibians. If the test scores do not distinguish between those who understand and those who do not, it would be pointless—and perhaps even damaging—to use the data in any sort of decision. A test score that is comparatively high should indicate that the student has a better command of the concepts than others. However, if the individual items are poorly constructed, or inappropriate for some other reason, scoring differences reflect something besides how well students understand. Perhaps what the score reflects is how well students can take tests, or how ably they can memorize large amounts of information. Clearly, those abilities are not the same as a grasp of the different types of animals.

Although we are interested in the quality of individual items, scores from the test as a whole can be particularly informative. They provide a gauge of students' performances, and because they represent a measure of students' performance on several individual items, they are a more stable information source than individual items provide. We will see that the total test score is the measure we need for evaluating individual items.

We identify those who scored highest and those who scored lowest and use the performance of the students in those two groups as benchmarks for analyzing the quality of individual items. Sometimes everyone understands a concept, but when there are relevant differences in how well students know, those with the higher total test scores should do better on any particular item than those in the lower group. The degree to which this occurs is the measure of how well the item discriminates between students of different levels of knowledge or skill.

When most of the items discriminate reasonably well, we have confidence that students with high test scores understand the content and those with low scores have not yet learned. We lack that confidence if several of the items from a test discriminate poorly.

When there are large numbers of test takers involved, item analysis is typically handled by computer, and some of the available software programs will be looked at in Chapter 11. Here we examine a simpler paper and pencil approach. One begins by administering the assessment and ranking the students' total scores. If the class size is 20 or more students, identify the 10 students who scored highest and the 10 who scored the lowest. If the class size is smaller, the two groups are the top half and the bottom half of the class. However, if the total class size is lower than 12 or so, this approach may not be very helpful.

The top 10 and the bottom 10 become the test groups for evaluating each of the items. As we review them one at a time, the idea is to determine how many students in the two groups scored each item correctly, and then calculate how well the item discriminates between those students who did well on the test as a whole and those who did not. We also want to calculate the level of difficulty for each item. This is the procedure followed in Figure 7.5.

The product of the procedure is an item discrimination index (d_i) that we calculate for each item. The statistic, which can range from +1 to −1, is an index of how well the particular item separates those in the two groups. An index of +1 indicates perfect separation. It can only occur if everyone in the top group scored the item correctly and everyone in the bottom group missed it. An index of −1 indicates that the low scorers all scored the item correctly and the top scorers all missed it. Actually, extreme scores are comparatively uncommon and indeed the author has never seen an item with an index of −1. Probably most discrimination indices occur near the middle of the range between 0 and +1.

Item Difficulty

The difficulty index (p) is a very simple calculation. One divides the number who scored the item correctly by the number who attempted the item. If you have 35 students in class who attempted the item, and 28 of them scored it correctly, $p = {}^{28}\!/_{35}$, or .8. The p designation is used because it stands for "probability." The probability that someone from this particular group scored the item correctly is .8.

Teacher-Prepared versus Standardized Testing

In most traditional standardized testing situations, item discrimination is all-important because assessors assume that what the test measures is distributed unevenly through a population. The test items are supposed to help separate test takers according to the characteristic. Consequently, an item that does not discriminate contributes nothing to the assessment, and those that either everyone scores correctly or no one scores correctly are set aside because they do not discriminate.

FIGURE 7.5 Calculating the Item Discrimination Index

Group Characteristics:

The class has 24 students.

We identify the top 10 and the bottom 10 students' scores and ignore the 4 who are between these two groups.

We will use the top 10 and bottom 10 to calculate d_i.

The assessment has 20 items.

The discrimination index is calculated as follows:

$$d_i = (g_1 - g_2)/g$$

where d_i = the discrimination index, which may range from -1 to $+1$

g_1 = the number in the top group who scored the item correctly

g_2 = the number in the bottom group who scored the item correctly

g = the maximum group size common to g_1 and g_2

The Discrimination Index

Item	Number Correct	g_1	g_2	d_i	Item	Number Correct	g_1	g_2	d_i
1	16	10	6	0.4	11	19	10	9	0.1
2	14	10	4	0.6	12	15	8	7	0.1
3	16	9	7	0.2	13	12	10	2	0.8
4	12	10	2	0.8	14	13	7	6	0.1
5	15	8	7	0.1	15	13	9	4	0.5
6	12	9	3	0.6	16	20	10	10	0
7	17	9	8	0.1	17	8	4	4	0
8	18	10	8	0.2	18	15	7	8	-0.1
9	16	8	8	0	19	10	10	0	1
10	8	8	0	0.8	20	12	4	0	0.4

In the classroom, our focus is different. We allow that sometimes there are no relevant differences among students on a particular concept. There are some things that we teach so carefully, and that are so fundamental, that we expect nearly everyone to score them correctly when they occur in a test. On the other hand, an item that everyone misses can also be valuable. Although it may indicate that the item is flawed, it may also indicate that we have missed something in the instruction.

In most school assessment, therefore, discrimination is just one of the criteria for judging test items. This is particularly true of achievement tests that are constructed for individual classrooms and may be administered only once. Here the discrimination index can be helpful, but it isn't as important, nor is it interpreted in the same fashion, as it is in the case of standardized tests. There are some characteristics that we know are not likely to reflect anything approaching a normal distribution. For example, everyone should know what to do in case of a fire, which means that if such an item were part of a test, results ought to reflect a complete lack of discrimination.

In any academic area, there is likely to be some distribution of achievement scores, but particularly in smaller groups. Scores are not usually evenly or normally distributed, however. Item analysis will assist the instructor to know something about class performance in specific areas, and the information should affect the decisions instructors make afterward. Generally the learning is uneven, and part of the assessment task is to determine who understands and who does not, or who can perform the task and who cannot. With that in mind, consider the items and indices in Figure 7.5.

To keep the example uncomplicated, we used a class of 20 students, with half the class falling into each of two groups that are defined by g_1 and g_2. Remember that g_1 refers to the top 10 students on this particular test, and g_2 refers to the bottom 10. Ordinarily, class sizes are large enough that two groups of 10 students each will exclude a group in the middle. Whether the class is 20 students or some number closer to 35, it is an advantage to use group sizes of 10 for the g_1 and g_2 groups because the math becomes very simple and the item analysis procedure less time-consuming.

Recall that the discrimination index is the measure of how well each item separates the group who had the greatest success on the assessment as a whole from the group who had the least success. An item that everyone in the top group (g_1) scores correctly, and which everyone in the bottom group (g_2) scores incorrectly, provides the maximum discrimination between groups. This is what occurred with item 19, which is why it has a d_i value of 1.0. This is the maximum value the index can have.

▇ | Speaking of Assessment

They are presented in separate figures, but item discrimination and item difficulty should be considered together. You will note that item 19 had a maximum discrimination value of 1.0. If you consider only the 20 students identified in the two sample groups, you should know without any more information exactly what the difficulty level is. Professional item writers are interested in maximum discrimination. Can you see why a difficulty level of .5 is their objective for each item?

Item 18 presents a situation that is unique for this test. Since more of the lower scoring group than the higher scoring group succeeded with this item, we have a negative discrimination index. While there is no magic formula to determine how low the discrimination index must be before rejecting the item, a negative index indicates a significant problem, and *items with negative indices should be set aside*. This means that our 20-item assessment now has only 19 useful items. One can be sure that those who scored the item correctly will protest losing the point, but students' performance on the item is apparently unrelated to what they have learned, and in the interest of fair assessment, we should eliminate the effect of this item from the test.

> As a rule of thumb, one should eliminate from the assessment items that yield negative discrimination indices, though it means adjusting the scores of those who scored them correctly.

Beyond the item's elimination, it is important to try to determine why it discriminated so poorly. Sometimes a careful rereading of the item will reveal an ambiguity or an error in construction that we missed when we initially constructed it. Or perhaps the answer key is incorrect. When the responses are unusual, one of the most important sources of information about test items is simply asking students to explain why they chose as they did. You may not be able to correct the error, but perhaps an adjustment can be made in the scores, or in the instruction, that makes the assessment fair to everyone and clarifies what we were trying to assess with the item.

In terms of the magnitude of the discrimination index, item 16 appears little better than item 18, but the scoring pattern suggests that we look a little more closely. Item 16 does not discriminate between the two groups, since everyone scored it correctly. However, if everyone understands the content, or has developed the skill, a discrimination of 0 does not indicate a problem item. On the other hand, perhaps the item did not discriminate because it was too easy. Or maybe there is some cue in the item that directs learners to the correct response even when they do not know the material. It is possible that something inadvertently left on the bulletin board revealed the correct answer. Understanding what the discrimination index reveals is both science and art.

Discrimination indices shouldn't be examined in isolation. Examine the first and last items in Figure 7.5 for a minute. They both have the same discrimination value (.4), but they have very different levels of difficulty. Only four respondents incorrectly scored the first item. But of the group of 20, 16 missed the last item. It appears to deal with something that learners should review. Because the discrimination index only tells part of the story, it should always be accompanied, at a minimum, by a measure of item difficulty.

> Item discrimination is an index of how well the particular item separates those who did well on the test as a whole from those who did poorly. When there is little discrimination among scores (everyone in the class has nearly the same score), calculating the discrimination index is of little value.

The difficulty index (Figure 7.6) reflects the probability that someone from this group of learners will score the item correctly. Its calculation is noted above. The maximum difficulty index is 1.0 just as it is for the discrimination index. It indicates that everyone who attempted the item scored it correctly. The lower range, however, is 0. A difficulty index of $p = 0$ indicates that no one scored the item correctly, or stated in terms of a probability, that the probability that someone selected from this group will score the item correctly is nil. Although it is called a difficulty index, the relationship between the value of the index and the difficulty of the item is actually an inverse relationship. The higher the value, the easier the item was for the group in question and the greater the probability of scoring it correctly.

In the *Speaking of Assessment* box, it was noted that an item with a difficulty level of $p = .5$ offers the maximum opportunity for discrimination. This occurs, of course, when the most able half of the students score the item correctly and the lowest scorers all miss it. These circumstances yield a discrimination index of 1.0 and a difficulty index of .5.

Distracters and Item Difficulty

As a footnote to item difficulty, one way to understand item difficulty—with multiple-choice items, at least—is in terms of how similar the distracters are to the correct choice(s). What we ask of respondents when they answer multiple-choice items is that

FIGURE 7.6 Calculating the Item Difficulty Index

The difficulty index is calculated as follows:

$$p = \frac{\text{number who scored the item correctly}}{\text{number who attempted the item}}$$

The Difficulty Index

Item	Number Correct	p	Item	Number Correct	p
1	16	.80	11	19	.95
2	14	.70	12	15	.75
3	16	.80	13	12	.60
4	12	.60	14	13	.65
5	15	.75	15	13	.65
6	12	.60	16	20	1.0
7	17	.85	17	8	.40
8	18	.90	18	15	.75
9	16	.80	19	10	.50
10	8	.40	20	4	.20

Since everyone (20 students) attempted every item, and the entire class is represented in either the top group or the bottom group in Figure 7.5, the number correct is the sum of $g_1 + g_2$. The difficulty index is that sum divided by 20.

> A difficulty index indicates the probability that someone from the particular group will score the item correctly. Employed with the discrimination index, it can yield a good deal of information. One can manipulate multiple-choice item difficulty by altering the relationship between the correct choice and the distracters. As the correct choice and the distracters become more similar, the item becomes more difficult.

they discriminate between the correct choice and the distracters. Item difficulty, then, is a function of the level of discrimination required of the respondent. The more precise the discrimination, the more difficult the item is. If we find that that the item discriminates poorly because it is too easy, we can fine-tune it by manipulating the level of discrimination. We can modify the distracters so that they are a little closer to the correct choice. The resulting item requires more precise discrimination by the respondents. By the same token, an item that is too difficult can be revised by making distracters less similar to the correct choice.

Distracter Analysis

Besides examining the item to determine who responded correctly and who did not, one can also evaluate the individual distracters. For someone who does not possess the learning or skill we are assessing, all of the distracters should appear plausible. If those who score poorly on the assessment as a whole select the distracters in approximately equal proportions, the distracters are equally plausible. When the low scorers consistently avoid a particular distracter, there is usually something in the distracter that "gives it away." Very much like an item that everyone scores alike, a distracter that no one selects contributes nothing to the assessment because it doesn't help us to discriminate between those who have the learning and those who do not.

Part of the item analysis should focus on the items missed by those who do well on the test as a whole, and it can be helpful to look at the particular distracter that they select. When those who otherwise score well on the test tend to select a particular distracter on an item they miss, there are several possibilities. Perhaps the distinction between the distracter and the correct choice is not clear enough, or maybe there is some other ambiguity in the distracter.

Formula Scoring

Because the choices are presented with the item, selected response items (multiple-choice, true/false, matching) lend themselves to guessing (which is probably one of the reasons students prefer them to constructed response items). On a multiple-choice item with four choices including one correct choice, the probability (p) that someone may blindly guess the correct choice is, of course, one out of four, or $p = .25$. True/false items carry an even greater ($p = .5$) risk.

Procedures called **formula scoring** (Fray, 1988) have been developed to adjust scores for the effect of guessing, but they are based on the assumption that there are only two options—either one knows or one guesses blindly. Under the related procedures, test instructions sometimes caution students not to guess. Often in the classroom, however, the alternative to knowing the correct answer is not blind guessing. Students can often eliminate at least one choice from among those offered in a multiple-choice item, and Fray demonstrated that, even with formula scoring, students who guess generally achieve higher scores than those who follow the directions. For this reason, it is probably unfair to caution students against guessing when they can eliminate one or

> Formula scoring is intended to adjust for the probable effect of guessing on selected response test items. It is not a "correction for guessing," since there is no way to establish what the score would have been had the student not guessed.

more of the distracters. If there is the potential to increase the score through guessing, one has an ethical responsibility to make that known to the respondents.[6] This must be balanced, however, against the sophistication of the respondents. Very young students may not understand a direction to "Guess, when you can eliminate one or more of the choices."

Although classroom teachers often do not use them, testing experts have developed mechanisms for adjusting for chance correct guesses. The various procedures collectively called "formula scoring" (Fray, 1988) are developed more fully in Chapter 13.

SUMMARY

This chapter began by considering Mrs. Bondy's concern regarding how she can evaluate tests to determine whether they are appropriate for her students. There isn't anything inherently wrong with using assessment materials that some third party develops.

After all, we commonly supplement our teaching with instructional materials that someone else has prepared. In every instance, however, the instructor must examine the appropriateness of the materials. Two very important criteria in that examination are evaluations of scores' reliability and validity. These issues aren't unique to this chapter. They were raised, also, when we were examining authentic assessment, which makes this a good time to make a point. Often, critics of traditional assessment practice try to make reliability and validity discussions characteristic only of standardized testing and relics of "the way things used to be." By now you ought to recognize that, although we must construct the concepts differently according to the type of assessment, the need for reliability and validity transcends the form of the assessment we might choose.

Will the published quizzes yield consistent data? If she will take the time to calculate reliability after she has collected data with the assessment, Mrs. Bondy can answer that question. Are results consistent with other assessment data, and are they comparable to what the teacher's own experience suggests will be the case? Although the latter question, particularly, calls for a more subjective judgment, they are both important considerations and they allow one to respond to questions about data validity.

An instructor need not wait until after using the assessment to have some sense of its value, however. Most content validity issues can be resolved when one reviews the test items to determine whether they adequately cover the content. This is why we introduced the table of specifications. If we prepare it carefully, it allows us to match the test coverage with the content coverage. It is also a mechanism that helps us to tie different elements of the educational plan together and to recognize the relationships among them. Carefully integrating planning, teaching, and assessment is central to establishing content validity.

Students' scores offer something of a global view of the assessment. We also need the micro-level view that individual items and item analysis provide. Chapter 6 dealt with the mechanics of item writing. This chapter has attempted to develop the item analysis techniques that will allow us to examine items, one at a time, in order to improve them. As careful as we might be in their construction, it is difficult to know how well they work until we have actually used them with students. We are not married to discrimination and difficulty indices, but they do provide an important source of information about item quality, and, by inference, the quality of the assessment as a whole.

The issues being raised here are the issues everyone who is involved with assessing learners ought to raise. There are certainly legal reasons to be responsible with the assessment activities, but there are ethical reasons as well. They will be examined more carefully in Chapter 12, but for now we might wonder who, in good conscience, would *not* take steps to minimize the errors that are possible in judging students' competencies or achievement levels. With important decisions and the students' own self-esteem frequently affected by assessment data, the stakes are simply too high to make a mistake that might be avoided with a little more care and understanding. Traditionally, classroom teachers have abandoned considerations of reliability and validity to "the experts," but becoming conversant with the issues raised here is a critical part of every truly dedicated educator's technology inventory. Whether we create our own assessments or modify those someone else has developed, we must be able to evaluate their quality.

Finally, books such as this are written to help people develop an expertise that is part of, rather than apart from, effective teaching. Your author has maintained from the beginning that instruction and assessment ought to reflect a symbiosis rather than a separation. We must recognize the potential that assessment data have to inform instruction and educational decision making.

ENDNOTES

1. The trade-off, of course, is that using calculators also makes it more difficult to assess the students' command of some procedures that calculators complete automatically.
2. Our language is a little deceptive. We speak of a valid or a reliable test, but it is actually the data from the tests that have those characteristics. It is the application made of the testing results that establishes quality.
3. Classical test theory is one approach to academic assessment and perhaps the most widely followed, at least until the 1990s. There are alternatives that will be spoken of briefly in Chapters 9 and 13.
4. Reliability is important, but it certainly is not the only indicator we are interested in. If we were developing standardized tests for a living, we would exclude any item that did not contribute to reliability. Although we want instruments that produce stable data, reliability is just one of the factors we examine. If everyone scores an item correctly, and we feel it's because we thoroughly covered the concept, the item remains.
5. As an aside, the reader should note that classifying educational tasks in terms of cognitive complexity involves assumptions about what the learners have already done. What is a problem-solving (or in the Bloom taxonomy, "synthesis") task today is a recall ("knowledge" to Bloom et al.) task tomorrow if the same learners are asked to do the same thing again.
6. This is not to say that there are not procedures that *do* penalize for guessing. Your author remembers true/false assessments from his experience as a primary school student during which the number of items incorrectly scored was subtracted from the number correct to arrive at a final score. Such a scoring method dampens enthusiasm for anything but the most conservative of response procedures.

FOR FURTHER READING

Traub and Rowley (1991) wrote an instructional module titled "Understanding reliability." The language is nontechnical and very readable.

See chapters by Feldt and Brennan, and Messick, in R. L. Linn (Ed.). (1989). *Educational measurement* (3rd ed.). New York: Macmillan and The National Council on Measurement in Education. They provide excellent discussions of some of the more technical aspects of reliability and validity.

Introduction to Measurement Theory by Allen and Yen (1979), Monterey, CA: Brooks/Cole Publishing Company, provides an excellent discussion of true score theory in the third chapter. Chapters 4 and 5 are very good on reliability and validity, respectively.

REFERENCES

Bloom, B. S. (Ed.). (1956). *Taxonomy of educational objectives, Handbook I: Cognitive domain.* New York: David McKay.

Carter, K. (1986). Test-wiseness for teachers and students. *Educational Measurement: Issues and Practice, 5*(4), 20–23.

Ebel, R. L., and Frisbie, D. A. (1986). *Essentials of educational measurement* (4th ed.). Englewood Cliffs, NJ: Prentice-Hall.

Fray, R. B. (1988). Formula scoring of multiple-choice tests (Correction for guessing). *Educational Measurement: Issues and Practice, 7*(2), 33–38.

Frisbie, D. A. (1988). Reliability of scores from teacher-made tests. *Educational Measurement: Issues and Practice, 7*(1), 25–35.

Millman, J., and Greene, J. (1989). The specification and development of tests of achievement and ability. In R. L. Linn (Ed.), *Educational measurement* (3rd ed., pp. 335–366). New York: Macmillan.

Nunnally, J. C. (1978). *Psychometric theory* (2nd ed.). New York: McGraw-Hill.

Secolsky, C. (1987). On the direct measurement of face validity: A comment on Nevo. *The Journal of Educational Measurement, 24,* 82–83.

Stiggins, R. J. (1991). Relevant classroom assessment training for teachers. *Educational Measurement: Issues and Practice, 10*(1), 7–12.

Subkoviak, M. J. (1988). A practitioner's guide to computation and interpretation of reliability indices for mastery tests. *Journal of Educational Measurement, 24,* 47–55.

Traub, R. E., and Rowley, G. L. (1991). Understanding reliability. *Educational Measurement: Issues and Practice, 10*(1), 37–45.

Wright, E. L., and Kuehn, P. (1998). The effects of academic language instruction on college-bound at-risk secondary students. *Journal of Educational Opportunity, 17*(1) 9–22.

Van Dalen, D. B. (1979). *Understanding educational research: An introduction.* New York: McGraw-Hill.

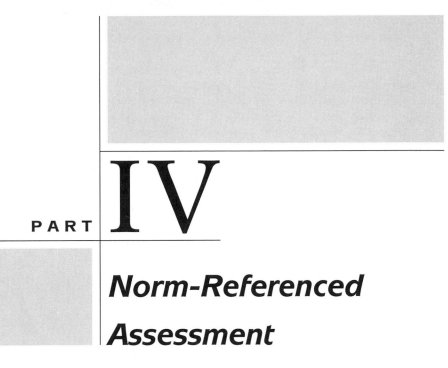

PART **IV**

Norm-Referenced Assessment

We are probably most aware of achievement testing, and the title of the text does suggest that emphasis, but much standardized testing has a different focus. There are personality assessments, intelligence tests, occupation inventories, and tests intended to provide a psychological profile of the individual, to name a few. In spite of the different objectives, the various forms share a number of important technical characteristics, and the content of Chapter 8 will examine at least some of them. As we shall see, these tests are not without controversy, but since the alternatives often introduce their own problems, the tests remain a fixture in educational settings.

In Chapter 9 we will step back a little from assessment and consider some of the issues that help to provide its structure. Assessment depends upon our ability to gather information in the form of particular kinds of data. What we are able to understand and the conclusions we are able to draw are both dictated to some degree by the nature of the data. For example, we use different procedures to analyze the ethnic makeup of a classroom than we use to describe the verbal aptitude of its occupants. Since a significant component of assessment involves describing the data, sections are included on central tendency, data dispersion, and correlation—some of the most frequently used descriptive statistics. This is followed in Chapter 10 by a discussion of the language of standardized testing. It will help the classroom teacher understand how standardized test data are reported by those who publish the tests, so that explaining those data to students and their parents is not so daunting a task.

Error is one of the realities of assessment. As careful as one might be, the variables involved in assessment are simply too complex and too numerous to be completely controlled. Classical test theory offers at least one approach to understanding error. There are competitors, as we shall see in Chapter 13, but classical theory provides an important foundation to classroom assessment, and it will be raised in Chapter 10.

8

Assessing Aptitudes and Attitudes

■ *The reader will compare and contrast achievement, aptitude, and attitude assessment in terms of how validity is construed and how data are gathered and interpreted.*

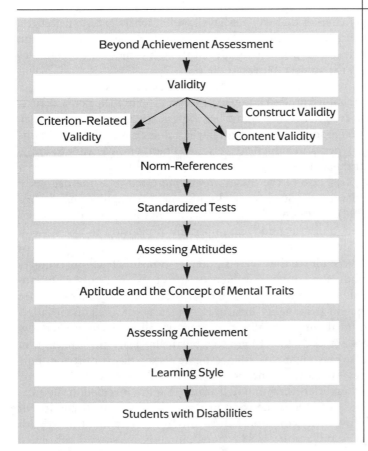

There are other things to assess besides student achievement. Aptitude and attitude, for example, are related to academic achievement. We noted earlier that there are multiple dimensions to validity. As the type of assessment changes, the quality indicators must also change. Depending upon the type of assessment, the focus might be content validity, criterion-related validity, or construct validity. ■

Mr. Meldrum surveyed his sixth-grade class as the students quietly performed their seat-work. Before he even began the composition unit, he knew some would embrace it eagerly and others would proceed under protest. The differences, he knew, were more than a curiosity because to some degree the learners' attitudes toward their task were reflected in the quality of their work. Mr. Meldrum wondered whether it might have been worthwhile to assess how they felt about composition before he developed the unit. Although he was committed to the need for the material, it occurred to him that perhaps he could design the exercises in a way that accommodated their attitudes and still maintained the integrity of the content. ■

OTHER LEARNER DIMENSIONS TO ASSESS

The concept of gathering information about students before we begin to teach them has been a common theme so far in this book, but usually our focus has been directed at preparing instructional materials that will mesh well with learners' past experiences. Here the focus will be broadened to include accumulating other relevant information that helps us understand learners' performance, even though it may be unrelated to what they have done with the subject matter in the past.

The truth is that information about learners' experiences with a subject or an activity tells us only part of what we need to know in order to explain their performance. Perhaps the most obvious evidence is that even when experience appears to have been consistent from student to student (they were all in the same class and did the same assignments), some of them perform at higher levels than do others. We want to know as much as we can about those differences.

As the prologue suggests, one of the things we're interested in is the degree to which the learners' **attitudes** toward academic tasks influence their achievement (Harter, 1988; Lefrancois, 1994). Attitude is associated with what is often called the individual's affective domain, and affect adds an important dimension to assessment. If there is a relationship between how students feel about a task and the quality of their performances, and we shall see that there is, then responsible teaching requires that we assess—and then do something to influence—affect. We not only want students to like what they do, we also want them to do it better. Attitude measures are part of the larger category of **personality measures.** This area of assessment is important because information about personality characteristics allows us to predict how similar groups of learners are likely to respond to a particular learning situation. In a general psychology course one might wish to investigate personality for broader purposes, but here our interest is just its connection to school achievement.

We are also interested in differences among learners that are revealed in their capacity for academic work. **Aptitude** is the concept we will use in our discussion of differences in mental ability. More commonly those differences are mentioned with **intelligence,** but as Hopkins and Stanley (1981) noted, intelligence should be viewed as a broader term that also encompasses abilities beyond those associated primarily with academic tasks. Aptitude, or more particularly scholastic or academic aptitude, narrows our focus to the potential for school achievement and those abilities that are directly related to academic performance differences.

Bond (1989) noted that, in actual assessment practice, the distinctions that are sometimes drawn between different kinds of assessments are more academic than substantive. Sometimes we are left to wonder whether the differences are structural or based only in the assessor's intent. He, perhaps with some cynicism, observed that often the distinction between the different kinds of assessments is a function of when the particular ability is used:

> *If a test is used as an indication of past instruction and experience it is an achievement test. If it is used as a measure of current competence, it is an ability test. If it is used to predict or forecast future performance, it is an aptitude test. Yesterday's achievement is today's ability and tomorrow's aptitude. (p. 429)*

It is common practice to use achievement tests as a record of both past and current levels of competence, and for that reason, and in terms of that dimension, we will not worry about what Bond (1989) treated as the difference between achievement and ability tests. The distinction between achievement and aptitude tests is central to a number of the topics to be raised in this chapter, however, and we will examine it more closely. Bond noted that when they are properly understood, those two kinds of assessments differ in at least three ways: (a) the amount of declarative knowledge they require, (b) the level of connection to a particular subject they represent, and (c) the level of cognitive functioning they require. Figure 8.1 elaborates these differences.

By virtue of how frequently we use them, and their variety, achievement tests represent the most dominant form of assessment. Achievement tests are grounded in the content and the skills associated with a particular curricular area. Millman and Greene (1989) observed:

> *Within recent advances in cognitive theory, achievement is conceptualized as the amount and nature of knowledge an individual has acquired about a specific subject area, the way in which this knowledge is organized or structured, and the functional uses an individual can make of this knowledge structure. . . . (p. 338)*

FIGURE 8.1 Contrasting Achievement and Aptitude Assessments

Achievement	Aptitude
Substantial amounts of declarative knowledge required.	Great emphasis on procedural knowledge.
Based in particular components of well-defined subjects.	Not associated with discrete disciplines or with any particular curriculum.
Frequently based primarily on memory ability.	Higher level processing skills called for. Particular emphsis on problem-solving and reasoning ability.

Achievement tests may be teacher-prepared, or they may be standardized instruments that are developed and published for use with many different groups in a variety of settings. Since teacher-prepared achievement tests were the focus of the discussions in Chapters 6 and 7, they do not have a major emphasis here. Standardized assessments are prepared by testing professionals and are typically used to make comparisons between students, and between groups of students. Although little is said about their development, we will examine some of their applications as we go along.

We should note that, even though little emphasis is placed on it in this book, motor ability or physical performance can also be related to academic performance. The idea of assessing motor ability isn't new. Grading penmanship, although not common today, was a consistent part of the historical academic regimen. In disciplines such as music, athletics, or industrial arts, motor ability turns out to be a very important component. In most traditional academic subjects, however, motor ability is relatively unimportant as an explanation of performance differences unless a handicap interferes with the student's ability to hear, see, or write, for example.

One of the differences between assessing motor ability and assessing attitudes or aptitudes is that the learner's motor ability represents a characteristic that can usually be examined directly. The assessor can often make an accurate judgment because direct observation alone provides enough physical evidence of the trait. This is not the case in the aptitude or affective domains, where assessment is based on inferences drawn from samples of a behavior that are selected because they represent the characteristic. Since aptitude cannot be weighed with a bathroom scale or measured with a meter stick, it is the individual's performance on specific tasks associated with the aptitude we are trying to measure that we are interested in. For this reason, some of the validity issues examined earlier in the book become very much a focal point in this discussion. What kinds of behaviors indicate positive attitude? What level of ability with which task represents an aptitude for academic performance? Because validity is central to the larger assessment discussion, we will discuss that topic here and create a context for our discussion of the different classes of assessments.

> Because the characteristics we assess are often cognitive characteristics that cannot be approached directly, validity is a more complex issue in educational assessment settings than it is in many other situations.

VALIDITY ISSUES

Validity was a topic in both Chapter 4 and Chapter 7. Remember that, from the standpoint of authentic assessment, the heaviest emphases are on face validity and on consequential validity. Face validity is the appearance of validity, and appearances are very important in a system where one intends for the assessment setting to emulate what students will encounter in the world beyond the classroom. Authentic assessment advocates pay particular attention to the collateral influence that assessment has on the related teaching and learning. Neither face validity nor consequential validity is easy to measure, so for advocates of authentic assessment, the discussion of validity can become quite subjective.

Different Constructions of Validity

Among advocates of more traditional assessment, validity is a more objective quality, and you will note much in common here with what was said in Chapter 7. As a starting point, the assessment ought to represent all of the important dimensions of the content area. This is the content validity for which a table of specifications was developed. When we measure characteristics such as aptitude and attitude, the subjects in this chapter, we are more interested in norm-referenced assessment than criterion-referenced assessment because, in a particular group, those characteristics have their greatest meaning when we examine them in relative terms. The issue is less "how does the student feel about doing math?" than it is "how does the student like math compared to reading?" There are actually a number of other differences between norm- and criterion-referenced assessments, some of which are suggested in Figure 8.2.

Recall that assessment data gain criterion-related validity when they are in harmony with some external measure of the same attribute or characteristic. The data from your reading assessment gain criterion validity when they predict how your students will perform in reading next year. In fact, that is an example of predictive validity.[1] When the external criterion is established at about the same time as the assessment data are gathered, concurrent validity is the issue. The distinction is more than just a matter of time. Predictive validity is based in what is likely to occur. Concurrent validity is directed at detecting conditions that already exist. The two kinds of validity reflect different testing objectives.

College entrance examinations are intended to predict the likelihood of students' success in college-level studies. College grade averages may become the criteria to which the entrance exam scores will be compared, and when those with high entrance scores do well in college, and those with low scores struggle in college, we could conclude that the entrance exam data have predictive validity.

Concurrent validity is the object when, for example, performance on an in-class reading exercise parallels students' scores on a standardized test of reading ability. Although it may sound a little cynical, for criterion-related purposes, it really does not matter what, exactly, the test measures, so long as the data agree with the external

FIGURE 8.2   Breadth of Coverage in Norm-Referenced versus Criterion-Referenced Assessment

I. Criterion-Referenced Assessment	II. Norm-Referenced Assessment
Can the student solve *these* multiplication problems correctly?	What is the student's level of computational ability?
Can the student define a series of vocabulary words?	What is the student's level of verbal ability?
Can the student complete a woodworking project involving softwood and hand tools?	What is the student's level of psychomotor ability?

criterion. Predictive validity is probably the more publicized and the more evident of the two forms of criterion-related validity.

Construct Validity

The point of this validity review is to illustrate that there are multiple aspects to validity. One or another becomes prominent depending upon the particular type of assessment. Although very little time was spent on earlier in the book on construct validity, it is important in this chapter.

Earlier it was noted that understanding student-to-student differences often means we need to know something about mental abilities when we have reason to believe those abilities explain performance variability. Such abilities are associated with particular mental traits or **constructs.** When an assessment is developed that allows us to measure a particular construct, the data have validity for that construct, or construct validity. That's what occurs when we establish that a test of problem-solving ability truly assesses problem-solving ability, or when we demonstrate that an anxiety scale actually measures one's level of anxiety. Construct validity is the most ethereal of the different types of validity. It can be quite difficult to demonstrate that data reflect the degree to which a particular construct is present. The process of establishing construct validity has three components, according to Kerlinger (1973). The assessor must:

1. suggest which constructs or traits account for performance differences,
2. develop hypotheses that involve the construct, and
3. test the hypotheses.

Assume for a minute that you teach math to seventh-grade students. Having recognized that there are substantial differences in your students' performance on a standardized math aptitude test, you review the test carefully and note that the test items use printed directions made up of words rather than symbols. You suspect that the heavy verbal component of the test has much to do with the scoring differences, and because your students have a variety of linguistic backgrounds, that perhaps verbal ability has more to do with the data than mathematics ability, in spite of the developers' intent. If this is so, a test of verbal ability should demonstrate scoring differences similar to that of the math test. This means not that the scores will be the same necessarily, but that those who scored well on the math test compared to the other students should also be among the higher scorers on the test of verbal ability. Those who struggled on the first test should also have

As was the case with authentic assessment, the **face validity** of an assessment is the fidelity with which the assessment appears to do what its developers claim. Data have **content validity** when the instrument from which they are drawn provides an adequate representation of the content or domain for which inferences will be drawn. We have **criterion-related validity** when the data agree with an independent measure of the same characteristic. **Construct validity** is evident when assessment data reflect the degree to which a particular mental construct or ability is present in the respondent. Although construct validity was largely ignored in the discussion of developing authentic assessment and constructing traditional paper and pencil tests, construct validity becomes very important in measuring attitudes.

difficulty with the second, and so on. You could test your hypothesis by administering a test of verbal ability and then checking for the predicted scoring pattern.

THE NORMATIVE ASSUMPTION

This review of the different validity dimensions should indicate that, although it is always a critical element, validity is viewed differently depending upon the type of assessment we employ. There is another consideration. In Part II of this book, learner performance was gauged by how well students met a standard or a set of criteria. In fact the process of setting a standard (Chapter 3) is really just the business of determining the criterion for judging student performance. This has great appeal when we can identify and defend a discrete standard, but there are times when a standard is fundamentally arbitrary. As an example, when criterion-referenced testing (CRT) was very popular, it was common to require that learners score 80 percent of the assessment items correctly in order to demonstrate "mastery" of an objective. Determining whether this is an appropriate standard depends almost entirely on the content validity, quality, and difficulty of the test items. With a little imagination, one could develop a test so easy that nearly everyone would score at the 80 percent level, and by that criterion, at least, demonstrate mastery. In a moment of perversity, one could also develop a test so difficult that the results would suggest that no one had mastered the content.

If some criteria are arbitrary, others are artificial. Many assessments evaluate reading comprehension in terms of the percent of comprehension, for example, with the implicit assumption that 100 percent comprehension is the objective. It is an artificial criterion. As Hopkins and Stanley (1981) asked, "Who [really ever] has 100% reading comprehension?" (p. 184).

The fact that a standard or a criterion is named, and even widely embraced, does not mean that it is appropriate. The issue is how the scores will be interpreted. We need to know whether the scores have meaning in isolation, or whether they yield the information we need only when we examine them relative to the other scores in the group. This, of course, is what defines whether we use a criterion or a normative reference.

Relationship between Criterion-References and Norm-References

In actual practice, the issue is often a little more complicated than the examples just given, and we can illustrate some of the complexity. Although the procedures for establishing them can be very formal and very detailed, criteria are also set with an eye to the effect they will have on the test takers. Indeed, many criteria tend to have a normative element. If results are substantially different from expectations, it isn't unusual to alter the criteria, even if the developmental process by which the criteria were established in the first place was rigorously followed.

A classroom teacher may determine that those who accumulate 90 percent of the points possible on all of the tasks during the semester will receive an "A" grade. However, that criterion's level of difficulty is probably adjusted from time to time based on how many people have qualified for an "A" in the past. When that occurs, the criterion is based at least partly on the performance of the students as a whole. The criterion often has a normative element.

For Further Discussion

Assessment criteria do not emerge out of isolation. Although classroom teachers rarely follow them, the procedures for establishing criteria can be quite formal and reasonably objective. However, criteria are also influenced by how the tested group performs as a whole. Once you have established the criteria for evaluating your students' performance in a particular subject, should you adjust them if results are unlike what you expect? Should performance criteria be fluid from term to term?

Different Tests and Different Interpretations of the Data

Employing a criterion-reference or a norm-reference involves different purposes and different assumptions. When data are criterion-referenced, the gauge of students' accomplishments is how well they "measure up" to the criteria. The following statement reflects a criterion:

> The kindergarten student will correctly name the colors of six out of eight pieces of colored construction paper.

Once the criterion is established, the purpose of the assessment is to determine which learners have met the criterion. Stated a little differently, the assessment allows one to discriminate between those who have met the criterion and those who have not.

By contrast, a norm-reference provides a comparison of the individual to the group's performance as a measure of the individual's performance. A university admissions committee may decide they have room for the top 30 percent of those who apply. Whereas the members of the committee are certainly interested in the candidates' level of aptitude for college-level work, the more important immediate indicator is the person's standing relative to the group of all applicants. Probably all of the applicants have some level of college aptitude. All may even have sufficient aptitude to succeed, but with limited space and resources, the decision makers will try to identify those with the greatest potential. The issue is to identify who is the *most* qualified.

As noted earlier, adopting a criterion-reference assumes that we can identify a criterion that we can defend because it represents the requisite level of student performance. There are several components to assessing students' performance on the criterion. First of all, the assessment must have test items that will allow one to assess whatever knowledge or skill is represented in the criterion. If the criterion score actually represents more than one skill or understanding, the assessment must include each of the emphases in appropriate proportion. If a criterion score is established that younger learners must achieve to meet a writing objective, for example, the assessment probably should include items dealing with grammar, spelling, usage, punctuation, and sentence construction. Each is an element of writing, and ignoring any will contribute to an assessment lacking content validity.

> Although data from both types of assessment must reflect content validity, criterion-referenced assessment usually has a more specific focus. It deals with specific objectives. Norm-referenced assessment is usually directed at broad topics and domains.

Assessments for which the data are to be norm-referenced must also demonstrate content validity. Although the focus is on the individual's performance relative to the others in the group, the basis for the comparison must be some knowledge or ability grounded in the content. If we are interested in assessing mathematics ability, the determination that a particular student is at the 70th percentile must come in reference to computation, problem-solving ability, or something else that is mathematically significant. We could certainly discriminate among mathematics students on the basis of their verbal ability, their musical ability, or perhaps their foot speed, but those characteristics are not relevant to the math ability construct.

Although both approaches must reflect content validity, criterion-referenced assessments tend to be directed at very specific criteria, and consequently, at a narrower portion of the discipline. Norm-referenced instruments usually assess much broader domains, which was illustrated in Figure 8.2.

Norm-Referencing and Discrimination

Criterion-referenced assessment answers the question, "Who have met the criteria?" Norm-referenced assessment responds to a different question: "In terms of a particular knowledge or ability, how does the individual compare to the group?" The contrast is more apparent when we begin to ask questions such as, "Who submitted the *best* essay?" or "How many of his classmates are ahead of him?"

Before we continue the discussion, let us note that much has been written in the scholarly literature about the damaging effects of placing students in competition with each other, and certainly there are times when student-to-student competition is destructive to the students and inconsistent with the goals of schooling. However, there are also times when it is essential to determine who has more of some relevant ability, or some needed trait, than the others who are also assessed. Consider a most obvious example.

Suppose an airline adopts a criterion that all of the pilots must be capable of flying their aircraft. Most of us would agree that the criterion makes sense, but we would also agree that it falls well short of what passengers may wish to know. Given a choice, most of us do not wish to fly with someone who has barely met the criterion. We wish to be piloted by the *best* pilot, and we're grateful for assessments that determine the most able pilots, the safest airlines, the most competent surgeons, and so forth. Indeed, we demonstrate great interest in normative assessments. Some years ago, *U.S. News and World Report* began ranking colleges and universities in terms of a number of criteria, to determine the best schools. The issue is awaited eagerly each year by the news media (and probably also by officials in those institutions that are ranked highly). The ordering probably appeals to our desire to organize and structure information.

Establishing the relative standing among group members means that we must be able to discriminate between the members. This is appropriate as long as the distinctions we draw are relevant. Recall that the point of criterion-referenced assessment was also to discriminate between learners, but in that setting it is between those who have met a criterion and those who have not. With norm-referenced assessment we try to develop as many discriminations as there are meaningful differences among subjects in the knowledge or ability we're assessing. This approach to discrimination is more demanding of the assessment instrument than criterion-referenced assessment, even if we are interested in the student's degree of accomplishment. Letter grading (A, B, C, and so forth) requires only that the test items help us determine who falls into a comparatively few categories. In some norm-referenced instances, there are as many categories as there are test takers because each student possesses a slightly different level of the characteristic.

The Normal Distribution

Much of the assessment literature is based on the understanding that cognitive abilities and mental traits are **normally distributed** in a population. This means that if the scores for everyone in a particular population were plotted on a frequency distribution, it would appear as the bell-shaped curve[2] illustrated in Figure 8.3.

Recall from Chapter 7 that the contours of the curve indicate that the frequency with which a score occurs is reflected in the height of the curve. Most scores occur in the middle of the distribution, and scores to the extreme left or right are the most rare. Normally distributed characteristics exhibit great variability. Any test of problem-solving ability in Iowa fifth graders, or verbal ability in university students in Montana, must reveal many different levels of ability.

For Further Discussion

The normal distribution provides a rationale for evaluating students by comparing them to each other in day-to-day achievement testing. If, one might reason, the students' learning is predictably distributed, why not just assign grades to particular areas of the distribution and grade students accordingly? The middle of the distribution, a specified number of points in either direction, from the mean might represent the "C" range. A specified number of points in either direction from "C" could designate the "B" and "D" areas, as so on.

Although this might work for large groups, how might circumstances with small groups call for a different approach?

What would you guess the probability might be that a class of 30 or so students might reflect a normal distribution of *any* academic characteristic?

Because of the problems implicit in these questions, the discussion of normal distributions and assessment was not raised in the early chapters of the book when norm-referenced assessment was first commented on.

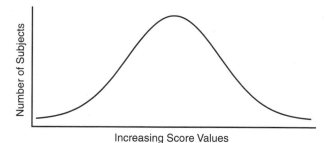

FIGURE 8.3 A Normal Frequency Distribution

The Role of Item Difficulty

When assessment is criterion-referenced, the items need only allow one to discriminate between those who have met the criterion and those who have not. The task is different in norm-referenced assessment, where one must be able to discriminate between individuals who have many levels of a characteristic. Here, the difficulty of individual items plays a critical part. An assessment item that everyone scores correctly is not necessarily a problem in criterion-referenced assessment as along as one has some certainty that all students have mastered the related learning. In norm-referenced assessment, any item that everyone scores alike is a waste of time because it does not contribute to the discrimination among test takers.

> Because test items must discriminate according to the degree to which a trait may be present, item difficulty is more important in norm-referenced assessment. In criterion-referenced assessment, even where there are categories for degree of accomplishment—such as letter grades—the discrimination is a more simple distinction regarding whether the learner has met the criterion.

ASSESSMENT AND STANDARDIZED TESTING

Recall that whenever we gather data regarding any characteristic related to aptitude, personality, or achievement, we risk allowing unrelated factors to become reflected in the score. The potential exists because those characteristics do not lend themselves to direct observation, and in the roundabout effort we must take to assess them, occasionally extraneous factors become part of the score. If a secondary school teacher administers a test to multiple sections of a class, and the amount of time for testing varies because several interruptions come in one class, some of the scoring variability may reflect time differences. Changing environmental factors compound the already difficult task of assessing what cannot be assessed directly. These problems characterize nearly all classroom assessment, since it is difficult to hold environmental conditions constant and most of what we're interested in is related to mental traits and abilities rather than to physical capabilities. Much of what we do in test construction, administration, and scoring reflects the effort to minimize the error component. It is one of the reasons assessments are standardized.

For Further Discussion

Error is often not immediately apparent in a student's score. Recall that the expression $x = t + e$ suggests that the error (e) and the true score (t) are both components of the observed score (x). There is a possibility that error may either inflate or diminish the student's observed score. What factors will erroneously inflate an observed score? Which will deflate it?

Instructor-constructed assessments are prepared for a particular classroom environment. Standardized tests are developed so that they can be used in a variety of settings. Rather than a specified classroom, the groups for whom standardized tests are developed are broadly defined. The assessments are for "fifth-grade students," for example, or "first-semester chemistry students," and the assessments tend to cover broad instructional goals rather than specific objectives.

Beyond the broader application and the more general goals of these tests, the "standardization" element relates to the manner in which the assessment is administered and the scores are interpreted. Millman and Greene (1989) wrote:

> *A standardized test is one for which the conditions of administration and the scoring procedures are designed to be the same in all uses of the test. The conditions of administration include the physical test setting, the directions to examinees, the test materials, and the time factors. Scoring procedures include both derivation and transformation of raw scores. The psychometric value of standardization is the reduction of variations in, and thus error arising from, administration conditions and scoring practices. (p. 340)*

Everyone receives the same directions (usually because they are read), the same supplementary tools and materials, and the same amount of time to complete the test. This is important because standardized test data are usually norm-referenced. The performance of the individual is compared to the performance of a norm group, and the inferences drawn are based on the individual's performance relative to that group. The comparisons make little sense if the assessment conditions are not common to all students. Data from a reading test are impossible to interpret accurately if some students are allowed to return to the reading selection while working on the questions and others are not.

Those who standardize tests go to great lengths to see that the norm group represents the relevant characteristics of the entire population. If gender, age, ethnicity, social class, or background characteristics might be relevant to a particular test, the norm group must reflect those characteristics in the same proportions as they exist in the general population. When that occurs, one can generalize the performance of the norm group to the performance of the general population. Because the norm group is representative, comparing the individual's performance to the norm group gives one a sense of where the individual fits in the population as a whole. The norm group may be a sample drawn from the entire country so that one may compare the individual to "all 10-year-olds," for example. On the other hand, school district researchers might develop a sample intended to reflect just "the primary grade students in Jordan School District." "The primary grade students in Jordan School District" and "all

10-year-olds" both define populations. Norm groups can be created to represent the performance of each as long as the group reflects the same characteristics as the population and the testing for the norm group occurs under the same conditions as it will for those who will be compared to the norm group.

Norms, then, represent a description of a group's performance. They are usually reported as a measure of central tendency (the arithmetic mean or the median) and may represent the entire group ("all high school seniors") or subcategories of the group ("female seniors," or "Hispanic female seniors"). Note, however, that norms are distinct from standards. The standard represents an aspiration, a desired or required level of performance (Chapter 3). The norm reflects what is characteristic, and there is usually a disparity between what is typical of a group and what the educational program aims to accomplish. A school district might adopt a standard that reads as follows: 90% of all students will read on grade level. At the end of the grading period, a standardized achievement test might reveal, however, that the reading level that is typical of fifth-grade students is a grade-equivalent score of 4.2, or two months into the fourth grade. If that is typical, it represents the norm, but it may be substantially different from the standard.

Sometimes other forms of standardized tests are ignored because the achievement and aptitude tests are so much more common. At least in the case of achievement instruments, classroom teachers are frequently involved in administering the tests and, in fact, the level of testing that occurs would probably be impossible without their participation. In other kinds of assessment, such as attitude and personality measures, instructors usually do not administer the instruments. The potential for misuse of standardized tests or of misinterpretation of the scores often requires specialized training, and those who administer these instruments are often psychologists or school counselors. Not all such measures are standardized, however. Some attitude instruments are intended for individual classroom application, and their use requires that we be reasonably familiar with them.

ASSESSING ATTITUDE

Probably every classroom includes students who perform below their abilities and others who succeed at a higher level than measures of their ability might have predicted. A performance that is inconsistent with the student's ability is often explained in terms of the student's attitude. Because we know that, to some degree, learners can compensate for lower levels of ability with superior motivation, and also that high ability can be tempered by low motivation, every instructor has a vested interest in knowing how to assess attitude. Furthermore, because attitudes are subject to change—indeed, are often affected by the learners' experiences—we want to have some mechanism for gauging attitude in the academic setting. These are important because we know that students' attitude helps explain academic performance.[3]

Sometimes attitudes change as a result of what's occurring in the classroom. When interest is improving, we try to capitalize by enhancing what appears to work well. When interest is waning, we should make appropriate changes.

As a footnote to this introduction to attitude assessment, you will want to consider the following: The assessment of affect is encouraged as a means, rather than an end. Students who like what they're doing are more likely not just to do well at it, but also to pursue it independently, and lifelong learning has become an objective that is valued very much (Jarvis, Holford, and Griffin, 1998). To some degree, helping students to become independent learners is every educator's responsibility. Since the willingness to operate independently is connected to students' attitudes, it makes sense to know how they feel about what we are trying to teach them.

Another point should be made about assessing attitude as a means rather than as an end. If the attitude is the only thing we care about, there is a tendency to separate it from the students' actual experience with learning, and that carries risks that we do not wish to incur. Baumeister (1996) has demonstrated that some programs that focus only on improving attitude actually disconnect students from the realities of their own performance. As a result, they can become self-congratulatory when actual achievement suggests that there is little to feel good about.

Attitude Scales

Attitude scales have been used for some time. Although they have several potential applications, their primary use has been in vocational counseling, where they are a mechanism for matching the individual to a potential profession on the basis of personal likes and dislikes. There are several forms of the attitude scale.

The Interest Inventory

The interest inventory first reviewed in Chapter 2 (Figure 2.4) is one of the less formal attitude scales and is quite easy to construct and use. One can develop some sense of how appealing a particular activity is by asking respondents to rank several activities— from what they prefer to do most to what is least appealing. Using the example in Figure 8.4, one might determine how students feel about writing compared to several other classroom activities.

FIGURE 8.4   A Composition Interest Inventory

Students: There are ten activities listed. Please rank from 1 to 10 the one you **most prefer** (1) to the one you **least prefer** (10).

_____ reading a history assignment	_____ solving a math problem
_____ preparing an oral report	_____ reciting poetry
_____ writing an essay	_____ writing a chemistry lab report
_____ working on a drama production	_____ listening to a recording of *Hamlet*
_____ debating the use of the atomic bomb	_____ taking a biology field trip

Two of the tasks involve extensive writing, and several might involve some written work. Once this instrument is administered, the instructor should know something about where writing activities fit among students' preferences. Note that this interest inventory really does not reveal anything about how well students like to write. What it indicates is whether a particular student likes one thing more or less than something else. For this reason, the other things to which the particular activity is compared ought to be selected with care, or the results are not meaningful. Asking typical high school seniors whether they would rather work in a chemistry lab or go to a movie isn't going to be very revealing. Asking whether they would rather work in a chemistry lab or write an essay for an English class might be a good deal more helpful because it suggests how competing academic requirements stack up against each other. Sometimes, however, nonacademic activities *are* included when we wish to know how disposed learners are to choose to do academic work over alternatives. The literature teacher who knows that most of the students often read for pleasure will probably prepare differently than one who has discovered that most of the students would rather not read.

> Teacher-constructed interest inventories are a simple way to establish how individuals rank a particular educational activity compared to alternatives. Used as pre- and postmeasures, they also allow one to establish whether students' views of an academic task have changed as a result of some planned activity.

Besides what the interest inventory reveals about preference, we can also use it a classwide indicator by summing the numerical responses for each item and dividing by the number of students. Using these item averages as pretest measures can help reveal whether interest among class members as a whole has changed during a learning activity when we administer it again after the activity concludes. We probably don't expect them to swap a computer game for a composition task, but it would be telling if, after a writing unit, the mean value for the class of "writing an essay" changed substantially (up *or* down) from what it was on the pretest.

Standardized Interest Inventories

One of the more widely used standardized attitude scales is the Strong-Campbell Interest Inventory (SCII). The example of the interest inventory in Figure 8.4 simply listed a series of activities and then we noted how students rank them. The SCII is a good deal more sophisticated. In his original work, Strong listed a variety of very different activities, most of them quite unrelated to particular occupations, and then administered the inventory to groups of people from different occupational areas. His idea was that people from the same occupation tend to respond similarly to the inventory items, even though the items are not directly related to their particular occupation. Those upon whom the instrument was normed were people who had some tenure in their occupation and professed to like what they did for a living. The scores were weighted according to whether the individual liked (a score of +1), disliked (–1), or was indifferent to (0) the particular activity. By averaging the scores of all those in the norm group from a given occupational group, Strong developed a score to which individuals who are administered the test can be compared. The occupational score that is most similar to the individual's score indicates the occupation with which that person is probably most in harmony.

Summated Rating Scales

Attitude scales, such as the Strong-Campbell, are examples of summated rating scales. One responds to each item in a series, with each response representing a particular score. The individual item scores are summed for the total attitude score. As we saw with the Strong-Campbell, the choices were like, dislike, and indifferent, with scores of +1, −1, or 0 assigned accordingly. Sometimes we wish to know how strongly respondents feel, in which case a summated rating scale is more helpful. Summated rating scales use a Likert format, which allows one to indicate how intensely one feels about the issue. Respondents may, for example, (1) strongly agree, (2) agree, (3) neither agree nor disagree, (4) disagree, or (5) strongly disagree with something such as the following:

I always do my homework before watching television.

In the "yes," "no," or "indifferent" classifications that instruments such as the Strong-Campbell employ, all of the items have equal assessment value. A positive response on one item, for example, carries the same significance in calculating the total scores as a similar response on any other item. The Likert format makes multiple responses possible—five in the example given. One must take care, however, to assign the values to the responses consistent with the way the item is framed. If the next item on the instrument containing the item above read as follows:

I generally dislike doing my homework.

the numerical values used on this item must be reversed in order for the scores to be consistent with the responses to the prior item. A "strongly agree" on the first item is likely to parallel a strongly disagree on the second. If scoring isn't reversed for the second item, a "strongly disagree" on item 2 will neutralize a "strongly agree" on the first item, even though both responses indicate a positive attitude toward homework.

The Likert form of the summated rating scale is very common in attitude surveys. Likert items yield more information about attitude than dichotomous "yes/no" or "like/dislike" responses because they reveal something about how strongly one feels rather than just the direction of the attitude.

Equal-Appearing Interval Scales

Equal-appearing interval scales are also a type of interest inventory, but they are different from some of the previous formats in that those who use them do not assume that all items reflect the same attitude intensity. Thurstone and Chave (1929) developed the procedure, which is more specialized than needed in this book, but the substance is that a large number of statements are collected that express an opinion about the issue being sampled. The statements are selected because the feelings about the subject range from the most favorable to neutral to the most unfavorable. An individual's responses allow the scorer to determine more than a ranking of respondents. Besides whether the person is favorably or unfavorably disposed, one can determine how strongly the respondent feels about what is assessed.

The Cumulative Scale

The cumulative scale is sometimes called the Guttman scale. It uses unidimensional items, which means that they assess just one variable. This is important because the instrument is planned so that responses on one item are related to responses on subsequent items. The instrument is constructed so that a positive response on item 1 will likely be followed by positive responses on all subsequent items. If the response to item 1 is negative, the response to item 2 can be negative or positive, but if it is positive, it is most likely that the item 3 response and subsequent responses will also be positive. In Figure 8.5 we have an example of an attitude survey employing a cumulative scale for assessing, in this instance, how high school students feel about the proliferation of chemical weapons.

An individual who answers in the affirmative to item 1 is likely to respond "yes" to the other three items also. Someone who answers "no" to item 1 but "yes" to item 2 is likely to answer "yes" to 3 and 4 as well.

An interesting characteristic of cumulative scales is that, when one knows the individual's final score, one can usually determine the pattern of responses. If scoring is 1 for a "yes" and 0 for a "no," and someone is known to have a score of 2, for example, it is most likely that the individual answered the first two items in the negative and the last two in the affirmative. Given the scaled nature of the items, it would be unlikely for someone to answer both of the first two items "yes" and the last two "no." If someone feels sovereign nations have the right to develop and place chemical weapons, it would be inconsistent to then indicate that he or she doesn't believe that a sovereign nation has the right to design and develop limited prototypes, for example.

Excepting interest inventories such as the one in Figure 8.4, summated rating scales are used most frequently when we want to gather formal information about

---

FIGURE 8.5   **Cumulative Scale for Assessing Proliferation of Chemical Weapons**

Following are four items dealing with the development and installation of chemical weapons of mass destruction by nations. If you agree with the statement, indicate "yes." If you disagree, indicate "no."

1. Should a sovereign nation have the right to develop and deploy chemical weapons?

   Yes _____   No _____

2. Should a sovereign nation have the right to develop and store chemical weapons for later deployment?

   Yes _____   No _____

3. Should a sovereign nation have the right to design and develop limited prototypes of chemical weapons?

   Yes _____   No _____

4. Should a sovereign nation have the right to design, but not develop, chemical weapons?

   Yes _____   No _____

students' attitudes. Of the more formal instruments, they are the easiest to construct and to interpret. As we noted, a survey such as the Strong-Campbell, or any other summated rating scale, will also yield more information than an interest inventory since it tells us something about how strongly respondents feel about an issue, a characteristic the interest inventory lacks. Depending upon how much information one wishes to gather, one might develop an attitude survey based on any one of the foregoing procedures. Although equal-appearing interval scale and cumulative scales offer the potential to provide more detail about attitude than summated rating scales, they are also more complicated to develop and to interpret. As a result, they are far less common in classroom settings.

Assessing Attitude versus Achievement

The different approaches to attitude assessment are actually different approaches to establishing individual preferences. There are other assessment settings in which this type of self-reporting can be very misleading, but in attitude surveys, stated preferences are quite revealing because part of the success the instructor and the students enjoy is related to how students feel about an area of study. Instructors also should be aware of changes in attitude as a result of the classroom experience.

When we are assessing just academic achievement, the student's individual preference becomes ancillary. The focus is generally on the learners' ability with the content or skill, rather than their feelings about it. A correct, or a complete, answer transcends individual preference. In attitude assessment, however, there are no "correct" answers. There are only "best" answers, and they are the responses that most accurately reflect the attitude of the respondent.

ACADEMIC APTITUDE AND THE CONCEPT OF MENTAL TRAITS

As noted earlier, the aptitude for completing academic tasks is a dimension of intelligence that should be viewed more broadly. The interest here is not in the global capacity that intelligence refers to, but in the student's "potential . . . for achievement," which is how Kerlinger (1973, p. 493) defined aptitude. In fact, the primary interest is in the even narrower dimension of *academic* aptitude.

The relationship between intelligence and academic aptitude is widely accepted. Hopkins and Stanley (1981) observed, "Most authorities feel that current intelligence tests are more aptly described as 'scholastic ability' tests because they are so highly related to academic performance . . ."(p. 364).

Distinguishing between academic aptitude and intelligence opens the way for the examination of other concepts that are related to the discussion of cognitive abilities. Academic aptitude, for example, is frequently subdivided into verbal aptitude and mathematical aptitude, a division that college admissions procedures reflect when discreet tests are

> Academic aptitude is that part of intelligence expressed in school-related achievement.

used to assess each. Separating verbal from mathematical ability is only the tip of an iceberg, however. There are actually multiple mental factors or traits, each of which is relatively independent. The existence of multiple characteristics can be verified by a statistical procedure called **factor analysis.** Although it is beyond the scope of this book, in factor analysis, correlation data are used to determine the number of different mental traits that test items call upon.

Perhaps a math test consists of 60 individual test items. Factor analysis may reveal that there are actually a comparatively few mental traits that the test assesses. Factor analysis does not name those traits, but someone who reviews the data might find that one subgroup of items reflects mostly the students' ability to calculate, that another group is connected to their ability with deductive logic, a third is based on their ability to estimate, and so on. The value of this technique is that it allows one to verify that the reasoning involved in solving algebraic equations, for example, is different from that ability required for completing computation problems. Although both are related to the more general "mathematics ability," they actually represent distinct mental traits.

Distinguishing among the different traits that contribute to academic achievement is very valuable from an assessment standpoint. In this example at least, a math assessment can provide information about several distinct traits rather than only about a generic "math ability." A college math placement test must provide data that will allow one to make intelligent decisions about an applicant's competence in basic mathematics computation, algebra I, geometry, algebra II, trigonometry, and perhaps even calculus. Math ability alone is not very revealing. In fact, were we to tabulate scores from each of those areas and also aggregate a total score, we might well find that performance in any one area was more highly correlated with the total score than with any other subcategory, suggesting that the subareas are relatively independent.

The Relationship between Intelligence and Academic Aptitude

Alfred Binet and his colleagues established the association between aptitude and educational achievement in work produced in France near the beginning of the twentieth century. Binet is recognized as the father of modern intelligence testing. His charge from French education officials was to develop procedures that would take the guesswork out of identifying mentally retarded children. Binet ultimately constructed a series of tests designed to measure children's intellectual capacity. He made an assumption in the development of the first widely used intelligence tests that underscored the connection we still assume between intellectual capacity and academic aptitude. As he began his research, Binet examined work on intelligence, which Galton and others had produced earlier, in which the approach had been to rely on factors such as sensory discrimination and reaction time as indicators of intelligence. Binet rejected such work because the data correlated poorly with academic achievement. The position he took presumed that whatever intelligence is, it must positively relate to one's level of success on academic tasks.

The product of Binet's work was a single, global measure of the individual's capacity. The assumption of one underlying characteristic was common among early theorists who subscribed to a **unitrait theory of intelligence.** The implicit assumption in unitrait theories is that one global mental trait can explain people's performance in all aspects of their intellectual functioning. Subsequent to the development of unitrait theories of intelligence, there were dual-trait, then multiple-trait theories.

Certainly a single aptitude can be correlated to an individual's performance in several different academic disciplines. Verbal ability, for example, can be an effective predictor of students' performances in a variety of subjects because learning in most disciplines involves large amounts of verbal material. The concept of one general measure also remains because it is easier for the researcher to manage than multiple scores. Be that as it may, most researchers agree that a profile of scores is a better way to represent a learner's aptitude, even if the scores from each of the dimensions are not completely independent. Anastasi (1976) maintained that when researchers argue that aptitude can be reflected in a single score, what they actually assess is a narrow slice of the aptitude, rather than the entire spectrum of ability.

The discussion of the number of traits or factors that constitute academic aptitude characterizes what has been called the psychometric view of mental ability. As the name suggests, the psychometric view assumes that aptitude can be assessed and represented with a number, or, when there are multiple traits, with several numbers. The psychometric approach has been dominant, but there are also other views of aptitude.

Developmental theory has contributed a "Piagetian perspective" (Wagner and Sternberg, 1984) of aptitude/intelligence suggesting that the mind, just like the body, follows a predictable developmental sequence as one matures. From this point of view, our expectations for intellectual performance should be adjusted for age just the way we modify our expectations for physical performance. We should expect different things, both physically and intellectually, from six-year-olds and from 16-year-olds. The heart of the developmental approach is that the differences may relate more to age than to experience. The differences reflect a developmental process that everyone passes through and that characterizes variations in the ways people think. From this point of view, academic aptitude is viewed in terms of the ways one thinks and the kinds of things one is capable of doing at a particular time. At least in some instances, this view of aptitude has had a great impact on the way we approach younger children in the classroom.

More recently, an information processing view of aptitude/intelligence has evolved that explains intellectual functioning in terms of "the ways in which people mentally represent and process information" (Wagner and Sternberg, 1984, p. 183). Often using the flow of information as a model, these approaches explain what occurs in human information processing between stimulus (input) and response (output). Information processing models focus heavily on memory and the characteristics of memory storage to explain differences in individuals' levels of cognitive functioning.

It is probably evident from their names (psychometric/Piagetian/information processing) that the formal measurement of intelligence is related much more to the psychometric view of intelligence than to the alternatives.

Conceptualizing Academic Aptitude

In reviewing the various aspects of validity earlier in the chapter, it was noted that different kinds of assessment may have different validity emphases. The heart of the issue for intelligence testing, for example, is construct validity. One must have some assurance that whatever one operationally defines as intelligence is what is actually measured.

With aptitude testing, we are primarily interested in criterion-related validity. When we administer an aptitude test, it is invariably an effort to identify a level of performance with which some other measure of achievement can be compared. We compare the aptitude data with how the student is performing presently in the related discipline, or we use the aptitude data as a predictor for how the student will perform on some other related task. We may be interested in the student's performance in the next course, the professional program, the work place, or the like. If there is no association between the two measures (there is no criterion-related validity), the aptitude data have very little value.

Academic Aptitude and College Entrance

Perhaps the most publicized application of academic aptitude assessments is their use in college entrance exams. In that setting, the tests have become a fixture. Kessel and Linn (1996) noted:

> *Multiple-choice college entrance examinations are a pervasive part of American life. Based on the notion that college admissions and scholarship should reflect merit, rather than privilege, standardized examinations have taken on roles undreamed of by their creators. (p. 10)*

Although they are widely used to make college admissions decisions, the tests are certainly not without their detractors. A book by Crouse and Trusheim (1988) is a scathing criticism of the Scholastic Aptitude Test (SAT). The authors argue that the test discriminates against black applicants and poor applicants, and that fundamentally it does not help admissions committees make better decisions. Although the Crouse and Trusheim arguments are not new, and many other critics have joined in the criticism, the SAT is still widely used for at least two reasons. First, SAT math and SAT verbal scores do correlate well with other measures of math and verbal ability, which is to say that the data have acceptable concurrent validity. Second, the predictive validity is quite good. The data predict subsequent college-level performance more accurately than high school grades predict them. College admissions tests provide a common measure of student aptitude. The measure cuts across other differences such as grade averages which, even when they contain identical numbers, often represent substantially different levels of performance because conditions vary so much from school to school.

ASSESSING ACHIEVEMENT

In contrast to aptitude assessment, where criterion-related validity is the focus, or attitude measurement, which requires careful attention to construct validity, those who assess academic achievement are more interested in content validity. The task is to construct an instrument that represents the entire content area from which inferences may be drawn. As a consequence, more than other types of testing, achievement testing is directly linked to curriculum and instruction.

Depending upon the application we make of the data, achievement tests may be administered before, during, or following instruction. Chapter 2 noted that assessment prior to instruction is often necessary for purposes of student placement and also for instructional planning. When we assess achievement while instruction is ongoing, it should be for formative purposes because we should be checking on the learners' progress and also on the effectiveness of the instructional plan. The criterion for our decisions *is* the learners' achievement, but the only people who are graded at this point are the instructor and the instructional planner. The only time that assessment for grading makes good sense is when it occurs after the learning activities are completed. Midway through an instructional unit is usually not such a time.

The final type of achievement testing is a component of what Bloom, Hastings, and Madaus (1971) called summative evaluation. Figure 8.6 provides a list of the different applications of achievement testing and indicates where each fits in relation to the instructional plan.

Figure 8.6 should remind you of what has become a repetitive theme in this book: Achievement data can be employed for a variety of quite different purposes. Whichever application is intended, however, the assessment must be constructed so that data lend themselves to the inferences we wish to draw. Pretest data are not helpful as a measure of final student achievement. Attitude data will not tell us what we need to know about who has the prerequisite skills and abilities, and aptitude test data reveal very little about students' attitudes toward their subject.

The business of making sure that the test data fit the assessment purpose is a major component of the content validity that is central to achievement assessment. Although both problem-solving ability and a grasp of Newton's laws of motion can fall under a secondary school physics umbrella, instruments designed to assess each objective will have very different kinds of content.

FIGURE 8.6   Assessing Achievement in Relation to Instruction

When Assessment Is Conducted	Issues Addressed with Assessment Data
Before Instruction	Does the individual have the prerequisite skills and knowledge?
During Instruction	Is the instructional plan working properly?
	Are the learners progressing appropriately?
	Were there deficiencies in either learner preparation or instructional planning that were not detected before instruction began?
After Instruction	Were the learning objectives achieved?
	What are the levels of the learners' achievement?
	How could the instructional plan be improved?

Source: Adapted from Millman and Greene (1989), p. 336.

ASSESSMENT AND LEARNING STYLE

Thoughtful educators have frequently wondered whether they ought to alter the way they teach and assess because of differences in students' personalities. Your author will make a judgment about that subsequently, but first let us review the concept of a student's learning style.

Identifying Learning Style

The subject of learning style came up in Chapter 2 in the discussion of impulsive versus reflective styles, and field independence versus dependence. Conceivably, there are several aspects of how students approach academic tasks that might be relevant to the teaching and testing materials we develop. Many of these characteristics become evident when we observe students' behaviors.

A more formal approach is to use an instrument such as the Myers-Briggs personality measure published by Educational Testing Service. The Myers-Briggs employs a self-report format to establish the dominance of particular personality characteristics. The individual responds to a series of questions about certain situations which, when the answers are aggregated, indicate a preference for introversion versus extroversion, thinking versus feeling, and judgment versus perception. The resulting personality profile has been used primarily in employment situations, but it might have a variety of applications. If you found that a student was quite introverted, an oral exam might be unnecessarily intimidating. Knowing that a student relied heavily on perception rather than judgment suggests differences in the way he or she analyzes visual stimuli. It might affect the way you present material in a laboratory experiment.

There are other dimensions to this discussion. It has become very common for authors to speak of learning style differences among students—which refer to the learning mode (visual, auditory, or kinesthetic) on which students rely most heavily during the learning activities. There are several interrelated issues stemming from the discussion of learning style.

For Further Discussion

If distinct learning styles can be identified, how did they come to be? Are learning styles an artifact of individual learner differences or do they reflect elements of ethnic, cultural, or gender group style? Do they describe both individual and group differences? Should instruction and assessment be adapted to those styles? Develop some tentative answers to these questions before you continue.

Adapting to Learning Style

Whether learners prefer different learning styles, the attempts made to adapt instruction to the mode upon which students rely most heavily have not borne fruit.

Stahl, Osborn, and Stein (1995/96) reviewed the existing research on reading instruction and came to the following conclusion:

> *Matching children by modality or learning style . . . is an approach to reading instruction that is neither useful nor effective, no matter how intuitive it may seem . . . Quite simply, the data do not support the use of different instructional methods with children classified as "auditory" and those classified as "visual." Given the failure of these approaches to produce results, given the amount of research invested in them, it would seem best to look elsewhere for ways to improve reading instruction. (p. 32)*

Guild (1994) noted what has become a very common theme, that particular cultural groups might exhibit particular learning characteristics in common. However, adjusting instructional materials based on the characteristics of the group creates its own difficulties. Notes Guild, it is "a serious error to conclude that all members of the group have the same style traits as the group taken as a whole" (p. 16). It is, of course, stereotyping to impose psychological traits that may be characteristic of a group on all individual members of the group.

> There is a great deal of discussion about learning style differences, and we have instruments that will allow us to determine individual students' preferred styles. Although a match between the students' learning styles and the teacher's presentation is logical enough, the research does not yet support the beneficial effects to the students, at least in terms of their academic achievement.

Incidentally, effective instructors make an effort to engage multiple learner senses in the learning setting, but this is less a reflection of learning style than an understanding that what is called "multiple coding." Employing multiple senses is more effective than using a single auditory or visual approach in the classroom. Even though we can conduct the assessments that help us determine learners' personality characteristics and even their preferred learning styles, there is not yet compelling evidence in any discipline that tailoring instruction to learning style impacts student performance. Your author hastens to add, however, that one may often adjust for linguistic differences, and those adjustments are necessary and important, but they reflect differences in the level of preparation students possess, not learning style differences stemming from personality.

Assessment and Individual Cognitive Style

Although efforts to adapt to group learning characteristics for instruction have not been helpful, and adapting to preferred learning mode does not seem promising, there other options dealing with cognitive style. As noted above, cognitive style was first mentioned in Chapter 2 in connection with field independence. Some students have a greater tendency than others to see an object separately from the background in which it occurs. Field dependent people see things holistically. Armstrong (1993) found that this difference could be important when it comes to assessment. Multiple-choice items sometimes take the form of asking the respondent to determine the choice that does *not* fit. A question that asks, for example:

Which of the following is **not** a noun?

employs a format that favors field independent thinkers. Students who cannot set aside a holistic view of the problem will struggle determining the choice that does not fit. Armstrong (1993) found that poorly written items that contain grammatical cues to the correct answers benefit field independent learners but not field dependent learners, who less frequently detect the cue because of their tendency to view the item as a whole. There may not yet be research support for adapting instruction to cognitive style, but there are implications for assessment. Field dependent people have difficulty responding to items of the form, "All but one of the following . . . ," and the like. Witkin, Moore, Goodenough, and Cox (1977) indicated a relationship between field dependence/independence and performance on intelligence tests when the items require one to use some element of a test item in a context different from the way it was presented.

STUDENTS WITH DISABILITIES

Two movements have converged to focus attention on disabled students. One is the growing presence of formal assessment. The other is the increased tendency to retain disabled students in the academic mainstream. In combination, they reflect the need to make all students accountable for their academic progress, in spite of the presence of a handicapping condition, but in a way that reasonably accommodates the disability. In the United States, at least, the legal requirement to accommodate the disabled is established by the "Americans with Disabilities Act" (ADA). Other countries have laws with similar intent.

Although accommodating physical disabilities can be difficult, it is rarely controversial. Providing signing for the hearing impaired or ramp access for those who are confined to wheelchairs are needs that any reasonable audience finds acceptable. Cognitive disabilities raise a different issue, however. Since test scores must have the same interpretation for all students in order to be valid (Phillips, 1996), any accommodation that is made for disabled students cannot compromise the assessment standard without also compromising the validity of the decisions made for the students.

As an example of the difficulty, if a learner has been diagnosed with a learning disability that affects reading, would it be appropriate to read assessment items for the student? What if the test is a reading comprehension test? As Phillips has pointed out, at least in the second instance, the accommodation is inappropriate:

> The courts have clearly indicated that reasonable accommodations must compensate for aspects of the disability which are incidental to the standard being measured but that policymakers are not required to change the standard being measured to accommodate a disabled student. *(p. 12, italics added for emphasis)*

At issue is determining when aspects of the disability are incidental to the standard and when, in the process of accommodating the disabled student, the standard itself is compromised. Phillips (1998) has illustrated some of the difficulty in a situation in which one is testing mathematics achievement. If the intent is to assess computational ability but a student has been diagnosed with a computational processing deficit that has been termed "dyscalculia," and is permitted to use a calculator, are the data compromised? Phillips points out that the student who uses a calculator does not have to properly line up the numbers in an addition problem so that the units columns and the tens columns line up. Neither will the student need to know the math facts, nor how to carry. All that is necessary is keying in the two numbers and the proper signs.

While there may be pressure to relax a standard for a student with a cognitive disability, in Phillips's (1998) words:

> *The courts have indicated . . . that accommodations are appropriate only for factors unrelated to the skill being measured. One is* not *required to make substantial modifications which alter the knowledge/skills that the test measures. Rather than compensating for an unrelated factor, allowing a calculator when the objective calls for computation of estimation provides a preferential advantage* not *available to other students who would probably increase their score if allowed to use calculators. (p. 2)*

Every educator has a legal and ethical responsibility to watch for handicapping conditions that diminish the learner's performance, but which are not directly related to what is assessed. When assessment reveals these conditions, appropriate adjustments should be made. Perhaps when time is unrelated to what is being assessed, more latitude can be given to complete the test. Perhaps a student who is easily distracted can take the test in a more isolated setting. If the adjustment is not incidental to what is assessed, however, it is important to recognize that changes diminish the data and compromise their validity.

For Further Discussion

Adjustments made to accommodate the handicapped are necessary and important. Accommodations must not, however, alter the characteristic being assessed or compromise the interpretation of the data.

At what point are differences between learners so great that the learner has a handicap?

How will you distinguish between conditions that are appropriate accommodations and those that may inflate the learner's performance?

SUMMARY

Although assessment is a broad topic, prior to this chapter the book has primarily concentrated on the dimensions dealing specifically with academic achievement assessment. There are very practical reasons, however, for examining learners' traits, attitudes, and aptitudes, and some of them relate directly to achievement. The prologue was intended to suggest one such reason. There are at least some instances when the student's attitude is reflected in the quality of the achievement. Consequently, we need to know something about students' attitudes toward an activity before the activity is implemented, and probably even before it is prepared.

We should be comfortable by now with the fact that validity is multidimensional. Beyond a fairly consistent concern for the appearance of the assessment termed face validity, the relative importance of content validity, criterion-related validity, and construct validity is specific to the assessment task. In achievement testing, for example, where adequate coverage of a discipline or a curricular area is very important, content validity is preeminent. If the task is screening applicants for entrance into a program or institution, criterion-related validity takes precedence, and if attitude assessment is the focus, one must be careful to establish construct validity. Only then do we have the assurance that what we are measuring is truly attitude.

Weaving through much of this discussion are the differences between norm-references and criterion-references. In those instances in which one can use objective methods to determine the level for individual performance, criterion-references hold sway. The current interest in specific academic outcomes makes liberal use of criterion-referenced testing. In settings in which individual performance is given meaning by comparing it to others' performances, norm-referencing is common, and it is particularly evident where assessing traits and aptitudes is the focus.

One of the more interesting trends in current educational practice is the move to tailor instruction to the individual learner. The issue was raised in connection with the handicapped, as well as in relation to learning style differences among learners. The approach suggests that where assessment reveals pronounced differences in the way students learn, we modify instruction accordingly. These accommodations have substantial intuitive appeal, but we need to be cautious. In the area of learning style differences there have been two directions taken; one approach deals with learning modality, and the other focuses on the characteristics of cultural and ethnic groups. The limited research available suggests that tailoring instruction to respond to differences in learning modality has not resulted in higher levels of achievement.

Neither has the effort to make this adjustment with groups been very successful, perhaps because group characteristics represent a general—but not necessarily individual—trait. The individual members of the groups may not exhibit the characteristic, and we must be cautious about framing instruction or assessment based on a generalization.

The circumstances are different with handicapped learners. Where assessment indicates a handicapping condition, we have a responsibility to make a reasonable accommodation, whether it appears to have an affect on the achievement data. One must take care, however, to distinguish between adjustments that neutralize the handicap and those that distort or inflate the characteristic we wish to assess.

This chapter took us beyond conventional teacher-made assessments. There are, however, concepts and principles common to both ordinary classroom testing and formal, standardized testing that we have mentioned but have had little occasion to develop. Chapter 9 will look more carefully at some of them.

ENDNOTES

1. Prediction, in this usage, does not necessarily mean of some future event. An assessment instrument can have "predictive" validity for events past as well as for events yet to come.
2. More properly, the name is a "Gaussian distribution"—named for Karl Gauss, the mathematician who first defined the normal distribution's properties.
3. As it turns out, most of the research examines the impact that particular instructional practices have on affect rather than the impact that improved affect may have on subsequent performance. That improved affect has a positive impact on academic performance is generally taken for granted. The issue is raised not to challenge the assumption, but to note it. Since the assumption that improved attitude has a positive

influence on achievement is widespread, procedures are introduced to conduct assessment in the affective domain.

FOR FURTHER READING

For those with an interest in attitude scales, Anastasi's (1976) chapter titled "Measures of interests, attitudes, and values" is very good. In nontechnical language, she explains how the different scales are developed and what their primary uses have been.

REFERENCES

Anastasi, A. (1976). *Psychological testing* (4th ed.). New York: Macmillan.

Armstrong, A. M. (1993). Cognitive-style differences in testing situations. *Educational Measurement: Issues and Practice, 12*(3), 17–22.

Baumeister, R. F. (1996). Should schools try to boost self-esteem? *American Educator, 20*(2), 14–19, 43.

Bloom, B. S., Hastings, J. T., and Madaus, G. F. (1971). *Handbook on formative and summative evaluation of student learning.* New York: McGraw-Hill.

Bond, L. (1989). The effects of special preparation on measures of scholostic ability. In. R. L. Linn (Ed.), *Educational measurement* (3rd ed.). New York: Macmillan.

Crouse, J., and Trusheim, D. (1988). *The case against the SAT.* Chicago: The University of Chicago Press.

Guild, P. (1994). The culture/learning style connection. *Educational Leadership, 51*(8), 16–21.

Harter, S. (1988). Developmental processes in the construction of the self. In T. D. Yawkey and J. E. Johnson (Eds.), *Integrative processes and socialization: Early to middle childhood* (pp. 45–78). Hillsdale, NJ: Erlbaum.

Hopkins, K. D., and Stanley, J. C. (1981). *Educational and psychological measurement and evaluation* (6th ed.). Englewood Cliffs, NJ: Prentice-Hall.

Jarvis, P., Holford, J., and Griffin, C. (1998). *The theory and practice of learning.* London: Kogan Page.

Kerlinger, F. N. (1973). *Foundations of educational research.* New York: Holt, Rinehart and Winston.

Kessel, C., and Linn, M. D. (1996). Grades or scores: Predicting future college mathematics performance. *Educational Measurement: Issues and Practice, 15*(4), 10–14.

Lefrancois, G. (1994). *Psychology for teaching* (8th ed.). Belmont CA: Wadsworth.

Millman, J., and Greene, J. (1989). The specification and development of tests of achievement and ability. In R. L. Lin (Ed.), *Educational measurement* (3rd ed.). New York: Macmillan.

Phillips, S. E. (1996). Legal defensibility of standards: Issues and perspectives. *Educational Measurement: Issues and Practice, 15*(2), 5–13, 19.

Phillips, S. E. (1998). Calculator accommodations, *NCME: National Council on Measurement in Education Quarterly Newsletter, 6*(1), 2.

Stahl, S. A., Osborn, J., and Stein, M. (1995/96). Research does not support matching instruction to learning styles. *Reading Today, 34,* 32.

Thurstone, L., and Chave, E. (1929). *The measurement of attitude.* Chicago: University of Chicago Press.

Wagner, R. K., and Sternberg, R. J. (1984). Alternative conceptions of intelligence and their implications for education. *Review of Educational Research, 54,* 179–224.

Witkin, H. A., Moore, C. A., Goodenough, D. R., and Cox, P. W. (1977). Field-dependent and field-independent cognitive styles and their educational implications. *Review of Educational Research, 47,* 1–64.

Assessment Data and Description

■ *Readers will become familiar with the differences in the reporting and treatment of assessment data, and with the different theories underlying current assessment practice.*

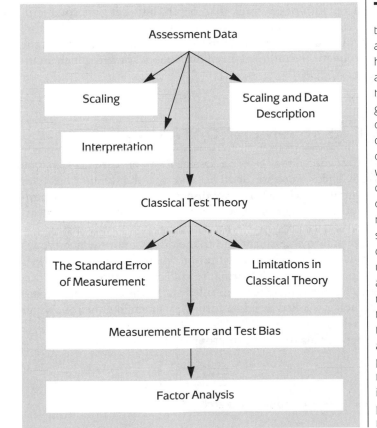

Assessment Data

Scaling

Scaling and Data Description

Interpretation

Classical Test Theory

The Standard Error of Measurement

Limitations in Classical Theory

Measurement Error and Test Bias

Factor Analysis

There are important differences in the things one may wish to measure, and some of the differences are inherent in the nature of the data. Data about students' ethnicity and about their academic performance are gathered differently, and those differences carry over to the way we describe groups of data. To some degree, the scale of the data dictates what is the appropriate measure of central tendency, or of dispersion, or correlation. The standard error of measurement (SEM) is also a measure of dispersion. When we rely on classical test theory, the SEM helps us define the amount of error associated with a test score. For measurement specialists, item response theory (IRT) stands as an alternative to classical test theory. With any approach to understanding student performance, we are interested in the possibility of bias in the test items, as well as in situations where performance is differential, even if the items are not biased. ■

Ms. Neilson took her assessment responsibilities seriously. She knew that assessment was part of teaching, and she prepared the tests and projects she assigned to her students very carefully. She was not naïve, however. She knew that the scores reflected factors unrelated to what her fifth-grade science students were learning, and she worried about the accuracy of her assessments. Besides great differences in preparation and ability, sometimes students were distracted by events elsewhere in the school, by their own social interests, and even by their physical and emotional well-being. Sometimes, Ms. Neilson acknowledged, students' performance reflected errors she made in her assessment procedures. She wondered whether there was some way to determine how accurately students' assessment scores reflected their learning. ■

BREADTH VERSUS DEPTH

An introductory textbook such as this one offers little opportunity to exhaust an issue. The focus is more on breadth of coverage than depth, but there are some tangents to the discussions held in other chapters that will be developed a little more thoroughly here; others will be pursued in Chapter 13. With some luck, some of the topics will whet your appetite for the more involved discussions toward which an introductory text can only hint.

DIFFERENT KINDS OF ASSESSMENT DATA

Much earlier in this text it was noted that before assessment can proceed very far, one must decide what to assess. There is no test for all occasions, and different objectives require different assessment approaches. When we discussed these matters in Chapter 6, we spoke of the different levels of thought learners are capable of demonstrating and the kinds of items that are appropriate for assessing each level.

There is another dimension to assessment and to the discussion of which type is appropriate. An anecdote will illustrate it. An institution where your author worked used a questionnaire that had an interesting format to collect data about the performance of student teachers. The instrument was one filled out by the classroom teacher with whom the student teacher worked. It had a form very much like the following:

The teacher prepared materials that were appropriate for the particular students.

———   ———   ———   ———   ———

strongly agree ——————→ strongly disagree

Study the example for a moment. There is not anything fundamentally wrong with the statement, which raises an issue that is very important in teacher preparation, or with the response format, called a Likert-type format. The problem is a mismatch between the two. The statement implies that the response will be yes/no (either the student teacher did or did not prepare such materials). The response format, on the other hand, requires the respondent to scale the student teacher's work somewhere along a continuum that implies much more than either "the student did," or "the student did not."

Scaling

The issue here is one of data scale. The statement calls for one scale of response, and the response format solicits another. Depending upon what they reveal, there are four grades, or scales, of assessment data. Nominal data are the simplest, followed by ordinal, interval, and ratio. Figure 9.1 indicates the different scales and provides a brief description of each.[1]

Nominal Scale Data
Nominal data are sometimes called categorical data, or count data. It is characteristic of them that they define categories, and "measuring" nominal data is nothing more

FIGURE 9.1   Scale of Assessment Data

Nominal	Data at this level define mutually exclusive categories.
	Gender, nationality, religious affiliation, and the like each represent nominal data. The categories are such that one is a member of one group or another. Technically, there are not "degrees" of membership.
Ordinal	Data at this level allow one to rank the subject.
	Ordinal data allow one to make informed judgments about greater-than or less-than characteristics. Larger numbers indicate more of a property, although precisely how much more is not defined. Ordinal data are characterized by such descriptors as higher, faster, older, and so forth.
Interval	Data at this level are characterized by equal intervals.
	The difference between any two consecutive points on an interval scale is equal. On an interval scale from 1 to 50, for example, the difference between 13 and 14 is the same quantity of the quality measured as the difference between 40 and 41. The same is true of the difference between pairs of numbers. The difference from 5 to 8 is the same amount of the quality as is the difference from 34 to 37.
Ratio	These data have interval characteristics, as well as a meaningful zero.
	Some scales, such as the Fahrenheit scale in temperature measurement, have no meaningful zero. It actually occupies an arbitrary place on the scale. Your checkbook, on the other hand, has a meaningful zero.

than counting how many subjects fall into a particular category. The categories are mutually exclusive, which means that what we are counting cannot occupy two categories. Gender is a case in point. One is either female or male, but not both, and in spite of what advertising would have one believe, there are not degrees of maleness or femaleness that will affect the count. Questions about how many students speak a language other than English, how many did their homework, or how many prefer a particular teaching style call for nominal data.

Ordinal Scale Data

When the data reveal how much of a quality a subject possesses relative to other subjects, we are dealing with at least ordinal data. We can say "at least" because data from interval and ratio scales will also allow us to rank subjects. Ordinal scale data do not indicate the quantity of the thing measured in absolute terms, but rather whether one has more or less of it than others. We use ordinal scale references a great deal in informal discussions. It is common to hear educators say that someone has become a better student, or that one person is a faster learner than another, or that an individual is taller than someone else. These are all descriptions that reflect ordinal measurement.

Sometimes test scores are reported as ordinal data, and percentile scores are a common example. A score at the 60th percentile indicates that the student's score falls at a point where 60 percent of the rest of the group scored at or below that level. The score doesn't tell us how much of the quality measured the student possesses. If the data are achievement data, for example, we don't know from the percentile score how many of the items the student scored correctly, because a percentile score is not the same as a percentage correct score. We only know how the student compares to the rest of the group.

Interval Scale Data

As Figure 9.1 suggests, the defining characteristic for interval data is equal intervals between numbers. Although we sometimes see percentile scores treated as though they were interval, they usually are not. As it turns out, interval data are quite common in assessment. If a spelling test is administered to a group of fifth-grade students, and scores are reported as the number of words out of 20 that were spelled correctly, the students' scores represent interval data. The difference between a score of 15 and 16 is the same interval as that between scores of 7 and 8. There are also equal intervals between percentages correct. A student who scores 19 scored 95 percent of the words correctly. The difference between 95 percent and 75 percent (a score of 15) is the same interval as that between 60 percent (a score of 12) and 40 percent (a score of 8). Note that these differences between percentages can be quite different from the differences between percentile scores. From the 30th to the 40th percentile might involve a substantially different performance interval than the difference between the 73rd and 83rd percentiles.

Ratio Scale Data

Although they are common enough elsewhere, ratio data are quite rare in educational settings—perhaps because none of the characteristics we might assess can have a meaningful quantity of zero. Certainly a student can score zero on an achievement test, and that does mean that none of the items was scored correctly, but remember that we are nearly always using the test score to draw inferences about some other quality that cannot be assessed directly. The spelling test is intended to allow us to make a judgment about a student's spelling ability. Unless we are comfortable with an inference that the student possesses none of the quality assessed—no spelling ability, in this case—a zero score means something else. In fact, the zero usually cannot be interpreted to mean none of the quality in any educational measurement, so, at least in the classroom, we have little to do with ratio scale measures. Consequently, we will concentrate only on data measured on nominal, ordinal, and interval scales from this point on.

Interpreting Data

The nature of scaling is that each level includes more information about what is being measured than the level preceding it. The difficulty with the statement from the questionnaire mentioned earlier is that it poses an issue for which the response should be nominal scale data (yes/no), but the response options require at least an ordinal scale judgment. Unfortunately, such mismatches are not uncommon, but they are at least easy to modify. Instead of presenting that original question as follows:

> The student teacher prepared instructional materials that were appropriate for the particular students.
>
> _____   _____   _____   _____   _____
>
> strongly agree ——————→ strongly disagree

the responses might have been changed to correspond with the item as follows:

> _____   _____
>
> did   did not

As an alternative, the item might have been framed to provide for the type of comparison that the "strongly agree" to "strongly disagree" options suggested.

> Compared to materials produced by others of this level of experience, how adequate were the teaching materials the student prepared?
>
> _____   _____   _____   _____   _____
>
> completely inadequate   completely adequate

By making either change, the item and the response format agree (and harmony is restored to the assessment world).

Scaling and Data Description

The issue is not only a matter of question-and-answer consistency, which is important in its own rite, but the latitude we have when we are describing large amounts

Descriptive statistics are "methods for organizing numerical descriptions of . . . phenomena" (Kurtz, 1999, p. 5). They allow us to describe sets of data in an abbreviated and symbolic fashion. Descriptive statistics usually involve a measure of centrality describing what is typical, as well as a measure of dispersion defining how the data are distributed.

of assessment data is also affected by the scale of the measurement. When large quantities of data are involved, we often rely on two **descriptive statistics** to summarize the data. Usually we employ one statistic, called a measure of central tendency, to describe what is typical of the group. The second statistic explains how much the various numbers tend to stray from the first statistic. This second statistic is, logically, a measure of variability.

Describing Nominal Data

Because nominal data measure the number of subjects who occur in the different categories, the statistic used to describe them indicates what is most common among the categories. It is called the mode, and the notation often used for it is M_o. Presume that you are collecting data on students' ethnicity in a particular elementary school. Upon reviewing school records you find the following:

ethnic group 1:   238 students
ethnic group 2:   145 students
ethnic group 3:   128 students
ethnic group 4:   95 students
all other groups: 44 students

For these data, M_o = ethnic group 1. Students from that group have the greatest numerical frequency at the school. Bar graphs are often used to display nominal data, and a graph of the ethnicity data allows one to come quickly to the same conclusion (see Figure 9.2(a)).

The first (tallest) bar in the chart, Figure 9.2(a), and the highest point in the frequency polygon, Figure 9.2(b), provide alternative ways to visualize the mode. The mode is the only measure of what is typical that makes much sense for nominal data. With only five groups, the visual representation doesn't clarify very much, but when there are more numerous categories, data presented in graphical form can make it much simpler to verify which category of subjects is most common.

Describing Ordinal Data

Recall that ordinal data are measured in relative terms. The measure of central tendency used to describe what is typical of a group of ordinal measures is the median, often abbreviated M_d, or perhaps M_{dn}. The median describes the midpoint in a distribution of measures, and it may be used with any type of data except nominal. Half of the scores in the group that is defined are above the median and half are below.

As noted previously, percentile scores are ordinal data. By definition, the 50th percentile is the median. Unlike the mode, it may not be the most common measure. In fact, it may not be a number that actually occurs within the group of measures at all. Consider the following sets of measures.

(a) 12   15   15   17   28   29   30
(b) 12   15   15   28   29   30

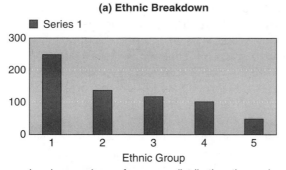

(a) Ethnic Breakdown

In a bar graph or a frequency distribution, the mode is easy to determine. It reflects the tallest bar, when the bars are arranged vertically as they are above, or the highest point in the frequency polygon below.

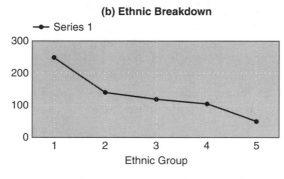

(b) Ethnic Breakdown

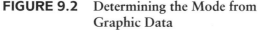

FIGURE 9.2   Determining the Mode from Graphic Data

In the first set, the number 17 represents the median (M_d = 17), since it occupies the point among six numbers where three numbers fall below 17 and three numbers are beyond. In the second set of numbers however, there is no middle-most number appearing in the set. In such cases, the median is the midpoint between the two middle numbers, so we average them to locate it. Since 15 + 20 = 43, and $^{43}/_2$ = 21.5, 21.5 is the median for the second set.

By the way, you will notice that in both sets of numbers, the most common number (the mode) is 15. Although the median makes no sense for nominal data, both median and mode can help us understand ordinal data.

Describing Interval Data: Measures of Central Tendency

The most informative measure of central tendency is the mean, the arithmetic average of all measures. It is usually abbreviated $\bar{X}$ or M_n, although simply M is becoming more popular. The mean is calculated (as you already know) by summing all scores and dividing by the number of scores. Symbolically, the calculation of the mean can be written $M = \frac{\Sigma X}{N}$, which should be read "the mean is equal to the summation of X divided by the number of scores." The Greek letter sigma means summation, or the total of. The X represents each individual score.

We use three different measures of central tendency to describe data. The mode describes what is most common. It is the only measure of what is typical that allows one to describe nominal data with accuracy. With ordinal data, we can rely on the mode, and the middle-most score, the median. If data are interval or better, we can use the mean, as well as the median and the mode.

Although the mean and median cannot be used to describe nominal data (neither average gender nor average ethnicity translates very well into usable information), all three measures of central tendency can be used to describe interval data, and it is not uncommon to see them reported together. The average score, the middle-most score, and the score that occurs most frequently provide one a good deal about the entire group of scores.

When scores are normally distributed, which means that they fit that bell-shaped or Gaussian curve, all three measures of central tendency occur at the same point. On the other hand, when a group of scores includes a few extreme scores, called outliers, which all occur in the same direction, the three measures of central tendency are all different. This is important because the mean can be greatly affected by outliers. Examine Figure 9.3 for a moment.

When the distribution of scores is "pulled" out of symmetry by a few extreme scores, the data are skewed. If it is a few scores in the upper end of the distribution [distribution (b) in Figure 9.3] that disturb the symmetry, the data have a positive skew. A few low scores without corresponding high scores to counterbalance them [distribution (c)] create negative skew.

For Further Discussion

If someone on your block won several million dollars in the lottery and you wanted to describe the net worth of people in the neighborhood, which measure of central tendency would be best?

This has an academic application. In Alberta, where your author attended elementary and secondary schools, all students in the province took the same government examinations. They were quite rigorous. A classmate of your author's was the only person in the province to score 100 percent on the Grade 12 physics exam. He was extraordinarily talented in things quantitative. In a class of a dozen or so students (it was a very small school), his "off the chart" scores could substantially skew a distribution. What would be the best way to describe the students' scores in that small group? What impact would the outstanding phyics student's scores have if performance were norm-referenced?

Measures of Dispersion

The measures of central tendency are helpful because we always wish to know what is typical of a group, but such statistics tell us very little about the balance of the scores. Measures of dispersion indicate something about how the other data are arrayed.

The simplest measure of dispersion is the **range.** It is simply that number found when we subtract the lowest number in a group from the highest number. If the lowest value in a data set is 13 and the highest is 47, the range is $47 - 13 = 34$. The range tells us

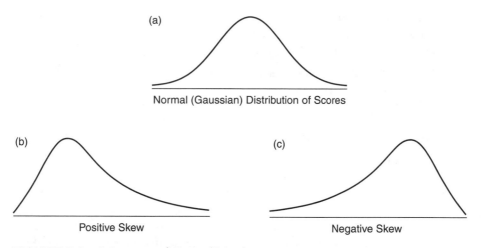

(a)

Normal (Gaussian) Distribution of Scores

(b)

Positive Skew

(c)

Negative Skew

FIGURE 9.3 Measures of Central Tendency

nothing about how many students scored either 13 or 47, or whether they are at all typical of the group. It only tells us what was lowest and highest.

The range can be quite helpful, however. You would probably be curious if a test were given to two groups that you thought were quite similar, and they had very different scoring ranges. If assessment scores represent achievement and the range of scores is different in what ought to be similar groups, something is affecting the range. Perhaps one group has benefited from a topic the teacher inadvertently missed in the other class. This would increase lower scores. Perhaps there is a cheating problem, allowing students to avoid the lower scores. There might be a variety of explanations.

The other common measures of dispersion are the **standard deviation** and the **variance**, two closely related statistics. The variance, which was used in Chapter 7 to calculate reliability for achievement test data, is the square of the standard deviation. Or, said the other way around, the standard deviation is found by taking the square root of the variance. Their notations suggest the relationship between the variance and the standard deviation. Although it varies some from text to text, usually s is the notation for the standard deviation of a sample,[2] and s^2 is the symbol for the variance of a sample. Since one is directly related to the other, and the standard deviation is used more commonly, we will refer primarily to that measure of dispersion.

The standard deviation has utility partly because of the amount of information it contains. Unlike the range, the standard deviation takes into account all of the scores in the distribution. Remember that with all measures of dispersion, we are describing how scores are spread out. Unlike the range, the dispersions of the standard deviation and variance are in reference to the mean of the distribution. As its name suggests, the standard deviation is a measure of the typical deviation from the mean for the scores in the group we are describing.

Perhaps we can grasp the concept of a standard deviation best by thinking in terms of **deviation scores** (Sprinthall, 1997). If you were to take a group of scores, calculate the mean for the group, and then subtract the mean from each of the individual scores, the differences are deviation scores. The typical or standard deviation from the mean is the measure reflected in the standard deviation statistic. The standard deviation is derived by the following procedure:

1. Derive the deviation scores for all scores in the group,
2. Square each deviation score,
3. Sum the squared deviation scores,
4. Divide the sum of squared scores by the number of scores, and
5. Calculate a square root of the result.

This procedure is followed in (a) of Figure 9.4.

Sprinthall (1997) has noted that, although the deviation method of calculating the statistic illustrated in Figure 9.4 helps us understand the concept of standard deviation, it isn't very convenient when working with large groups of numbers. A more useful "calculation formula" is presented in part (b) of the figure. Although its logic is not quite so transparent, it will yield the same answer and is a good deal easier to use with larger groups of data, for example, the 150 students from your seven sections of eighth-grade English. As a footnote, inexpensive hand calculators are available that will calculate standard deviation quickly and painlessly, but however they are derived, it is important that we understand what they mean.

There are several **measures of dispersion,** or *measures of variability,* as they are sometimes called. The most common are the range and the standard deviation. The range indicates the interval between the highest and lowest scores in a group, and provides no information about the other scores. As its name implies, the standard deviation is a measure of how much individual scores typically deviate from the mean of the group. The way standard deviations are calculated, except in small groups, this statistic indicates how much scores in the group generally are distributed, and even where particular proportions of scores fall.

Measures of Association

As previously noted, the statistics we use most often to describe data measure their central tendency and their variability. Because most of the student data we work with are interval data, the respective statistics are most often the mean (central tendency) and the standard deviation (variability or dispersion). Sometimes we need a third statistic. One may suspect, for example, that students' verbal ability is a very good indicator of their academic performance generally. To test this relationship, we need to determine how closely measures of verbal ability and general academic performance are connected. This is the purpose that correlation coefficients serve. They provide a numerical representation of how closely two things covary. When they covary, or co-relate, movement in one is associated with movement in the other.

Correlation coefficients have many uses, but one of the more important is that they allow us to make predictions. Since, as it turns out, verbal ability and grade point average *are* significantly correlated, knowing a student's verbal ability score permits us a better than random chance opportunity to predict what his or her grade averages are likely to be. As the strength of the relationship increases, the precision of the prediction increases correspondingly.[3]

Before we look at the mechanics of calculating correlation coefficients, we should recognize that we can find visual evidence of an association between two variables, and some

FIGURE 9.4   Calculating the Standard Deviation

The scores: 1, 4, 4, 5, 7, 9

(a) The Deviation Method d = the deviation score $(X - M)$

Step 1. Calculate the difference scores (d)
Step 2. Square the difference scores (d^2)
Step 3. Sum the difference scores (Σd^2)
Step 4. Divide the sum by the number of scores $(\frac{\Sigma d^2}{N})$
Step 5. Take the square root of the result

$X - M$	d	d^2
1 − 5 =	−4	16
4 − 5 =	−1	1
4 − 5 =	−1	1
5 − 5 =	0	0
7 − 5 =	2	4
9 − 5 =	4	16
30		38

$$S = \sqrt{\frac{\Sigma d^2}{N}}$$

$$= \sqrt{\frac{38}{6}}$$

$$= 2.52$$

$$M = \Sigma \frac{X}{N} = \frac{30}{6} = 5$$

(b) The Calculation Formula

Step 1. Square each score (x^2)
Step 2. Sum the squares (Σx^2)
Step 3. Divide the sum of squares by the number of scores $(\frac{\Sigma x^2}{N})$
Step 4. Subtract the square of the mean (M^2) from $\frac{\Sigma x^2}{N}$
Step 5. Take the square root of the result

X	X^2
1	1
4	16
4	16
5	25
7	49
9	81
	188

$$S = \sqrt{\frac{\Sigma x^2}{N} - M^2}$$

$$= \sqrt{\frac{188}{6} - 5^2}$$

$$= 2.52$$

indication of the strength of the relationship, in a scatter plot. Figure 9.5 shows three different scatter plots.

The key to understanding scatter plots is to remember that each point in the graph represents the intersection of two separate measures. In scatter plot (a), each point in the graph indicates both the study time and the level of performance for one person. If the relationship is such that, as one variable increases, the other does likewise (as study time increases, so does performance), we have a **positive correlation.** The data points in a scatter plot with a positive correlation will reach from the lower left to the upper right of the graph. There will usually be more data points in the middle of the graph than at either extreme.

If the relationship between two variables is negative, the points range from upper left to lower right. This is the case in plot (b) when the graph represents the relationship between percent of body fat and the individual's quickness in a physical education drill. Other things being equal, as body fat increases, one's quickness declines. This relationship is depicted in plot (b) in Figure 9.5.

Some variables are not correlated—shoe size and intelligence, for example. When there is no correlation between variables, either there is no pattern to the scatter plot, or, for reasons related to normal distributions that we will not bother with here, the many points reflect a circular pattern. An arbitrary scatter is the condition depicted in the third plot (c).

Unless the relationship between the two variables is perfect (a most unlikely occurrence in educational assessment), more than one level of each variable will correspond to a single score in the other variable. In plot (a), imagine a horizontal line from that point on the vertical axis that represents average student performance, through all

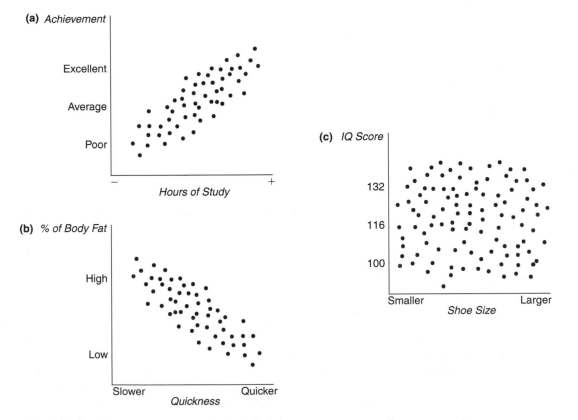

FIGURE 9.5 Visual Representations of Positive, Negative, and Zero Correlations

of the points in the graph to the right. Notice that the line, which is associated with just one level of performance, passes through several data points. This indicates that, for this data set at least, several different amounts of study time can potentially produce this one level of performance. This is true because variables other than study time affect performance, and the scatter plot accounts only for the relationship between the two variables. The extent of the scatter in plot (a) provides visual evidence that the relationship between the two variables, although positive and substantial, is far from perfect.

For Further Discussion

As previously noted, knowing that two characteristics correlate gives us predictive power. Does correlation also suggest a causal relationship? Presume, for example, that we determine that the number of hours students study correlates well with their academic performance.

Does that mean that more hours of study causes higher grades?
Could the relationship be the reverse (high grades motivate some students to study more than they would otherwise)?
Could there be some other variable causing both higher grades and more study time?

Calculating Correlation Coefficients

Producing the correlation coefficient quantifies the strength of the relationship between two variables. Correlation coefficient values can range from −1 to +1. A value of −1 represents a perfect negative relationship between two variables, such as that suggested in plot (b) in Figure 9.5. A coefficient of +1 is portrayed in plot (a). The fact that these relationships are perfect means that there is no "scatter" in either plot. One level of one variable is associated with only one level of the other. Be careful to note, however, that in the positive correlation the increase in one variable is accompanied by increases in the other, and in the negative correlation, as one increases, the other declines.

There are many formulae available for calculating correlation. When the data are interval scale, most of the formulae are derivations of what is called a **Pearson correlation,** named for its author, Karl Pearson. The formula used in Figure 9.6 is a variation of **Pearson's formula** (Sprinthall, 1997).

The data in Figure 9.6 are contrived. They answer the type of question one might ask when interested in the relationship between intelligence and academic performance. In effect one asks, "To what degree are intelligence and grades related?" The $r = .69$ suggests that there *is* a degree of covariation, but it also begs another question about how to interpret the number. Guilford (in Sprinthall, 1997) gave us a subjective guide to the interpretation of correlation coefficients. When the relationship is strong enough that it is not likely to have occurred by chance (that is, it is statistically significant[4]), Guilford suggests the following labels to describe the strength of the correlation:

$r < .20$	the relationship is slight
$r = .2$ to $.39$	low correlation
$r = .4$ to $.69$	moderate correlation
$r = .7$ to $.89$	high correlation
$r \geq .9$	very high correlation

FIGURE 9.6 Calculating Correlation (*r*) for Interval Scale Data

Assume we have intelligence (*x*) and grade point average (*y*) data for 8 students. We can calculate the correlation between the students' intelligence (*x*) and grade point average (*y*) using a variation of Pearson's formula:

$$r = \frac{\frac{\Sigma xy}{N} - (\bar{x})(\bar{y})}{(s_x)(s_y)}$$

where Σxy = the sum of the product of each score pair

$\bar{x}$ = the mean of the *x* variable

$\bar{y}$ = the mean of the *y* variable

s_x = the standard deviation of the *x* variable

s_y = the standard deviation of the *y* variable

N = the number of *pairs* of scores

Use the following data and the formula above to calculate the correlation between *x* and *y*.

Student	x	y	xy
1	95	2.2	209
2	110	2.8	308
3	100	3.0	300
4	110	2.7	297
5	115	3.2	368
6	98	2.0	196
7	112	3.0	336
8	104	1.9	197.6

$$r = \frac{\frac{2211.6}{8} - (105.5)(2.6)}{(6.82)(.46)}$$

$$r = \frac{2.15}{3.14}$$

$$r = .69$$

$\bar{x} = 105.5$ $s_x = 6.82$

$\bar{y} = 2.6$ $s_y = .46$

$\Sigma xy = 2211.6$

Source: The formula appears in Sprinthall (1997).

Perhaps you have noticed that the notation for correlation is the lowercase *r*, and maybe you remember that *r* also is used as notation for test reliability (Chapter 7). This isn't an accidental duplication. There is a natural relationship between test reliability and correlation coefficients. Recall the statement in Chapter 7 that we can gauge the reliability of assessment data by conducting an assessment twice and then comparing the data, as long as we hold the relevant conditions constant. We measure how closely the data from the first test parallel those from the second. In effect, this is a correlation issue. The reliability of the data can be thought of as the degree of correlation between the two sets of scores.

A Correlations Coefficient for Ordinal Data

The correlation formula makes certain assumptions about the nature of the data we are working with. First, the data must reflect at least interval scale measurement; and, second, both distributions of scores must be reasonably close to fitting a normal distribution, which means that if each were arranged in a frequency distribution, it would appear bell-shaped. When either of the assumptions does not hold, we can use another formula, and **Spearman's rho** (ρ) is one of the most common.

Rho is a correlation statistic that requires only ordinal scale data, and the procedure makes no assumption about how the data are distributed. In Figure 9.7 we have the formula for an example problem.

The Spearman formula allows one to quantify the strength of the relationship between two variables when the data are ordinal, or when the data are interval but are not distributed normally. Occasionally the data we collect from our students have different scales. If your students were ranked on some characteristic, say problem-solving ability, and you also had their scores on an algebra test, you could correlate the two sets of scores with rho. The Spearman test requires the data to be ordinal, so you would begin by converting the algebra test scores to rankings, and then correlate the

FIGURE 9.7 **Correlating Ordinal Scale Data**

Assume that you are researching the relationship between class rank and the score on a math test. You can use the formula for Spearman's rho and the sample data in the following table to do this.

Student	Class Rank	Test Score	Test Rank	d	d^2
1	1	37	2	1	1
2	8	28	5.5	2.5	6.25
3	2	43	1	1	1
4	9	25	8.5	.5	.25
5	7	27	7	0	0
6	10	22	10	0	0
7	6	28	5.5	.5	.25
8	3	32	3	0	0
9	4	30	4	0	0
10	5	25	8.5	3.5	12.25
				Total	21.00

Because the class rank is already ordinal, you must (1) rank the test *scores*. Note that there were two test scores of 28, and two of 25. Rank duplicates by adding their places in the score ranking together (5 and 6 for the 28s, 8 and 9 for the 25s), and divide by the number of rankings represented: $5 + 6 = 11$, $11/2 = 5.5$. (2) Determine the difference (d) between the rankings without regard to whether they are positive or negative. (3) Square the difference scores (d^2). (4) Sum the squared differences (Σd^2). (5) Solve for r_s in the formula for Spearman's rho:

$$r_s = 1 - \frac{6\Sigma d^2}{N(N^2 - 1)}$$

$$r_s = 1 - \frac{6(21)}{10(10^2 - 1)}$$

$$r_s = 1 - .13 = .87$$

There are several ways to measure the degree to which variables vary in concert. One of the factors in selecting an approach is the scale of the data. The Pearson correlation is used with data that are interval scale, and which reflect a normal (bell-shaped) distribution. The Spearman formula requires only ordinal (ranked) data and makes no assumption about whether the data are normally distributed.

two sets of ranks. The Spearman coefficient is not difficult to calculate, but it is less precise than the Pearson test, so when we have a choice, we use Pearson's *r*.

CLASSICAL TEST THEORY AND THE STANDARD ERROR OF MEASUREMENT

Some of the issues associated with classical test theory were first raised in Chapter 7, when we considered the distinction between learners' observed scores, which is what we called the scores they received from the test, and their true scores. The distinction between the two is based in this reality: Whenever we assess a characteristic or trait, the score that is assigned to the individual probably obscures the true measure of the characteristic by including some component of error. The expression we used to symbolize this was $x = t + e$, with x symbolizing the observed score, t the true score, and e, error. In most classroom settings, we almost never have direct access to what we wish to measure. Because we must measure indirectly, we have an ever-present potential for measurement error. This brings us to the **standard error of measurement (SEM)**. Calculating the SEM is a method of quantifying the error component contained in a group of scores. You will see that it is related to the standard deviation previously discussed.

As noted before, error emerges because factors other than students' skill level, knowledge, or command of the content affect their test scores. Luck, the environment in which the test is administered, and, in fact, any uncontrolled, random event that affects the assessment outcome contributes to error (Harvill, 1991). Although it seems ironic, test bias is not technically a component of error. This is because bias is systematic rather than a random occurrence. It occurs consistently and that, of course, is the difficulty. Some group is consistently at an advantage or a disadvantage for reasons unrelated to what one is trying to assess. Although test bias does not constitute random error, we certainly take pains to identify it and make the necessary corrections.

Variability and the Standard Error of Measurement

Recall that assessment data reliability increases as the error component of the observed score is minimized. This is logical because the measure of data reliability is repeatability and it is difficult to repeat scores unless the random errors are eliminated. Although elusive, measurement error is not a hypothetical construct. In fact, we can learn something of its magnitude by calculating the standard error of measurement (SEM).

Recall that the standard deviation is a measure of how scores typically deviate from the mean of a group of scores. The SEM is also a measure of variability. It is the standard deviation of all the error components in the scores of those who were administered the test (Harvill, 1991). Classical test theory holds that these random

Technically, the standard error of measurement (SEM) is the standard deviation of the error scores among a group of scores. Because we have no direct access to error scores, we estimate the SEM. Since the SEM is inversely related to data consistency, test reliability values provide an indirect indicator of error. Higher reliability means the error component is relatively small, and so forth.

errors are distributed according to—you guessed it—a bell-shaped curve. The errors that deflate observed scores are counterbalanced in the distribution by those that make the students' scores higher than they ought to be. This makes the mean of the distribution of error scores zero.

Although this may help us to understand the concept of measurement error, it is of little practical value, because we have had no access to the error scores and hence no opportunity to calculate their standard deviation; but help is on the way. The standard error of measurement can be *estimated* with the formula in Figure 9.8.

In words, we calculate it this way: (a) determine the standard deviation of the test scores, (b) calculate the reliability of the test (Chapter 7), (c) take 1 minus the reliability value, (d) calculate the square root of that result, and (e) multiply by the standard deviation.

It has been noted that, as test data become more reliable, the error component is minimized. By inference, this makes reliability a measure of error as well, but the reliability coefficient only suggests the level of error present in a group of scores, and it reflects an average error for that group. It is not helpful for determining how much might be present in the scores of individual test takers.

FIGURE 9.8   Estimating the Standard Error of Measurement

The formula for estimating the standard error of measurement is

$$SEM = S_x\sqrt{(1 - r)}$$

The procedure for estimating this error follows:

Step 1. Determine the standard deviation of the test scores (S_x).
Step 2. Calculate the reliability of the test (r).
Step 3. Take 1 minus the reliability value.
Step 4. Calculate the square root of 1 minus the reliability value.
Step 5. Multiply the squre root by the standard deviation.

Using this procedure and the formula, we can calculate the standard error of measurement for a set of test scores with the following characteristics:

$$standard\ deviation = 4.6$$
$$test\ reliability = .74$$

$$SEM = 4.6\sqrt{1 - .74}$$
$$= 2.35$$

Source: The formula appears in Harvill (1991).

The Standard Error of Measurement and the True Score

Since Chapter 7, from time to time the student's "true score" has been introduced. Although there are limitations on the approach to be taken here (Harvill, 1991) and the conclusion still represents an estimate, calculating the standard error of measurement also allows us to estimate the true score for an individual. Using the concept that error scores are distributed symmetrically, which means that the positive and the negative errors in a group of scores are balanced, we can predict, with a certain level of probability, where an individual's true score will fall. The area is within a range of scores we can define if we use both the observed score and the SEM.

The standard deviation (and remember that the SEM is a standard deviation of error scores) defines proportions of scores that occur under certain areas of the curve in a distribution of scores. For example, in a distribution of scores,

- from −1 to +1 standard deviation includes about 68 percent of the scores in any distribution of scores
- from −2 to +2 standard deviations includes about 95 percent of scores
- from −3 to +3 standard deviations includes about 99 percent of scores

When these are stated as probabilities, we can say that the probability that a score will fall from −1 to +1 standard deviations is $p = .68$. We always know, at least with the help of a table that statistics texts include, what proportion of a group of scores falls between the mean and any particular standard deviation value.

We apply the same logic to identifying true scores. Once the standard error of measurement has been calculated, we can use the student's observed score as the reference and predict with $p = .68$ probability that the student's true score will fall within the range from the observed score minus one SEM to the observed score plus one SEM. Harvill (1991) has explained that there are times when the observed score may not be exactly in the middle of this band. This contingency has to do with whether the student's score is typical of the group or atypical because it is either lower or higher than most others. Although it won't be pursued further here, the concept of identifying true score within a band created by the observed score and the SEM remains a useful tool for recognizing the impact that error may be having on a group of scores. For now, note that a large calculated SEM indicates a substantial error component—which means that we could not have the confidence in the students' scores possible if the SEM were smaller.

Some Limitations in Classical Test Theory

One of classical test theory's characteristics is that since the true score and the standard error of measurement are both calculated from the students' scores, it is most likely that they are accurate only for that particular test. One might well find that both measures vary from test to test, even when the different tests deal with the same content. Simply put, the way we calculated true score and the standard error of measurement makes them both test dependent.

There is another problem. The way we approached the standard error of measurement means it has the same value for all learners—from those who score at the lowest levels and have the poorest command of the material to those who have mastered the content. In the *Speaking of Assessment* box, reasons are suggested for why that approach might be deceptive.

Speaking of Assessment

Set aside their scores for a minute and think in terms of two students in the same class. One of them is very attentive and prepares very carefully for every assessment. The other is perennially the low achiever who is easily distracted from the subject, fails to study for the tests, and guesses wildly on multiple-choice test items. By definition, luck is random, and is therefore one potential source of measurement error. Does it not seem likely that luck will have a different impact on the scores of these two students? If one of them is feeling sick during the assessment, that may influence the one student's performance but have no impact on the other. The way the standard error of measurement is calculated, however, individual students' errors become part of a "pooled error" component that is applied equally to all who take the test. Each student's errors help define the other students' errors and, consequently, also the other students' true scores. Some errors do affect an entire group of students, but an error in the scoring key or a problem with a biased item are examples of the nonrandom errors that the SEM does not include. The SEM is a great help when we are trying to determine how precisely we have measured a characteristic, but one should know something about how it is derived.

> The SEM is a standard error of measurement. One measure of error is applied equally to all in the group. The truth is that, like any average, it will overestimate error for some students and underestimate for others.

Let's consider another dimension to the problem. If you administered a conventional paper and pencil test made up of several multiple-choice items, you could calculate a difficulty index for each (the p values that we spoke of in Chapter 7). The indices (or indexes) provided a measure of the probability that a student selected randomly from the group who took the test would score the particular item correctly. Reviewing the difficulty indices will illustrate what you already know: Some items are more difficult to score correctly than others. However, if each item carries the same score value, say one point for a correct response and zero for an incorrect answer, under conventional scoring procedures, two students may have identical scores on a test but have a very different grasp of the material. If we really wanted to understand students' performances, we might be concerned about *which* items they scored correctly and which they missed, rather than just how many.

Item Response Theory: An Alternative to Classical Test Theory

One reaction to these difficulties is represented in **item response theory (IRT)** or **latent trait theory.** Classroom teachers do not employ IRT in the design of their own tests. It is simply too complicated and time consuming, but it has become increasingly common as a foundation for standardized testing. For example, the Comprehensive Test of Basic Skills, which is administered so commonly to elementary school students in the United States, is based on IRT (Mehrens and Lehman, 1987). There is a minimal treatment of item response theory in Chapter 13, but "the nickel tour" is appropiate here.[5]

According to item response theory, students are able to answer a test item correctly because they possess a sufficient quantity of whatever trait or characteristic the item assesses. In conventional assessment, we may draw a similar conclusion, but it is usually based on how many items one scores correctly, rather than which. In conventional testing, we pay relatively little attention to item-to-item differences. With IRT systems, however, it is important to know what each item measures and how much of the underlying trait one must possess in order to score the item correctly. Therefore, each item must be analyzed, or scaled. Two students who scored the same number of items correctly might receive quite different scores if their respective correct answers were on items with different scale values.

Note the difference between determining how much reasoning ability someone possesses, on the one hand, and what percentage or what number of questions the student scored correctly on the other. If we measure the quantity of some underlying (latent) trait the student possesses, we have measured a characteristic that transcends the test. This represents one of the most important advantages related to IRT. The results are not dependent upon a particular instrument. With testing based on classical test theory, the student's standard error of measurement and true score are test specific (Hambleton and Jones, 1993).

Speaking of Assessment

If a crude analogy is helpful, think of the difference between IRT procedures and conventional assessment this way: We wish to measure someone's weight, and we have an accurate bathroom scale as well as several rocks of carefully graduated sizes. The bathroom scale represents IRT procedures; the series of rocks, conventional testing. In either case, we can derive a measure—perhaps a very precise one. With the scale, the result (115 pounds) has meaning beyond the context of this specific scale. However, the measure associated with rocks (4 large rocks, 3 middle-size rocks, and 2 very small rocks) is specific to them; it does not translate well into another setting.

As anyone who is familiar with classroom activities knows, there is a great deal of variability in the way students respond to academic tasks. If, like so many experts, we conclude that students perform differently because they possess different levels of such underlying traits as verbal ability, analytical ability, and the like, IRT gives us a better view of the student's performance than conventional testing. On conventional tests, there is, typically, no distinction drawn between very easy and very difficult items, which may make the total scores inaccurate indicators of the student's performance and ability.

Measurement systems that focus on item difficulty offer another advantage. The typical instructional pattern is to begin a new topic with comparatively simple concepts and increase the degree of difficulty as we proceed. Standardized tests based on IRT tend to follow the same procedure (Shermis and Chang, 1997). The less difficult items come first. This means that curriculum is aligned with assessment, even when each is developed independently of the other.

MEASUREMENT ERROR AND TEST BIAS

A passing reference was made to test bias a little earlier, and it is a major topic in Chapter 12, on ethics in assessment, but some comment is appropiate here as well. As a statistical term, *bias* indicates the presence of *systematic* error in a set of scores (Scheuneman and Slaughter, 1991). This is in contrast to the *random* error previously quantified in estimating the standard error of measurement. Because there are so many extraneous factors that can affect assessment scores, we will probably always have some level of random error when we measure cognitive abilities. Systematic error is not inevitable, however, and anyone who conducts assessments has a responsibility to watch for bias and make the necessary corrections when it emerges.

In the discussion of classical test theory, we considered the true score. At least theoretically, we could derive a student's true score by averaging the scores from repeated administrations of the same test, assuming that testing conditions remain constant (still a most unlikely assumption, but yet another point is needed). You will recall that because random errors are normally distributed, over repeated administrations they factor each other out. The errors that inflate observed scores and those that deflate them sum to zero, but this is not true for systematic errors. If there is a bias problem and test scores systematically err in either direction, the average of all scores cannot be the true score.

A similar logic holds for groups of learners. Rather than administering the test repeatedly, one might gather a sample from a defined population that is large enough to represent the characteristics of that population, and then average all of their individual scores as an estimate of the true score for the group. If the group's average systematically under- or overestimates the average true score, the test is biased.

What complicates the discussion is that group differences are not, by themselves, an indicator of bias since there may

---

Item response theory assumes that there are latent traits such as verbal ability, problem-solving ability, and so forth underlying one's ability to respond correctly to test items. IRT procedures establish how much of a characteristic one must possess in order to score the item correctly. The scaling results in a differential weighting of each item and scores that is not specific to the particular items or test. In testing based on classical test theory, results (the standard error of measurement, the true score) are specific to the instrument.

The standard error of measurement is a measure of random error. The randomness allows us to assume that, among a group of students, those errors will sum to zero. The deflating errors are cancelled out by the inflating errors. Bias is also error, but it is nonrandom and the positive errors and negative error do not cancel each other out. Bias is a systematic over- or underestimation for all members of a particular group.

be actual differences in average ability levels between the groups. Scheuneman and Slaughter (1991) were addressing this issue when they observed:

> *Some critics of testing have asserted that the performance of two groups in an unbiased test should be identical, but this argument assumes the true score means of the two groups are the same, an assumption that is often not warranted in the light of other evidence. (p. 17)*

If there are differences in groups' true scores, one cannot detect bias simply by comparing the mean of the groups' observed scores. There are other approaches, however. Recall that according to IRT, candidates of equal ability should have an equal probability of a correct score on a particular item, regardless of ethnic, gender, or cultural differences, or the social class they happen to belong to. Actually we can extend this position to any sort of assessment. If two candidates have an equal grasp of the learning material, they should have an equal probability of scoring any individual item correctly. We can apply this to a total test score. If the test is constructed well and testing conditions are equivalent, people of equal ability and learning should receive equivalent scores. The difficulty, of course, is in equating the ability and learning of two individuals or two distinct groups because, if ability is equivalent but learning opportunities are not, scores are likely to vary.

Differences charged to bias may reflect a variety of factors not related to bias at all. Besides potential differences in ability, there might be differences in the quality of the earlier instruction, level of parental support, or availability of relevant resources, or a host of other factors. The term used to describe item performance differences that do not constitute bias is differential item functioning (DIF). DIF is a more appropriate description of what is occurring when it is clear that there are group differences but they are unrelated to the quality of the test item (see Walstad and Robson, 1997, for example).

If one intends to explain that performance differences are unrelated to bias, it is not enough to suggest that there are other sources of the scoring variability. One must try to locate the source of the differences. Perhaps you teach the seventh grade in an intermediate school that is fed by several different primary schools. Reviewing the scores from a particular test that includes an essay item may reveal that not all students did equally well, and that those who came from an inner-city school, who are also largely ethnic minority students, did least well. Rather than rushing to a judgment of testing bias, it might be helpful to research the English curricula followed in each of the feeder schools. It might also be helpful to know how much writing was asked of students in subjects other than English.

> Sometimes there are different levels of performance that do not reflect bias. If students from distinct groups perform differently on particular items because they have varying levels of command of the subject matter, we speak of differential item functioning (DIF).

We are not suggesting that one discount the possibility of bias. If the essay question requires that students write a description of their last experience "surfing the (Inter)net," those who respond least well may be those without computers, or those living in homes where there is hardware, but no Internet access. In those instances the item is biased against the children coming from the poorer homes.

Sometimes in the attempt to reach students on the academic periphery, we design test items around something interesting to them. However, if we construct items using sports language, for example, the item may be biased against those unfamiliar with sports.

A CLOSER LOOK AT WHAT WE'RE ASSESSING: FACTOR ANALYSIS

Item response theory presumes that we know which characteristic or trait a test item measures, and yet we have said very little about how that might be determined. Anyone with expertise in a content area can make a judgment, of course, but ordinarily we want a procedure that is more objective and perhaps a little more precise. This brings us to factor analysis, a procedure that does not identify traits as such, but makes it easier for us to do so.

Factor analysis will indicate, for example, whether all of the items on a test appear to measure the same characteristic, or whether there are multiple characteristics. Alternatively, if we have scores from multiple tests, we can determine whether all of the tests measure the same—or multiple—characteristics. To pursue the second example for a moment, we might review eighth-grade students' scores on five different kinds of math tests:

> a test of computation ability that the instructor developed (C)
> a mathematical reasoning test included with the textbook (R)
> a standardized test of problem-solving ability (P)
> a standardized introductory algebra test (A)
> a teacher-developed geometry test (G)

Having reviewed data from the instruments and in spite of what the tests are called, one might become suspicious that they actually reflect fewer than five different traits, or factors. A first step in factor analysis is to determine the level of correlation between pairs of scores. If scores covary they may both be measures of the same characteristic. If that is so, some of the assessment is redundant. If it is not so, then each of the tests has an independent value because it contributes information that none of the other tests includes. An easy way to visualize the association between sets of scores is with a correlation matrix such as that in Figure 9.9.

The scores from the tests are all correlated, which is not surprising since they are all math related, but the relationships between some are much stronger than for others. Note that the boldfaced correlation coefficients are all above .8. According to the Guilford criteria cited earlier (Sprinthall, 1997), those are "high" correlations. They suggest that each of those tests is measuring a mathematical characteristic, or "factor," also common to the others. The computation and geometry tests provide a measurement component that is unique to each, but there is a good deal of measurement duplication among the reasoning, problem-solving, and introductory algebra tests. It may not be practical to use all three. In summary, instead of five separate traits or factors, these five tests may yield only three.

We could do the same thing with data from one test. Analyzing learners' responses on all of the test items might reveal that data from several items are so closely related

FIGURE 9.9   A Correlation Matrix for Five Math Tests

C is the test of computation ability
R is the math reasoning test
P is the standardized test of problem-solving ability
A is the standardized introductory algebra test
G is the teacher-developed geometry test

	C	R	P	A	G
C		.59	.61	.55	.56
R			**.85**	**.87**	.61
P				**.86**	.64
A					.61
G					

Note: The correlation data in this matrix are contrived.

that we suspect that they measure the same characteristic. If that is so, perhaps we can abbreviate the test by diminishing the quality of the assessment.

As objective as correlation coefficients are, there is a subjective element to factor analysis. It does not name the measured characteristic. That is up to the person performing the analysis. One might review the items on the reasoning, problem-solving, and introductory algebra tests and decide that the common element is reasoning ability, but there really is no way to verify the accuracy of the judgment. All we really know is that, whatever the characteristic is, it is common to all three tests.

There is much more to factor analysis than correlation matrices. The procedure is so complex that, before computers were common, only the most determined researchers pursued it. Factor analysis is very helpful, however, because although the procedure does not name traits, it provides the sort of information that allows one to make a reasonably well-informed judgment about the nature of the trait. This makes it very helpful in item response theory and other areas of test construction.

SUMMARY

Data classification and description are important parts of assessment. The ability to be accurate and precise is probably reason enough to deal with the scaling issues and the discussion of descriptive statistics presented early in the chapter. There is more than clear communication at stake, however. An effective educator must be a capable assessor, and the questions we can ask and the answers we derive depend at least to some degree upon the nature of the data. We measure a variety of different characteristics. Some of them reflect nominal data and must be summarized in terms very different from the questions regarding students' analytical ability, which usually involve interval data.

Some discussions that have been undertaken—such as those of measures of central tendency, dispersion, and association—show up more often in statistics texts than in assessment books. Remember, however, that the lines we draw between disciplines often define convenience as much as they suggest natural relationships. In this case, descriptive statistics serve a variety of important classroom assessment purposes, and, in fact, the concepts will be fundamental to some of the discussion of standardized testing, to be taken up in the next chapter. But whether one is conducting standardized testing, it is a great advantage to have some systematic way to describe what is typical of a data set, how variable data tend to be, and how strong the relationship is when data are correlated.

Some of the topics dealt with here technically go beyond the scope of an introductory assessment textbook, but they are important enough to warrant some mention. The discussion of item response theory is usually reserved for more advanced courses, but so much of current testing practice utilizes IRT that perhaps the exposure will let us be conversant with the theory on something of a conceptual level, at least. A similar argument might be made for raising the issue of error, and the standard error of measurement. Most readers will not have occasion to calculate the standard error of measurement, but there is considerable value to a concept that reminds us that, when we measure unobservable characteristics, there is an ever-present opportunity for error. In the beginning of the chapter, Ms. Nielson recognized this, as would most of you, but she did not know how to pursue the issue of error in measurement. We are now in a position to understand how it is quantified. We can also distinguish random errors from the systematic errors that we classify as testing bias.

Much of the discussion about assessing students' performances assumes that we have a clear fix on what we are measuring. Without wishing to belabor the point, there may be a substantial difference between what we intended to measure and what the scores actually represent. That was the point of introducing factor analysis. Most educators will not conduct the procedure, but it is important to recognize that, although there may still be some guessing involved in identifying the characteristics, we can at least determine how many characteristics we are measuring.

ENDNOTES

1. By the way, if you are looking for a mnemonic device to help you remember the scales in order, you can make your first-year French useful. The first letter of each scale makes up the French word for black, "noir."
2. Statisticians are obliged to distinguish between the characteristics of samples and those of the populations from which samples are drawn. A population is all subjects that fall within a defined group. "All women," "all 12-year-olds," and "Hispanic elementary school children" each define particular populations. In statistical notation, the characteristics, or parameters, of populations are signified by Greek letters. The Greek letter mu (μ) is the sign for the mean of the population, and the standard deviation is indicated by the Greek letter sigma (σ). Samples are subsets of populations, and their characteristics are designated by statistics such as x with the bar over it $(\bar{x})$, the M we use for the mean, and the s or SD used to designate the standard deviation of the sample.
3. The business of predicting one variable from the other brings us to regression analysis. Although beyond the scope of this book, it is a statistical technique employing correlation coefficients to make predictions from one or a set of variables that are known to a variable whose specific value is unknown, although its relationship to the predictor variable(s) has been established. If it is known, for example, that there is a significant correlation between the scores on two different tests, knowing the score a student received on the first will allow one to predict what the value of the second

score would be, even in the absence of the second score. When the relationship between the variables is strong, the prediction can be quite accurate. When the relationship is weak, the prediction, although discrete, includes a larger amount of error.

4. Statistical significance is a function of both the size of the correlation coefficient and the number of pairs of data involved in the analysis. As the number of pairs increases, the size of the coefficient needed to assume that the relationship is not a chance occurrence diminishes. Statistics textbooks provide tables that indicate the point at which a coefficient is statistically significant.

5. For those interested in the origins of item response, or latent trait theory, the formative work was done in a series of important works by Lord, beginning in 1953, and later in work that he completed with Novick. Note the suggestion in "For Further Reading."

FOR FURTHER READING

There are several good statistics textbooks written in nonthreatening language. Sprinthall (1997), for example, places more emphasis on students' ability to reason than on their mathematics background.

For those wishing a primer in measurement theory, including both classical test theory and item response theory, Allen and Yen (1979) is something of a classic. An article by Lord (1953) and a book by Lord and Novick (1968) trace the origins of item response theory. Both require a better-than-average foundation in statistics and psychological measurement.

REFERENCES

Allen, M. J., and Yen, W. M. (1979). *Introduction to measurement theory.* Monterey, CA: Brooks/Cole.

Hambleton, R. K., and Jones, R. W. (1993). Comparison of classical test theory and item response theory and their applications to test development. *Educational Measurement: Issues and Practice, 12*(3), 38–47.

Harvill, L. M. (1991). Standard error of measurement. *Educational Measurement: Issues and Practice, 10*(2), 33–41.

Kurtz, N. R. (1999). *Statistical analysis for the social sciences.* Boston: Allyn & Bacon.

Lord, F. M. (1953). The relation of test score to the trait underlying the test. *Educational and Psychological Measurement, 13,* 517–548.

Lord, F. M., and Novick, M. R. (1968). *Statistical theories of mental test scores.* Reading, MA: Addison-Wesley.

Mehrens, W. A., and Lehman, I. J. (1987). *Using standardized tests in education* (4th ed.). New York: Longman.

Scheuneman, J. D., and Slaughter, C. (1991). *Issues of test bias, item bias, and group differences and what to do while waiting for the answers.* (ERIC Document Reproduction Service No. ED 400 294)

Shermis, M. D., and Chang, S. H. (1997). The use of item response theory (IRT) to investigate the hierarchical nature of a college mathematics curriculum. *Educational and Psychological Measurement, 57,* 450–458.

Sprinthall, R. C. (1997). *Basic statistical analysis* (5th ed.). Boston: Allyn & Bacon.

Walstad, W. B., and Robson, D. (1997). Differential item functioning and male-female differences on multiple-choice tests in economics. *Journal of Economic Education, 28*(2), 155–171.

Understanding Standardized Tests

■ *The reader will analyze the purposes and assumptions for which standardized tests are developed and administered and become conversant with the more common terms employed when discussing standardized test data.*

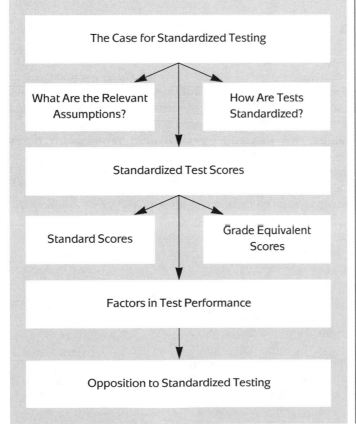

The Case for Standardized Testing

What Are the Relevant Assumptions?

How Are Tests Standardized?

Standardized Test Scores

Standard Scores

Grade Equivalent Scores

Factors in Test Performance

Opposition to Standardized Testing

Standardized testing is an efficient mechanism for assessing large numbers of people from different backgrounds and learning circumstances, which is why the tests have become so pervasive in the schools. Standardized testing involves a set of assumptions that critics challenge quite openly, and the tests employ scores and a scoring language that is unique to this form of assessment. ■

In the smaller towns, there are generally only a few people available who are willing, and qualified, to substitute in the schools. As a result, those few tend to have a variety of different assignments and develop a perspective that is probably more informative than what occurs for most other observers of education. As a substitute, Mrs. Hindley watched the students as they worked their separate ways through the history section of the Stanford Achievement Test. This test wasn't new, and the practice of administering standardized tests was certainly not novel, but the tests seemed to have a higher profile than she remembered in past years, and their influence appeared to cut across grade levels. She remembered a time when such tests were administered once or twice in a year, and then largely forgotten for the balance of the term. In contrast, Mrs. Hindley knew the results from these tests would be scrutinized carefully and judgments made about student progress, teaching quality, and curricular effectiveness. Furthermore, the classroom teachers would probably be called upon to do part of the explaining. If Mrs. Hindley faced a curious parent in a parent-teacher conference, she wondered whether she would be able to explain the data. ■

THE CASE FOR STANDARDIZED TESTING

Probably everyone associated with formal education acknowledges that test use is more prevalent than ever. There are likely many reasons why this is so and, without defending or criticizing the wider application, we need to explore it. Mrs. Hindley's situation is not isolated. All elementary and secondary school educators encounter standardized test data from time to time, and classroom teachers generally are much more involved in the administration of the tests than they once were. They are far more likely to be called upon to explain the tests and the results to a variety of audiences. If we become acquainted with some of the concepts and language most commonly associated with standardized testing, we are in a stronger position to explain to others when we are asked.

In simple terms, the purpose of standardized testing is to allow one to assess the performance of large numbers of people from a variety of dissimilar backgrounds on some common trait or characteristic. The prevalence of the tests in current practice has at least something to do with how well they serve these purposes. Standardized tests are generally more convenient, require less time, and are less expensive than most assessment alternatives.

Because they provide information relatively efficiently, standardized tests often help us solve difficult problems, a point we can illustrate with a historical example. For most of the major nations, World War I began in 1914. The United States was an exception, not formally entering the conflict until 1917. There was a great urgency to classify men quickly. The numbers involved made it a monumental problem for those whose responsibility it was to make the judgments. Who among them should be trained for leadership? Who had the aptitude for wireless communication? Which recruits could be taught to calculate ballistics tables?

Developers working for the army created two standardized tests—Army Alpha and Army Beta—that allowed users to scrutinize large numbers of inductees quickly and make reasonably good judgments about which had the aptitude to perform the different tasks. As a result, American participation in the war effort came sooner than it would have otherwise. As it turns out, these tests were two of the earliest group-administered intelligence measures.

Classroom teachers have almost no involvement with intelligence testing, but the point is that standardized tests allow one to make informed decisions about large numbers of test takers from dissimilar backgrounds. We use other standardized tests for the same purposes.

"Standardizing" a Test

At the heart of standardized testing lies the ability to draw comparisons and arrive at meaningful conclusions, even when test takers' experiences and circumstances differ. The reason we can have a common interpretation of scores from test takers in Shelby, Montana, and Rockville, Maryland, is that we know that the same administration and data-interpretation procedures were employed in both settings. To state it differently, the conditions under which the test is administered and interpreted are standard for all test takers. They all hear the same instructions (usually because they are read), they all work under the same time limitations, and all test takers have access to the same tools and materials during the test.

Standardized tests may be designed for group or for individual administration. When tests are individually administered, as many intelligence measures are, standardization extends even to the voice tone and facial expression characteristics that the administrators must control, lest their reactions guide respondents' choices.

Scoring procedures are also uniform. Although they are not exclusive, selected response test items and particularly multiple-choice items predominate in standardized testing. This is primarily because they allow one to present larger numbers of items than the most logical alternatives, and they lend themselves to reliable scoring. When scoring procedures are consistent, one can exclude scoring procedure as a factor in score differences. Remember that part of the task is to conduct the assessment so that scoring variability reflects only differences among test takers in the measured characteristic.

Some standardized tests have no predetermined pass or fail point by which to gauge the student's score, but are norm-referenced instead. This is usually the case with psychological measures, but it is not uncommon for the scores from achievement tests to be interpreted in terms of what is typical of the group. In this instance, we need norms suggesting the score

Standardized tests derive their name from assessment that makes the procedures for administering and scoring a test standard for all test takers. All who are administered the tests hear the same instructions, work under the same time limitations, and have access to the same tools and materials during the test. The procedures for scoring the test and interpreting the data must also be standard. Often (although certainly not always), those who construct standardized tests elect to use multiple-choice test items in order to minimize the scoring reliability problems.

that one might expect for students of a particular age group, or the amount of time that students typically need to complete the assessment task.

The Assumptions Associated with Standardized Testing

One of the conclusions implicit in the use of standardized tests is that they measure what they claim to measure. This issue appeared in Chapters 7 and 8 as one of construct validity. It emerges when someone administers a standardized reading comprehension test and we wonder whether we are measuring reading comprehension, or the learner's memorization ability, test-wiseness, or something else. To compound the problem, sometimes a statement about what a test is intended to measure is not very helpful because the construct itself is unclear. A test booklet that proclaims that the test is one of "mathematical ability," for example, might mean a variety of things, not all of them synonymous. We might be speaking of a variety of abilities, including perhaps calculation, analysis, problem solving, or critical thinking. A reputable test will include very clear information about what the test measures.

We expect standardized tests to provide data that reflect measurement without bias. Remember that bias occurs when there is systematic error in the assessment such that someone or some group is consistently at an advantage or a disadvantage, for reasons unrelated to what the instrument is intended to measure. The evidence for bias is that test data provide different levels of predictive validity for different groups or individuals. A college admissions test, for example, should predict future college performance equally well for everyone who takes the test. The data must indicate those who will do well in college and those who are likely to struggle. This issue is a particularly knotty problem because there was at least a historical effort to adjust tests so that the differences in the groups' scores disappear—even without compelling evidence that the differences reflect a biased assessment. If the differences actually reflect differences in the quality measured, the effect of manipulating them to reduce the differences will be to diminish their predictive validity and, as a consequence, the value of the scores as predictors.

Particularly with standardized achievement tests, one must be able to assume that the instrument will produce data with adequate content validity. A standardized test of writing ability for eighth-grade students ordinarily must provide an opportunity to evaluate several components. The students' spelling, their grasp of grammatical rules, their understanding of sentence and paragraph structure, and their skill with vocabulary are all components of verbal ability. A test intended to provide a measure of verbal ability that deals exclusively with spelling falls far short of representing the length and breadth of the entire content area. It lacks content validity.

Remember that each of the different validity questions assumes that the data are reliable. However it is construed, we must have some assurance that when an informed scorer makes a judgment, others with a similar background will draw the same conclusion. As your author noted earlier, this explains part of the appeal of multiple-choice items. Several people scoring the items independently will usually come to the same conclusion. As you know, however, reliability is more than scoring reliability. It is also a quality in the assessment reflected in the fact that test takers respond the same way each time unless there is a change in the characteristics assessed. If we measure the tendency to be impulsive, we need to be able to assume that the score for a particular student will be the same if we measure a second time and the student's tendency to act suddenly or impetuously has not changed in the meantime.

For Further Discussion

It is generally easier to establish the reliability of psychological measures than it is for achievement measures. You already know that reliability is consistency or repeatability. Why do you think that it is easier to demonstrate reliability for something such as impulsive behavior or anxiety than it is for reading comprehension or one's grasp of history? (The key is in which characteristics are most likely to change over the short term.)

Finally, we assume that there is a certain level of expertise associated with understanding and explaining standardized tests, and that those whose task this is understand the tests well enough to explain their output. Perhaps because the tests have become so common, we no longer give much thought to them, but Scheuneman and Slaughter (1991) have made an observation that contains an implicit warning:

> In our society, we do not let individuals drive our streets without a permit or license; one cannot become a doctor without rigorous training; and yet thousands of individuals . . . spend some of their time using test scores to help make decisions about individuals' lives without ever being required to read about the test and its uses or take a course in statistics, or tests and measurement. (p. 23)

Considering the gravity of the decisions made with standardized test data, classroom teachers should at least be able to explain them. They are rarely the sole criterion in any important judgment about a learner, but they are increasingly a major information source, and those who use them owe a certain level of expertise.

The Focus of Standardized Tests

Standardized tests are ordinarily used to help us measure broad characteristics (such as verbal or math ability, analogical reasoning, critical thinking), rather than the more specific objectives around which we might plan a particular day's instruction. This serves at least two purposes. From a marketing point of view, of course, it allows test developers to prepare an instrument with broad appeal. They need not be overly concerned about what might occur in a particular school or district. The more important purpose from our point of view, however, has to do with the conclusions we can draw. Broader assessments allow us to measure characteristics that will not be unduly sensitive to the inevitable, minor differences in curriculum and experience that occur from place to place. Consequently, we can make comparisons and judgments about performance and educational progress across several different groups.

The judgments that attract the most attention are those associated with what is called high-stakes testing. The prominence of this type of testing reflects a confluence of several different interests, but none of it would exist if the relevant standardized tests were not available. They have made it possible to include data from those tests in decisions about whether students will graduate, be certified, receive scholarships, and so on. Standardized tests are an integral part of the most important academic and occupational decision making.

Because their profile is so high, the tests receive very close scrutiny, and their assumptions are sometimes challenged. The assumptions were stated above, but particularly those who are critical of test use often do not accept them.

Although it is not universal, remember that one conducts much of the standardized testing in order to compare test takers to other test takers, individuals to groups of test takers, and groups' performances to other groups'. This depends upon data in a format that has meaning beyond the particular group or student from which it is drawn, and this requirement brings us to the discussion of scores.

STANDARDIZED TEST SCORES

Beyond the fact that scores from standardized testing are typically norm-referenced, note that there are several different kinds of scores reported. A variety of formats are employed, depending upon the primary use anticipated for the data. Knowing how the different scores are derived will help us understand the logic behind each score and also suggest how the scores might be helpful.

Standard Scores

There are several different kinds of scores referred to as "standard scores." **Standard scores** fit a distribution of scores whose characteristics are known and are fixed. As a consequence, one can interpret scores in a way that is unaffected by the particular test or by the testing circumstances. The nature of the scores is such that, whatever the test, one knows immediately whether a particular score is typical of others who took the test—whether it is higher or lower, and what the magnitude of the difference is.

The z Distribution

Remember that in Chapter 9 we were introduced to the mean as a measure of central tendency and the standard deviation as a measure of how much data vary from the mean. When a group of raw scores is transformed into a z distribution, they are recalculated to fit a distribution in which the mean is equal to 0 and the standard deviation is 1. Transforming raw data into z scores, or the T scores that we'll discuss next, does not alter the shape of the distribution of scores. Although the topic won't be pursued here, one can normalize z and T scores, in which case, whatever the shape and characteristics of the original distribution, the transformed distribution takes on the familiar bell-shaped character. This unimodal (one highest point), symmetrical shape reflects the distribution of many characteristics in large groups. There are many different kinds of normal distributions. However, a mean of 0 and the standard deviation of 1 create what is called a **standard normal distribution,** of which there is only one. Figure 10.1(a) represents the standard normal distribution.

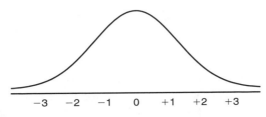

(a) Calculating a *z* score

A group of scores have a mean of 37.5 and a standard deviation of 4.35. What is the *z* score for a student who scores 43?

$$z = \frac{x - m}{s} = \frac{43 - 37.5}{4.35} = \frac{5.5}{4.35} = 1.26$$

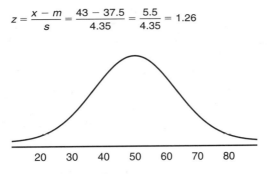

(b) Calculating a *T* score

For the group described above, and individual scores 30. What is the equivalent *T* score?

$$z = \frac{x - m}{s} = \frac{30 - 37.5}{4.35} = \frac{-7.5}{4.35} = -1.72$$

$$T = (z \times 10) + 50 = (-1.72 \times 10) + 50 = -17.2 + 50 = 32.8$$

FIGURE 10.1   Examples of the *z* and *T* Distributions

The formula for transforming raw scores into *z* scores is as follows:

$$z = \frac{x - m}{s}$$

where *z* = the standard score
  x = the individual's score
  m = the mean for the group
  s = the standard deviation of the group's scores

In words, one student's *z* score is derived by taking the test average away from the individual's test score, and then dividing the difference by the standard deviation for all scores in the group. (It may be helpful to review the Chapter 9 discussion of the standard deviation and the mean.) By virtue of this transformation, the group mean takes on a score of 0. Individuals scoring above the mean will have positive scores, and scores below the mean are negative. The individual scores are reported in units of standard deviation. Someone with a *z* score of 1.0 has scored 1 standard deviation above the mean, and another test taker with a score of −.5 has scored half a standard deviation below the mean. Figure 10.1(a) provides an example of calculating a *z* score.

The *z* score of 1.26 indicates that the particular individual scored 1.26 standard deviations beyond the mean. Part of the value of *z* scores is that besides the distance of a single score from the mean, they can suggest something about the distribution of the other scores, at least when the group sizes are comparatively large. Recall that the normal distribution is such that a particular number of standard deviations from the mean always identifies a specific proportion of the total distribution of scores. One standard deviation beyond the mean denotes an area between the mean and that point that includes 34 percent of those in the total distribution. Plus *and* minus 1 standard deviation involves the middle 68 percent of the distribution (2 × 34), and so on. Statistics textbooks always contain a table, generally with a title such as "Area Under the Normal Curve," that will indicate, for the different *z* scores, the proportion of the distribution included between the particular score and the mean of the distribution. As it turns out, the area between the mean and the *z* score of 1.26 marks the point that includes about 40 percent of the distribution. If you add in the half of the distribution below the mean, we can now say that the test taker with a score of 43 scored beyond about 90 percent of those in the group.

> The *z* score is a standard score. In the distribution of scores that result from a *z* transformation, the mean of the distribution is 0 and the standard deviation is 1. The *z* score reports raw scores in units of standard deviation from the mean, with positive scores beyond the mean and negative scores below.

The T Distribution

By definition, half the scores in the *z* distribution are negative—those below the mean, of course, since the mean is 0. Because negative scores tend to have a connotation that one may not wish to convey (after all, half the scores *must* fall below the mean), a variation of the *z* transformation called a *T* score was developed. The distribution of *T* scores has an appearance identical to the *z* distribution (and, therefore, the original distribution of raw scores). The differences are that the mean of the *T* distribution is 50 and the standard deviation is 10. This creates a situation in which all except the most extreme of low scores[1] are positive.

> The *T* transformation alters raw scores in the same manner as the *z* transformation except that the distribution has a mean of 50 and a standard deviation of 10. A *T* score of 40, for example, represents a raw score one standard deviation below the mean.

The easiest way to calculate *T* scores is to complete the *z* transformation first, and then use the *z* score to determine the *T* score as follows:

$$T = (z \times 10) + 50$$

Stated verbally, the *T* score is the *z* score times 10 (the standard deviation of the *T* distribution), plus 50 (the mean of the *z* distribution). Figure 10.1(b) demonstrates the calculation of a *T* score (see p. 255).

Comparing Dissimilar Tests

The *z* and *T* scores are simple transformations that make it possible to restate raw test scores in terms that communicate more clearly. Without changing the scoring distribution, z and T scores recalibrate scores according to predictable dimensions. In the case of the z distribution, they have a mean of 0 and a standard deviation of 1, and for a T distribution scores have a mean of 50 and a standard deviation of 10. After the transformation, it makes no difference whether the range of raw scores was 40 or 400, nor does it matter whether the mean was 38 or 104.5. Whatever their original characteristics, scores from very dissimilar tests have common dimensions after a z or T transformation.

Besides providing a ready ranking of scores, standard scores make it a simple matter to compare scores from different tests, even when they have different ranges and different levels of difficulty. Perhaps you have data on the analytical ability and on the reading comprehension of your seventh-grade students. In the interest of analyzing students' different relative strengths, you wish to compare their scores on these two dissimilar tests. The problem is that the tests each have very different characteristics. We can resolve this by calculating a standard score (either a z or T) for the individuals' performance on both tests. We can then compare the two scores directly and determine whether a particular student has better reading comprehension or analytical ability. In Figure 10.2 we calculate a z score, but the interpretation is no different for a T score.

When we calculate standard scores such as the z and T, we can tell at a glance how the individual's performance compares to that of the group, and we can make direct comparisons between different tests. We must have access to the test mean and

---

FIGURE 10.2   Using Standard Scores to Compare Data from Dissimilar Tests

We have data from tests of analytical ability and reading comprehension and wish to know on which test the student performed best.

Step 1. Gather the relevant data.

	Test Mean	Standard Deviation	Individual's Raw Score
Analytical Ability	73.45	14.88	64
Reading Comprehension	42.73	12.16	36

Step 2. Calculate a standard score for each raw score.

The z score for analytical ability (z_1) is

$$z_1 = \frac{x - m}{s} = \frac{64 - 73.45}{14.88} = -.64$$

The z score for reading comprehension (z_2) is

$$z_2 = \frac{x - m}{s} = \frac{36 - 42.73}{12.16} = -.55$$

Step 3. Compare the two standard scores.

Because both raw scores were below the mean for the group, the z scores for both will have negative values, but the larger negative z value for analytical ability indicates that it is lower, relative to the rest of the group, than the z value for reading comprehension. Relative to the groups, this student did a little better on the reading comprehension test than on the test of analytical ability.

standard deviation, of course, but those descriptive statistics are always available from one source or another.

Percentile Scores

We initially encountered percentiles in Chapter 9. The 50th percentile defines the median, a measure of central tendency representing that point at or below which half the scores in a distribution occur. The definition generalizes to all **percentile scores.** The 37th percentile is the point at or below which 37 percent of the scores occur, and so on.

Although they are usually associated with large groups, percentile scores may not represent a normal distribution. They divide the distribution into 100 parts, and they identify that part in which the score occurs, but in doing so they reveal very little about how the other scores are arrayed.

A score at the 38th percentile (the most common notation is P_{38}) occurs at a point such that 38 percent of all scores in the reference group are equal to, or below, that score. There is no other information provided about how distant the other scores are. Percentiles indicate only the point among the scores at which a score occurs. From a percentile score alone, we are unable to answer questions about how many items the student may have correctly scored, or how much of the content the student may have mastered. The percentile score's value is the immediate normative reference it provides, but we need to be careful with the concept. Ordinarily, someone with a rank of 1 possesses the highest score. A percentile rank of 1, however, indicates the *lowest* end of the scale.

Because they are rankings, percentile scores do not necessarily have equal intervals. In terms of the Chapter 9 discussion of scaling, percentile scores represent ordinal scale measure. One may not assume that the distance between the 38th and 39th percentiles is the same as that between the 63rd and the 64th. This will become more apparent if you remember that percentile scores separate the scoring distribution into segments. Remember, however, that some possible scores occur many times and others may not occur at all. Therefore, the intervals between scores do not represent equal numbers of questions answered correctly, or content mastered, or the like. If the raw scores reflect a bell-shaped curve, most of the scores will occur in the middle. This means that a particular percentage of cases in the middle of the distribution will cover a much shorter distance than the same percentage when it occurs in either extreme of the distribution, where scores are less common. (This effect is evident in Figure 10.4).

Unless the data sets are much larger than what we generally encounter during normal school activities, there will be little need to calculate percentile scores, and the matter will not be directly pursued here. However, percentile scores can be determined easily enough, based on the use of the z scores previously discussed. The approach is as follows (Diekhoff, 1992):

1. Calculate a z score for the raw score in whose percentile you have an interest.
2. In any statistics textbook, consult the table (typically the first listed in the appendix) that provides the "area under the normal curve."
3. The proportion of the curve that falls below the relevant score, multiplied by 100, is the percentile score.

Figure 10.3 provides an example of how one might determine the percentile score using this procedure.

FIGURE 10.3 Determining the Percentile Score via the *z* Score

Assume that you have reading scores for a large group of 12-year-olds. The group average and the standard deviation are 24.6 and 6.35, respectively. At what percentile does a score of 27 occur?

Step 1. Calculate a *z* score for the raw score in whose percentile you have an interest.

$$z = \frac{x - m}{s} = \frac{27 - 24.6}{6.35} = .38$$

Step 2. Consult a statistics textbook to determine the "area under the normal curve."

proportion $= .615$

Step 3. Multiply by 100 the proportion of the curve that falls below the relevant score.

$.615 \times 100 = 61.5$, or the 62nd percentile

> Percentile scores establish where a score falls in a distribution relative to the other scores. A score at the 20th percentile occupies that point at or below which 20 percent of the other scores occur. Percentile scores reveal nothing about how great the interval is between scores.

It is important not to confuse percentile ranks with percentages. Test percentages are raw scores that indicate how many items a student scored correctly. Percentiles are transformations of raw scores expressed, not in terms of percentage correct, but in terms of the percentage of persons who fit a category (Anastasi, 1976).

Stanines

In conventional classroom situations, we often measure student performance with scores ranging from 0 to 100. This provides a familiar frame of reference, but sometimes a somewhat less precise reference can provide the essential information. Stanines, a name evolving from "standard 9-point scale," divide a distribution of scores into nine categories, each of which covers a band of the distribution rather than a discrete point. Each stanine has the width of half a standard deviation in a standard normal distribution. The first stanine is that band occurring at the extreme low end of the distribution of scores. A stanine of 5 covers the mean of the distribution. And the highest portion of the distribution occurs in the 9th stanine. Although the stanines are visually the same width, in normal distributions at least, the scores are not distributed evenly. The farther from the middle of the distribution the stanine falls, the fewer scores the band will contain. The percentages of scores that will occur within a particular stanine are as follows:

1st stanine: the lowest 4 percent of scores
2nd stanine: the next higher 7 percent of scores

3rd stanine: the next higher 12 percent of scores
4th stanine: the next higher 17 percent of scores
5th stanine: the middle 20 percent of scores
6th stanine: the next higher 17 percent of scores
7th stanine: the next higher 12 percent of scores
8th stanine: the next higher 7 percent of scores
9th stanine: the highest 4 percent of scores

> Although the stanine is a standard score, it represents a band rather than a point. There are nine stanines, each representing a distance of ½ the standard deviation in a normal distribution. The first stanine is the lowest extreme of the distribution, the fifth stanine is the middle of the distribution, and the ninth is the highest.

Note the symmetry between the percentage of scores the 1st and 9th stanines contain, the 2nd and 8th, and so on.

Stanines are useful when the issue is the area in which a particular score occurs, rather than the precise point. Like z and T scores, they are standard scores and they provide a metric for comparing scores from the same test or for comparing performance on different tests. Because the stanine is a band rather than a point, it is less likely that one will overemphasize numerical differences that are actually unimportant. If a student scores at the 57th percentile on one test and the 55th percentile on the next, there is a tendency to think of it in terms of a decline, but is the change really significant? Since both scores occur in the same stanine, there is a lesser tendency to overstate such results.

Once z scores are calculated, deriving stanines is quite simple. The formula is:

$$\text{stanine} = (2 \times z) + 5$$

A student who has a z score of 1.3 has a stanine of $(2 \times 1.3) + 5 = 7.6$. Rounded to the nearest whole number, the stanine is the 8th.

Normal Curve Equivalents

One of the reasons that T scores are appealing is that the T distribution has a mean of 50, something that is easy to identify with since we often think in terms of scales that range from 0 to 100. Another standard score, the **normal curve equivalent** (**NCE**), offers the same advantage, but with some important differences. The T distribution has a standard deviation of 10. The standard deviation in the distribution of NCE scores is 21.06. This rather odd-sized measure of dispersion allows NCE scores of 1 to be equivalent to a percentile rank of 1, and an NCE of 99 to equal a percentile rank of 99. Scores of 50 are equivalent in NCE and percentile scores as well, although the other scores are not parallel.

NCE scores use integers from 1 to 99. The relationship between NCE scores and stanines is such that each stanine contains approximately 11 NCE scores, something that is evident in Figure 10.4. The transformation from z to NCE is very much like that from z to T. One first calculates a z score, then multiplies the z score by the standard deviation of the NCE distribution (21.06), and adds the mean of the distribution (50) to the result:

$$NCE = (z \times 21.06) + 50$$

Someone who had a *z* score of 1.3 (who scored 1.3 standard deviations above the mean of the group) has a comparable NCE of $(1.3 \times 21.06) + 50 = 77.38$, or 77.

> Normal curve equivalent (NCE) scores are standard scores that range from 1 to 99. Their similarity with the usual classroom practice of using scores that range from 1 to 100 is part of their appeal. The mean and standard deviations in a distribution of NCE scores are 50 and 21.05, respectively. In a normal distribution of scores, NCE scores of 1, 50, and 99 match the same percentile scores.

If we assume that we have a set of normally distributed scores, we can construct a model that indicates how the different standard scores compare and where they fall in reference to each other in a distribution. This is what Figure 10.4 illustrates.

The *z* scores, *T* scores, and NCE scores are all associated directly with the standard deviation of the distribution of scores. Even the stanine unit is half a standard deviation. The figure indicates the percent of cases that fall into each category. Note that if you add up the percentages that relate to *z*, *T*, and NCE scores, the total is 99.98 percent. What happened to the other .02 percent? The percentage total less than 100 indicates that there is always at least a theoretical possibility of a score that is yet more extreme. The fact that the 1st and 9th stanines are open-ended allows for the same possibility. If we can measure a characteristic precisely, someone can always present a yet lower or higher score, although the possibility becomes increasingly remote as scores become more extreme.[2]

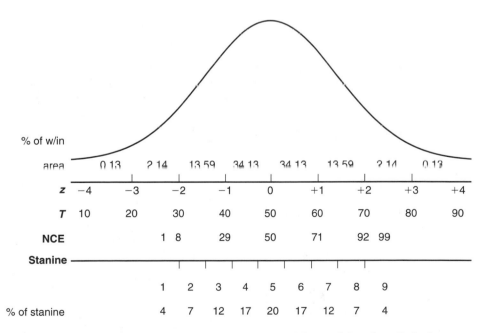

FIGURE 10.4   **Positioning *z* scores, *T* scores, NCEs, and Stanines Relative to Each Other, in a Normal Distribution**

Grade Equivalent Scores

Although they are norm-referenced scores like those discussed previously, grade equivalent scores are not standard scores. Rather, they are developmental level scores. They are quite common, and as simple as they seem, they are frequently misinterpreted.

A grade equivalent score of 4.7 indicates the level of performance *on the particular instrument* that is typical of fourth-grade students in the seventh month. This is not a general statement that the student is performing as well as students in the seventh month of the fourth-grade year. We will explain this more thoroughly, but note that the grade equivalent scores are supposed to serve as a normative reference point, not a standard. *They are not placement scores.*

Grade equivalent scores probably get the most notice when they are substantially different from the individual's grade level. If a sixth-grade student who is halfway through the school year scores 9.8 on a mathematics test, how should we interpret the score? We may be sure that the student is functioning beyond grade level, but maybe not on a par with the typical ninth-grade math student. The key revolves around this important interpretation: A grade equivalent score of 9.8 means that if a group of ninth-grade students in the eighth month of the year took the same test, 9.8 is their average. The test may not be a ninth-grade test at all. In fact, if it is administered to sixth-grade students, it most likely is not, so it is difficult to generalize to the ninth-grade curriculum.

As a related issue, grade equivalent scores may overstate their level of precision. Arguing that a grade of 9.8 is the average for a group of ninth-grade students in the eighth month suggests that the test developers collected data from such a sample. The test organization has almost certainly not determined the typical score for every combination of grades and months. The cost would be exorbitant. The scores are actually extrapolated from data gathered from the students in those grades most likely to take the test. It is safer to treat the scores as rankings. A score of 9.8 is certainly a higher level of performance than, say, 9.6. The improvement in performance between 9.8 and 9.6, however, may not be the same as the difference between 6.5 and 6.7, in spite of the fact that the interval suggests two months in either case. To couch it in terms of the scale of the data, it is safer to view grade equivalent scores as ordinal rather than as interval data.

Finally, remember that grade equivalent scores represent what is typical. If the tested group has a normal distribution, half of those who take the test are going to fall below the mean for the group.

For Further Discussion

If grade equivalent scores have the same characteristics as other norm-references, it means that the scores are scattered both above and below whatever is typical of the group. In light of that understanding, consider the following questions:

1. Speaking generally, what proportion of the group is beyond grade level?
2. What proportion is below grade level?
3. How would you respond to charges in the popular press that half the students who took a particular test received grade equivalent scores that fall below grade level?

FACTORS THAT MAY INFLUENCE TEST PERFORMANCE

We use standardized test data for a variety of purposes, including program admissions, employment, licensure, and educational placement decisions. As it turns out, these are all examples of "high-stakes testing," and because the outcomes are so important, there is a great deal of effort to improve test scores. In some instances, test score improvement is only tangentially related to the learning or the characteristic the test was intended to measure. Said a little differently, test preparation programs sometimes focus on the increase in test scores—not as an indicator that the trait or characteristic has increased, but as an end in itself. Assessment experts refer to the associated techniques as test "coaching," and besides becoming a commercial growth industry, the topic has become an important part of measurement discussions.

Defining coaching and determining the coaching effect can be difficult because the distinction between coaching and conventional instruction sometimes is not very clear. Bond (1989) suggested (tongue in cheek) that, from one point of view at least, coaching is a function of the amount of time one devotes to the test-preparation activity. If one spends comparatively little time to improve test scores, there is a tendency to speak of "test coaching." If the preparation is lengthier, we may refer to the efforts as "further instruction in the subject matter."

There is more to consider than how much time we devote to score improvement, however. Coaching procedures tend to focus on tactics that are unrelated to the student's grasp of the content or skill measured. The strategies include elements of test-wiseness such as:

planning one's time carefully
learning to recognize choices that cannot be correct
knowing when to guess

Perhaps because testing is so widespread, many students are test-wise without the benefit of coaching strategies. They simply develop the techniques because of their own experiences. For other students, coaching in test-taking strategies may make a significant difference in their scores.

Logically, people are most inclined to coach, and students are most likely to seek coaching, for tests that are widely used and that have far-reaching consequences. Bond (1989) noted, "With the possible exception of the IQ controversy, the controversy surrounding the 'coachability' of standardized measures of academic aptitude such as the Scholastic Aptitude Test and the Graduate Record Examination is perhaps the leading measurement dispute of our time" (p. 429). The Scholastic Aptitude Test (now the Scholastic *Assessment* Test) is widely used in college admissions decisions, so for both students and the institution the stakes are very high. There is a good deal of literature on the coachability of that test dating back to the late 1950s.

We have an interest that ranges substantially beyond the SAT, however, because test coaching is probably common to all widely administered standardized tests. Someone willing to browse through most bookstores will inevitably find books that are published to help students improve their scores on admissions tests for professional schools, certification and licensing exams, language exams, and a host of other high-stakes tests. Some of the issues with coaching are primarily ethical considerations, and they will be reviewed in Chapter 12, but there are other problems that raise what are fundamentally measurement considerations. Some of them are represented in the following questions:

> *What is it that standardized tests assess?*
>
> *If coaching prompts score improvements, what does that reveal about data validity?*
>
> *When coaching is not successful, does that suggest a problem with the coaching strategy, or is there something revealed about the nature of what is assessed? (Bond, 1989)*

Some standardized tests are intended to measure characteristics thought to be comparatively stable. Although the way it is expressed may vary, most mental measurement experts believe that intelligence, for example, changes little from the later primary school years to adulthood. If the characteristic measured is stable, coaching efforts should be largely ineffective. If scores yield to coaching efforts, then either the characteristic measured is not stable—in which case whatever is being measured is not intelligence but something else being represented as intelligence—or the measuring procedures themselves are flawed. This could occur because the test is badly constructed. As an alternative, perhaps the test taker is unfamiliar with the format of the test on an initial administration. Perhaps someone makes an error in administering the test, resulting in more time allowed for some test takers than for others. The research is not exhaustive, but experiments on retaking the Stanford-Binet suggest that, although intelligence scores may improve when test takers repeat the test, the changes tend to be quite modest, and larger for those with no previous test-taking experience. This suggests that the difference may be primarily a function of familiarity with the test and with testing procedures.

In this regard, assessing academic achievement is more complicated. We aim most of our educational testing at characteristics that change because of the students' experiences. After all, changing what we know or can do is the point of receiving an education. The students' spelling ability, their grasp of mathematics computation, and their understanding of historical concepts are fluid characteristics. We measure them periodically because, happily, they change over time. The problem is that some of the changes result from alterations in the related academic characteristic, and some may reflect an improvement in test-taking technique.

Consider a situation with a standardized reading test. Comprehension is affected by a variety of factors including how much one reads, how effective the reading instruction has been, and how motivated the test taker is. It might be difficult, therefore, to separate coaching effect from substantive changes in the test taker's achievement level. As a rule, however, the better assessments tend to be less sensitive than poorly constructed tests to coaching effects.

When it is easy to coach test results, there is probably an implicit message about the validity of the test data. On the other hand, when coaching strategies are unsuccessful, it can be difficult to determine the reason. When coaching appears ineffective, one may not know whether it reflects the quality of the assessment or of the coaching.

Speaking of Assessment

Think of differential coaching effects in these terms: Which would be easier to coach, a secondary school literature teacher's test when the teacher is known to favor Coleridge among early nineteenth-century British poets, or a standardized literature test with several dozen test items on a cross-section of nineteenth-century literature?

With our discussion about coaching and learning, note that, if someone repeats a test, sometimes scoring changes reflect nothing more than the characteristics of large groups. When they are measured on a large scale (districtwide, statewide, nationwide), much of the data reflect the familiar bell-shaped curve. This means that the preponderance of scores, those that are most typical, will occupy the middle of the distribution. Extreme scores in either direction are most likely to be followed by less extreme scores in a retest. Probabilities favor a less extreme score the second time, and we can make a better-than-chance prediction about what will happen when students are retested. The probabilities suggest that very low scores will most often be followed by higher scores on a retest, and those with high scores are more likely to have a lower score the next time. Predicting the scores for students who were initially in the middle of the distribution is more difficult.

We can make predictions such as these because no standardized test of any mental trait or characteristic has perfect reliability. Scores will vary from administration to administration even when circumstances are "standardized."[3] This is an issue that those promoting the virtues of a coaching program usually do not explain when they report how much low scorers improve when they take the improvement course and then retest.

The tendency for extreme scores to become less extreme on a retest assumes that all other relevant variables remain constant, however, and this may not always be the case. There are indications that retaking a standardized test affects some students differently than others, depending upon their ability. More able students may benefit more than less able students from having seen the test previously. Any scoring gains decrease as the repetitions of the test increase, however. The differential impact may reflect unique responses to coaching as well as differences in the aptitude, motivation, and certainly the experience of the individual.

It also appears that some disciplines are more susceptible to coaching than others. Verbal abilities may be a little more responsive to coaching than math-related abilities, for example, perhaps because verbal abilities have more frequent application in our day-to-day activities. We have more opportunity to practice them. The effect of coaching exercises is only one of several variables that may have an impact on a score. If classroom instruction continues in the discipline, the passage of time alone should have a positive effect on subsequent test scores (Bond, 1989).

Probably the largest score increases occur when students practice taking the test. It is common for test-preparation booklets to include items of the sort that the test will include, for example, and some test-preparation programs will include practice on earlier forms of the instrument. Logically, the scoring increases are greatest when students can practice on identical forms of the test, and, also logically, the coaching effects diminish as the practice tests differ from the actual test. Whether it is ethical to prepare for a test by practicing on an identical form of that test is an issue taken up in Chapter 12.

It was mentioned that coaching activities are most intense in connection with tests that have the most important consequences. College admissions tests such as the SAT are frequently at the top of the list of high-stakes tests. After his detailed review of coaching and the SAT, Bond (1989) observed:

> Testing organizations, the College Board and Educational Testing Service in particular, insist that all verifiable evidence indicates that abilities measured by the SAT and similar admissions tests develop slowly, are largely insensitive to brief interventions involving drill and practice, and are quite valid for their intended purposes. The majority of the published evidence in the technical literature supports this view. It is unfortunate that the most dramatic claims to the contrary come, with rare exceptions, from outside the peer review process characteristic of modern scientific practice. (p. 442)

Bond's lament is that there is a healthy research literature reporting that coaching on some of the most prominent high-stakes tests indicates only minor gains. If one moves outside the scholarly literature, the claims are more elaborate. Those promoting the value of commercial coaching are, or course, quite optimistic about its benefits.

If the effects of coaching on SAT performance are minimal, and if what occurs with the SAT is characteristic of what happens with other high-stakes tests, excepting the opportunity to practice the actual test, it seems that coaching may not be a good investment of time, or of money. In the case of tests that measure a nonstable characteristic, it might be wiser to simply spend more time with whatever learning nurtures the characteristic. The dilemma is that, although coaching gains may be minimal, the stakes are sufficiently high that for some the cost seems worth the gamble, particularly when there has already been a substantial investment in the outcome. This is the case, for example, when someone completes a university course of study but can be denied a license or a credential by failing to successfully navigate an assessment prepared to provide a final measure of competency.

OPPOSITION TO STANDARDIZED TESTING

Only those who are isolated from educational discussions can be unaware of how strong feelings become when the discussion turns to standardized testing. There appear to be two primary objections to the tests. Critics question (1) whether what is assessed with standardized tests has any value beyond the classroom and (2) whether standardized tests bring with them a bias that works against particular ethnic, gender, or social class groups.

Does What Standardized Tests Measure Matter?

In large measure, we can answer questions about whether standardized test data are really worth their costs in two parts. We need to know whether standardized test data make educational activities more productive, and whether the scores are significant beyond the classroom. Standardized testing is a very cost-effective way to assess large numbers of students from different backgrounds, but that does not mean that what the scores represent is important. If standardized tests measure only the students' ability to take tests and they predominantly reflect background characteristics, they may not be worth their costs.

Perhaps the best way to approach these issues is in terms of the validity discussion in Chapter 7. Sometimes we test so that we can make better predictions. If prediction is the primary purpose of the test, what the test actually measures may not matter. The SAT scores predict college grades, and the Law School Admittance Test (LSAT) indicates how well applicants to law school will likely perform. Some tests predict actual job performance. A test of manual dexterity might be used to measure how quickly and accurately a potential assemblyline worker can perform some intricate manual task.

The value of the measure depends on whether those who use the data can make better selection decisions by using the data. If the test data do not contribute to better decisions, or if the improvement is inconsequential, their problems outweigh their benefits. Crouse and Trusheim (1988) direct this very argument at the SAT. They suggest that committees can make accurate admissions decisions about college and university applicants without using the test. No one suggests that the tests do not predict college performance. The question is whether they predict it well enough to justify their use, so there is a subjective component to the decision. One must decide how much better the decision must be, and there is no simple formula for that determination. We only note in passing that, notwithstanding Crouse and Trusheim, the SAT has good predictive validity. It provides a measure of students' performance common to all since all take the test under the same conditions. One can generalize the results beyond the school district or the state, which is increasingly important in the midst of concerns about grade inflation and regional curricular differences.

One dimension of the value of standardized tests, then, is the strength of their predictive validity. We are more likely to judge achievement tests, on the other hand, on the strength of their content validity. If we award a high school diploma by testing the content areas, we want some assurance that the English test samples the relevant components. Such matters are particularly important to those who worry that students lack the competencies they ought to have. From this point of view, we can define the importance of the tests in terms of their ability to sample the content area fairly and to provide an accurate measure of learners' grasp of the subject.

We already know that validity can be difficult to establish (Messick, 1980). The critics of standardized testing decry the attention given to what seem to be very elusive concepts. Advocates of alternative assessment, for example, suggest that rather than worrying about validity, it might be more productive to focus on practical outcomes such as the test of manual dexterity mentioned earlier. Some might argue that it is the one example here that has meaning beyond the assessment setting. This logic suggests that the SAT and LSAT could be replaced by something that measures skills and abilities that are more authentic. Perhaps the college applicant's verbal ability can be assessed via a writing sample developed during the final year of secondary school. Maybe aspiring attorneys should demonstrate their analytical ability by explaining to a panel Locke's concept of the social contract outlined in his *Second Treatise on Civil Government*. In either case, the abilities are those that have clear application beyond the assessment.

Advocates of alternative assessment also place great stock in the *appearance* of authenticity reflected in an assessment exercise. In traditional assessment discussions, this is face validity, and there is some irony in the fact that it really expresses only the test taker's perception.

Alternative assessment procedures hold some promise, but they too pose some difficulty. One of the reasons standardized tests evolved the way they did is because of the need to assess large numbers of people. It has been emphasized that alternative assessment procedures do not respond very well to the need to assess large numbers of students quickly and economically.

Some standardized tests are certainly more useful than others, and some may focus on content or a skill that the student may never use beyond the classroom. That represents a problem with the content of the test rather than with the form, however.

On a more fundamental level, the criticisms of standardized testing are not easy to answer because the discussion is largely a philosophical one about the merits of the different approaches. Those who wish assessment to reflect local priorities and specific outcomes often criticize standardized testing, which is much better suited to assessing general characteristics among large numbers of people from dissimilar backgrounds. Perhaps we will find some resolution—not in changing minds as much as in appealing to practicality and pursuing whatever form of assessment seems to produce the relevant information. When conditions are appropriate, however, the economy and efficiency of standardized testing have great appeal.

Standardized Testing and Bias

Along with several other topics raised briefly here, bias in testing is examined more carefully in Chapter 12, but in the meantime, note a comment by Castenell and Soled (1993) regarding standardized tests used to license teachers in the various states:

> Without exception, the validity of these measures is invariably debated by psychometricians, policymakers, and influential others. Given that there is some measure of standard error in all assessments and that many minorities are trained in institutions that are frequently not included in the norming process, one can argue that ethnic bias does exist. Thus, ethnic bias has resulted in African Americans, Hispanic Americans, and most other minority groups being severely penalized by testing practices that clearly favor the majority culture. This and other well-documented cases of test bias, including gender bias, linguistic bias, religious bias, and geographic bias, all serve to remind us that most educational tests are written by and normed using white, middle-class Americans. (p. 43)

This particular quotation appeared in a publication by what is perhaps the major national organization of teacher education colleges and universities in the United States. Implicit in this quite broad criticism is the suggestion that standardized tests provide such an easy target that critics sometimes feel no responsibility to validate their claims. Cole and Moss (1989) alluded to this when they noted that many different people observe standardized testing, and they often scrutinize according to quite different values and a variety of prior assumptions. More particularly, different people apply different standards of evidence to determining whether test data are valid. Some of the assumptions Castenell and Soled (1993) have made, and some of the positions they hold, are revealed in the preceding quotation. One can bring the assumption into sharper focus by asking questions such as the following:

Is measurement error a characteristic only of standardized tests?

If students from all institutions are not included in the norming process, does whatever other sample is used necessarily make the test data non-representative?

If some students are excluded from a process or an opportunity because of low test scores, is the test punitive by definition?

If members of some groups have greater success on the test than members of other groups, is the test biased by definition?

Do the test scores allow one to make accurate inferences regarding the individual?

The questions are not asked merely for rhetorical effect, but your author will respond only briefly because he has dealt with their substance elsewhere. Measurement error is not the exclusive domain of standardized tests. Its potential is present whenever one conducts an assessment, but it is particularly problematic when the focus is a characteristic that we cannot measure directly. That means that error is characteristic of educational assessment, whatever its form. It is not a characteristic only of standardized testing.

A sample of students used in a norming process can be representative without being exhaustive. The issue is not whether everyone is represented, but whether the characteristics of the population to which results may be generalized are represented in correct proportion. If the general population is 20 percent ethnic group A, then a norm group that is also 20 percent group A, even though it is smaller numerically, can represent the larger group's characteristics.

Tests, particularly admissions tests, are sometimes gatekeepers. Often their purpose is not to determine whether respondents possess a certain characteristic, but to reveal who possesses it in greatest abundance. This is a necessity because, in some instances, the number of openings, or university admissions, or desks in a classroom is fewer than is the number of applicants. There may be a compelling argument favoring open admissions or applications, but economic realities usually make it infeasible. When someone is excluded, it is very tempting to place blame on the messenger.

As will be evident from your reading of Chapter 12, differential performance does not necessarily indicate bias. There are a variety of reasons, some of them relating to access and opportunity, that groups might perform differently. Some of them are revealed in, but not necessarily caused by, the assessment data. The issue should not be whether there are differences so much as whether the data indicate how well a test taker will perform, or how well a test taker understands. While there are certainly important, documented cases of test bias, the truth is that the legal and financial implications are so important in high-stakes testing that developers scrutinize instruments for bias and for validity very carefully.

SUMMARY

Those who are involved with formal education will certainly encounter standardized tests. They are ubiquitous in contemporary public—as well as private—elementary and secondary schools. They affect both the students who must take them and the educators who must administer them and explain their results. Your author intends to be no apologist for standardized tests, but the fact is that they remain very popular because they allow one to evaluate large numbers of people relatively efficiently, even when they may have dissimilar backgrounds. This is possible because the tests generally measure rather broad characteristics that tend to be unaffected by minor changes in curricular emphasis from place to place, and everyone takes the tests under similar circumstances. The time requirements, instructions, and testing facilities are as common to all test takers as they can reasonably be made to be.

In order for the reporting language to be common also, standardized test data are often stated in terms of standard scores. They provide information about an individual's performance relative to others in a way that is unaffected by the characteristics of the particular test. They also allow one to compare an individual's performance on two dissimilar tests.

The stakes on standardized tests can be very high for the individual and sometimes for the institution. As a result, efforts to boost scores by coaching students and by encouraging their test-wiseness are common. The degree to which test results can be affected by coaching is one standard for judging their quality.

There has always been some opposition to standardized testing. As test use has grown, so has the criticism. There are generally two areas of focus: Are the tests biased? and Are the tests justified by what they measure? We will pursue the bias question at some length in Chapter 12. The other question reflects matters of personal choice as much as anything. Advocates of alternative assessment are critical of testing procedures that seem removed from what the students will face beyond the classroom. One must balance that criticism against the value of being able to predict future performance, to measure trends among large numbers of students, and to evaluate progress in a fashion not unnecessarily sensitive to local conditions.

ENDNOTES

1. There is a possibility that a *T* score could be negative, but it would have to be more than 5 standard deviations below the mean, a probability so remote that statistical tables do not even provide the necessary data. Even the probability that a score would be 4 standard deviations below the mean (the most extreme possibility listed in any of the statistics texts on your author's shelf) is about $p = .00003$, or three in one hundred thousand.
2. In the language of statistics, the tails of a normal distribution are "asymptotic to the curve," which means that although the tails of the curve get closer to the abscissa as scores become more extreme, they never touch. The practical expression of this bit of esoterica is that, theoretically, if our capacity to measure were unfettered by any of the usual limitations that contribute to error, there would always be the possibility of a score higher or lower than what we have yet witnessed.

3. The related statistical term is *regression to the mean,* and, although that refers to prediction problems, the principle is the same. Extreme scores tend to be followed by less extreme scores.

FOR FURTHER READING

A number of books are available that deal in some measure with standardized testing. Mehrens and Lehman (1987) wrote one of the more readable publications. It deals specifically with standardized testing in the classroom rather than with employment testing, psychological evaluation, or the like. The language is direct and the authors assume no prior background in the subject.

REFERENCES

Anastasi, A. (1976). *Psychological testing* (4th ed.). New York: Macmillan.

Bond, L. (1989). The effects of special preparation on measures of scholastic ability. In R. L. Linn (Ed.), *Educational measurement* (3rd ed.). New York: Macmillan.

Castenell, L. A., Jr. and Soled, S. W. (1993). Standards, assessments, and valuing diversity. *Essays on emerging assessment issues.* Washington, DC: The American Association of Colleges of Teacher Education.

Cole, N. (1982). The implication of coaching for ability testing. In A. K. Wigdor and W. R. Garner (Eds.), *Ability testing: Uses, consequences, and controversies.* Washington, DC: National Academy Press.

Cole, N. S., and Moss. P. A. (1989). Bias in test use. In R. L. Linn (Ed.), *Educational measurement* (3rd ed.). New York: Macmillan.

Crouse, J., and Trusheim, D. (1988). *The case against the SAT.* Chicago: The University of Chicago Press.

Diekhoff, G. (1992). *Statistics for the social and behavioral sciences: Univariate, bivariate, and multivariate.* Dubuque, IA: William C. Brown.

Mehrens, W. A., and Lehman, I. J. (1987). *Using standardized tests in education* (4th ed.). New York: Longman.

Messick, S. (1980). Test validity and the ethics of assessment. *American Psychologist, 35,* 1012–1027.

Scheuneman, J. D., and Slaughter, C. (1991). *Issues of test bias, item bias, and group differences and what to do while waiting for the answers.* Princeton, NJ: Educational Testing Service. (ERIC Document Reproduction Service No. ED 400 294)

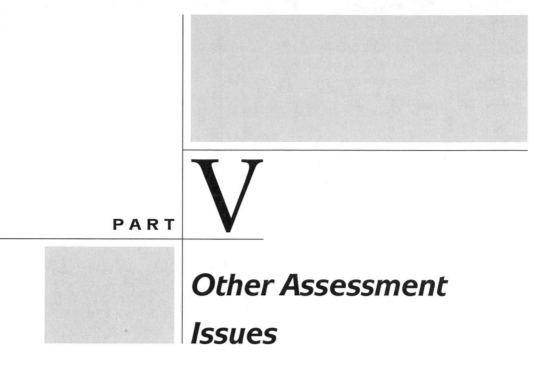

PART V

Other Assessment Issues

It is difficult to identify any area of education not affected by computer use, and assessment is no exception. Whether as a score manager, or a mechanism for constructing, administering, and scoring assessment instruments, computers have become a ubiquitous part of educational assessment. At the least, they save labor; but in many instances, analytical tools previously unavailable to classroom teachers have become accessible. Some of the more common applications will be examined in Chapter 11.

As the stakes associated with educational assessment rise, so do the ethical considerations associated with assessment. Every educator will face them. The way we respond will guide the way we help our students prepare for high-stakes tests, the way we interpret assessment data, and a host of other related questions that will be hinted at in Chapter 12. There is a good deal of wisdom in considering the ethical issues early in one's career so that one might develop a position regarding some of the more common potential problems before they are encountered. Ignoring ethical issues will not eliminate them.

Inevitably, a book such as this raises some topics we have occasion to develop only superficially. A few will be revisited in the final chapter. Although one might ordinarily expect them only in a second course in assessment, they are basic to some of the earlier discussion and it is appropriate to give them some treatment here. They will help the reader fix passing standards on tests and understand the risks and issues involved in making incorrect judgments about students' performances.

The Computer as an Assessment Tool

■ *The reader will review the use of the computer as a component in developing, administering, and scoring tests, analyzing the data, and managing learners' grades.*

The Computer Revolution

Computers and Assessment

Test Development

Administering Tests via Computer

Data Analysis

Item Discrimination

Equating Scores

Criterion-Related Validity

Scoring Essays

Scoring Interest Inventories and Personality Assessments

Static versus Dynamic Measurement

Computer-Adaptive Testing (CAT)

Generations of Computer Assessment

Group Differences in Computer Use

For the typical classroom teacher, computers affected instruction first. Gradually, however, teachers have recognized the potential that computers offer in connection with assessment. As a first step, educators use them to store copies of items and assessment instruments, and to manage grades. The potential is now available to use computers to reach populations that have been inaccessible, and to produce assessment data that can inform instruction in great detail. ■

Mr. Forsythe stared idly at the computer on the table beside his desk. He was no novice to the machine, but he was certainly not as comfortable with the technology as many of his students—who often demonstrated applications of the computer for his classroom that were new to him. The students did not hesitate to use the technology, and the possibilities open via the Internet were a source of constant interest, but student use was not his focus just then. It occurred to Mr. Forsythe that in recent years he had spent increasing amounts of time monitoring students' progress and managing performance information. He knew that some of his colleagues used the computer as a platform for creating their assessments and for managing students' performance data, but he had always been a little skeptical. Mr. Forsythe was unconvinced that, simply because computer technology was employed, education necessarily improved. Indeed, there were times when it appeared that the technology got in the way, that people spent an inordinate amount of time doing "gee whiz" things on their machines that, he suspected, did not translate into educational gains for students. Still, he was willing to try. He disliked the business of weighting and totaling grades with calculator in hand at the end of each grading period, and some of the other instructors were automating this process with computer spreadsheets. In addition, a faculty development course he took demonstrated that assessment data can be statistically analyzed with specially prepared computer software to reveal a good deal about the quality of both the assessment and the students' performances. He resolved to begin an investigation. ■

THE COMPUTER REVOLUTION IN EDUCATION

Probably very few innovations have the potential to impact education as have computers. Although the interest here is in the possible influence that computer use has on assessment applications, there is much more to educational computing than assessment. Instructional software has proliferated to the point that computer tutorials are now available in virtually any subject and at any level of sophistication that the typical elementary, secondary school, or even college student will likely need. Simulation software allows students access to "virtual" laboratories, conducting experiments without most of the associated costs. With Internet access, students and instructors conduct worldwide searches for materials. Beyond instruction, computers have changed the way educators manage students' records. Computer-managed data allows more information to be more accessible.

Perhaps the most startling part of the change is how quickly it occurred. In an important article written as the changes in computer testing were just beginning to take shape, Bunderson, Inouye, and Olsen (1989) spoke of the changes relative to other revolutionary advances affecting formal education. They wrote, "Although other major innovations in education, like writing and printing, took centuries and even millennia to become the common possession of every person, the distribution of computing resources has occurred within decades" (p. 367).

The wording, "within decades," actually *under*states the velocity of the change. Experimental work at Stanford University and the University of Illinois in the early 1960s employing the large machines of that time to tutor younger reading students suggested that computers offered great educational promise (Atkinson and Fletcher, 1972). This work served as an important foundation for further exploration, but the greater computer revolution in education awaited the advent of microcomputers. They became available from the Apple Corporation in the late 1970s, from IBM in 1981, and then from many others. At the printing of this book, most of the changes resulting from computer use in education are less than two decades old.

COMPUTERS AND EDUCATIONAL ASSESSMENT

Just as assessment is a subordinate part of education, computer assessment is a subset of general assessment. It reflects the intersection of assessment and computer technology (Bunderson et al., 1989).

Computers affect all areas of educational assessment, but not all instructors use them. They are far more prevalent among those who analyze standardized test data as a major part of their occupation than among classroom teachers administering the assessments they construct themselves. We want to make some mention of several of the areas in which computers have affected assessment practice, but with particular attention to the applications likely to be most helpful to the individual instructor.

> Computers have affected all areas of educational assessment, in spite of the fact that not all instructors make use of them. They are far more common in instructional and data management applications than they are in classroom assessment.

One if this book's themes is that we err when we treat assessment separately from the other components of a complete educational plan. This idea was developed in Chapter 2 with the goal-referenced model. Just as we can reduce the model to its components (the objectives, preassessment, teaching strategies, and the like), we can also subdivide the assessment component. This is what Bunderson et al. (1989) have done, and Figure 11.1 makes it easier to see where computer technology fits in.

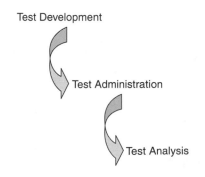

Test Development

Test Administration

Test Analysis

FIGURE 11.1   The Three Major Assessment Processes

COMPUTERS AND TEST DEVELOPMENT

Test development tasks are different for the typical instructor than they are for someone whose job description is "test developer." The components from Figure 11.1 are common to both, however. If we break the components down still further, we have the micro view of assessment that Figure 11.2 presents, as well as a chance to examine the pieces of assessment that are most affected by computer use.

Some of Figure 11.2 should look familiar from the treatment of test construction in Chapter 7, but there we had a simpler focus. Developing assessment instruments was primarily a matter of selecting test items that were appropriate for both the content we needed to cover and the level of thought we wanted to gauge. Because of their capacity to analyze and manage data, computers make it easier to move beyond content validity and the cognitive level of the test item.

Every assessment has a purpose. Once the purpose is explicit, one can also explain how it will be served. This is what test specifications accomplish, and they become a blueprint for the balance of the assessment activities. The testing purposes are statements about the kind of information we need. The specifications outline how this will be achieved. If we were explaining the purpose and developing the specifications for a math facts test, they might look this way:

The assessment's *purpose:*

- Assess third-grade students' command of the addition and subtraction of two-digit numbers.

FIGURE 11.2   Component Elements in the Processes of Assessment

1. **Test development** activities require
   - establishing the purposes of the test
   - developing the tasks, or test items
   - testing the items
   - revising the items
   - combining the items into the finished instrument

2. **Test administration** includes
   - gathering the students' responses to the test items
   - scoring test items for correctness
   - interpreting the individual student's performance (grading)

3. **Analyzing test data** includes
   - evaluating item, or task, difficulty
   - scrutinizing items to ensure that they discriminate between students who have the skill or characteristic measured and those who don't (validity)
   - determining whether identifiable groups of students respond to particular items, or particular groups of items, differently than do members of other groups (differential item functioning)

Source: Adapted from Bunderson et al. (1989).

The assessment's *specifications:*

- The assessment will employ 20 two-digit items, 10 addition and 10 subtraction.
- The items will be constructed response type.
- Half the items will involve problems in carrying (addition) or borrowing (subtraction).

At this point, the activities are primarily conceptual, and there is little opportunity to use the computer except to store the file containing lists of different kinds of test purposes and specifications. Keeping them in a file makes it easy to revise and modify specifications. With the purpose and the specifications established, one can select the assessment items.

Truly effective test items can be very time-consuming to develop, so it makes sense to develop the habit of "banking" them in a computer file for later use. Although it is generally poor practice to use the same test twice, it makes very little sense to construct new test items every time one must evaluate a particular component of learning. If they exist in a file, one can modify the items with the benefit of the scoring data, the students' comments, and one's own experience. Test items are much easier to revise than to create. In time, instructors can develop enough test items that even the more ambitious (devious?) gatherers of prior copies of tests will have only a few of the items from the current instrument.[1]

Commercial software is available to help one construct and store assessment items. One of the leading marketers is the Assessment Systems Corporation, but most classroom teachers do not need test construction programs. Word processing software works well for most basic applications. In the example used here one might create two files, perhaps one named something like "twoadd" for two-digit addition items and another for "twosub." As one constructs two-digit addition items, they can be maintained in the "twoadd" file and then modified and improved over time. The process of adding new examples is ongoing.

> Instructors who "bank" their test items in a computer file can save themselves a good deal of time when they must assess similar material at some later time. One can also revise the items and improve their quality based on the earlier experience.

Database programs offer a more powerful approach to the same task of storing and accessing test items. The advantage is that such software allows one to store and then later access assessment items in terms of certain characteristics that the educator defines as "fields." One field might be the topic ("two-digit addition problems"), another might indicate the level of difficulty (whether the student must carry to solve the problem), and a third field might be length (two, two-digit numbers versus three, and so forth). By selecting items that fit particular characteristics, one can tailor an assessment to test specifications.

Once we have the items, it is a good idea to test them, perhaps by administering a few of the new items to students as seat work or homework assignments. Students' performance and their comments will be very helpful. Such feedback allows us to revise the items before we combine them into a finished instrument. Each time one receives information and revises the items, one ought to revise the computer file containing the master list. For those who use the computer to store test items, this is a continuing process, since items effective with one group of students may miss the mark with others and need adjustment.

COMPUTERS AND TEST ADMINISTRATION

The next of the assessment processes is administering the test. Although experimenters were initially interested in the computer as a tutor, computer-administered tests were a logical follow-up to computer-aided instruction (CAI). If the computer represents a more effective way to present instruction, then why not use the same medium for student assessment? One of the most compelling rationales for any type of individualized instruction, of which computer-aided instruction is one example, is that students learn best when they can proceed according to their individual needs. If instruction proceeds individually, students are ready for assessment at different stages in the process. Computer-managed testing is a logical companion to computer-aided instruction.

Speaking of Assessment

We have just suggested that if we individualize the students' learning by using CAI, students will proceed at different rates and a common assessment period makes little sense. Is this situation unique to CAI, or to individualized instruction? Were you ever in any classroom where everyone proceeded at the same rate? Does this suggest to you that even if one does not individualize instruction via CAI or some other method, there is some logic to computer-managed testing?

Computerized testing includes more than multiple-choice types of tests, although they are probably the most common. Simulation exercises, case studies, and nearly any other type of assessment we see in traditional testing are increasingly common. There is also more to computer-managed testing that just preparing the items and administering the test. One might use the computer to record, score, and analyze students' responses according to a number of different criteria. One might wish a record of which content areas were the most troublesome, or the extent of difficulty of particular items. Such data can inform subsequent instruction. Beyond the implications that test results might have for further teaching, computer administering and scoring eliminate some of the data reliability and validity problems associated with conventional testing. The presentation and the directions test takers receive will be entirely consistent with computer-administered tests. Scoring procedures will also be uniform as long as the software is not altered.

Using computers to administer tests may make inaccessible assessment available. The personality and intelligence tests that yield the most reliable data are often tests that a trained professional administers one at a time, a procedure that makes them very expensive. In some instances, one may elect not to test because of the cost, and data that might improve the educational program may go uncollected.

When computers and software allow one to automate testing, at least the labor costs involved in administration become negligible. Many of the clinical tests, particularly those in which some element of subjective judgment is required to interpret a respondent's answer, will probably continue to rely primarily on trained professional administration, but computers will automate much of the other testing.

Computer testing does not eliminate the need for people to be involved in assessment procedures. Someone must oversee the testing activities, but rather than requiring testing experts, with their greater attendant costs, procedures can be managed by paraprofessionals (Bunderson et al., 1989). Their responsibilities are generally removed from the technical side of testing and focus instead on the computer operations, test security, and the questions test takers ask about testing procedure.

These benefits balance some of the computer assessment costs. One must modify the assessment for computer presentation, and, of course, computer equipment and software must be available. Logically, cost savings are most dramatic for instruments that are traditionally administered one person at a time, but there are labor savings whenever we adapt a test to the computer.

In addition to the cost benefits, computer-administered assessment offers flexibility advantages. Nearly all standardized tests include time limits. Often they are only for convenience rather than because testing time is relevant to the assessment. The administrator cannot spend an unlimited amount of time administering the test, so reasonable limits are set. When the assessment is computer administered, one may allow learners to take as much time as they wish. It is easy enough to impose time limits with computerized testing, by the way, but it usually is not necessary.

Administering assessments with computers also makes them available whenever students are ready to take them. When we examined formative and summative assessment in Chapter 2, it was suggested that grading (from summative assessment) should occur when students have had an adequate opportunity to learn, rather than when learning is in process. The difficulty, of course, is that students progress through learning materials at quite different rates. If we use computers, theoretically at least, we can test whenever students are ready and eliminate the need for a common testing period that will either hold some students up or catch others unready. Any type of individualized instruction makes it a central tenet that one tests when the student is ready. This is much more feasible when the computer manages the testing procedures.

Administering standardized tests via the computer diminishes the need for certified professionals to conduct testing sessions. Computers can also make tests accessible to populations who have no access to testing because of their locations, and so help resolve an important equity-of-access problem.

There are other administrative advantages to testing with computers. Some might find it very difficult to meet face to face with a trained test administrator or in a testing center because of their schedules, or perhaps because of their locations. Traditionally, they would have represented an inaccessible group, but computer administration makes it possible to gather measurement data in remote locations and at unconventional hours.

Computer use also makes it easier to use simulations in assessment. There has been a great deal of development in multiple media presentations for the computer. Integrating sound and video makes it much easier to develop scenarios for an assessment that might include a simulated chemistry exercise, a virtual classroom, or a variety of other situations contrived to evaluate students' learning. By definition, simulations are more authentic than testing when there is no effort to represent the relevant conditions. Although the developmental costs may be significant, they are one-time expenditures, and the resulting simulation can offer real-world exposure without the costs and risks that accompany the actual experience.

COMPUTERS AND TEST ANALYSIS

Test analysis is the third component in assessment (Figure 11.1). Besides evaluating the learner's performance, we also wish to know as much as we can about the instrument, the curriculum that preceded it, the progress of the group, and so forth. Much of this information is available only after we have administered the test.

When assessment results are scores rather than a qualitative description, the analysis is statistical. Statistical analysis involves a great deal of calculation, some of it very time-consuming if completed by hand, but it takes only an instant for the computer. Indeed, numerical analysis is the computer's forte.

Machine scoring of test data was common before computer analysis and, in fact, even before computers were widely available. Probably the most familiar form of machine scoring is optical scanning, a procedure that involves "bubbling in" the correct choice on a specially formatted answer sheet.

Psychological measures have no "correct" answer, but scoring achievement tests begins with a scoring key. One first runs the scoring key through the scanner. This creates a scoring pattern to compare with the learners' responses. Learners' scores that match the key pattern are correct. Optical scanners developed by the Scantron Corporation, IBM, and others can provide summary data on individual items, including the proportion of test takers scoring the item correctly, for example, as well as other item statistics.

Generally, scanners indicate only when there is a match between the key and the student's answer sheet. If one connects the scanner to a computer, however, besides scoring answer sheets, the appropriate software program allows one to manipulate the data and then store them for analysis later. One has the option to weight some responses differently than others, so that a correct response on item 9 can carry twice the point value as a correct response on item 8, for example.

The item analysis we can conduct with computer help is conceptually similar to the procedure explored in Chapter 7, but there are some important differences. Rather than determining whether selected samples of high- and low-scoring students respond differently to a particular item, computer analysis generally includes data from everyone who participated. This makes item difficulty and item discrimination data more comprehensive. When responses are highly unusual, some item analysis programs will even indicate what may be an error in the scoring key. Perhaps the greatest advantage, however, is that the computer will usually perform the calculations much more quickly and accurately than we can perform them by other means. An item analysis for a 20-item quiz given to 25 students might take 20 to 30 minutes if we follow the Chapter 7 procedure. That is not an inordinate amount of time for the information one gains, but the more comprehensive computer analysis takes only a second or two.

Computers can also be programmed to interpret test scores. Software can instruct the computer to assign a particular verbal comment to all scores that fall within a defined numerical range. A score on an achievement test that falls in the first quartile, for example, may automatically key a response to the reader indicating that "Performance is substantially below what is typical of others in this age group. The student may need significant remedial help in order to perform at the level of her/his age peers."

Such programmed comments can help one who is unfamiliar with the testing procedure and who may need assistance to understand the results. Note that that there is some risk involved with an automatic explanation, however, because even when comments are prepared carefully, they are generalizations at best (Thorndike, 1997). Any score in a specified range of scores keys the same explanation. For example, students who score in the first quartile because they do not speak the language well probably receive the same comment as those whose scores stem from illness and distraction. While we can program the computer to respond to scoring differences, it usually will not determine the reason for the differences.

It is not feasible to develop a comment for every possible score so, ordinarily, one uses the same comment for a range of scores. Logically, it is less of a chore for the instructor to cover a wide range of scores with the same comment, but the comment is also less informative. In our example, the student at the 1st percentile will be assigned the same explanation as one at the 25th percentile, even though there are substantial differences in their performances.

Speaking of Assessment

When one uses software that provides verbal descriptions of students' performance to go with their scores, the comments are as good as the programming. Perhaps a language minority student takes an English assessment and scores at the 10th percentile. A second effort, scoring at the 25th percentile a month or so later, suggests remarkable progress, but if the verbal comments are the same for all scores in the first quartile, the instructor must intervene. When computer-generated assessment is inconsistent with information from other sources, someone must deal with the subjective judgment that the computer is ill-equipped to handle.

Computer-generated responses are very helpful with large groups of test takers. They are generalizations, however, with all of their attendant weaknesses.

Computing and Item Discrimination

A number of important decisions hinge on the information that comes from test analysis. Therefore, we try to see that the information is as good as it can be, which is what makes item analysis so important. Assessment must allow us to discriminate among the different levels of a characteristic that each test taker possesses.

If we gauge students' interest in drama, ordinarily we need to know the degree of their interest, rather than simply whether they are interested. For an achievement test, although we sometimes evaluate students "pass" or "fail", more often we expect the data to verify as many different levels of understanding as exist among the students. The degree to which an item discriminates among learners on the measured characteristic is the item's discrimination ability. Achievement items that discriminate well are items that those who have the learning will score correctly. Those who lack the learning will miss the item.

As we saw in Chapter 7, we can quantify the discrimination by calculating an index. There are actually several ways to measure discrimination. One way is by determining how well students' performance on an item correlates with their performance on other items measuring the same characteristic. If there are 10 items on the use of commas in composition, the students' performance on any 1 item should mirror their performance on all of the other comma items, so long as the item quality is consistent. Likewise, those who struggle with the item should also struggle with the other 9 items dealing with the topic. The degree to which the item discriminates is its discrimination index.

When we first looked at item discrimination, we relied upon the performance of two representative groups to help us make decisions about individual items. Recall that, from the total group of test takers, we identified one group who performed best on the test as a whole, and a second group of equal size made up of the lowest scoring students. We then calculated the discrimination index as a function of the difference between the number in each group who scored a particular item correctly. Items with the highest indices were the items that the higher students scored correctly and the lower students scored incorrectly. The accompanying assumption is that students who score well on the test as whole will have higher levels of the measured characteristics than those who do poorly on the test as a whole.

This approach to item discrimination provides very helpful information about the quality of test items. It is simple enough that we can calculate it quickly, but it also involves an assumption that may not always hold true. We assume that the entire instrument measures a single characteristic. Many of the assessments we use in the classroom cover more than one type of knowledge or skill, and they require more sophisticated item analysis procedures, which is why we turn to computer-managed item analysis programs.

Our pencil and paper approach obliged us to examine one item at a time. The computer can almost simultaneously accommodate all students' responses on all of the items from the assessment. The Chapter 7 approach is not fundamentally flawed it is just very crude compared to what the computer can generate with a program such as TESTAT™ (Assessment Systems Corporation, 1998). One could complete the same calculations that computer programs produce, by the way, but it would consume a great deal of time and require more than a passing knowledge of statistics and measurement theory.

The software that makes this possible was once the exclusive domain of measurement specialists who had programming ability in esoteric computer languages such as FORTRAN. Today, item analysis software is a good deal more "user-friendly."[2] One must still use a command structure to set up the analysis, but the steps outlined in the manuals are easy for the nonexpert to follow.

Computing and Validity

Computer data can provide answers to questions about criterion-related validity. Perhaps an intermediate grade instructor has developed a world history test. Although there are standardized tests of world history, perhaps the teacher wishes for something a little shorter and less intimidating to the students. If data from the two essentially agree, perhaps the teacher can rely less on the standardized test and so save the school the cost, and the students some of the related travail. First, however, the teacher must measure the level of agreement between the two measures.

The question is of the correlation between scores from the teacher-made test and those from the standardized test. Although the scoring ranges may be very different on the two tests, the students' rankings should be very similar if the data are valid. Those who achieve the higher scores on one test should also score well on the other. If those who perform well on one instrument tend to fall in the middle or the bottom relative to their classmates on the other, the data from at least one of the tests lack validity.

When they first appeared, computer spreadsheets were for business applications. Their on-screen array of horizontal rows intersecting with vertical columns looks very much like a traditional accountant's ledger, but it makes it much easier to enter data, change data, and recalculate the results. Many outside the business world who manipulate numerical data find spreadsheets helpful, including classroom teachers keeping track of scores and grades, but they offer more than an electronic record. Many of the popular spreadsheet programs incorporate statistical functions, including correlation. The correlation coefficient for the teacher's test and the standardized instrument will answer questions about the level of criterion-related validity reflected in two sets of scores.[3] There is an example in Appendix 11.1 that illustrates how one can calculate a correlation for two sets of (contrived) data using a computer spreadsheet.

The commands for calculating the correlation are quite similar from program to program, but they are certainly not identical. The example in Appendix 11.1 provides the commands for Excel (Microsoft Office, 1997). Those for other programs will differ. The point is that one can adapt spreadsheet programs, which have become very common and quite easy to use, to provide validity information. Correlation coefficients are not difficult to calculate without a computer (Chapter 9), but computers make it much easier. Of course, this is helpful only when the assessment is the type that yields a score. Qualitative results require quite different handling, but when the assessment data are numeric, a little work with a computer spreadsheet will answer a variety of questions, including those about criterion-related validity.

Equating Scores

One way to evaluate testing fairness is to see whether students of different groups (gender, ethnic, linguistic, social class, and so forth) respond to particular test items differently than those of other groups. When one has access to group membership data,

Significance tests such as *t*-test and analysis of variance allow one to determine whether particular groups' average scores are sufficiently different that the variability is not random. When two groups are at issue, *t*-test is often the choice. Analysis of variance allows one to examine the mean differences among multiple groups.

Electronic spreadsheets lend themselves to providing statistical answers to assessment questions that deal with topics ranging from criterion-related validity to group differences.

computers make this comparatively easy to determine. Appendix 11.2 is a sample problem in which the question is whether gender groups have significantly different scores on an attitude survey. The statistical test used in the example is a *t*-test, and it will help one determine whether there are statistically significant differences in the average scores of two groups. The example includes a list of the commands needed to complete the test, but one should note that some computer spreadsheets have a *t*-test option built in.

The *t*-test is usually fine for examining significance differences between two independent groups.[4] The test is limited, however, in that it accommodates only two groups, such as male/female, English speaking/non–English speaking, and so forth. A test called **analysis of variance (ANOVA)** examines the differences among more than two groups using a similar logic, the comparison of the groups' average scores.[5]

Questions of group differences precede a knottier question—whether the differences reflect test bias. There are many reasons that particular groups might score a test item differently than members of other groups, some of them having nothing to do with item or test bias. If, however, one can demonstrate that (1) there are statistically significant differences, and (2) those differences are unrelated to anything except the individual's group membership, there is a bias problem. Computer analysis can be a great help in such investigations.

Using the Computer to Score Essay Items

On at least one level, recent developments in assessment seem *in*consistent with the increasing use of computers. Historically, those who developed standardized achievement tests made almost exclusive use of dichotomously scored (the response is either right or wrong) assessment items. Those items lend themselves very well to computer scoring for reasons noted in the prior discussion of optical scoring. The computer does not "grade" the right or wrong responses in the sense of evaluating their characteristics except to see whether the learner's response matches the scoring key.

In recent years, however, there has been much more emphasis on the essay and other constructed response items. These items do not lend themselves to a simple keyed scoring procedure. Ordinarily we examine a response to see whether the learner addresses the main points, develops a logical argument, provides supporting detail, and so forth. This seems inconsistent with optical scanning and scoring with a key, but there have been some important developments. The largest test-developing organizations are experimenting with scoring procedures that, although they do not entirely eliminate human participation, include elements of machine scoring (Page, 1994; Page and Petersen, 1995).

One measure of essay scoring quality is the level of agreement among multiple essay scorers, usually called interrater reliability. Work by the Educational Testing Service

(ETS) suggests that interrater reliability with machine-scored essays is at least as high as when people do the scoring (ETS, 1998). The great advantage, of course, is that it occurs much faster. First, human evaluators score a series of sample essays. Different elements of their findings—including the length of the essay, the complexity and variety of word usage, and the structure of the writing in the best responses—become the basis for a scoring protocol. Computers determine the degree to which other essays match the characteristics of the best ones and assign high scores to similar essays and lower scores to responses that differ substantially on the essential characteristics. Researchers described the scoring process:

> *Longer essays incorporating a variety of sentence structures and a sophisticated vocabulary, for example, may receive a relative higher score . . . because these traits are valued highly by human scorers, and [the computer scoring procedure] is able to identify such traits. (p. 6)*

In some situations, researchers eliminated essay length as a scoring variable. They did not want those who wrote more lengthy essays to receive higher scores than those with shorter pieces if the responses were otherwise comparable. Those interested in improving scores might simply tell learners to write as much as time permits, even if it is not directly relevant.

On one level, the computer is still looking for a match, just as with traditional machine scoring. Rather than examining student responses for the presence of a pencil mark in the appropriate space, however, the computer searches for several possible characteristics in a variety of combinations.

> Although they are largely experimental at this point, programs exist that allow one to use the computer to score constructed response items such as essays. The grammar, spelling, thesaurus, and sentence structure aids that word processing software contains operate on the same principles.

As evidence of software that can identify and even correct writing errors, consider the capabilities of the typical word processing program. The software used to draft this book, for example, indicates when the author has misspelled one of the words contained in its dictionary. The software detects common punctuation errors. It indicates the readability level of the text. It even indicates (often to your author's irritation) when the author uses the passive voice, since that characteristic is not associated with a formal writing style. The capacity to recognize these characteristics is the same ability that allows computers to score essays.

Scoring Interest Inventories and Personality Assessments

Most of the scoring examples so far have been situations in which we are measuring student achievement, but computer-managed assessment is quite common in psychological testing. Here one often weights items differentially or perhaps combines certain items into subscale scores to determine the presence of particular characteristics or attitudes. This sometimes makes the scoring procedure quite involved, but the complicated scoring so common in interest and personality instruments is the computer's forte.

Automated scoring can dramatically improve both the speed and the precision of the procedure, but it does not come without a cost. Computer scoring has a tendency to depersonalize an activity that, especially in the case of assessing interest and personality characteristics, is highly personal by its nature. Someone who scores the assessments by hand and one at a time might recognize some characteristic or trend that a machine-scoring process cannot reveal unless it happens to be programmed to recognize it. What one gains in assessment efficiency one must counterbalance with what may be lost in individual insight.

STATIC VERSUS DYNAMIC ASSESSMENT

Traditional assessment procedures offer what one might call a snapshot of the learner's performance. A test, homework assignment, report, or the like provides a view of what the student knows or can do at the assessment point, but it usually reveals little of the learners' progress during a period of time. A report card primarily reflects how well a student performs at the end of the term, not what occurred during the term. Bunderson and his co-authors (1989) call this "static" measurement, and it reflects what is most common in student assessment. As the number of assessments over the course of a learning experience diminishes, measurement is increasingly static. In the extreme, we have a situation in which a single project or final exam reflects the learner's performance over an extended period.

Static measurement specifies a point (Bunderson et al., 1989). It is an important point because what the student knows at any juncture matters, especially when it occurs at the end of the course, but it is still only one point. If one wishes to use a static measure to develop a view of the student's progress over time, there are some notable risks involved. One is obliged to extrapolate a trend from the point and make educated guesses about what the learner knew before that point, as well as what the direction and progress of the learner will be after the measurement.

Static measurement generally has another important characteristic. It employs the same assessment procedures and instruments for all recipients. Assessors avoid adjusting the instrument or the procedure to an individual learner's circumstances because of fears that changes will compromise one's ability to generalize about the assessment data. Indeed, the usual standardization procedures call for a testing environment that is as similar as possible for all test takers.

There is a great deal of assessment in the ordinary classroom, however, that does not constitute standardized testing. For the bulk of that activity, perhaps it is better to examine student progress as a continuous process rather than a point, or even a few points. When we think in terms of a process, it is easier to view what occurs with the student as a modifiable sequence that we can fine-tune whenever conditions in either the learners or the environment change. This, however, calls for a program of continuously monitoring all of the variables known to affect the student's achievement. It calls for **dynamic assessment** (Bunderson et al., 1989), which offers the potential to be a more comprehensive and sensitive assessment procedure.

We often speak of learning curves, and the student's learning curve or learning trajectory is a good way to visualize dynamic assessment. This system of continuous monitoring allows one to plot the student's progress rather than extrapolating tendencies from a single point. The final point in the trajectory is equivalent to what static measurement reveals when one assesses the student's performance only at the conclusion of the learning period. As valuable as a final exam is, the score cannot indicate how the learner arrived at the point. It does not suggest what might have been the periods of greatest growth for the student, nor does it indicate what may have been the areas of difficulty. Figure 11.3 illustrates these differences.

The static measurement in (a) indicates that there were just two assessments administered during the instructional period, one at the beginning and a second at the end of the unit. There was assessment throughout the dynamic measurement in (b) however. If the figures both represented the same instructional unit, note how differently one might understand students' performance according to the different types of measurement. Static assessment does not illustrate the flatness of student progress early in the unit. Only the dynamic measurement in (b) indicates that the most rapid growth was during the very late elements of the unit.

Tracking relatively minor changes in students' performance calls for multiple measures, and the process increases in difficulty and complexity as the group size increases. The time requirements for dynamic measurement are so great that static measurement is far more common in the traditional classroom.

(a) Static Measurement

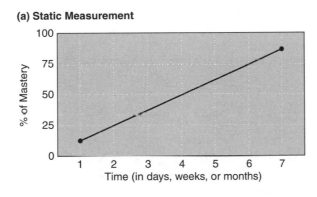

(b) Dynamic Measurement

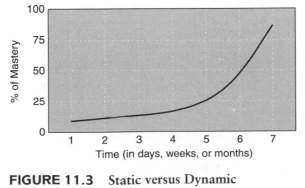

FIGURE 11.3 Static versus Dynamic Measurement

Computers offer the potential to alter this. Developing assessments that we can administer by computer is no small task, but once we have them, the computer can administer the instrument, analyze the data, and record the results. Theoretically, at least, the instructor need not interrupt other activities in order to measure the students' progress. There is an even greater opportunity for dynamic assessment when the instructional activities are also computer managed. In that instance, assessment can become a component of the instruction and provide constant monitoring as the student responds to instructional activities.

> Student assessment is of two kinds: static assessment, which allows one an "at the moment," snapshot view of students' performance, and dynamic assessment, which permits one to track the progress of learning over time. Although computer technology enhances both, dynamic assessment is much more feasible when instruction and assessment are both managed by the computer.

A student's learning trajectory can be linear, which specifies a uniform rate of learning over a period. It is more likely, however, that most students' trajectories are curvilinear. They experience some periods of accelerated learning and others of slower progress. Ordinary static assessment cannot reveal a curvilinear learning trajectory. Static assessment may suffice when all one wishes to know is the student's final location relative to an objective, but remember that there are other questions to answer. When one can identify the times at which the pace of learning changes substantially, one can begin to examine some of the factors in the student's progress more carefully. If a student's progress drops off noticeably, and particularly if progress declines for several students, it might be advisable to examine the subject, and perhaps the learning materials that are used to help deliver the curriculum. It is much more feasible to pursue these questions if one can rely on the computer to manage elements of the assessment.

COMPUTER-ADAPTIVE TESTING

In academic assessment generally, the data reflect how well respondents perform with a series of tasks designed to indicate what they know. Although the tasks may represent a part of exactly what we expect learners to be able to do beyond the classroom, they can almost never represent the entire domain. A math test, for example, is a sample of problems drawn from a much larger universe of potential test items. Because of time constraints, teachers must set aside some of the problems they might have posed to the students. The test is a subset of the larger population of possible questions, which makes it an approximation of the curriculum offered the student. Consequently, any score or evaluative comment based upon assessment results represents only an estimate of the learner's performance. The estimation allows one to draw inferences about learners based on their performance with the sample of test items, but because the test items are only a sample, one always runs the risk of drawing inaccurate conclusions. If some of the items are not characteristic of the content area, or if the sample of questions is too small to reflect the discipline, the score will probably not reflect what the learners know.

Note something else. The usual assessment procedure presents the same tasks to all respondents. Although this approach to assessment is common enough, and seems at first blush at least to be the fairest tactic, it does not stand scrutiny very well. With the great differences among learners in background experiences, learning styles, aptitude, preferred mode of expression, and the like, a clear picture of what they know may call for assessment instruments that are tailored more closely to their individual circumstances.

Two students, for example, may have similar capacities for solving mathematics multiplication problems, but because of experience differences, one may struggle with multiplication problems involving "carrying" while the other does not. A cursory view of the student's performance might indicate that the student does not know the multiplication tables. If, however, the instructor were able to adapt the problems to the individual learner, it might become clear that how to carry—not math facts—is the problem. At that point, it is easier to help the student with some remedial instruction. To generalize this, we might say that if one wishes the clearest picture of a learner's knowledge or ability, one might need to pose different test items to different learners.

These are some of the problems that **computer-adaptive testing (CAT)** was designed to address. It offers the potential to reveal more about what the respondent knows, believes, or can do than conventional assessment, and it relies squarely on the use of computers. Where conventional assessment represents a static system, remaining fixed for all recipients from the time it is developed, CAT is a dynamic assessment procedure. By design, it adjusts according to the respondent's performance during the assessment procedure by allowing the sort of probing that instructors often use during an in-class discussion, but which is uncommon in conventional assessment.

If the learner scores an item correctly, a CAT procedure responds by selecting a subsequent test item that is slightly more demanding. On the other hand, if the response is incorrect, the next item presented is less difficult. The logic is as follows: Scoring an item correctly means that the learner can respond at the level of difficulty the item represents. Once that is established, there is little point in belaboring the issue and lengthening the assessment by continuing to present similarly difficult items on the subject or skill.

On the other hand, if the item is incorrect, one could conclude that (1) other, similar items will also be too difficult and (2) the respondent lacks the skill of knowledge that the item is intended to gauge. More of the same items will reveal nothing more about the respondent. This process of adapting to responses continues until a profile of the learner's ability emerges. All who are tested begin with the same item, but as the procedure unfolds, it tailors the assessment to the test taker. Because the assessment procedure adapts, there is a separate profile for each person. Nitko (1989) called the profile a representation of the learner's **zone of proximal proficiency**. It offers the potential for a much more complete view of what the learner knows or can do than a score from

> Computer-adaptive testing (CAT) selects items from an item bank depending upon the learner's responses to earlier items. By selecting both items with a lower difficulty level than previously missed items and items more difficult than those scored correctly, CAT produces a profile of the learner's ability/achievement that is more complete than conventional testing provides.

a conventional test where everyone responds to the same items without regard to individual differences.

CAT and Formative Assessment

In addition to testing that can adapt to the individual learner's skill and ability levels, these same characteristics make CAT an excellent source of remedial information to the instructor. The test items the learner can complete correctly, as well as those which continue to pose problems, represent a profile of the areas of instruction the student has a command of, and those where additional learning is still needed. An Educational Testing Service bulletin (ETS, 1998) dealing with these procedures explained:

> *In each of the major skills groups addressed . . . students are asked to demonstrate their abilities through a number of tasks. Those who cannot fulfill these . . . requests are routed into the remediation phase, which provides up to three levels of review with increasingly basic exercises or questions for people to work through. (p. 3)*

Mosenthal (1998) explains that computer-adaptive testing is completely compatible with the teacher's instructional duties. Besides providing a profile of the student's abilities, CAT can also provide an important learning experience as the student works through test items selected because they are incrementally easier—or more difficult—than those preceding. The sequence of items also provides important information to one who is interested in monitoring the learner's progress. This can be very informative if it occurs during the course of learning, rather than only after the learning is completed. It permits the instructor to recognize the student's learning trajectory.

Mosenthal's (1998) reference to monitoring the learning while it is in progress is what earlier was called formative assessment. Recall that this is assessment for evaluating instructional quality and the learners' progress, rather than for grading students. It is an element of diagnostic assessment and indicates an area in which computer-adaptive testing might become particularly helpful as a tool for identifying how to alter the instructional program for the learner's benefit.

In order to implement CAT, we must align the assessment items with the related content. More specifically, we must be able to state what the learner must know in order to respond to the item correctly. When we establish what the student had to know in order to respond, we can develop a meaningful profile of what the student knows, or can do, and what is yet to be learned. The profile ought to be a great help to the instructor and to the student. The profile might indicate, for example, that a student lacks a command of the basic facts associated with the subject, or that problem-solving items tend to be more difficult than items in which the respondent must define a term. Armed with such information, the instructor can alter lesson plans and learning activities to strengthen areas of weakness, and spend less time on abilities that students have already developed.

Since the computer's program selects subsequent items based on performance on prior items, CAT procedures make sense only when one controls the assessment domains. The test specifications that are prepared before the instrument is constructed must indicate what to assess, and each topic or skill area addressed by the assessment will require a separate learner profile. Remember that the computer's task is to presents items based on the correctness of prior responses. This presumes that items reflect a common theme, or at least a series of related ideas. When the focus of the assessment shifts to some new curricular area, the procedure must begin anew.

Because this procedure will detect what the learners do and do not know more quickly than conventional assessment, there are two likely results. There will probably be more precise measurement, and there will be less time spent in testing (Bunderson et al., 1989). This is possible because the procedure will not administer assessment items that are likely to provide redundant information. The items like those already answered correctly, and those answered incorrectly, will remain unused.

CAT and Item Response Theory

Not very much has been said about classifying item difficulty, but it is central to the use of CAT. From one point of view, computer-adaptive testing is possible because of procedures stemming from the item response theory (IRT) techniques mentioned in Chapter 9 and to be elaborated in Chapter 13. Recall that IRT allows us to analyze performance by how much of a trait students possess and the probability that they will score an item correctly. This information makes it possible to classify test items so that they are usable in CAT procedures.

COMPUTER GENERATIONS IN EDUCATIONAL ASSESSMENT

When there are definable points of progression, sometimes a developmental process is easiest to understand in terms of stages. Bunderson and his coauthors (1989) described the growth of computer use in assessment in terms of successive computer generations. With each generation, the computer performs a greater share of the assessment task, and finally, because artificial intelligence is available, the computer becomes the assessment "expert." Figure 11.4 summarizes the developments that make up the four generations that Bunderson et al. described. As you read, note that the progression from generation to generation is cumulative. Each level includes the advances of the prior levels in its own increasingly sophisticated approaches.

First-Generation Applications

With first-generation computer applications, actual assessment practices changed very little. Rather, educators used the technology as a means to automate some of their more ordinary and repetitive assessment procedures. At this level of computer integration, the practice is to adapt existing software to assessment purposes. Instructors may save their tests in computer files. Often simple word processing documents fill this need, although software designed specifically for test construction is available.

In the early 1980s, electronic spreadsheets that were developed for use in business and accounting became widely available, but it was not long before educators

FIGURE 11.4   Generations of Computer Use in Assessment

First Generation	Computers are used primarily to bank test items and store grading data.
Second Generation	Computer-adaptive testing (CAT) is available. This technology allows the computer to adapt the assessment to the student's responses to develop a clear picture of the student's "zone of proximal proficiency."
Third Generation	Continuous measurement allows the use of dynamic assessment. Learning trajectories can be developed for each student.
Fourth Generation	Artificial intelligence allows the computer to be used as an assessment expert to analyze assessment problems.

Source: Adapted from Bunderson et al. (1989).

discovered that they are also very effective grade-management tools. The capability of spreadsheets to sum, average, and automatically recalculate lengthy lists of numbers make them very helpful in classrooms where there are many assignments and projects to record and large numbers of students. The more sophisticated applications discussed previously that allow us to evaluate criterion-related validity and group differences came later. Over the years, the command language that spreadsheets employ has become quite simple, and many instructors adapt them to educational uses. Such situations in which, for efficiency reasons, computer software originally developed for some other purpose is adapted to educational and psychological assessment are characteristic of first-generation computer applications.

Second-Generation Applications

The next generation of computer applications in assessment introduces us to computerized testing (CT). Unlike first-generation applications, which primarily streamline existing assessment procedures, CT allows educators to pursue objectives that were unreachable before. When one translates assessments and adapts them to a computer format, the instructors gain much more flexibility. Assessment can occur whenever the student is prepared, and neither teacher nor student must adhere to a rigid testing schedule. One can also structure computerized testing to provide a descriptive profile of the learner's performance. It is common with standardized testing, for example, to receive a normative comparison of the individual to what is typical of the others who have taken the test. As an extension of this, the CT report may also contain a verbal description of where the student's strengths and weaknesses lie.

The CT applications can also yield important information about the instrument. Item analysis procedures belong to this level of computer use. Item analysis can indicate how well a test item discriminates among test takers on levels of the characteristic measured. It will also indicate the item's difficulty. This opens the way for the testing choices that are characteristic of the second generation.

In a CT environment, all respondents may receive the same instrument, as they would in a conventional testing setting, or the procedure may include the computer adaptive testing (CAT) examined above. Recall that CAT uses an extensive item bank to select and administer particular items, each successive item dictated by the individual's earlier responses. CAT is possible because one can program the computer to scale test items according to item response theory (IRT) procedures. Although this is still possible without the use of computers, it is not practical because of the level of analysis required. It would ordinarily be far too time consuming to bother with if we had to do it by hand.

Perhaps the greatest advantage this level of assessment offers is the speed and accuracy with which learners' scores and the item analysis information become available. Although computer applications can be no better than the programs that make them operational, if the programming is accurate and one enters the scoring key correctly, the data are highly reliable.

As we discuss third- and fourth-generation applications, the reader will note that this work is largely experimental. First- and second-generation applications, however, are very evident—both in the schools and in the work done by professional testing organizations. For some time, researchers and educators have used the microcomputer to write test items, to bank them in computer files, to construct the tests, and finally to administer the tests. Applications that focus on test scoring, response analysis, and the reporting phases of testing are also quite common. The MICROCAT Corporation (Assessment Systems Corporation, 1998), for example, produces assessment systems that will handle item banking, test construction, online testing, and item and test analysis, as well as the detection of scoring irregularities that suggest that cheating might have occurred.

Third-Generation Applications

The third computer generation represents the dynamic assessment procedures discussed earlier. Remember that dynamic assessment is continuous throughout the instructional period. In fact, Bunderson and his coauthors (1989) call it the generation of continuous measurement (CM). Rather than separating assessment from instruction, which is what ordinarily happens, the assessment elements become an unobtrusive but important part of the instructional sequence. In addition to the continuous updates of the learner's progress, the flow of assessment information allows one to modify the instruction whenever needed. Although it is largely experimental, note how consistent dynamic assessment is with our goal of thoroughly integrating assessment with instruction.

In some scenarios, computer-adaptive testing is an integral part of continuous measurement. The individualized assessment instrument that CAT produces becomes a guide to the learner's strengths and weaknesses. The result is a CM program tailored very closely to what the individual needs. Those involved in a CM episode potentially receive both assessments and instructional materials that are unique to their own circumstances.

The idea of an instructional sequence modified by assessment data is not a novel one, of course. We have noted repeatedly that integrating assessment with other elements of the educational plan is simply good teaching. Continuous measurement has an element that sets it apart from this more general idea, however. A CM program allows us to construct an accurate learning trajectory for students. We can see not only their different levels of performance, but also differences in their rates of learning. That information, in turn, reveals something about what resources we will need as the students continue their progress toward defined objectives.

Each generation of computer assessment is more complex to set up than the last, and this is certainly true of a CM system. It requires extensive cooperation between curriculum specialists and assessment experts, who must determine together what to measure. A continuous measurement program cannot emerge from either group in isolation, at the risk of solid instruction for which there is poor assessment, or sound measurement of shoddy instructional materials (Bunderson et al., 1989). Beyond the general need to cooperate, let us restate the other elements of CM:

1. The measurement is continuous throughout the curriculum.
2. Besides being continuous, the testing is an integrated, rather than a separate, part of the instruction.
3. The assessment items in the exercise modules reflect a CAT program. The computer selects each item based upon the learner's response to a prior item in the module.
4. The assessment data emphasize the progress of the individual rather than of the institution. The assessment data are available to both the student and the instructor.

Fourth-Generation Computer Assessment Applications

This fourth generation, called intelligent measurement (IM), is still primarily an experimental attempt to use artificial intelligence (AI) in assessment tasks. If past developments are any guide, however, it will become accepted practice in the not-too-distant future.

Early computer applications for assessment were primarily efforts to relieve educators of some of the time burdens associated with assessment, but time is not the only problem. Educational assessment is becoming increasingly technical and remarkably complex, and perhaps educators sometimes fail to possess the expertise that even some of the common assessment tasks require. The IM systems use the computer, programmed with an expert's knowledge, to assist local educators to collect data and properly interpret them. Potentially, an IM system will assist the educator to construct items and develop an assessment instrument, administer the test, and analyze the results— all within the context of the instructional plan. The concept is attractive. The computer becomes a resident assessment consultant that the educator can access in order to work through the various measurement tasks and understand the assessment data. The implicit assumption is that someone can reduce all of the necessary information to computer commands and then create a system that is simple enough that ordinary educators can use it to guide them through sometimes very complex questions.

The danger in such a system, of course, is that even if one condenses the expert's understanding to accessible computer files, it will be difficult to build into the system

Computer use in assessment has four discrete stages, or generations. First-generation developments are essentially the use of the computer to store and manipulate items and test data. The second includes computer-adaptive testing (CAT) and computerized test preparation and analysis. The third generation includes continuous measurement and its associated dynamic assessment. In the fourth generation, the computer uses artificial intelligence in the role of expert assessor.

all of the needed safeguards. By intent, IM systems will provide an expertise that the user lacks. The companion problem is that one has a potential to make poor decisions with the system, or to misunderstand the results because one lacks the understanding upon which the system rests. By way of an analogy, high-performance automobiles now come equipped with braking and handling systems that will compensate in some measure for the driver's ineptness or the car's sudden loss of traction. They allow one to drive more safely at relatively high rates of speed. However, neither braking nor handling systems are helpful to the driver who simply makes poor decisions and inadvertently directs the vehicle into a tree. Even if IM systems are developed and widely adopted, they will still require some level of understanding by the educator who uses them. There is no way to make assessment systems foolproof.

Computer Testing Problems

With any emerging technology, there are problems to solve, and computer assessment is no different. Some of the problems relate to format. Many students prefer to flip through the pages of a test once it is completed, looking for items they may have been unsure of earlier. They may also wish to revise an earlier response in light of something that they thought of later in the assessment. These options are a little more difficult with electronic presentation, where assessment items ordinarily are on screen one at a time. Although this could be changed, current format usually does not allow one to review or change test items once they are entered.

There is also less flexibility in the testing site. Most of us have taken standardized tests in gymnasiums or cafeterias converted for the purpose when the circumstances demanded it. The requirements for conventional testing are quite simple: a space where students can work in reasonable comfort, with minimal disturbance, and where proctoring their work is possible. Computer testing requires a far more specialized environment. At the least, one must have access to a laboratory where the hardware and software are available. Many computer laboratories are too small to accommodate larger assessment groups, and often computers are so close to one another that proctoring students' work is difficult.

Not only can the labs be very confining, they may not be available at all. While new hardware developments and the economies of scale that accompany computers' widespread popularity have brought prices down, not every school has a dedicated computer lab. Such facilities still require a very substantial investment, and software costs are ongoing as newer versions replace dated copies of an assessment program.

Perhaps these problems are only transitional. Virtually all newly constructed schools include plans for computer labs. Although most existing labs were not set up with assessment in mind, as the practice becomes more common, the physical setting will probably be more conducive to computerized assessment.

GROUP DIFFERENCES IN COMPUTER USE

One of the concerns raised regarding computer use is whether computerized testing may produce different effects for different groups of students. If it does, this approach may have the effect of widening the disparities that educators often work to narrow. Cyberphobia (the buzzword for fear of computers) is quite common, particularly among older students with very limited computer experience. Some experts have asked whether testing anxiety may be higher for those unfamiliar with the hardware who are administered tests by the computer. The Educational Testing Service examined the issue experimentally. Using students whose experience with computers varied, researchers administered a common language assessment, first in the conventional paper and pencil fashion, and then a second time via the computer. "The research team concluded, once language ability was controlled for, there were no meaningful differences in performance between the paper-and-pencil test and computer-based . . . items" (ETS, 1998, p. 3).

There has also been some concern that test takers' attitudes might be a factor in test taking. Although the research in this area is still emerging, the conclusions suggest that test takers generally have favorable feelings regarding the use of computers in assessment. Legg and Buhr (1992) point out, however, that much of this research is grounded in differences related to ethnic group, gender, or age. The data on attitude differences remain sparse. Legg and Buhr conclude that whatever differences emerge in learners' attitudes are not statistically related to their groups. They also indicate that attitude differences appear unrelated to the learners' ability levels. Low-ability students indicate no greater problems in testing by computer than the higher ability students. [6]

At least one application of computerized testing offers to redress a disparity that emerges in conventional paper and pencil testing. In much of the mathematics achievement testing, males tend to achieve more extreme scores (high and low) than female learners. There is also evidence that male and female students may excel at different kinds of mathematics test items, perhaps because they employ different kinds of problem-solving strategies. For example, some gender differences emerge because males are more comfortable taking short-cuts to a solution, and female students are more inclined to follow an established problem-solving procedure (ETS, 1998). Standardized tests often have time limits imposed, more for administrative convenience than for any psychometric reason. As the time limit becomes more restrictive, it favors learners who look for shortcuts. The problem, of course, is that the assessment was to measure mathematics achievement, rather than the willingness to take a short-cut. Because computers can handle many of the administrative chores involved in testing large numbers of students, there may be no need to impose time limits, and the shortcut as a factor in the score can be minimized.

SUMMARY

In truth, most classroom teachers make comparatively modest use of computers in their assessment activities. They usually restrict computers to the business of storing copies of their tests in word processing files and managing students' grades. There are indications that more change is coming, and there is also some suggestion of how difficult it will be to further those changes.

It has become something of an article of faith that the key to greater progress in education, and indeed a focal point in educational reform, is more assessment. More assessment clears the way for more accountability; and that, the reasoning goes, is the remedy for disappointing levels of performance. Without analyzing the merits of this argument, note that learners, educators, curricula, and in fact all elements of the educational program are subject to great scrutiny. The quantity and the complexity of the data produced make computer use a necessity. There is simply too much to manage otherwise, and happily, the developments of recent years render the relevant software quite easy to use. The products of computer analysis need no longer be the esoterica that only a specialized few will understand.

That said, the average classroom teacher will probably see some of the most sophisticated applications associated with item response theory and computer-adaptive testing primarily from a distance. This will occur as teachers continue to participate in the administration of standardized tests. Although the level of specialization that using computer technology requires may have been a bottleneck to computer use in the past, Schilling and Schilling (1998) observed that many of those issues have been resolved. Educators who use computers at one level or another are presently the rule rather than the exception.

Fundamental changes depend on more than advances in hardware and software, as significant as those advances are. The other element is the disposition of the people who are involved in delivering and interpreting educational products (Bunderson et al., 1989). Basic educational practice is very difficult to modify because teachers tend to do what they have seen done in the classroom, not just during their professional preparation, but also during their earlier years, as students. This cycle can be very difficult to overcome. The computer applications the educators adopt are usually the minor adjustments in the way they manage data, rather than the more basic adoptions of new assessment practices.

The way the major testing agencies administer standardized tests has brought more significant changes, and here there are a number of distinct advantages. Several of them are logistical. Data from computerized testing are often available almost immediately. Computerized testing often does not require testing professionals to be on-site, a factor that makes it more convenient to offer the assessment to populations that were inaccessible, and which also lowers the administrative costs. Computerized testing may also eliminate the need to impose a time limit for testing, unless it relates somehow to the quality assessed.

We noted the progress made in scoring essays with computers. Because there is a great deal of interest in thinking that can be assessed with constructed response test items only, those applications are destined to become increasingly important. A word of caution is in order, however. The computer can do what one programs it to do. It can do it with remarkable efficiency and with untiring perseverance, but it can respond no better than the commands that direct it, and programming is a skill most educators do not have. They must rely on others for their assessment programs, a circumstance that places them in the same position they occupy with those who produce the other materials they use. Someone who does not know their particular students is designing the materials that will help define their students' progress.

Computer systems—particularly desktop microcomputer systems—have become relatively inexpensive, and the software developers have produced programs that make them very easy to use. The level of interest in educational reform has had a spillover effect on assessment activities, and many educators will use computers to help manage the data they are required to gather on individual learners. Computer-adaptive testing (CAT) and continuous measurement (CM) both rest on a sound theoretical basis. They each offer the potential to alter and improve classroom procedure. At the writing of this book, their level of sophistication is beyond the reach of most classroom teachers, however. Past practice suggests that CAT and CM will become fixtures in the classroom, although not immediately.

ENDNOTES

1. One of your author's erstwhile professors had the practice of using his items repeatedly in a course in test construction. This soon became common knowledge, of course, and because graduate students are no slouches when a short-cut is available, classmates set about collecting all of the former tests they could locate. The reality, however, was that Dr. Barker had an item bank containing several hundred items, and he was quite content to have students locate and learn the correct answers to as many as possible. From his point of view, it was simply a part of the learning process.

2. One such software provider is MICROCAT Systems, referenced below.

3. Should you have a spreadsheet, but no ready option to calculate correlation, Appendix 11.1 provides an example of calculating correlation for Excel (*Microsoft Office*, 1997), one of the more popular spreadsheets (which has a statistical option, by the way).

4. There are actually several assumptions implicit in the use of this *t*-test. Discussions of group independence, equality of variance, and interval scale measure (raised in Chapter 9) are primarily the purview of statistics texts. Sprinthall (1997) provides a very good introduction.

5. Most statistical testing is beyond the scope of this book. However, as an example, should one wish to determine whether students from two different language groups have distinct responses to a question, or to a test, a simple independent *t*-test would probably answer that question. The test is a ratio of numerator to denominator. The numerator is the difference in the groups' average scores. The denominator is the variability in the scores of all involved in the analysis. When the ratio of scoring differences to variability is large, one concludes that the two groups' scores are significantly different, which means that the difference probably did not occur by chance. Tables available in statistics texts indicate how large the ratio must be before one can conclude significance. Appendix 11.2 is an example of completing an independent *t*-test with spreadsheet data to resolve such an issue.

   Analysis of variance is similar in principle. Excel (*Microsoft Office*, 1997) has options both for the *t*-test that is used for two groups and for the analysis of variance test that allows one to analyze data from any number of groups.

6. The difficulty with this type of research, by the way, is that the researchers rely on self-reported feelings by respondents. While they are interesting and may be valuable, they are not always reliable.

FOR FURTHER READING

Several times in this chapter an article has been cited by Bunderson, Inouye, and Olsen (1989). When the domain of computer testing was still very much in the formative stages, Bunderson et al. outlined it well. Citations of their article are common in the literature dealing with computer testing. They are particularly helpful for one attempting to understand the structure of computerized assessment.

Although computer spreadsheets often provide statistical functions including the correlation, *t*-tests, and analysis of variance (ANOVA) mentioned here, one ought to consult a statistics text to understand the tests more fully. Sprinthall (1997) provides an excellent introduction and requires a minimal math background.

REFERENCES

Assessment Systems Corporation. (1998). 2233 University Ave., Suite 200, St. Paul, MN.

Atkinson, R. C., and Fletcher, J. D. (1972). Teaching children to read with a computer. *Reading Teacher, 25,* 319–327.

Bunderson, C. V., Inouye, D. K., and Olsen, J. B. (1989). The four generations of computerized educational measurement. In R. L. Linn (Ed.), *Educational measurement* (3rd ed., pp. 367–407). New York: Macmillan.

ETS. (1998). Coming to your test soon—computerized scoring of essays. *ETS Developments, 43*(3). Princeton, NJ: Educational Testing Service.

Legg, S. M., and Buhr, D.C. (1992). Computerized adaptive testing with different groups. *Educational Measurement: Issues and Practice, 11*(2), 23–27.

Microsoft Office. (1997). Copyright Microsoft Corporation.

Mosenthal, P. B. (1998). Defining prose task characteristics for use in computer adaptive testing and instruction. *American Educational Research Journal, 35,* 269–307.

Nitko, A. J. (1989). Designing tests that are integrated with instruction. In R. L. Linn (Ed.), *Educational measurement* (3rd ed., pp. 447–474). New York: Macmillan.

Page, E. B. (1994). Computer grading of student prose, using modern concepts and software. *Journal of Experimental Education, 62,* 127–142.

Page, E. B., and Petersen, N. S. (1995). The computer moves into essay grading: Updating the ancient test. *Phi Delta Kappan, 76,* 561–565.

Schilling, K. M., and Schilling, K. L. (1998). "Proclaiming and sustaining excellence: Assessment as a faculty role." *ASHE-ERIC Higher Education Report, 26*(3).

Sprinthall, R. C. (1997). *Basic statistical analysis* (5th ed.). Boston: Allyn & Bacon

Thorndike, R. M. (1997). *Measurement and evaluation in psychology and education* (6th ed.). Columbus, OH: Merrill.

Using Microsoft Excel to Calculate Criterion-Related Validity

Criterion-related validity is the correlation between two sets of scores. Both sets of data should reflect the same relative standing among the students if the data are correlated. Assume that the data in the following sample spreadsheet represent test scores. The scores in column B are from a teacher-made achievement test, and the scores in column C are from a standardized test.

	A	B	C
1	Student	Score #1	Score #2
2	A	21	74
3	B	14	61
4	C	16	60
5	D	11	51
6	E	18	65
7	F	21	70
8	G	22	71
9	H	17	63
10	I	24	74
11	J	15	58
12	K	14	59
13	L	19	64

In spreadsheets, the columns are lettered and the rows are numbered. Column letters and row numbers identify individual cells. The data are entered in columns A, B, and C. The first test score for student A, therefore, appears in cell B2. The commands to complete the correlation calculations in an Excel spreadsheet are as follows:

Click the "Tools" option on the tool bar.
Click "Data Analysis."
Highlight "Correlation" and click "OK."
Enter B2:C13 in the box for input range and click "OK."

The calculated correlation rounds to .96, a very high level of concurrent validity.

APPENDIX 11.2

Using Microsoft Excel to Determine Group Differences

The *t*-test allows one to determine whether, with a given level of probability, two groups' scores are significantly different. The test is a ratio of the differences in the mean scores of the two groups and a measure of the variability in the scoring of both groups. Assume that the data in the following sample spreadsheet are the scores from students representing two different ethnic groups.

	A	B	C
1	Student	Group 1	Group 2
2	A	21	26
3	B	14	21
4	C	16	12
5	D	11	15
6	E	18	20
7	F	21	25
8	G	22	13
9	H	17	18
10	I	24	22
11	J	15	16
12	K	14	17
13	L	19	15

When the ratio of the difference between groups compared to the differences within the two groups is large, the test indicates that the difference is probably not a chance difference: The two groups are scoring differently. We wish to know whether the scoring differences in our data are statistically significant. Once the data are entered in the spreadsheet, we use the following commands:

Click "Tools."
Click "Data Analysis."
Highlight "*t*-test: Two samples assuming equal variances." Click "OK."
In "Variable 1 Range" enter B2:B13.
In "Variable 2 Range" enter C2:C13. Click "OK."

The test compares the calculated ratio to a critical value. If absolute value (ignore the sign) of the calculated number exceeds the critical value, we conclude that the scoring differences are statistically significant. In this instance, the calculated value rounds to −.39. The critical value is 1.72. Therefore, the differences between the students in these two groups are not statistically significant.

12

Ethical Considerations in Assessment

■ *Readers will examine assessment factors relating to the rights and the interests of those assessed and those who use the assessment data.*

Teaching to the Test	
Interests at Odds	Interpreting the Data
Test Coaching	

Test Bias	
Group Differences	Culture and Ethnicity
Item and Content Bias	Data versus Application
Gender	Aptitude
Language	

A Code of Fair Testing	
Test Selection	Data Interpretation
Fairness	Informing

Assessment data are the basis for many educational decisions, some of them relatively mundane and some very important. Because of the important decisions, those who develop the assessments, those who administer them, and those who use the data to make the decisions each have a stake in the validity and the fairness of the data. Since the ethical decisions involve questions of degree, it is important for educators to confront them in the abstract before the decisions directly affect their own students and classrooms. ■

Mrs. Ririe teaches in the same small farming community where she grew up, and for much of her career in the elementary school, the makeup of the town changed little. Conflict elsewhere in the world brought changes, however, as refugees sought calm in her town, and the immigrants had a profound effect on the schools. Educators accustomed to students who spoke a common language scrambled to cope with languages and cultures quite different from the traditional mainstream. In the quiet of her classroom at the end of the day, she reviewed tests that were awaiting scoring. She wondered whether she ought to make allowances for students who did not yet read the primary language as well as most of their classmates. She also wondered how she ought to prepare them for the battery of placement tests that the school district required of all sixth graders before their intermediate school experience. Having participated in the development of those very instruments, she knew the range of skills and knowledge the tests would require. Would it be wrong, she wondered, for her to develop instructional materials that would prepare her students for specific elements of the tests? ■

CONSIDERING ASSESSMENT ETHICS

The opening scenario is very familiar for many classroom teachers. Even without the complications wrought by international upheaval, everyone at one point or another must determine where to draw the line separating what is appropriate from what is not when preparing students for tests. Those issues fall under a more general topic dealing with the ethical considerations in assessment. While there has always been a moral/ethical dimension to assessing performance, the issues are more pressing now because testing is more prominent than it has ever been. Early in one's career is the time to resolve issues of appropriateness—rather than waiting for them to emerge, which they most surely will.

TEACHING TO THE TEST

The issues associated with teaching to the test are not new. Certainly every instructor whose plan includes formal assessment has made decisions about the propriety of framing the day-to-day instruction, or perhaps the review that precedes the test, in such a way that the learners are well prepared. Perhaps it has become a more pressing issue in contemporary times because educational accountability movements have raised the stakes for learners and educators alike. When test performance is a criterion for gauging not only the students' progress, but also their instructors' and administrators' competencies, there is a great deal of pressure to improve test performance. When one has personal knowledge of the test, it is very tempting to teach it directly.

For Further Discussion

When assessment data become the criterion by which both the students' progress and the educators' competence are judged, there is a great deal of pressure to teach to the test. In the school district where your author once taught, there was a good deal of pressure on some of the teachers to prepare students for college. This was particularly evident when it came time to administer Advanced Placement exams. This program allows students who successfully write a final exam to receive credit at a participating college or university. Parents and administrators both placed significant pressure on the relevant teachers to ensure the students' success. Since teachers may not administer or proctor tests in the subjects they teach, a teacher of Advanced Placement history pursued the practice of debriefing the students immediately after the testing concluded. He made a list of as many of the test items as his students could remember, and then used them in his preparations in subsequent years.

In your judgment, is this practice ethical?

If you hold the teacher responsible for an ethical violation, do the administrators and parents also bear some responsibility?

Is it fair to hold the teacher accountable for the students' performance?

On a general level, there is nothing inherently wrong with trying to prepare the learners for an assessment. Indeed, it seems an abrogation of responsibility not to do so when the stakes are as high as they sometimes are for the test takers. At issue is the extent of instructors' knowledge of the assessment, and how closely they can tailor the preparation materials to the actual assessment without compromising the assessment data. Before making a judgment about the propriety of particular activities, there are at least three interrelated factors one ought to consider. They deal with:

the nature of the content to be assessed
the degree to which the assessment covers the content domain
the application that will be made of the data

We can examine these factors by using a framework employed by Mehrens and Kaminski (1989). Their approach was to arrange test preparation activities along a continuum ranging, as a starting point, from activities that are generally accepted as ethical to activities that are increasingly suspect (see Figure 12.1).

While the list in Figure 12.1 is not exhaustive, it reflects what we might view as a series of incremental steps from what most people agree is acceptable to what most probably view as inappropriate test-preparation procedures. There is little disagreement, for example, that we can gear both instruction and assessment to the same objectives. If we know our students will be given a vocabulary test asking them to define a list of words, we may decide to spend more time helping students to learn to match words and definitions. No one has much difficulty with this activity because it is instructive regardless of whether the assessment asks students to do the same thing. It would probably be a different matter, however, if one knew *which* words were on the test and the same words appeared on the practice exercises.

FIGURE 12.1   Choices along the Way: From Appropriate to Inappropriate
Activities in Test Preparation Practice

To prepare students for an assessment, one might exercise any of the following choices:

1. Preparing instructional materials that are based on a general familiarity with what will be assessed, but without examining the specific objectives assessed on the test.
2. Teaching test-taking skills.
3. Preparing instruction responding to the objectives that an outside organization has determined to be the objectives or skills that will be assessed by a particular test.
4. Preparing instructional materials designed to specifically match the objectives that a particular assessment addresses.
5. Preparing practice materials that duplicate the format employed by the assessment.
6. Employing a parallel form of the assessment for test-preparation practice.
7. Employing the test to practice for a subsequent administration of the test.

Source: Adapted from Mehrens and Kaminski (1989).

Another area in which there is general agreement about what is appropriate concerns the value of teaching test-taking skills. One of the realities of contemporary education is that public and governmental concern over disappointing educational performance has paved the way for very frequent student assessments. We can level the playing field somewhat if we see that all students are able to

1. recognize when they will be penalized for guessing,
2. complete the items they know before laboring over those they are less sure of, and
3. balance time between the different portions of an instrument according to how heavily they are weighted.

Beyond issues such as those reflected in items 1 and 2 of Figure 12.1, Mehrens and Kaminski (1989) indicate that there is less clarity about what may be appropriate.

One of the complicating factors is whether we are assessing the complete domain of the subject or whether what is tested is only a portion of the discipline. How closely we tie instruction to an assessment instrument is dictated in large part by the degree to which the test covers the content domain. When the test actually samples comparatively little of the related content, teaching directly to the test becomes unethical. A high score suggests a command of the entire discipline, when actually the student may know only the portion presented on the test.

Speaking of Assessment

Maybe two stories can make a point about how much of the subject domain an assessment represents.

When your author was in the seventh grade, his vice-principal challenged the class to a contest. If on a designated day everyone could spell the Soviet Premier's name correctly (it was Khrushchev in those days), he would give each student a piece of chewing gum. On the other hand, everyone had to do the same for him if anyone in the class made an error. All knew exactly what would be asked and the class (most, at least) prepared to spell the precise name.[1] It represented the entire content domain, and in that instance at least, there were no inferences to be drawn from the results.

On the other hand, there is a story told of Churchill who, as a boy, had not been a very dedicated student. In a particular course of study covering the period when Britain had a worldwide empire, he and his classmates were told that they would be required to reproduce a map of one of Britain's colonial possessions as part of a final examination. Intending that the students would study *all* of the territories, they were of course not told which colony that they would have to draw. On the night before the assessment, recognizing that he no longer had time to study all of the colonies, Churchill placed the name of each colony into a hat and drew out one. His thought was to be well prepared in at least one area. The name he drew was New Zealand. As it turned out, that is also the colony whose map he was asked to draw the next day. As happy as the result was for the student and ultimately for his country, it created an opportunity for a badly distorted inference based on the test results. The instructor probably assumed that the student could have done equally well had the task been any other territory.

We can teach the exact content of the test and commit no ethical violation if the test reflects the entire content area, as it did in the Khrushchev story above. The only question there was whether we could spell the name correctly. If the assessment items are a subset of a larger content domain, and we use test performance to predict achievement in the entire domain, the circumstances change, however. In that instance teaching directly to the assessment items diminishes the validity of the data and represents an ethical problem. Students' preparations are likely restricted only to the actual test items, not to all possible test items.

The issue of inferences is very important. Even the most comprehensive assessments rarely sample the entire content or skill domain. The time limitations are simply too confining. A driving test, for example, in which the student actually drives the vehicle and performs according to the examiner's instructions, certainly is representative. The skills the learner demonstrates are completely relevant to the circumstances, but there is no way to represent all possible driving contingencies in a 20-minute test. The examiner does not know how the driver will react if a tire fails at highway speeds, or if someone unexpectedly pulls in front, unless such things happen to occur during the test.

Likewise, all of the relevant academic issues can rarely be sampled in a one-, or two-, or even a several-hour exam. A test of verbal ability cannot be exhaustive for anyone except learners at the most beginning levels, so assessment presents test items that are selected because they are *representative*. If we direct the learners toward the tested objectives (choice 3 in Figure 12.1), or if students practice the same assessment tasks we intend to use (choice 4), we may compromise the test data. It then becomes difficult to draw inferences to the larger content area. Said a little differently, when preparation is focused too specifically on what will be tested, the test data are likely to reflect a level of competency or ability that learners do not have because their preparations were selective rather than comprehensive.

An assessment need not be comprehensive, but it must be at least representative. That reflects the content validity presented in Chapters 7 and 8. We usually assess content validity with the assumption that students do not know precisely what the individual test items are to be. When they do know, and they ignore those areas of content that will not be assessed, the validity of the results suffers.

Interests at Odds

The problem, of course, is that there are competing interests at work. Those who interpret test data are usually interested in scores that can be extrapolated beyond the particular set of items to the universe of skills or abilities they represent. However, those who take the test and perhaps those who help students prepare may be interested only in scores that are as high as possible. That desire translates into the need to prepare test takers as specifically as they can be prepared. Smith (1991) analyzed these competing interests and observed:

> *If external audiences use [the] scores as measures of school effectiveness and accountability and as triggers for reform, school personnel will focus their efforts on improving the scores without respect to, and to the neglect of other equally plausible and valuable outcomes. The boosted indicator will not likely generalize to alternative indicators, such as the number and quality of books the children read, their writing, projects they undertake, or even to other achievement tests. (p. 541)*

Beyond choice 2 in Figure 12.1, there is an increasing tendency for the preparation activities to undermine the interpretation of the data. One audience's means becomes the other audience's end.

For Further Discussion

Some years ago, a primary school near your author's institution came under particular scrutiny by district officials because sixth-grade students' math performance scores on a standardized test were quite low. Educators probably made a number of important adjustments, but one of the more desperate was to secure and then circulate copies of the year-end math test a few weeks before it was administered. As one might imagine, learners' math scores improved dramatically over those of the prior year. However, educators in the seventh grade used the scores to make placement decisions for the new students.

According to Figure 12.1, which choice did educators exercise?

What sort of test makes what occurred most objectionable?

What testing conditions could occur that would make such a situation ethically acceptable?

Assuming that the test was a small subset of possible math questions, what is the likelihood that students who are placed in advanced classes as a result of high scores will succeed in those classes?

For the students referenced in the *For Further Discussion* box test data suggested a level of competency that the learners did not have. In this particular instance, the need to develop the students' grasp of mathematics so that they could perform better was short-circuited by the interests of some other population.

The conclusion that Mehrens and Kaminski (1989) drew is that choice 1 (Figure 12.1) is always ethical, choice 2 is usually considered ethical, and choices 6 and 7 are never ethical. Choices 3 to 5 constitute marginal areas. Whether they are ethical choices depends upon how the assessment data are used.

Your author does not wish to suggest that it is never ethical to teach the test, a point he tried to make with the Khrushchev story. Although the opportunity to sample the entire content area disappears with the passing of the lower grades, there are times when the test items are exactly the skills and abilities one wishes to develop. This may occur particularly in criterion-referenced assessment, where it is sometimes entirely appropriate to share the criteria with the students. Perhaps one objective from a grammar unit calls for students to identify each noun in a sample paragraph. Practicing the very skill makes perfect ethical and practical sense. The difficulty is not in telling students ahead of time what they will have to do on the unit test, but in telling them with *which* paragraph they will work with when the test comes.

Part of the issue is that what appears to pose an ethical problem when it is considered by a dispassionate audience may be justified in the minds of the learners who will be directly affected. Taylor and Nolen (1996) reported that students were surprised to learn that testing professionals considered it cheating for teachers to teach the specific content that was shortly to be covered by a test. The students reasoned:

> Were they not being admonished, by both the instructor and the course textbook . . . to see whether students were learning what had been taught? To these students, if vocabulary words were to be tested, they should be taught. If science or social studies concepts and facts were to be tested, they should be taught. Even if the test expected students to generalize a concept or skill to the new situation, the concept or skill should have been taught first! (p. 3)

Having considered some of the difficulties associated with teaching to the test, we should note that some of the fault lies not with preparation procedures, but with the test itself. A test with well-established content validity, for example (it fairly represents the entire subject area to which inferences are drawn), will be a great deal more difficult to compromise than a test with sketchy content validity. In fact, Smith (1991) expressed little concern about the negative effects of teaching to the test. She suggested that if doing so can easily alter test results, the instrument may not be a valuable source of data in any case:

> When an indicator is so fallible that it changes in relation to short-term test preparation and test-wiseness training or the social and ethnic composition of the population, it is worth little in public debate over school effectiveness or in the disbursing of rewards and punishments from society. (p. 541)

Test Coaching

Although commercially prepared test preparation programs are not new, the amount of emphasis on testing for admissions, certification, promotion, and the like has moved what might have been described as a "cottage industry" a few years ago to a major commercial enterprise today. Probably every high school and college bookstore offers manuals and handbooks that assure users that they can improve test scores by learning a few important techniques. Formal classes offering test preparation are common as well. Because the activities that these programs provide vary a good deal, one would do well to evaluate them in terms of the options listed in Figure 12.1. There is no doubt that involvement in a coaching course often will prompt score improvements, and the producers of these programs advertise the gains prominently. Some of the reasons were offered in the Chapter 10 discussion. Let it suffice here to say that it is difficult to separate the amount of improvement from coaching from what would have occurred simply because students are taking a test they have seen before. Gellman's (1995) review of research suggests that gains attributable to coaching on the SAT, for example, average 1 to 3 points on the verbal portion and approximately 17 points on the math portion. With total scores ranging from 200 to 800 points on each portion of the test, and a standard deviation of 100 points, gains of this magnitude are comparatively unimportant.

> Because they are reported as averages, the increases in test scores that occur because of test coaching obscure the fact that some scores actually decrease. Scores on most standardized tests are distributed such that an increase will be most likely among those who score lowest on the first administration, and decreases will be most likely among those who score highest on the first test. Extreme scores in either direction tend to regress toward the mean on a second effort.

If what the learner knows or can do changes, valid assessment data will reflect the change, but the alterations in test scores that are a result of coaching only, rather than differences in learning, are usually minor. One final note on coaching. Bear in mind that when coaching results are reported, the data may be stated as the average increase that occurs after one has completed some prescribed program of preparation. Buried in the averages with those scores that increased are those that *decreased* on the retest, and you can be sure that some students' scores decline the second time.

Interpreting the Data

When we get to the point of reporting assessment results, another consideration emerges. Assume for a moment that you develop instructional materials for a particular subject, and that, as you work with students and the material over several years, you become increasingly adept at teaching the material (a not unlikely scenario). Because of your progress, yesterday's typical performance is significantly lower than today's. Instruction has improved and student performance has increased to the point that nearly everyone is now performing beyond what was originally the norm. Recognizing this, would it be ethical to report that all of your students are above average? (Think a minute about the implications of such a statement before continuing.)

As odd as it sounds, what we described has happened on a state level. Cannell (1988) reported what others have called the "Lake Wobegon effect," a name that conjures up that mythical place where "all the children are above average." Cannell argues that the effect occurs because educators widely teach to the most common standardized tests, and then officials gauge student progress with outdated norms. The reform movements of the early 1980s brought about greater interest in educational accountability and increased pressure to improve student performance. Since a comparatively few tests became the gauge for student progress throughout the United States, educators focused on them quite specifically. As student performance improved (at least in terms of their test scores), reporting officials were in a position to enhance the picture of state and school districts' progress by comparing current performance to several-years-old testing norms. In doing so they compromised the integrity of the reporting process.

TEST BIAS

Test bias occurs when test data are inaccurate for a group or an individual because of a systematic error. *Systematic* means that although the error is unintentional, it is consistent. The error cannot occur because of sickness, because of an unanticipated interruption during testing, or any other random factor that occurs in some settings but not others. It must be something that persists as an artifact of the test, of the administration of the test, or of data interpretation.

The issue with bias is not just one of the accuracy of the data, or even of their fairness, but rather of a systematic over- or underprediction of test takers' performances on some criterion. We expect college admissions tests, for example, to predict the candidate's academic performance in college. Employment tests are used to predict one's level of job performance. Math placement tests are intended to help a decision maker determine which mathematics course of study will be the most profitable for a particular student. We can identify testing bias when an assessment has better predictive validity for some groups than for others. When an assessment consistently under- or overpredicts how well someone, or some group, will fare, the data are biased. The point is neither that all groups must perform equally well nor that assessment data must have perfect predictive validity for everyone to be free from bias. Rather, however well the data predict, the validity must be equal for all groups.

> Testing bias is revealed when a test systematically provides lower predictive validity for some populations than for others. Under current usage, the issue is not whether there are scoring differences but whether the data are more valid for one group than another.

The bias issue would not matter so much if the testing stakes were not high. As has been stated previously, results often determine who is admitted and who is not, who graduates and who does not, and so on. We will look at the issues relating to gender bias subsequently, but by way of illustration, Kessel and Linn (1996) reported that Scholastic Assessment Test (SAT) data "tend to underpredict the grades of females relative to those of males in mathematics courses" (p. 11). They note that in studies where the courses taken were similar for both males and females, females earned higher grades but had lower SAT scores. This systematic underprediction suggests a possible bias problem.

The range of people affected by assessment decisions based at least in part on test data is very broad, and for some, of course, the consequences will be negative. As a result, bias is frequently discussed in the popular as well as the scholarly press, but the terms have different meanings for different audiences. In general discussions, bias has a quite negative connotation, and when the issue comes up it is often framed in terms of a test or a decision procedure that is coldly discriminatory for certain populations of test takers.

Among measurement specialists, bias is a neutral statistical term that has a quite explicit meaning. It means systematic over- or underprediction. As a consequence of different constructions of bias, one should take some care regarding its discussion. The term attracts a great deal of attention and more than its share of emotion. Scheuneman and Slaughter (1991) noted, "the debate [about bias] rages as if all participants were talking about the same concept" (p. 5), when there is actually little common understanding.

Group Scoring Differences

Recall that any time we assess academic characteristics, we run the risk of measurement error. Measurement error distorts scores, but we should not confuse it with testing bias, although the two may be indistinguishable in the score of any individual. In a group, the measurement errors that distort individual scores are likely to factor out each other. Errors that inflate the scores of some students counterbalance those that deflate the scores of others. By contrast, bias distorts the scores of the members of the entire group in just one direction. Bias can certainly affect the score of one person, but it is difficult to detect in a single score—where one cannot easily separate bias from random measurement error.

Some of those who most consistently criticize testing argue that the performance of two groups should be identical if the assessment is unbiased, but differences between group averages do not necessarily signal bias. Several factors might explain different average scores, including differences in educational opportunity, in instructional quality, in the quality of the facilities, and so forth. There is a more fundamental question that asks whether group averages are the same if environmental conditions are uniform, but since the evidence for bias is unequal predictive validity, that becomes our focus. Whatever the scoring differences, test data must have equal predictive validity for all groups. If the data from an English placement test consistently allow educators to place members of some groups much more accurately than they place other group members, students for whom placements are less accurate are victims of bias.

Blaming the Messenger

The issues associated with test bias are complex and contentious enough that various parties sometimes seek legal remedies where there may be a question of bias. Although groups' scoring differences appear to suggest a bias against the lower group or in favor of the higher group, the most current legal decisions indicate that score differences alone do not establish bias. The elements that do establish bias include scoring differences that emerge each time the data are gathered and that are unrelated to the object of assessment. As an example, consistent differences in reading scores must be unrelated to differences in reading ability. This last point deserves some amplification because it has not always been the case.

At one point, scoring that differed by group was accepted as sufficient evidence of test bias. That position has been modified with the understanding that there may be a variety of reasons unrelated to the test for scoring differences and that bias exists only when it is an artifact of the test itself, or of related testing procedures.

In the United States, at least, a 1971 Supreme Court decision (*Griggs v. Duke Power Co.*) provided a legal definition of bias that was much easier to satisfy. The court took the position that test scores that correlate with an ethnic or racial group constitute what is called *prima facie* (a phrase meaning "self-manifested") evidence of test bias (Gottfredson, 1994). By such a standard, a statistical correlation between scoring and test takers' ethnic memberships, for example, is sufficient to establish that the test is biased, and therefore flawed. This definition imposes no requirement to determine the origins of the scoring pattern and no consideration for the possibility of real differences in what is being assessed. The test was blamed for the differences.

Although such thinking dominated legal definitions of bias for 20 years, it was modified in the 1990s. The current position is that there may be a variety of reasons for scoring differences. However, the differences themselves, even though they may prompt scores to vary, do not automatically imply a testing bias. The differences do, however, suggest a reason for close examination of assessment data.

Factors in Scoring Differences

Scheuneman and Slaughter (1991) noted that there are several elements that help explain group-to-group scoring differences. Although they are not mutually exclusive, it will be simpler to explore them as discrete categories. The factors are briefly outlined in Figure 12.2.

Scoring differences that might have their origin in a community's history include conditions such as the disruption in education that occurs when there is civil strife and the inequities that accompany racial segregation. In many modern societies, education is the one institution experienced by most citizens, but any number of factors may conspire against a common experience.

FIGURE 12.2   Factors in Group Scoring Differences

Factor	Cause
Historical	Some past practice that can be traced to a performance difference in present practice.
Cultural	A learned behavior that is identified with a cultural group and that has been identified to be a factor in test performance.
Biological	An innate difference that is directly related to a performance difference.
Educational	Differences in the exposure one has had during formal educational experiences.
Psychometric	Scoring differences that are an artifact of the tests themselves.

Source: Adapted from Scheuneman and Slaughter (1991).

Speaking of Assessment

In the area of western Canada where your author grew up there are several communities of pacifists united by a common religion. These very interesting people live in a communal order and are successful farmers, but they eschew any education beyond what the law requires—the eighth grade. Should a standardized academic test be administered to 17-year-olds, there would likely be significant differences in scoring between the young people from these settlements and those of the other communities surrounding them. The difference, however, has its origin in a cultural distinction, not the test. Scoring differences, at least in this case, and by current definition, do not reflect bias.

When all other environmental variables are controlled, we use a biological explanation to explain persistent differences between groups. If girls have superior verbal abilities because they are girls, rather than because they are treated differently from the way boys are treated, scoring differences have a biological explanation.

Educational differences are perhaps the easiest to document. Students in suburban schools typically have higher test scores than do those from inner-city schools. There are probably several explanations, one of which may be that there are differences in the resources available in each setting. Schools are generally funded at least partly from real estate revenue, something typically more plentiful in suburban areas—with their more robust tax bases—than in what are sometimes blighted urban centers.

Each of the factors above describes a situation in which groups' scoring averages may differ for reasons unrelated to the test. Among these sources of scoring variability, the test is the only one that can be at the root of a bias problem. The test itself must create the scoring differences.

Sources of Bias

Having noted that scoring differences themselves do not constitute bias, we ought to examine those factors that *do* give rise to biased testing. They are the subject of Figure 12.3.

FIGURE 12.3   Possible Factors in Biased Test Results

- Differences in the adequacy of *instructions* for persons from different groups, especially when the task or the material is novel.
- An *item format* or mode of presentation that is more familiar to some audiences than to others.
- Elements of *content* that are more appealing to some audiences than to others.
- A *test length* that may result in differential speededness penalizing those who tend to work more slowly.
- Assessment elements requiring a *strategy* that learners from some backgrounds are discouraged from using.

Source: Adapted from Scheuneman and Slaughter (1991).

Instructions as a Source of Bias

If the members of several groups who receive the assessment each understand their tasks differently because they receive different instructions, and the differences give rise to scoring differences, the data are biased. Think, for example, of a science achievement test with multiple-choice items. If some students are told to guess when they are not sure of the correct answer, and others are cautioned against guessing, there will probably be score differences that have nothing to do with the learners' achievement. Contradictory directions are particularly confounding when parts of the assessment are new to students, because they rely more heavily on the instructions when the form of the assessment is unfamiliar.

Language and Testing Bias

The language of the assessment also includes the potential for test bias, a problem that we can illustrate with a mathematics achievement test. For example, solving word problems is a very important ability, and math assessments with a story problem component can be very effective measures of reasoning ability. However, where many students speak a primary language other than the language of the assessment, those who are not fluent may have lower scores because of the language rather than because of their mathematics and reasoning abilities.

The language in which we teach students might also prompt scoring differences if some students are not fluent, but be careful about rushing to a bias judgment. Differences in students' facility with a language may reflect just that—differences—just as we might note differences in one's facility with any content or skill in a testing situation. Remember that one of the purposes of assessment is to discriminate among learners according to their levels of learning. The problem comes in mistaking language differences for content mastery differences. If we understand the mathematics differences to reflect primarily language skill differences, the data are still useful to us. If we mistake language differences for math ability differences, we may have a bias problem.

Timed Tests and Bias

Ordinarily, how quickly learners complete an assessment is not a factor we care to measure. If this is so, we must be careful with the number of test items, because lengthy instruments make it difficult for those who may choose to work slowly. Although some standardized tests impose stringent time limitations, they are quite different from the tests we usually develop for classroom application. The speeded tests typically employ comparatively easy test items. The measure of the students' ability is how many items they can complete.

Ordinarily the issue for learners is more whether one can construct, or select, a correct response than whether one can do so quickly. Although classroom instructors must work within the confines imposed by academic periods, beyond that general consideration time is usually not an issue. In fact, if we were to place stringent time limitations on classroom assessments, we might very well measure the students' tendency to be impulsive rather than their command of the material. In your author's experience, the students' command of the material and the time they take to complete an assessment are largely unrelated.

Test-Wiseness

The amount of experience certain groups have with testing may contribute to test bias because what are termed test-wiseness skills can play a role in scoring differences (Scheuneman and Slaughter, 1991). In secondary schools where large numbers of students traditionally attend college, educators may assist students with a test intended to familiarize them with the admissions test. The pretest is given to help students, not necessarily with what the test asks, but with the format and the best tactics for responding to items. The more experienced students may become more familiar, more test-wise, than others who have not practiced. If the scoring variability stems from greater familiarity with testing procedure rather than from differences in the aptitude for college study, there is a bias issue.

When two students have a similar command of the content, but one is able to detect—or construct—a more correct response because the student understands the testing procedure better, the student is test-wise. Such students receive scores that are too high, in light of their actual grasp of the material. Students who write well can sometimes sway a scorer by developing a well-constructed response that may be only tangentially related to the item (a particular kind of bias called **rater bias**). Test-wise students recognize that the longest choice on multiple-choice items is frequently the correct choice, and they learn to recognize other unintentional clues that may help guide them to the correct answer.

Experience alone is clearly not sufficient for the development of test-wiseness, however. Scheuneman and Slaughter (1991) noted that a more important factor may be a level of comfort with formal assessment. Some test takers may view the test as a challenge they rise to, rather than a situation best avoided when one has a choice.

Charging that an assessment procedure is biased is not the same as substantiating it, but one must always respond to evidence of bias. The charges should not be ignored, nor should evidence be minimized. Jensen (1980) argued, "Where test bias is discovered, the test in question should either not be used on the group for which it is biased or should be used only in ways that permit the particular bias to be precisely and explicitly taken into account" (p. ix).

Cultural and Ethnic Group Biases

In the United States, at least, the primary and secondary school populations often reflect great ethnic diversity. Scores on the more widely used tests are often reported in terms not only of national changes from year to year, but of group-to-group differences. Although it is difficult to generalize, most of the research dealing with ethnic group differences shows variations of from one to one-and-one-half standard deviations between minority and nonminority test takers (Scheuneman and Slaughter, 1991). Although they constitute an ethnic minority, frequently the scores of Asian American students do not follow this pattern (Scheuneman and Slaughter, 1991). In fact, theirs are typically the highest scores in measures of quantitative ability. Although scoring differences are no longer self-evident indicators of bias, the differences continue to attract attention and may persist for several reasons. Although they were mentioned briefly earlier in the chapter, it is useful to elaborate them again here.

Different backgrounds and experiences may prompt members of different groups to employ different learning strategies. In a culture in which obedience is prized and emphasis is placed on using specified algorithms to solve problems, scoring that rewards creativity may effectively penalize those who feel compelled to follow prescribed procedures.

The content around which some items are constructed might prompt more or less interest, depending upon the group to whom the assessment is administered. A test item that requires the student to determine the area of cultivatable land contained in a farm with specified dimensions may favor those who come from an agrarian background. At the same time, an item constructed around the price a farmer will receive at market for his hogs, when what is offered is a specified cost per pound, may be offensive to students from cultures where pork is not eaten and hogs are viewed as unclean.

In an effort to gauge higher level thinking abilities, sometimes items are constructed requiring that the respondent develop a reasoned argument for a position that is fundamentally controversial. Sometimes the controversy exists because of the complexity of the moral issues involved. Perhaps a test item calls for the student to develop "A defense of Truman's authorization to drop the atomic bomb on Hiroshima and Nagasaki," but this may place some respondents in a position that is contrary to their strong, personal feelings. The resulting conflict may be sufficient that some students cannot represent their best grasp of the issues in a response.

When personal characteristics are distributed differently in some groups than in others, they too could be reflected in scoring variations that reflect a bias. Some students come from a cultural environment in which they are expected to be submissive and nonassertive. Assessment settings that require that they stand before their classmates to deliver oral reports, or join a debate over some controversial issue, may place them at a considerable disadvantage.

It is very difficult to determine the presence of bias with only the group average to refer to. As noted above, there might be a variety of explanations for group scoring differences, some having nothing to do with the test. Consequently, a desirable approach is to select some other measure as a reference point with which the test score ought to be in harmony. College admissions scores are supposed to predict college performance. Our research might indicate that students who score 550 and above on the SAT verbal, for example, tend to have college grade point averages of 3.3 on a 4-point scale. If the scores predict well for a particular group, we could conclude that the admissions scores represent an unbiased estimator for the group. If college grades are higher, or lower, than admissions scores suggested that they ought to be, we may conclude that the scores are biased (Scheuneman and Slaughter, 1991).

| Tests that yield biased data measure different characteristics for members of some groups than for others. | One way to view bias is to recognize that a biased test measures a different characteristic for some groups than for others. Perhaps an instrument is constructed to assess problem-solving ability in 14-year-olds. If all of the problems are presented in algebraic terms, the scores of those who completed Algebra I may be higher than the scores of those who have not, for reasons more related to their math experience than their problem-solving abilities. Those who are most familiar with |

algebra may be able to move directly to the problem and their problem solving ability may be overpredicted, or perhaps the scores of those unfamiliar with algebra will be underestimated.

Because they are viewed as gatekeepers, college admissions tests probably are more scrutinized for bias than most other tests (see Crouse and Trusheim, 1988, for example). Readers should know that a number of studies have been conducted using admissions test scores as predictors of subsequent college performance by members of particular ethnic groups. The results do not generally indicate that test scores underpredict the college performance of students who are members of ethnic minority groups. There may be some instances of overprediction, however, with admissions scores suggesting that college grades will be higher than they turn out to be (Hunter, Schmidt, and Rauschenberger, 1984; Jensen, 1980).

Besides analyzing test bias from the standpoint of predictive validity, one may also detect bias with a statistical procedure called factor analysis. It is discussed in both Chapter 9 and Chapter 13, but it will help us with bias to discuss the procedure here, briefly. Tests typically use a number of items to assess a smaller number of underlying mental characteristics called factors. On a test of verbal ability, there might be several items dealing with parts of speech, another group of items dealing with sentence construction, and so on. Factor analysis is a procedure by which a larger number of test items is reduced to a smaller number of *groups* of items. Each group measures the same underlying factor.

Having clarified the factors involved in a particular assessment, we can use factor analytic studies to examine test data to determine whether a test appears to measure the same psychological factors or traits for members of different groups. The research indicates that the factor structure in the more commonly used tests is consistent for different ethnic groups. Scheuneman and Slaughter (1991) reviewed the studies and concluded:

> *In summary, the evidence from this work strongly supports the validity of the tests for minority groups for the same purposes as they are used for Whites, given that the examinees have sufficient English language competence. Further, the results seem to indicate that gross amounts of bias in the scores of minority group members do not exist. [That is not to say that] no bias exists [however]. (p. 11)*

Gender Bias

One of the areas of bias study that have been particularly dynamic in recent years is scoring differences that correlate with gender. Probably the most publicized differences are in the area of college aptitude, where test scores are supposed to predict the applicants' subsequent college-level performance. Generally, the tests work well, but there are exceptions. Kessel and Linn (1996) found that, in some instances, SAT data may underpredict college grades for women in mathematics. The scores suggest that females' performances in college-level mathematics will be lower than they turn out to be. Although the underprediction may be comparatively minor, it provides impetus for continuing work with the instrument. It also underscores the need to rely on multiple criteria for making admissions decisions.

As with ethnic and racial group differences, the group average is ordinarily what researchers examine when they look for gender bias. Recently, however, attention has turned to how scores vary from the averages. This analysis allows one to consider the possibility that, even if averages are similar, the way in which scores are distributed might be significantly different. Perhaps, for example, the top (or bottom) 5 percent of one group have a different average score than the corresponding students in the other group (Hedges and Friedman, 1993). This approach permits one to ask whether similar proportions of each group occupy the same area of the scoring distribution. Hedges and Friedman suggest that the distributions of scores by gender group may sometimes be different.

To illustrate why this may be significant, consider the distributions in Figure 12.4. Although they are contrived, these distributions suggest that two groups might have very similar group averages but quite different overall score distributions. In Figure 12.4, there are striking differences between the lowest and the highest scores for each group.

A good deal of the attention to gender group scoring has been focused in the math and science areas, where the differences were most pronounced in the past, and where there is a very active debate regarding the origins of the differences. Prominent in the discussion are questions about whether educators treat male and females students differently, whether the instructors communicate different expectations of students based on their gender, and the degree to which the choices students make affect their courses of study. Gipps and Murphy (1994) explained how these factors might be interrelated:

> *One of the reasons for differential success in . . . exams . . . is different entry patterns. Girls tend to be allocated to easier routes in math than their ability warrants because they are seen as hard working rather than bright and because they may be anxious about failure . . . There is evidence, too, that ethnic minority pupils are more likely to be allocated to lower-level . . . routes. (pp. 3–4)*

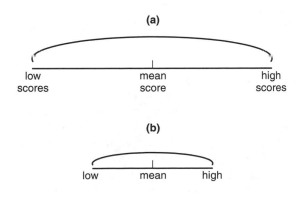

FIGURE 12.4   Comparing Scoring
Distributions

Historically, female students demonstrated an advantage in verbal skills and males in mathematics, but the differences are diminishing and in some areas are comparatively unimportant. After looking at several dimensions of this problem, Marsh (1989) reported "a relative lack of strong sex differences" (p. 217). He concluded that the only area in which the differences between the groups were particularly significant was in attitudes toward the subjects, rather than in course selection differences or in actual performance.

Although performance differences represent a very interesting area of study, and the reasons for scoring differences are important, our interest is in the degree to which scoring differences stem from biases, or systematic errors, *based in the assessment procedures*. As was the case with ethnic or cultural group differences, when the content used in test items is more familiar to one gender than the other, we risk a biased outcome. Computation problems based on batting averages may favor those who are most familiar with baseball. Reading selections that are grounded in a setting unfamiliar to one group, or which use words that one group of students has not encountered, may give rise to a systematic error in their reading scores. The task is to base test items in content and language that provide us some certainty that we are not assessing something unrelated to what we wish to assess.

Academic Aptitude and Other Group Differences

We have suggested a variety of factors that explain differences in groups' performances. When we test, we expect to discriminate between individuals on the basis of their command of the knowledge or skills being assessed. Scores that vary because students prepare differently, or because their instructors or parents treat them differently, may be a problem, but they do not indicate a flaw in the instrument that happens to illustrate the differences. Only if the differences are an artifact of the assessment itself, rather than some quantitative or qualitative difference between groups, or members of the groups, is there any point in finding fault with the test. This understanding has not always governed our approach to test bias in the past.

We noted earlier that, in the 1970s, court decisions established that if the test data revealed consistent group scoring differences, they could be ruled unlawful. This led to the development of procedures intended to "correct" the differences, one of which was **race-norming** test data. In this procedure, the scores of those belonging to groups whose average scores were lower than those of a comparison group were adjusted by a factor that eliminated any difference between the averages of the groups. This procedure allowed for variability within groups, but none between groups.

The difficulty with race-norming is that, although one can eradicate differences in groups' scores, doing so may not strengthen predictive validity, which is often the point of testing in the first place. If the original scores have better predictive validity, adjusting them diminishes their value.

> Race-norming data will eradicate groups' scoring differences by adjusting the scores of the members of one group so that the average of those scores is identical to the average of the comparison group. One of the collateral effects, however, is that the transformed scores may not predict future performance as well as the unadjusted data.

Cultural and Language Elements in Assessment

With care and effort, the impact that linguistic and cultural differences have on academic assessment data can be minimized, but it is not possible to develop what might be termed a culture-free assessment. Indeed, the very choice of what is assessed reflects a cultural value. The ideal in assessment is to be as equitable as possible, or "culture fair" (Hopkins and Stanley, 1981), by limiting the effects of any elements we do not wish to assess. When language is not the assessment object, sometimes we can simplify the directions and present them orally rather than in written form. If the instructions are not lengthy, the differential impact that language may have, while not eliminated, is at least limited.

The difficulty is that, by limiting the effects of language, sometimes we also diminish the value of the test data. Gellman (1995) observed that tests from which the influence of language is minimized typically have lower predictive validity than the instruments they replace. One must temper the desire to minimize language with the knowledge that directions and item language must be clear enough to enable one to assesses the appropriate knowledge or skill rather than some other.

For Further Discussion

In an area in which linguistic diversity is common, students in the schools and those who may wish to teach them may have many different levels of ability with the language of instruction. Certainly it is an advantage to have teachers in place who can speak the students' primary languages.

Is it wise, therefore, to attempt to "level the playing field" among the applicants by developing assessments that minimize language differences?

In what instances are language differences unrelated to the candidate's ability to teach effectively?

If applicants must pass a reading and writing competency in the primary language, is the test biased against those whose primary language is not the language of the schools?

It is clearly a problem for students to demonstrate their abilities when their primary language does not match the primary language used at the institution. Remember, however, that there is a logical relationship between academic achievement and verbal ability. When one alters an instrument to minimize the impact of language, one often also compromises what one may learn about an aspiring teacher, or students making their way through the grades. Gellman (1995) has cautioned: "Cultural differences often do impact on a child's success in school and, to the extent that language or cultural factors are interfering with the attainment of needed knowledge and skills, they cannot be ignored as a factor in predicting school performance" (p. 81).

Item Bias

The scoring differences we have discussed to this point stem from differences in the way particular groups respond to the test as a whole. Generally, however, it is individual test items that lie at the root of bias problems. Think in terms of an achievement test. Since it is achievement we wish to assess, and not group membership, we must develop items that students of equal levels of achievement have an equal probability of scoring correctly, regardless of their group membership.

When students respond to the items differently, we want some assurance that the differences are related to what we are measuring, but differences for any reason can be difficult to ignore. As a case in point, the Educational Testing Service (ETS) developed a licensing exam for insurance agents. Data indicated that African American candidates had significantly lower passing rates than Caucasian Americans, and the Golden Rule Insurance Company in Illinois filed a lawsuit. In an out-of-court settlement ETS agreed to reconstruct the test by selecting items for which racial group differences were more limited than was the case for many items on the original instrument.

Item Analysis

There is often a better opportunity in the individual items than on the assessment as a whole to detect the presence of some characteristic that may give rise to bias. In the examination of item analysis procedures in Chapter 7, it was noted that one way to view item quality is in terms of the degree to which an individual item discriminates between those who do well on the assessment as a whole and those who do poorly. We can use a similar approach to examine item bias. Instead of the two groups representing high- and low-scoring students, however, they represent students of distinct racial, ethnic, or gender groups. If the two groups have students of equal ability and experience, their performance on an unbiased item should be indistinguishable. In terms of the Chapter 7 discussion, the item discrimination index should be near zero. Although testing agencies such as ETS use a more sophisticated procedure, the concept is the same, and it is a helpful way to think about recognizing item bias. We still want items that discriminate between students of different levels of achievement, but the discrimination must not extend to characteristics that are not relevant to their achievement, such as ethnic group membership. Scheuneman and Slaughter (1991) offered a caution, however:

> The problem with the item bias methods is that one group can do particularly well or particularly poorly on a test item when compared to another group for reasons other than bias in the item. That is, any systematic difference in the way two groups respond to an item can be reflected in a significant bias statistic. Differences in performance between two groups of examinees may thus be related to differences in life experiences and cultural values as well as to differences in previous exposure to the material in the item or to opportunity to learn. If such differences result in genuine differences in the level of the knowledge, skill or ability being measured by the test, which are reflected in performance differences on an item, such differences would not be considered bias. (p. 11)

Differential Item Functioning

Scheuneman and Slaughter (1991) explained that a more appropriate description of group performance differences may be **differential item functioning** (DIF). This concept provides a way to describe groups' scoring differences without automatically attributing the differences to bias.

We spoke of the need to use language equally familiar to students of different groups. If one does not, language differences can become confused with achievement differences, but there is a distinction we need to draw. Sometimes it is the language of the discipline that students lack, and their inability is something we *do* wish to assess. In a government class for secondary school students, for example, one may raise such topics as sovereignty, federal system, representative democracy, and so forth. If the curriculum calls for one to teach those concepts, circumventing them only subverts what students are supposed to learn. Differences on items involving those concepts are likely important learning differences, not something we chalk up to DIF.

Content Bias and DIF

When ethnicity and culture are not factors, but the language of an assessment favors some students over others, we speak of a **content bias.** Sometimes learners understand the assessment task but they do not understand the language that provides the context for the item. Perhaps the assessment in a ninth-grade geography class evaluates students' ability to grasp the impact of climate upon one's vocation. The relevant item might read as follows:

> Although spring rains are at normal levels, low snowfall during the preceding winter has yielded much-lower-than-expected snow pack in the mountains. Who will be *least* affected by these conditions?
>
> a) sport fishermen in the mountain streams
> b) those who farm irrigated land
> c) urban centers who rely on mountain reservoirs
> d) dry farmers

Students with a background in agriculture recognize that a "dry farmer" is not a farmer without water, but someone who farms land that is not artificially irrigated. Students who are unfamiliar with farming terminology (which probably means those from the cities in particular) probably operate at a disadvantage. If lack of familiarity with the term contributes to scores that underestimate some students' grasp of the impact of light precipitation, the item is biased.

Besides a bias in terminology, some tests perpetuate a bias by disproportionately representing members of some groups more prominently than others in the examples. It may constitute content bias if the assessment is intended for members of all groups but the items depict primarily members of one ethnic or gender group.

Separating the Data from the Application

Because there can be differences that do not reflect bias, we keep returning to predictive validity, rather than the equality of the scores, as the measure of the quality of assessment data. One must recognize, however, that validity is specific to a particular application. What may be an excellent predictor of a criterion in one situation can be less effective in another situation, or for some other group. A test of verbal ability may be an excellent predictor of success in college for the relevant

> Validity is a property, not of the test, but of the use of the assessment data. We can quickly undermine careful test construction procedures by using the test or the data poorly. In order to maintain the integrity of the data, we have an obligation to use both the instrument and the data in a fashion that is consistent with the original intent.

populations, but the same test is probably a poor predictor of driving ability. For this reason, it is something of a misnomer to speak of "a valid test." It is actually the data that reflect validity, and more particularly the use to which the data are put.

A test of verbal ability under the guise of a driver's license exam is going to be biased against those less able with the language, in spite of how well developed their driving skills may be. These issues should be primary to educators. With the amount of assessment that occurs, one must take great care to see that assessments and their data are used properly. How carefully an assessment is designed and how much attention we direct at validity and reliability matter little if the test is administered—or the data are used—incorrectly. Under these circumstances, the ethical problems that crop up stem not from content or scoring problems, but from mistakes instructors make when they select the test and attempt to interpret the data.

A CODE OF FAIR TESTING

The growth in testing and testing issues in the early 1980s brought with it a good deal of criticism of some testing practices. Some of the criticisms have been implied in discussions of teaching to the test and the bias issues, but the problems really have a broader context. Interest grew in developing a set of guidelines for all of those who are involved with testing. It was in this spirit that Fremer (1986) called for a testing code that would "specify the essential principles of good practice that define the obligation of professionals who develop, administer, or use educational tests" (p. 26). What came to be called "The Code of Fair Testing Practices in Education" was designed specifically for educational testing, rather than for employment, certification, or psychological testing.

Several national organizations involved in assessment issues collaborated in the development of the testing code. The American Educational Research Association (AERA), the American Psychological Association (APA), and the National Council on Measurement in Education (NCME) each participated in the formative work (Diamond and Fremer, 1989). The developers intended the code for an audience broader than only the testing professionals that Fremer (1986) mentioned. The code was written in a way that allows the general public to understand its language and intent. The substance of the code is presented in Figure 12.5.

The code helps to clarify the responsibilities held by those who develop or select the tests and those who actually administer them. Note that the primary issues are selecting tests appropriate to the assessment task, taking care with data interpretation, and ensuring that the test takers are properly informed of assessment procedures and results.

FIGURE 12.5   The Code of Fair Testing Practices in Education

Area of Responsibility	Test Developers' Duties	Test Users' Duties
Developing or Selecting Appropriate Tests	Provide information that will allow users to select the appropriate test	Select tests that provide the necessary information and are appropriate for the intended population
Interpreting Score	Guide users' score interpretations	Interpret scores correctly
Striving for Fairness	Develop or adapt tests that are as fair as possible for students of different ethnic groups, gender groups, handicapping conditions, and so forth	Select tests that treat the intended population fairly
Informing Test Takers		Inform test takers regarding a) what the test covers b) the format of the test c) securing a copy of the test or answer sheet d) repeating the test e) taking a different form of the test f) having the test rescored g) having the scores canceled h) how long the scores are kept on file i) how scores are released

Source: Adapted from Diamond and Fremer (1989).

The reader will note that the emphasis in the code is primarily on those who develop and administer assessments professionally, rather than on instructors who conduct assessments as part of the teaching task. The code addresses issues that are very relevant to the classroom, however.

Selecting Tests

Instructors must select assessments that will yield what they need to know. In the classroom, this often means that one must develop a new instrument instead of pressing into service an existing instrument that is not well suited to the situation. Assessment instruments take time to construct and refine. Their convenience makes the tests and the items that come with textbooks very attractive, and they are certainly appropriate on occasion, but sometimes they do not fit the instruction very well. Perhaps a history unit dealing with the 1930s has been primarily a study of the worldwide effects of the Great Depression. If the in-class focus treats the decade as an interlude between the

World Wars, test items prepared for the book are unlikely to help the instructor. A change in focus calls for one to develop a new instrument.

A little study should reveal why an instrument was prepared, and what one should come to know by using it. When the objectives are not consistent with the instructional objectives, or if we cannot discern the objectives, it is better to set the prepared instrument aside. The test one may have used last year for the unit on poetry probably isn't appropriate for this year's literature class if the focus has changed from Elizabethan sonnets to twentieth-century writers. Even when the content remains relatively stable, there are often differences in the students from class to class that require us to make significant changes in the assessment previously used.

Interpreting Assessment Data

Recall that validity is an element of the data more than of the instrument. To extend that idea a little, fairness is also often a function of how one uses the assessment data. If one uses grammar test scores to indicate the students' general verbal ability, the data may be poor predictors. Note that the problem is with the application, however, not with the instrument. Some time ago, Cronbach (1969) raised this issue and assigned some responsibility when he noted that *those who interpret test data have the primary responsibility for appropriate use of the test*. Tests yield information. Interpreting the information falls to those who intend to use them to make placement decisions, assign grades, or check progress.

In order to avoid a misinterpretation, those who use the data must be clear about how to interpret the scores so that, at a minimum, they can explain the scores to others. When students are young, the audience is often their parents. If the students' reading scores are reported as percentile scores, but an instructor explains them as the percentage of items the student scored correctly, the instructor's interpretation is misleading. As noted elsewhere in this book, educators and professional testing agencies report test data in a variety of forms. Whether they are stated as standard scores, grade equivalent scores, or perhaps as a simple percentage correct, one must be able to explain test data to an audience. More than one instructor has befuddled both the instructor and an unwary parent by misinterpreting standardized test data in a parent-teacher conference.

One's ability to interpret assessment data is part of the more general subject of being properly qualified. For classroom instructors this probably means that they must have sufficient command of the discipline to prepare an appropriate assessment and explain how one derives the scores and how one should interpret them. Because the data tend to be of such a personal nature, those administering psychological tests must meet a set of criteria imposed upon them by the test publisher. These represent the conditions under which one may purchase instruments, scoring sheets, and the like.[2]

Maintaining Fairness

When a test isn't fair, the problem is almost never intentional. Rather, it occurs because educators lose sight of what they were trying to measure in the first place. An assessment of the students' grasp of photosynthesis can become a memory test if the items are heavily recall-type items requiring no interpretation.

Speaking of Assessment

Some years ago, one of your author's colleagues asked whether the language academics use to present their subjects (not the language of the subject itself) might be a stumbling block to students. Your author gave a lecture introducing the discipline of Educational Psychology. He mentioned that it is "a comparatively youthful discipline." When Dr. Kuehn (personal communication, 1997) asked students how they understood that phrase, it became clear that some had construed it to mean something to do with punishing youth—they put that together from the "youth" and the "discipline" parts. In at least this instance, the general academic language was a barrier to what students understood. Perhaps fairness will prompt us to spend a little more time clarifying the language so that the concepts are easier to grasp.

When scores vary, we want to have some confidence that the differences reflect differences in the learners' grasp of the concept or command of the skills, rather than seeing them as evidence of something unrelated.

Informing Interested Parties

The rule of thumb is that those to whom we administer an assessment are entitled to as much information as we can give them about the assessment and the scoring without compromising test results. One can disseminate some of this information before administering the test. One can usually answer questions about the number of items and their form. Perhaps one can share other information during the administration, such as the weighting assigned to different items and questions about whether students ought to guess when they are unsure of the correct response.

Many of the questions arise after the assessment is given. May the test be repeated? Are copies of the test or the scoring sheets available to the test takers? May one ask that a test be rescored? How long will the instructor keep the scores on file? Who may request to view the scores? Many of these issues are more relevant to standardized tests than to teacher-prepared instruments, but there is some overlap. In any case, the typical primary or secondary school teacher will have a great deal of experience with both types of assessment.

SUMMARY

The chapter prologue raised questions about how closely an instructor may teach to the test without crossing the ethical boundary. Two facts converge to make this issue increasingly important. First, diversity among learners—or at least our willingness to acknowledge diversity—is increasing. The diversity has linguistic, cultural, racial, and even religious facets, and some instructors are tempted to try to eradicate some of the group-to-group differences by teaching to the test. The second fact is that high-stakes tests, assessments with important consequences for the student, are more prominent than they have been, and they bring with them pressure to help students improve their chances.

When there are group differences in scores one should not necessarily presume a test biased against the lower scoring group. The standard for establishing bias is a scoring difference based on systematic errors in measurement. The evidence of these errors is poor predictive validity. When data predict the future performance of members of some group less accurately than they predict the performance of members of other groups, we have evidence of bias. Gellman (1995) explained that to establish that a college aptitude test, for example, is biased, one would need to determine that lower performance on the test is not related to lower performance in the college classroom.

One who spent his share of time in the midst of the mental measurement storm is Arthur Jensen. In a 1980 work he summarized the state of the bias issue in standardized testing when he concluded:

> *My exhaustive review of empirical research bearing on this issue leads me to the conclusion that the currently most widely used standardized tests of mental ability—IQ, scholastic aptitude, and achievement tests—are, by and large,* not *biased against any of the native-born English-speaking minority groups on which the amount of research is sufficient for an objective determination of bias, if the tests were in fact biased. For most nonverbal standardized tests, this generalization is not limited to English-speaking minorities. (p. ix)*

The amount of testing that occurs and the level of publicity that test data receive in the scholarly literature, let alone the popular press, make tests a very visible target. However, we should temper criticism with some appreciation of the assessment alternatives. College admissions committees, for example, often require letters of recommendation, records of earlier grades, and, sometimes, personal interviews. But each of these procedures provides for at least some opportunity for subjectivity. Would such an approach to admissions be more ethical than standardized testing? The question is not only, Are the current methods unbiased? but, Are there better alternatives available?

We need to make a final point or two about group comparisons and bias. Although racial group and gender group differences in standardized test scores have diminished over time, they persist and are easy to misconstrue. Some of the arguments make it seem that being a member of a particular group *causes* the difference. If one accepts that thinking, it follows that membership in a lower scoring group diminishes one's advancement opportunities. Perhaps there is a different line of thought.

Note that, although they are statistically significant, which means that the differences are not likely to have been a random occurrence, the differences between groups are often quite small in absolute terms. The real variability is within the group. Group characteristics do not define the individual student. To say it more directly, knowing the characteristics of a group reveals next to nothing about the performance of an individual who happens to fall within the group. To believe otherwise is to stereotype.

The educator's ethical responsibility is to be as fair and accurate as possible. We can avoid many of the pitfalls by remembering that assessment is a data-gathering mechanism and we wish the data to be as precise as they can be. In turn, this allows us to make decisions that are as effective as possible for the learners. Compromising one's responsibility to maintain high ethical standards in assessment is unlikely to improve the quality of any aspect of the educational program.

ENDNOTES

1. Alas, even a week's practice was insufficient to the day. The vice-principal smugly took his hoard of "Black Jack" chewing gum and left everyone wondering who it was that let the class down.
2. It is typical for organizations that market psychological tests to require of anyone who orders their materials, membership in a relevant professional association, his or her state certification or licensing number, and the name of the certifying agency.

FOR FURTHER READING

The summer 1987 issue of *Educational Measurement: Issues and Practice* is a series of articles on implications of the agreement in the Golden Rule Insurance Company case mentioned in connection with item bias. The articles, as well as the editorial in the issue, are interesting for their discussion of the issues related to test and item bias.

REFERENCES

Anastasi, A. (1976). *Psychological testing* (4th ed.). New York: Macmillan.

Cannell, J. J. (1988). Nationally normed elementary achievement testing in America's public schools: How all 50 states are above the national average. *Educational Measurement: Issues and Practice, 7*(2), 5–9.

Cronbach, L. J. (1969). Validation of educational measures. Proceedings of the 1969 Invitational Conference on Testing Problems: Toward a theory of achievement measurement. Princeton, NJ: Educational Testing Service.

Crouse, J., and Trusheim, D. (1988). *The case against the SAT.* Chicago: The University of Chicago Press.

Diamond, E. E., and Fremer, J. (1989). The Joint Committee on Testing Practices and the Code of Fair Testing Practices in Education. *Educational Measurement: Issues and Practice, 8*(1), 23–24.

Fremer, J. (1986). Code of fair testing in education. *Educational Measurement: Issues and Practice, 5*(2), 26.

Gellman, E. S. (1995). *School testing: What parents and educators need to know.* Westport, CT: Praeger.

Gipps, C., and Murphy, P. (1994). *A fair test? Assessment, achievement, and equity.* Philadelphia: The Open University Press.

Gottfredson, L. S. (1994). The science and politics of race-norming. *American Psychologist, 49,* 955–962.

Hedges, L. V., and Friedman, L. (1993). Gender differences in variability in intellectual abilities: A reanalysis of Feingold's results. *Review of Educational Research, 63,* 94–105.

Hopkins, K. D., and Stanley, J. C. (1981). *Educational and psychological measurement and evaluation* (6th ed.). Englewood Cliffs, NJ: Prentice-Hall.

Hunter, J. E. Schmidt, F. L., and Rauschenberger, J. (1984). Methodological, statistical, and ethical issues in the study of bias in psychological tests. In C. R. Reynolds and R. T. Brown (Eds.), *Perspectives on bias in mental testing.* New York: Plenum Press.

Jensen, A. R. (1980). *Bias in mental testing.* New York: The Free Press.

Kessel, C., and Linn, M. D. (1996). Grades or scores: Predicting future college mathematics performance. *Educational Measurement: Issues and Practice, 15*(4), 10–14.

Marsh, H. W. (1989). Sex differences in the development of verbal and mathematics constructs: The high school and beyond study. *American Educational Research Journal, 26,* 191–225.

Mehrens, W. A., and Kaminski, J. (1989). Methods for improving standardized test scores: Fruitful, fruitless, or fraudulent? *Educational Measurement: Issues and Practice, 8*(1), 14–22.

Scheuneman, J. D., and Slaughter, C. (1991). *Issues of test bias, item bias, and group differences and what to do while waiting for the answers.* Princeton, NJ: Educational Testing Service. (ERIC Document Reproduction Service No. ED 400 294)

Smith, M. L. (1991). Meanings of test preparation. *American Educational Research Journal, 28,* 521–542.

Taylor, C. S., and Nolen, S. B. (1996). What does the psychometrician's classroom look like? Reframing assessment concepts in the context of learning. *Education Policy Analysis Archives, 4*(17), 1–18. Retrieved January 26, 2000, from the World Wide Web: http://olam.ed.asu.edu/epaa/

Selected Advanced Topics in Classroom Assessment

■ *Readers will examine some of the more technical aspects of current assessment.*

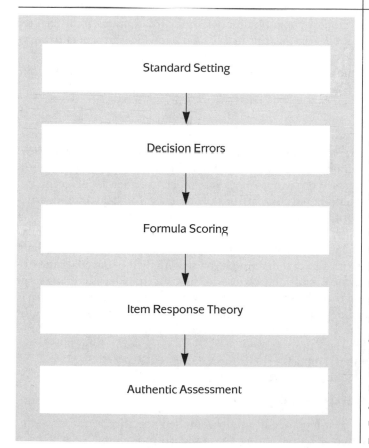

Standard Setting

Decision Errors

Formula Scoring

Item Response Theory

Authentic Assessment

The very high profile that assessment enjoys in primary and secondary schools opens discussions that might have seemed out of place only a few years ago. Determining the point that defines students' success and coping with the consequences of making errors in those judgments represent two such discussions. Although there are important exceptions, and authentic assessment frequently emerges as one, assessing large numbers of students usually involves selected response items. One of their shortcomings is the distortion possible when students guess. Formula scoring allows one to make an adjustment for guessing. Item response theory offers an alternative to traditional assumptions about how to measure students' understanding with selected response items. ■

Mrs. Robinson's interest in teaching was borne of a fascination with the way things work and a desire to share her understanding with others. Her curiosity ranged across many disciplines, a factor that kept her involved in the elementary school, where she could teach all subjects. Her current interest, however, was less in what her students should learn than in how their learning was gauged. The assessment rules appeared to have changed, and rather than simply administer the new instruments, Mrs. Robinson wanted to understand how they were developed and how the data were interpreted. ■

BREADTH VERSUS DEPTH

Books such as this one introduce a range of topics and offer little opportunity to exhaust any of them. The intent, after all, is to survey the subject rather than attempt to completely penetrate it. That said, in the effort to understand assessment we often encounter topics that are related to classroom assessment, but which are probably not critical to most classroom teachers. We can implement an educational plan, including the assessment component, without delving too deeply into the topics listed in the chapter outline; but as the prologue suggests, it is probably characteristic of teachers to wonder why things are as they are. There is still no opportunity to be exhaustive, but in this chapter we will pursue some of the topics we hinted at in earlier sections of the book.

STANDARD SETTING

Very early it was noted that we might gauge students' performance by comparing them either to other students (a normative-reference) or to a set of descriptors (a criterion-reference). There are elements of both approaches very much in evidence. It is common, for example, to read of international comparisons of students who belong to a particular age group. Their performances are compared to each other. Criterion-references in the guise of district, state, or national standards are also common, but because relative performance is not the gauge, there must be some other way to determine how good is good enough. Historically, that determination was implicit in the goals and objectives that individual teachers made on a classroom-by-classroom basis. Today, standards are often set beyond the level of the classroom, or even the school, and there is no single approach that guides all standard-setting procedures. **Judgmental models** focus on the content of the tests, and fix standards based on judgments of the difficulty of the test items. Although there are alternative models that focus on the ability of the test takers as well, judgmental models are the most common (Cizek, 1996).

Judgmental Standard-Setting Models

Nedelsky (1954) developed a judgmental model intended specifically for tests employing multiple-choice items. Those setting the standard must judge each item in terms of how a hypothetical "minimally competent person" will respond. The standard is a function of how many of the choices in an individual item this person will likely reject as incorrect. For example, for a test item with four choices, the judge(s) may determine that a minimally competent person will probably reject choice (b) as incorrect. The item rating is found by taking the reciprocal of the remaining three choices and then using its decimal equivalent as the item rating.

Recall that the reciprocal of a number is the number inverted, with its denominator becoming its numerator and the numerator becoming the denominator. Whole numbers are understood to have 1 as their denominator even though we do not usually write it. The number 3 can be written $\frac{3}{1}$, for example. Because there are three choices remaining in the item (a, c, and d), and the reciprocal of $\frac{3}{1}$ is $\frac{1}{3}$, the item's rating is the decimal equivalent of $\frac{1}{3}$, which is .33.

If the next item is one for which the minimally competent person is expected to reject choices (c) and (d) as implausible answers, the item's rating is .5 because the two choices not rejected have a reciprocal of $\frac{1}{2}$, and the decimal equivalent of $\frac{1}{2}$ is .5. The passing score, or standard for the test, is the sum of the individual item ratings. Figure 13.1 gives an example of standard setting using Nedelsky's (1954) approach.

FIGURE 13.1   Standard Setting Using Nedelsky's Approach

Item	Number of Choices	Number of Choices Rejected by a Minimally Competent Person	Rating	
1	4	1	.33	($\frac{1}{3}$)
2	4	2	.5	($\frac{1}{2}$)
3	4	1	.33	($\frac{1}{3}$)
4	4	3	1.0	($\frac{1}{1}$)
5	4	2	.5	($\frac{1}{2}$)
6	4	1	.33	($\frac{1}{3}$)
7	4	0	0	($\frac{1}{0}$)
8	4	2	.5	($\frac{1}{2}$)
9	4	1	.33	($\frac{1}{3}$)
10	4	3	1.0	($\frac{1}{1}$)
11	4	2	.5	($\frac{1}{2}$)
12	4	1	.33	($\frac{1}{3}$)
13	4	2	.5	($\frac{1}{2}$)
14	4	1	.33	($\frac{1}{3}$)
15	4	1	.33	($\frac{1}{3}$)
16	4	2	.5	($\frac{1}{2}$)
17	4	1	.33	($\frac{1}{3}$)
18	4	3	1.0	($\frac{1}{1}$)
19	4	2	.5	($\frac{1}{2}$)
20	4	1	.33	($\frac{1}{3}$)
		Total becomes the test standard	9.47*	

*The practice is to round up to the next whole number, in which case 10 would be the standard for this test, according to the Nedelsky method.

Ebel's (1972) approach actually requires multiple assessments to set a standard. The first two judgments assess the difficulty and the relevance of the item. There are typically three difficulty levels, such as "easy," "moderate," and "hard," and four relevance categories perhaps ranging from "marginal," to "relevant," to "important," and those of "critical" importance. With each item placed in one category from each dimension, the judges estimate the proportion of "minimally competent students" who will be successful with each group of items.

The Ebel (1972) method places a significant burden on the judges. If items fall into each possible combination of difficulty (three levels) and relevance (four levels), judges will have 12 separate groups of items to evaluate (Figure 13.2). As Cizek (1996) suggested, classifying the items is not an easy process since one must keep the multi-

FIGURE 13.2   Standard Setting Using Ebel's Method

The number in each cell represents the number of items fitting the category. The number in parentheses indicates the percentage of "minimally competent persons" who are judged to be successful on 20 items in this combination of item difficulty and item importance.

Item Difficulty	Item Importance			
	Critical	*Important*	*Relevant*	*Marginal*
Hard		2 (50)	2 (35)	1 (0)
Moderate	3 (75)	3 (65)	1 (50)	
Easy	4 (100)	3 (90)	1 (60)	

The ratings are found by multiplying the number of items by the number in parentheses. For example, the rating for the critical/moderate category is 3 × 75 = 225. The individual ratings are then totaled as shown.

critical/moderate	225
critical/easy	400
important/hard	100
important/moderate	195
important/easy	270
relevant/hard	70
relevant/moderate	50
relevant/easy	60
marginal/hard	0
Total	1,370

This total is divided by the number of items judged to determine the recommended passing standard.

In this example, the total number of items judged = 20 and the sum of the ratings = 1370. The recommended passing standard is $1,370/20$ = 68.5 correct. On a 20-item test this amounts to 13.7 or 14 items correct.

ple levels of difficulty and relevance distinct. The standard is an estimate of how the minimally competent student will fare with each group of items.

The Angoff (1971) procedure, too, relies on judgments of the "minimally competent person's" performance, but this approach is a little simpler to use than either of the other methods. One approach is to simply review the items one at a time and estimate whether minimally competent students would likely score the item correctly. If an assessment includes 20 items and the judge's review determines that the minimally competent person is likely to score 14 items correctly, 14 becomes the performance standard.

There is a slightly more involved approach to Angoff's (1971) procedure that requires that judges estimate the *probability* that the minimally competent person would score the item correctly. In this instance, a hypothetical group of minimally competent students becomes the sample and the probability is the proportion of students estimated to be able to respond correctly to each item. If three of a hypothetical group of 10 minimally competent students are judged to be able to respond to item 1 correctly, the rating for the first item is .3. The sum of the individual item probabilities becomes the performance standard for the assessment. Figure 13.3 illustrates standard setting using Angoff's (1971) approach.

FIGURE 13.3 Standard Setting Using Angoff's Method

Item	Number of Students Expected to Score Correctly	Proportion
1	6 of 10	.6
2	3 of 10	.3
3	10 of 10	1.0
4	8 of 10	.8
5	8 of 10	.8
6	4 of 10	.4
7	9 of 10	.9
8	7 of 10	.7
9	9 of 10	.9
10	8 of 10	.8
11	4 of 10	.4
12	9 of 10	.9
13	7 of 10	.7
14	9 of 10	.9
15	5 of 10	.5
16	6 of 10	.6
17	7 of 10	.7
18	8 of 10	.8
19	6 of 10	.6
20	2 of 10	.2
	Total	13.5

The standard equals the sum of the probabilities, which is 13.5 rounded to 14 items.

Sometimes the standard is related to a specific objective, and what we need to know is whether students have met the standard that the objective represents. Petersen, Kolen, and Hoover (1989) addressed this situation with a procedure similar to Angoff's (1971). First, all of the items relating to the objective are grouped together and then, in a procedure that you should be able to predict by now, one estimates how many of the items the minimally competent student will score correctly. Although the judges' estimate might fall at any number of items, Petersen et al. suggested that the minimally competent student should answer 90 percent of the items correctly in order to meet the standard.

Speaking of Assessment

The 90 percent standard should at least puzzle you a little. It seems to be established without reference to the complexity of the test items, to their difficulty, or to the conditions of the assessment (is the test to be timed?). When a standard is set in isolation of these other conditions, the potential for an arbitrary standard is very great. Why not an 80 percent standard, a performance level very popular among criterion-referenced test advocates of the 1970s? Ironically, an arbitrary standard is the very condition that standard-setting procedures are designed to help one avoid.

Back to the "how good is good enough?" issue for a moment, selecting the standard is only that part of the task visible to the casual onlooker. Note that it is actually the culmination of a series of judgments, each of which involves its own complications. We can develop this a little with the discussion questions in the *For Further Discussion* box.

For Further Discussion

The quality of the standard-setting procedures hinges in large part on the effectiveness of the judges' decisions. What we have examined to this point keeps returning us to that hypothetical "minimally competent person." The "average" student is a good deal easier to identify because we can do so mathematically by calculating the average score for the group. This ought to help one understand the appeal of normative-references. As the following questions suggest, minimal competence is more problematic:

Suppose we define the minimally competent learner as one who has just barely mastered the skill or developed the understanding, does that simplify the task?

How would one define a minimally competent third-grade reader?

Is the definition dependent upon the students' characteristics?—Is there a different standard for those who speak English as a second language, for example?

No matter how technical and involved the approach is, the business of judging means that there remains some element of subjectivity involved in standard setting.

By definition, the judges are people who can make the needed determinations, but the process is not entirely objective.

Although there is no assessment "fail-safe," the average estimations of several judges (teachers) offer more security than an individual's. When several judges are participating, one adds their respective standards together and then divides by the number of judges to determine *the* standard. In the earlier example, perhaps there are 12 items and three judges. If two of the judges estimate that the minimally competent person would correctly answer 8 and the third estimates a score of 10, the standard is $(8 + 8 + 10)/3 = 8.67$ or 9 items.

Because the judge must be competent in the subject matter, and also recognize how respondents are likely to respond to the items, perhaps no one is in a better position to fix standards than the classroom instructors. Even then, consensus among the several instructors will require training and practice.

In Ebel's (1972) procedure, there are multiple places to go awry as one attempts to determine how relevant an item is, how difficult it is, and how successful those marginally competent students are going to be when responding. Although each of the judgments makes intuitive sense, it is probably safer to keep procedures as simple as possible, and perhaps simplicity is what makes variations of Angoff's (1971) procedure the most common.

> There are different ways to determine where to set a performance standard. When we establish the standard based on how difficult the test items are, we use a judgmental model. Those using an empirical model fix the standard by judging the level of ability a minimally competent student possesses. Combination models include elements of item difficulty and students' ability (Cizek, 1996).

The concept of meeting standards implies that students' learning increases by degrees until they become competent in the subject or the task. This idea has greatest appeal in content areas that are well-ordered and incremental, such as mathematics or language learning. In many other disciplines, the step-by-step feature is less evident. Identifying the particular point at which students become competent in a social science course, for example, is less straightforward. (As an aside, identifying the point at which a teacher candidate becomes a competent teacher can also be very difficult.) These difficulties give rise to the potential to make mistakes when one judges competence. We call those mistakes **decision errors.**

DECISION ERRORS

Any time one makes a decision about students' performance there is the potential for an error. Mistakes in measurement, data tabulation, or analysis may all be culprits. One might also have made a mistake in standard setting. In turn, such mistakes give rise to erroneous judgments. The incompetent might be judged competent, or the competent not competent.

> False positive judgments are called type I, or alpha errors. False negative judgments are called type II, or beta errors.

In assessment language when one lacking a quality is judged to possess it, a false positive or type I error is committed. Type I errors are symbolized by the Greek letter alpha (α), and are also called alpha errors. If someone who has a quality has been misjudged as lacking it, a false negative, or type II error, has been committed. Type II errors are symbolized by beta (β).

The relationship between errors and the standard is depicted in Figure 13.4.

The students who fall just either side of the standard are most likely to be affected by measurement errors because a comparatively small measurement error can result in a decision error. The area just below the standard is where candidates are most likely to have the required learning, but because of measurement problems, erroneously to be judged not competent. Those are type II errors. Of those who are judged competent, the students just above the standard are most likely to actually lack the quality and so reflect type I errors. There is no potential for type II error among those judged competent, nor type I error among those judged not competent.

One can manipulate the standard to minimize a particular decision error, but note that decreasing the probability of one type of error increases the probability of the other. If we relax the cut-off score by moving it lower, the probability increases that those who are competent will be judged correctly. The trade-off, however, is that a higher number of those who are not competent will also be judged competent because the cut-off is easier to achieve. By the same logic, making the cut-off point more stringent will reduce the number of false positive classifications, but it will increase the number of false negative classifications.

Since one cannot minimize one type of error without increasing the other, the issue is which is more palatable. When the risks associated with incompetence are high, the tendency is to exclude those at the lower levels of competence (type II error) rather than risk including those who lack the quality by small margins (type I error). These decisions take on a very personal dimension. Classroom teachers work so closely with students and competency decisions that they usually know those who

FIGURE 13.4   Cut-Off Scores and Decision Errors

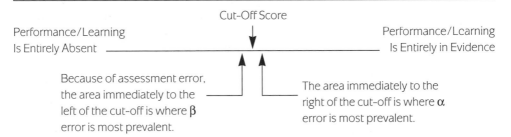

If we were worried about judging someone competent who is not, we could correct for alpha error by moving the cut-off score to the right (higher), but doing so increases the probability of beta error (false negatives). By the same token, moving the cut-off score to the left (lower) will eliminate some of the errors made when the competent are judged not competent, but doing so increases the probability of alpha error.

are likely to be affected, and it is sometimes difficult to determine which type of error poses the greatest threat.

For Further Discussion

Errors in collecting, tabulating, and interpreting data cannot be avoided entirely, which means that there is an ever-present risk of classification errors. Whether type I or type II errors are more acceptable depends upon the circumstances and the risks associated with misclassification.

Is it better to certify a student who may lack the quality by a small margin but scores well enough on the test to exceed the cut-off, or not certify students who may be competent, but who do not test well enough to demonstrate it?

Are the wishes of the student ever more important than the integrity of the standard?

There are no simple answers to the questions in the *For Further Discussion* box. One must recognize that there are competing interests involved and weigh the consequences of each type of error.

FORMULA SCORING

By comparison, formula scoring presents circumstances that are a good deal simpler to cope with than choosing the more acceptable decision error. Selected response test items predominate in much of the standardized testing. They offer extensive content coverage in a relatively short time, they provide objective scoring, and they yield a good deal of information via item analysis. However, because their format makes it easy for students to guess, scores from instruments using selected response items may also obscure what students have actually learned. Testing agencies sometimes adjust scores to counter some of the influence of guessing. Although such procedures are less common in the classroom, individual instructors sometimes use them as well.

Fray (1988) contends that formula scoring is the most appropriate name for such adjustments. The more common phrase is "correction for guessing," but that term carries the presumption that one derives the score that would occur if the respondents had not guessed. This is misleading, since there is no way to determine precisely what the score would have been. Furthermore, students are often inclined to interpret "correction for guessing" as a penalty for guessing, which formula scoring is not.

An early approach to formula scoring assumed that one responding to test items either recognized the correct answer or guessed randomly among the available choices. This gave rise to a formula for adjusting the individual's score that is demonstrated in Figure 13.5.

For the individual in the example, the logic of this adjustment is as follows: Each item has four choices including the correct choice. Therefore, the probability of

FIGURE 13.5   **Formula Scoring Data from a Multiple-Choice Assessment**

In words, we are subtracting, from the number of correct answers, a value equal to the number of wrong answers divided by the number of choices minus 1. Stated symbolically we have

$$S_{adj} = C - \left(\frac{I}{ch - 1}\right)$$

where S_{adj} = the adjusted score
C = the number of items scored correctly
I = the number of items scored incorrectly
$ch - 1$ = the number of choices in each item, minus 1 (presumes just one correct choice)

Consider a 35-item test constructed of multiple-choice items.

The student's number correct = 22
The number incorrectly scored = 9
The number of choices for each item = 4, only one of which is the correct choice.

$$S_{adj} = 22 - \frac{9}{3}$$
$$= 19$$

Source: Adapted from Fray (1988).

blindly guessing the correct choice on any given item is one chance in four. Symbolically, we can say the probability is $p = .25$ of a correct guess. The assumptions associated with formula scoring, and the nine items missed on this particular assessment indicate the following:

1. The student guessed on the items the student was unsure of.
2. Based on random probability and the number of choices for each item, the student should have missed three out of four of the items that were guessed, and guessed one out of four correctly.
3. The score of 22 includes correct guesses.

The formula uses the number of items missed to estimate the number the student correctly guessed. The calculations suggest that this student guessed the correct answers to three items. Consequently, reducing the student's score from 22 to 19 produces a more accurate measure.

> Selected response items increase the potential for distorting scores by guessing. Formula scoring, while not a correction as such, is at least an adjustment for guessing that probably produces a more accurate score than the unadjusted score.

Although 19 is probably a more accurate score than 22, we made some assumptions in the example that sometimes do not hold. The alternative to knowing the correct answer is usually not just blind guessing. Students can often eliminate at least one of the choices in a multiple-choice item. For that reason, those who guess wildly at the remaining choices will still receive higher scores than those who do not guess (Fray, 1988) and cautioning students against guessing places them at a disadvantage. In fact, when they can increase their scores through guessing, one probably has an ethical responsibility to inform the students accordingly.

ITEM RESPONSE THEORY: AN ALTERNATIVE TO CLASSICAL TEST THEORY

Part of the problem with traditional testing procedures is that they yield scores that are test-specific. A fourth-grade math test score tells us whether the student has learned to work those particular test problems, but we may not be able to generalize beyond the test. Item response theory (IRT) or latent trait theory represents an alternative. This approach assumes that answering an assessment item correctly depends on students' possession of a sufficient quantity of the particular mental trait called for by the test item. Verbal ability, problem-solving ability, and reasoning ability are all examples of mental traits that allow us to complete common academic tasks. The true and observed scores discussed in Chapter 9 reflect particular tests, but the latent trait is test-independent (Hambleton and Jones, 1993). The quantity of the trait varies from person to person, which is why some people can respond to a particular item correctly and others have difficulty.

One can describe each assessment item with an **item characteristic curve**. It reflects two kinds of data, the levels of the trait that students possess, and their scores on the items. The curve defines the probability that learners who possess the different levels of the trait that the item measures will score the item correctly. Part (a) of Figure 13.6 is an item characteristic curve for a multiple-choice test item.

The item characteristic curve can be interpreted for individuals, or for groups. The horizontal axis can be thought of as a continuum representing, as one moves from left to right, increasing levels of the ability or trait the item measures. The vertical axis represents the increasing probability of scoring the item correctly. Moving horizontally from any probability on the vertical axis to the item curve, and then vertically down to the ability axis, indicates the level of ability one must possess to have a specified probability of scoring the item correctly.

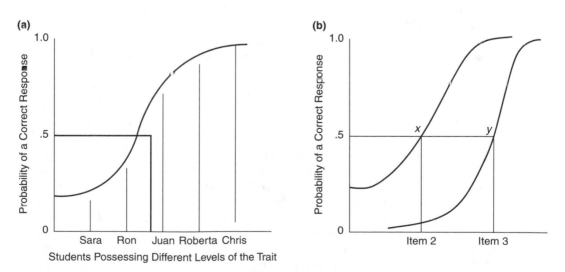

FIGURE 13.6 An Item Characteristic Curve for an Algebra Problem

For individuals, the curve indicates the probability that students of various levels of ability will score the item correctly. Students who have the same ability level as Sara will correctly score about 15 percent of the items with this difficulty level. Students of Chris's ability level are likely to score all such items correctly. Note that there isn't a zero probability of scoring the item correctly for anyone of any ability level. This is because the items are in multiple-choice format and there is always the possibility that someone may guess correctly, even if he or she completely lacks the trait the item is intended to assess. If there were seven possible answers offered, the probability of a random correct guess is just less than .15.

The figure shows a right angle line drawn through the middle of the curve horizontally to that point at which there is a .5 probability of scoring the item correctly. The line then proceeds vertically to the level of ability the student must have in order to enjoy that 50/50 chance of a correct choice. This line defines item difficulty. For more difficult items, that point will occur farther to the right on the horizontal axis, and to the left for easier items.

The other element of the item revealed by the curve is the degree to which the item discriminates between respondents who possess different levels of the trait. Chapter 7 described item discrimination and calculated a discrimination index as a function of the way top scorers versus bottom scorers performed on a particular item. That statistic (d_i) made the quality of the item a function of how well it reflects total test performance. It is a useful—but not a very sophisticated—measure of how well the item distinguishes between the differently performing groups.

Item response theory uses a different approach. The level of discrimination the item provides is indicated by the steepness of the vertical part of the curve. In part (b) of Figure 13.6, the curves are plotted for two different items. Think of item 2 as a multiple-choice item with five choices. For someone without the trait the item is intended to measure, there is still a probability of p = .2 ($^1/_5$) of guessing the item correctly. This is reflected at the point where the curve begins on the vertical axis. This item discriminates moderately well, but item 3 discriminates more precisely. The increasing discrimination is reflected in the steeper curve at the point at which the probability of a correct score equals .5. This can be interpreted to mean that relatively little increase in the trait measured separates those who will likely score the item correctly (their probability of scoring the item correctly is above .5) from those who probably will not (their collective probability is below .5).

When we have selected response items, the item characteristic curve always begins part way up the vertical axis to allow for correct guesses. Although the student speaks no French at all, the student may still guess correctly that the French word for cheese is *fromage*. This does not occur with constructed response items. When learners possess a level of the measured characteristic that is lower than a certain level, respondents can sometimes be expected to have no probability of responding to a constructed response item correctly. No matter how lucky he is, the average eight-year-old will have a zero probability of explaining the Pythagorean theorem in an essay. Although children of that age will certainly have some level of mathematics ability, what the item measures places the probability of a correct response out of reach.

Besides discriminating better, item 3 is also more difficult. This is revealed in the fact that the place on the horizontal axis directly below that point on the curve at which there is a .5 probability of scoring the item correctly, point *y* in the figure, is to the right of the equivalent point (*x*) for item 2. Remember that this axis is a scale of the trait measured. Item 3 requires more of the trait than item 2.

Items can have the same level of difficulty, but different levels of discrimination. This is the case when the "*x*-point" that we established for item 2, for example, is the same for some other item, but the curve is less or more steep. On the other hand, different items can have the same type of curve but different levels of difficulty, which is the case when items have identical curves but they are located at different points on the horizontal axis.

The early portion of item characteristic curves, and particularly the later parts, are typically flatter than the middle section. This suggests that there are points before which, and after which, the item does not discriminate well. Initially, moderate increases in the trait measured are not sufficient to significantly affect the probability of scoring the item correctly. The flatness of the later part of the item suggests that beyond the point at which the curve flattens, increases in the trait have little impact on correct responses, since the probability of a correct response is already near 1.0.

> When item response theory governs assessment, the focus becomes the trait that underlies the ability assessed. Item characteristic curves indicate the level of the trait that one must possess in order to answer an item correctly. One of the great advantages of IRT is that results are not specific to a particular test.

Although the early work in item response theory was done before computers were widely available, the calculations were complicated enough that few people got involved with the work. Even now, IRT work is restricted primarily to measurement specialists and researchers, but it holds great promise. Item response theory gives the test developer the opportunity to tailor an assessment very carefully by selecting assessment items on the basis of the trait they measure, and of their level of difficulty for particular students. This allows one to develop alternate forms of a test that are truly equivalent in terms of what it is they assess and the difficulty of the items.

AUTHENTIC ASSESSMENT

Most of the discussion in this chapter has been connected to traditional assessment procedures and issues. As something of a counterbalance we need to return to an aspect of authentic assessment first raised in Chapter 4.

One of the strengths of authentic assessment is the way this approach deals with content validity. Good authentic assessment procedures involve tasks that are completely embedded in the related content so that the students' performances can be a direct indicator of their grasp of the discipline. Authentic assessors are also very attentive to face validity, going to great lengths to make the assessment exercise(s) consistent with the world beyond the classroom. Remember, however, that there are other elements of validity besides content coverage and appearances, and some of them are not equally secure. Kamphaus (1991) asked, "What aspect of psychometric practice is addressed by authentic assessment? Is this approach aimed at increasing the predictive, concurrent, or factorial validity of educational achievement measures? I do not get a clear sense that this is the case" (pp. 300–301).

Predictive validity and concurrent validity are aspects of criterion-related validity. They both deal with the effectiveness with which the assessment predicts the individual's behavior in specified situations. However authentic the sixth-grade student's science presentation may appear, it should have some value as a predictor for the student's seventh-grade science performance as well. Champions of authentic assessment have not been very attentive to this element.

Factorial or construct validity is the degree to which the assessment measures a theoretical construct such as problem-solving ability. An eighth-grade science teacher might develop a laboratory activity in which students must solve pollution problems resulting from overusing chemical fertilizers on city lawns. Instead of analyzing how well the activity actually gauges problem-solving ability, however, the tendency is to appeal to the authenticity of the setting. But face validity is no substitute for construct validity. The fact that criterion-related validity and factorial validity are associated with traditional testing, which is widely criticized does not mean that those elements of validity are not relevant also to authentic assessment.

SUMMARY

This chapter is a vehicle for examining some of our earlier topics more closely. Your author has based it on the assumption that, like the prologue's Mrs. Robinson, the reader wishes to know how things work and is willing to dig a little deeper than usual to understand.

Standard setting first came up in Chapter 3 as part of the larger discussion of criterion-referenced assessment. Much of that topic's weight and importance hinges on the question of how one identifies the standard. With that in mind we examined standard-setting approaches based on the difficulty of the test items (judgmental models) and upon the ability of the students (empirical models). Neither those approaches nor the combination approach that involves elements of each provides an ideal solution to the problem of determining where to locate the standard. Each approach offers less guesswork than most of the alternatives, however.

Even if one settles on a standard that is completely acceptable to all parties (a most unlikely contingency), decision errors still hold the potential to make evaluating students contentious. Because of measurement error, sometimes those who lack a quality appear to possess it and one is responsible for a type I (α or false positive) error. If one judges someone who lacks the quality to have it, the error is type II (β or false negative). Under normal circumstances, one cannot eliminate either type of error without increasing the probability of committing the other. While there are instances when one type of error is clearly preferable to the other, the educator is generally left to choose the lesser of evils.

Formula scoring addresses a weakness in selected response test items, the potential for distorting scores because of guessing. It is not entirely accurate to describe formula scoring as a "correction," but it may be a helpful adjustment—allowing one, as it does, to neutralize at least some of the effect of guessing the correct answers.

Assessments produced by most traditional procedures yield results tied directly to the particular test one has used. Instead of the number of items correct, item response theory allows one to develop tests that indicate how much of a particular trait a student possesses. As such, one may generalize results beyond the particular instrument. While developing tests according to IRT procedures is beyond the reach of most of us, the concept is not, and it is helpful to understand the theory that provides the foundation for much of modern standardized testing.

The comments on authentic assessment sound like more of a critique than an explication. There is no intent to denigrate an important element of what all teachers should include among their assessment techniques, but there are reasons for caution. Ignoring the technical characteristics of authentic assessment does not mean that this procedure should not meet some of the same standards to which experts hold the traditional assessments.

REFERENCES

Angoff, W. H. (1971). Scales, norms, and equivalent scores. In R. L. Thorndike (Ed.), *Educational measurement.* Washington DC: American Council on Education.

Cizek, G. J. (1996). Setting passing scores. *Educational Measurement: Issues and Practice, 15*(2), 20–31.

Ebel, R. L. (1972). *Essentials of educational measurement.* Englewood Cliffs, NJ: Prentice Hall.

Fray, R. B. (1988). Formula scoring of multiple-choice tests (Correction for guessing). *Educational Measurement: Issues and Practice, 7*(2), 33–38.

Hambleton, R. K., and Jones, R. W. (1993). Comparison of classical test theory and item response theory and their applications to test development. *Educational Measurement: Issues and Practice, 12*(3), 38–47.

Kamphaus, R. W. (1991). Authentic assessment and content validity. *School Psychology Quarterly, 6,* 300–304.

Nedelsky, L. (1954). Absolute grading standards for objective tests. *Educational and Psychological Measurement, 14,* 3–19.

Petersen, N. S., Kolen, M. J., and Hoover, H. D. (1989). Scaling, norming, and equating. In R. L. Linn, *Educational measurement* (3rd ed.). New York: Macmillan.

Bibliography

Airasian, P. W. (1988). Measurement driven instruction: A closer look. *Educational Measurement: Issues and Practice, 7*(4), 6–11.

Airasian, P. W. (1991). Perspectives in measurement instruction. *Educational Measurement: Issues and Practice, 10*(1), 13–16, 26.

Allen, M. J., and Yen, W. M. (1979). *Introduction to measurement theory.* Monterey, CA: Brooks/Cole.

Ames, R. (1982). Teachers' attributions for their own teaching. In J. M. Levine and M. C. Wang (Eds.), *Teacher and student perceptions.* Hillsdale, NJ: Erlbaum.

Anastasi, A. (1976). *Psychological testing* (4th ed.). New York: Macmillan.

Andrews, T. E., and Barnes, S. (1990). Assessment of teaching. In W. R. Houston (Ed.), *Handbook of research on teacher education.* New York: Macmillan.

Angoff, W. H. (1971). Scales, norms, and equivalent scores. In R. L. Thorndike (Ed.), *Educational measurement.* Washington DC: American Council on Education.

Archbald, D. A. (1991). Authentic assessment: Principles, practices, and issues. *School Psychology Quarterly, 6,* 279–293.

Archbald, D. A., and Newmann, F. M. (1992). Approaches to assessing academic achievement. In H. Berlak, F. M. Newmann, E. Adams, D. A. Archbald, T. Burgess, J. Raven, and T. A. Romberg (Eds.), *Toward a new science of educational testing and assessment* (pp. 139–180). Albany: State University of New York Press.

Armstrong, A. M. (1993). Cognitive-style differences in testing situations. *Educational Measurement: Issues and Practice, 12*(3), 17–22.

Armstrong, C. L. (1994). *Designing assessment in art.* Reston, VA: National Art Education Association.

Armstrong, D. G., Denton, J. J., and Savage, T. V. (1978). *Instructional skills handbook.* Englewood Cliffs, NJ: Educational Technology Publications.

Assessment Systems Corporation. (1998). 2233 University Ave., Suite 200, St. Paul, MN.

Atkinson, R. C., and Fletcher, J. D. (1972). Teaching children to read with a computer. *Reading Teacher, 25,* 319–327.

Barros, J. H., Neto, F., and Barros, A. M. (1989). Socio-cognitive variables of teachers and their influence on teaching. (ERIC Document Reproduction Service No. ED 346 032)

Baumeister, R. F. (1996). Should schools try to boost self-esteem? *American Educator, 20*(2), 14–19, 43.

Belk, J. A., and Calais, G. J. (1993). Portfolio assessment in reading and writing: Linking assessment and instruction to learning. Paper presented at the annual meeting of Mid South Educational Research Association, New Orleans, November 10–12. (ERIC Document Reproduction Service No. ED 365 732)

Berlak, H. (1992). The need for a new science of assessment. In H. Berlak, F. M. Newmann, E. Adams, D. A. Archbald, T. Burgess, J. Raven, and T. A. Romberg, *Toward a new science of educational testing and assessment* (pp. 1–21). Albany: State University of New York Press.

Bloom, B. S. (Ed.). (1956). *Taxonomy of Educational Objectives, Handbook I: Cognitive Domain.* New York: David McKay.

Bloom, B. S., Hastings, J. T., and Madaus, G. F. (1971). *Handbook on formative and summative assessment of student learning.* New York: McGraw Hill.

Bond, L. (1989). The effects of special preparation on measures of scholastic ability. In R. L. Linn (Ed.), *Educational measurement* (3rd ed.). New York: Macmillan.

Bormuth, J. R. (1968). The Cloze Readability Procedure. *Elementary English, 45,* 429–436.

Bower, G. H., and Hilgard, E. R. (1981). *Theories of learning* (5th ed.). Englewood Cliffs, NJ: Prentice-Hall.

Bracey, G. W. (1992). What assessment and research say about the condition of education. *Educational Measurement: Issues and Practice, 11*(4), 5–6, 41.

Breland, H. M., Danos, D. O., Kahn, H. D., Kubota, M. Y., and Bonner M. W. (1994). Performance versus objective testing and gender: An exploratory study of an advanced placement history examination. *Journal of Educational Measurement, 31,* 275–293.

Brookhart, S. (1999). Teaching about communicating assessment results and grading. *Educational Measurement: Issues and Practice, 18*(1), 5–13.

Bunderson, C. V., Inouye, D. K., and Olsen, J. B. (1989). The four generations of computerized educational measurement. In R. L. Linn (Ed.), *Educational measurement* (3rd ed., pp. 367–407). New York: Macmillan.

Cannell, J. J. (1988). Nationally normed elementary achievement testing in America's public schools: How all 50 states are above the national average. *Educational Measurement: Issues and Practice, 7*(2), 5–9.

Carter, K. (1986). Test-wiseness for teachers and students. *Educational Measurement: Issues and Practice, 5*(4), 20–23.

Castenell, L. A., Jr., and Soled, S. W. (1993). *Standards, assessments, and valuing diversity: Essays on emerging assessment issues.* Washington, DC: The American Association of Colleges of Teacher Education.

Christenson, S. L. (1991). Authentic assessment: Straw man or prescription for progress? *School Psychology Quarterly, 6,* 294–299.

Cizek, G. J. (1996a). Setting passing scores. *Educational Measurement: Issues and Practice, 15*(2), 20–31.

Cizek, G. J. (1996b). Standard-setting guidelines. *Educational Measurement: Issues and Practice, 15*(1), 13–21, 12.

Cole, N. (1982). The implication of coaching for ability testing. In A. K. Wigdor and W. R. Garner (Eds.), *Ability testing: Uses, consequences, and controversies.* Washington, DC: National Academy Press.

Cole, N. S., and Moss, P. A. (1989). Bias in test use. In R. L. Linn (Ed.), *Educational Measurement* (3rd ed.). New York: Macmillan.

Cronbach, L. J. (1969). Validation of educational measures. Proceedings of the 1969 Invitational Conference on Testing Problems: Toward a theory of achievement measurement. Princeton, NJ: Educational Testing Service.

Crouse, J., and Trusheim, D. (1988). *The case against the SAT.* Chicago: The University of Chicago Press.

Darling-Hammond, L., Ancess, J., and Falk, B. (1995). *Authentic assessment in action: Studies of schools and students at work.* National Center for Restructuring Education, Schools, and Teaching. New York: Teachers College, Columbia University.

Diamond, E. E., and Fremer, J. (1989). The Joint Committee on Testing Practices and the Code of Fair Testing Practices in Education. *Educational Measurement: Issues and Practice, 8*(1), 23–24.

Diekhoff, G. (1992). *Statistics for the social and behavioral sciences: Univariate, bivariate, and multivariate.* Dubuque, IA: William C. Brown.

Ebel, R. L. (1972). *Essentials of educational measurement.* Englewood Cliffs, NJ: Prentice Hall.

Ebel, R. L., and Frisbie, D. A. (1986). *Essentials of educational measurement* (4th ed.). Englewood Cliffs, NJ: Prentice-Hall.

Elliott, S. N. (1991). Authentic assessment: An introduction to a neobehavioral approach to classroom assessment. *School Psychology Quarterly, 6,* pp. 273–278.

Entwisle, D., and Hayduk, L. (1981). Academic expectations and the school achievement of young children. *Sociology of Education, 54,* 34–50.

Estrin, E. T. (1993). Alternative assessment: Issues in language, culture, and equity (Brief #11). San Francisco: Far West Laboratory.

ETS. (1998). Coming to your test soon—computerized scoring of essays. *ETS Developments, 43*(3). Princeton, NJ: Educational Testing Service.

Fitzpatrick, R., and Morrison, E. J. (1971). Performance and product evaluation. In E. L. Thorndike (Ed.), *Educational Measurement* (2nd ed., pp. 237–270). Washington DC: American Council on Education.

Fray, R. B. (1988). Formula scoring of multiple-choice tests (Correction for guessing). *Educational Measurement: Issues and Practice, 7*(2), 33–38.

Fremer, J. (1986). Code of fair testing in education. *Educational Measurement: Issues and Practice, 5*(2), 26.

Frisbie, D. A. (1988). Reliability of scores from teacher-made tests. *Educational Measurement: Issues and Practice, 7*(1), 25–35.

Fry, E. (1968). A readability formula that saves time. *Journal of Reading, 11,* 513–516, 575–578.

Furst, E. J. (1981). Bloom's taxonomy of educational objectives for the cognitive domain: Philosophical and educational issues. *Review of Educational Research, 51,* 441–453.

Gagne, R. M. (1963). Learning and proficiency in mathematics. *The Mathematics Teacher, 56,* 620–626.

Galluzzo, G. R. (1993). The standards are coming! The standards are coming! In *Essays on Emerging Assessment Issues.* Washington DC: American Association of Colleges for Teacher Education.

Gardner, H. (1991). *The unschooled mind.* New York: Basic Books.

Gellman, E. S. (1995). *School testing: What parents and educators need to know.* Westport, CT: Praeger.

Gipps, C., and Murphy, P. (1994). A fair test? Assessment, achievement, and equity. Philadelphia: The Open University Press.

Glaser, R. (1963). Instructional technology and the measurement of learning outcomes: Some questions. *American Psychologist, 18,* 519–521.

Glaser, R. (1994). Instructional technology and the measurement of learning outcomes: Some questions. *Educational Measurement: Issues and Practice, 13*(4), 6–8.

Glass, G. V. (1978). Standards and criteria. *Journal of Educational Measurement, 15,* 237–261.

Glatthorn, A. A. (1993). Outcome-based education: Reform and the curriculum process. *Journal of Curriculum and Supervision, 8*(4), 354–363.

Gottfredson, L. S. (1994). The science and politics of race-norming. *American Psychologist, 49,* 955–962.

Guild, P. (1994). The culture/learning style connection. *Educational Leadership, 51*(8), 16–21.

Hambleton, R. K., and Eignor, D. R. (1980). Competency test development, validation, and standard setting. In R. M. Jaeger and C. K. Tittle (Eds.), *Minimum competence achievement testing: Motives, models, measures, and consequences* (pp. 367–396). Berkeley, CA: McCutchan.

Hambleton, R. K., and Jones, R. W. (1993). Comparison of classical test theory and item response theory and their applications to test development. *Educational Measurement: Issues and Practice, 12*(3) 38–47.

Harter, S. (1988). Developmental processes in the construction of the self. In T. D. Yawkey and J. E. Johnson (Eds.), *Integrative processes and socialization: Early to middle childhood* (pp. 45–78). Hillsdale, NJ: Lawrence Erlbaum.

Harvill, L. M. (1991). Standard error of measurement. *Educational Measurement: Issues and Practice, 10*(2), 33–41.

Hedges, L. V., and Friedman, L. (1993). Gender differences in variability in intellectual abilities: A reanalysis of Feingold's results. *Review of Educational Research, 63,* 94–105.

Holmes, C. T., and Matthews, K. M. (1984). The effects of nonpromotion on elementary and junior high school pupils: A meta-analysis. *Review of Educational Research, 54,* 225–236.

Hopkins, K. D., and Stanley, J. C. (1981). *Educational and Psychological Measurement and Evaluation* (6th ed.). Englewood Cliffs, NJ: Prentice-Hall.

House, N. G. (1997). How 'good' is good enough? *SEF News, 11*(2). A publication of the Southern Education Foundation.

Hunter, J. E., Schmidt, F. L., and Rauschenberger, J. (1984). Methodological, statistical, and ethical issues in the study of bias in psychological tests. In C. R. Reynolds and R. T. Brown (Eds.), *Perspectives on bias in mental testing.* New York: Plenum Press.

Jaeger, R. M. (1976). Measurement consequences of selected standard-setting models. *Florida Journal of Educational Research, 18,* 22–27.

Jaeger, R. M. (1989). Certification of student competence. In R. L. Linn, *Educational Measurement* (3rd ed.). New York: Macmillan.

Jarvis, P., Holford, J., and Griffin, C. (1998). *The theory and practice of learning.* London: Kogan Page.

Jensen, A. R. (1980). *Bias in mental testing.* New York: The Free Press.

Johnson, D. W., and Johnson, R. T. (1999). *Learning together and alone: Cooperative, competitive, and individualistic learning* (5th ed.). Boston: Allyn & Bacon.

Kamphaus, R. W. (1991). Authentic assessment and content validity. *School Psychology Quarterly, 6,* pp. 300–304.

Kerlinger, F. N. (1973). *Foundations of educational research.* New York: Holt, Rinehart and Winston.

Kessel, C., and Linn, M. D. (1996). Grades or scores: Predicting future college mathematics performance. *Educational Measurement: Issues and Practice, 15*(4), 10–14.

Koelsch, N., Estrin, E. T., and Farr, B. (1995). *Guide to developing equitable performance assessments.* Washington, DC: Office of Educational Research and Development. (ERIC Document Reproduction Service No. ED 397 125)

Kurtz, N. R. (1999). *Statistical analysis for the social sciences.* Boston: Allyn & Bacon.

Labaree, D. F. (1997). Public goods, private goods: The American struggle over educational goals. *American Educational Research Journal, 34,* 39–81.

Lambdin, D. V., and Forseth, C. (1996). Seamless assessment/instruction = good teaching. *Teaching Children Mathematics, 2,* 294–299.

Lefrancois, G. (1994). *Psychology for teaching* (8th ed.). Belmont CA: Wadsworth.

Legg, S. M., and Buhr, D.C. (1992). Computerized adaptive testing with different groups. *Educational Measurement: Issues and Practice, 11*(2), 23–27.

Lord, F. M. (1953). The relation of test score to the trait underlying the test. *Educational and Psychological Measurement, 13,* 517–548.

Lord, F. M., and Novick, M. R. (1968). Statistical theories of mental test scores. Reading, MA: Addison-Wesley.

Lu, Chin-hsieh, and Suen, Hoi K. (1995). Assessment approaches and cognitive styles. *Journal of Educational Measurement, 32,* 1–7.

Mantzicopoulus, P., and Morrison, D. (1992). Kindergarten retention: Academic and behavioral outcomes through the end of the second grade. *American Educational Research Journal, 29,* 182–198.

Marsh, H. W. (1989). Sex differences in the development of verbal and mathematics constructs: The high school and beyond study. *American Educational Research Journal, 26,* 191–225.

Marzano, R. J. (1994). Lesson from the field about outcome-based performance assessments. *Educational Leadership, 51* (March), 44–50.

McKernan, J. (1993). Some limitations of outcome-based education. *The Journal of Curriculum and Supervision, 8*(4), 343–353.

Medley, D. (1985). Issues and problems in the validation of teaching and teacher professional behaviors. Paper presented at the annual meeting of the American Educational Research Association, Chicago.

Mehrens, W. A. (1992). Using performance assessment for accountability purposes. *Educational Measurement: Issues and Practice, 11*(1), pp. 3–9, 20.

Mehrens, W. A., and Kaminski, J. (1989). Methods for improving standardized test scores: Fruitful, fruitless, or fraudulent? *Educational Measurement: Issues and Practice, 8*(1), 14–22.

Mehrens, W. A., and Lehman, I. J. (1987). *Using standardized tests in education* (4th ed.). New York: Longman.

Merriam-Webster's Collegiate Dictionary: Tenth Edition (1994). Springfield. MA: Merriam-Webster.

Messick, S. (1980). Test validity and the ethics of assessment. *American Psychologist, 35,* 1012–1027.

Messick, S. (1989). Validity. In R. L. Linn (Ed.), *Educational measurement* (3rd ed.). New York: Macmillan.

Microsoft Office. (1997). Copyright Microsoft Corporation. One Microsoft Way, Redmond, WA, 98052–6399.

Millman, J., and Greene, J. (1989). The specification and development of tests of achievement and ability. In R. L. Linn, *Educational measurement* (3rd ed.). New York: Macmillan.

Mosenthal, P. B. (1998). Defining prose task characteristics for use in computer adaptive testing and instruction. *American Educational Research Journal, 35,* 269–307.

National Council of Teachers of Mathematics. (1991). *Professional standards for teaching mathematics.* Reston, VA: The Council.

Nedelsky, L. (1954). Absolute grading standards for objective tests. *Educational and Psychological Measurement, 14,* 3–19.

Newmann, F. M., and Archbald, D. A. (1992). "The nature of authentic academic achievement." In H. Berlak, F. M. Newmann, E. Adams, D. A. Archbald, T. Burgess, J. Raven, and T. A. Romberg, *Toward a new science of educational testing and assessment* (pp. 71–83). Albany: State University of New York Press.

Nitko, A. J. (1989). Designing tests that are integrated with instruction. In R. L. Linn (Ed.), *Educational measurement* (3rd ed., pp. 447–474). New York: Macmillan.

Novak, J. D. (1998). *Learning, creating, and using knowledge,* Mahwah, NJ: Lawrence Erlbaum.

Nunnally, J. C. (1978). *Psychometric theory* (2nd ed.). New York: McGraw-Hill.

O'Connor, M. C. (1989). Aspects of differential performance by minorities on standardized tests: Linguistic and sociocultural factors. In B. Gifford (Ed.), *Test policy and test performance: Education, language and culture.* Boston: Kluwer.

Page, E. B. (1994). Computer grading of student prose, using modern concepts and software. *Journal of Experimental Education, 62,* 127–142.

Page, E. B., and Petersen, N. S. (1995). The computer moves into essay grading: Updating the ancient test. *Phi Delta Kappan, 76,* 561–565.

Petersen, N. S., Kolen, M. J., and Hoover, H. D. (1989). Scaling, norming, and equating. In R. L. Linn, *Educational measurement* (3rd ed.). New York: Macmillan.

Peterson, P. L., Janicki, T. C., and Swing, S. R. (1981). Ability X treatment interaction effects on children's learning in large-group and small-group approaches. *American Educational Research Journal, 18,* 453–473.

Peterson, S. E., DeGracie, J. S., and Agabe, C. R. (1987). A longitudinal study of the effects of retention/promotion on academic achievement. *American Educational Research Journal, 24,* 107–118.

Phillips, S. E. (1996). Legal defensibility of standards: Issues and policy perspectives. *Educational Measurement: Issues and Practice, 15*(2), 5–13, 19.

Phillips, S. E. (1998). Calculator accommodations, *NCME: National Council on Measurement in Education Quarterly Newsletter, 6*(1), 2.

Principles and indicators for student assessment systems. (1995). Cambridge, MA: National Center for Fair and Open Testing. (ERIC Document Reproduction Service No. ED 400 334)

Reckase, M. D. (1995). Portfolio assessment: A theoretical estimate of score reliability. *Educational Measurement: Issues and Practice, 14*(1), pp. 12–14, 31.

Resnick, L. B. (1987). *Education and learning to think.* Washington, DC: National Academy Press.

Scheuneman, J. D., and Slaughter, C. (1991). *Issues of test bias, item bias, and group differences and what to do while waiting for the answers.* Princeton, NJ: Educational Testing Service. (ERIC Document Reproduction Service No. ED 400 294)

Schilling, K. M., and Schilling, K. L. (1998). Proclaiming and sustaining excellence: Assessment as a faculty role. *ASHE-ERIC Higher Education Reports, 26*(3). Washington, DC: The George Washington University Graduate School of Education and Human Development.

Secolsky, C. (1987). On the direct measurement of face validity: A comment on Nevo. *The Journal of Educational Measurement, 24,* 82–83.

Shepard, L. A. (1995). Using assessment to improve learning. *Educational Leadership, 54*(5), 38–43.

Shepard, L. A., Flexer, R. J., Hiebert, E. H., Marion, S. F., Mayfield, V., and Weston, T. J. (1996). Effects of introducing classroom performance assessments on student learning. *Educational Measurement: Issues and Practice, 15*(3), 7–18.

Shermis, M. D., and Chang, S. H. (1997). The use of item response theory (IRT) to investigate the hierarchical nature of a college mathematics curriculum. *Educational and Psychological Measurement, 57,* 450–458.

Skinner, B. F. (1987). *Upon further reflection.* Englewood Cliffs, NJ: Prentice Hall.

Smith, M. L. (1991). Meanings of test preparation. *American Educational Research Journal, 28,* 521–542.

Solity, J. (1991). An overview of behavioral approaches to teaching children with learning difficulties and the National Curriculum. *Educational Psychology: An International Journal of Experimental Psychology, 11*(2), 151–67.

Spady, W. G. (1988). Organizing for results: The basis of authentic restructuring and reform. *Educational Leadership, 46,* 4–8.

Sprinthall, R. C. (1997). *Basic statistical analysis* (5th ed.). Boston: Allyn & Bacon.

Stahl, S. A., Osborn, J., and Stein, M. (1995/96). Research does not support matching instruction to learning styles. *Reading Today, 34,* 32.

Stiggins, R. J. (1987). Profiling classroom assessment environments. Paper presented at the annual meeting of the National Council on Measurement in Education, San Francisco.

Stiggins, R. J. (1991). Relevant classroom assessment training for teachers. *Educational Measurement: Issues and Practice, 10*(1), 7–12.

Stodolsky, S. (1985). Teacher evaluation: The limits of looking. *Educational Researcher, 13*(9), 11–18.

Subkoviak, M. J. (1988). A practitioner's guide to computation and interpretation of reliability indices for mastery tests. *Journal of Educational Measurement, 24,* 47–55.

Sugrue, B. (1995). A theory-based framework for assessing domain-specific problem-solving ability. *Educational Measurement: Issues and Practice, 14*(3), 29–35, 36.

Tanner, D. E. (1988). Achievement as a function of abstractness and cognitive level. *Journal of Research and Development in Education, 21*(2), 16–21.

Taylor, C. S., and Nolen, S. B. (1996). What does the psychometrician's classroom look like? Reframing assessment concepts in the context of learning. *Education Policy Analysis Archives, 4*(17), 1–18. Retrieved January 26, 2000, from the World Wide Web: http://olam.ed.asu.edu/epaa/

Tessmer, M. (1993). *Planning and conducting formative evaluations: Improving the quality of education and training.* Philadelphia: Kogan & Page.

Thorndike, R. M. (1997). Measurement and evaluation in psychology and education (6th ed.). Columbus, OH: Merrill.

Thurstone, L., and Chave, E. (1929). *The measurement of attitude.* Chicago: University of Chicago Press.

Tomchin, E. M., and Impara, J. C. (1992). Unraveling teachers' beliefs about grade retention. *American Educational Research Journal, 29,* 199–223.

Traub, R. E., and Rowley, G. L. (1991). Understanding reliability. *Educational Measurement: Issues and Practice, 10*(1), 37–45.

Tyler, R. W. (1949). *Basic principles of curriculum and instruction.* Chicago: University of Chicago Press.

Van Dalen, D. B. (1979). *Understanding educational research: An introduction.* New York: McGraw-Hill.

Wagner, R. K., and Sternberg, R. J. (1984). Alternative conceptions of intelligence and their implications for education. *Review of Educational Research, 54,* 179–224.

Walberg, H. (1984). Improving the productivity of America's schools. *Educational Leadership, 41*(8), 19–27.

Walberg, H. (1986). Synthesis of research on teaching. In M. C. Wittrock (Ed.), *Handbook of research on teaching* (pp. 214–229). New York: Macmillan.

Walstad, W. B., and Robson, D. (1997). Differential item functioning and male-female differences on multiple-choice tests in economics. *Journal of Economic Education, 28*(2), 155–171.

Whitney, D. R. (1989). Educational admissions and placement. In R. L. Linn, *Educational measurement* (3rd ed.). New York: Macmillan.

Witken, H. A., Moore, C. A., Goodenough, D. R., and Cox, P. W. (1977). Field-dependent and field-independent cognitive styles and their educational implications. *Review of Educational Research, 47,* 1–64.

Woolfolk, A. E. (1995). *Educational Psychology* (6th ed.). Boston: Allyn & Bacon.

Wright, E. L., and Kuehn, P. (1998). The effects of academic language instruction on college-bound at-risk secondary students. *Journal of Educational Opportunity, 17*(1) 9–22.

Yen, W. M. (1997). The technical quality of performance assessments: Standard errors of percents of pupils reaching standards. *Educational Measurement: Issues and Practice, 16*(3), 5–15.

Youngman, H. (1991). *Take my life, please!* New York: Morrow.

Glossary

Note: Many of the terms listed in the Glossary occur in multiple chapters. The designation here indicates the chapter in which the term occurs initially.

alpha error is another name for type I decision error. Alpha error occurs when someone lacking a behavior is mistakenly judged to possess it. The symbol is the Greek letter alpha, α. Chapter 3

alternate forms reliability is a measure of reliability taken by comparing the data from two different forms of the same test. Chapter 7

analysis of variance (ANOVA) is a statistical test employed to determine whether scoring averages that differ from group to group are systematic or random. Chapter 11

aptitude describes one's general aptness or suitability. A measure of academic aptitude, for example, indicates one's talent for academic performance. Chapter 8

assessment includes all of the data-gathering and evaluative processes that allow one to affect outcomes by making informed decisions. Chapter 2

assessment relevance is another term for assessment authenticity. It describes the degree to which the assessment setting represents the situation for which the learner is being prepared. Chapter 4

attitudes reflect the intensity of one's feelings toward or against something. Chapter 8

attitude scales are instruments designed to measure one's affect, or feelings toward an object. Chapter 8

authentic assessment is a movement whose supporters have little confidence in traditional standardized testing. Rather, the emphasis is on assessment activities, which are more closely connected to learning and skills that the learner will use when formal schooling ends. See also **performance assessment.** Chapter 3

banking test items is the process of saving items once they are constructed, usually in a computer file, to avoid reconstructing them every time one must assess the relevant material. Chapter 11

beta error is another name for type II decision error. Beta error occurs when someone who actually possesses a behavior is mistakenly judged not to possess it. The symbol is the Greek letter beta, β. Chapter 3.

bias. See **test bias.** Chapter 12

Bloom Taxonomy is one of several available classification systems for thinking tasks. Bloom and his coauthors suggested that all thinking tasks can be classified into one of six cumulative hierarchical categories, from simple rote memory to evaluation. Chapter 6

choices in the context of multiple choice items, are the alternative answers listed below the stem. They consist of one or more distracters that are incorrect and (usually) a correct response. Chapter 6

classical test theory holds that any assessment score reflects two components—a true score and some component of error. As the data become more reliable, the error component is minimized. Chapter 9

Cloze procedure is a reading assessment that helps one determine whether the reading level of a particular passage is appropriate for a specified group of learners. Chapter 2

coaching, or test coaching, represents any tactic that one adopts to assist test takers to improve their test scores with procedures that are unrelated to their content knowledge or skill levels. Chapter 10

code of fair testing was developed by the major educational and psychological measurement groups so that a set of ethical guidelines would be available for those involved with testing. Chapter 12

cognitive style describes differences in individual's preferred learning modality—visual, auditory, tactile, and so forth. Chapter 2

competency tests are procedures designed to measure the presence of some minimally acceptable level of knowledge or performance. Chapter 3

computer-adaptive testing (CAT) is an assessment procedure in which the computer develops the test taker's instrument as the assessment proceeds. When the test taker demonstrates that she can correctly answer items of a particular level of difficulty, subsequently the computer selects only items on that subject that are more difficult. The reverse is also true. When the test taker misses items of a particular level of difficulty, the computer selects subsequent items of reduced difficulty. The result is a shorter test, since redundancy is minimal. Chapter 11

computer-generated verbal responses. See **programmed comments.**

concurrent validity is reflected in the degree to which results from two different instruments employed to measure the same type of learning are in agreement. One has concurrent validity when those who do well on one assessment also do well on the other, and vice versa. The ranking of the students on the two tests will agree. Chapter 7

consequential validity refers to the impact that a particular type of assessment has for the related teaching and learning. If an assessment activity, besides gauging learners' performance, also encourages further learning or better teaching, it has consequential validity. Chapter 3

constructed response items are assessment items for which the test taker must develop, rather than simply choose, the response. Essay, fill-in, and short-answer items are examples of constructed response items. Chapter 6

construct irrelevant is something that is evident—but unrelated—to the characteristic one wishes to assess. One of the common assessment pitfalls is that a student's score will reflect something irrelevant to what was to be measured. If the scores on a history test are higher among the students who write the most legibly, the portion of the score that reflects legibility is construct irrelevant. Chapter 2

constructs are mental traits or characteristics that explain the individual's ability with a particular mental task. Each of the mental tasks we perform is related to a particular construct. Chapter 8

construct validity is the degree to which one measures some mental construct (motivation, aptitude, and the like) that one intended to measure. Chapter 8

content bias exists when test items use a content that is more familiar to some groups of test takers than to others. Exclusive of the quality assessed, the content of the item places some test takers at a disadvantage. Chapter 12

content validity is a measure of the degree to which an assessment represents the discipline or subject area it was intended to reflect. Chapter 4

correlation coefficient is a number that quantifies the strength of the relationship between two variables. The range of values is from −1 to +1. As the coefficient approaches either negative or positive 1, one is able to predict the value of the second variable with increasing accuracy. Variables that are unrelated have a coefficient of 0. Chapter 9

criteria are quality indicators in educational assessment. Chapter 3

criterion-based standards are the quality indicators by which assessment data are evaluated. They are usually associated with authentic, or performance, assessment. Chapter 4

criterion-references are employed when test scores are interpreted by comparing one student's score to a set of criteria that define the various grading and passing standards. Chapter 2

criterion-related validity is the consistency between test data and some other measure of the same trait taken either at the same time (concurrent validity), or at some future time (predictive validity). Chapter 4

criterion situation describes that setting beyond the immediate classroom for which the student is being prepared. To the degree that it is feasible, instructors attempt to duplicate the criterion situation in instruction and in assessment. Chapter 4

cut-off scores, or simply **cut-scores,** are the minimum score one may achieve and still be judged to have met the standard or objective. Chapter 3

decision errors reflect mistakes made when erroneous judgments are made about a learner's competency or level of mastery. The errors are of two kinds: type I, or alpha (α) errors, also called false positives; and type II or beta (β) errors, also called false negatives. Chapter 13

descriptive statistics are used to provide a brief summary of larger amounts of data. Descriptive statistics include measures of central tendency and dispersion, and, when the strength of association is an issue, measures of correlation. Chapter 9

deviation scores are those scores derived by subtracting the individual's "raw" score from the mean score for the test. Deviation scores are used often in statistical formulae such as that for the standard deviation. Chapter 9

dichotomously scored assessment items are items that are either correct or incorrect. For these items there cannot be degrees of correctness. The responses are right or wrong. Chapter 11

differential item functioning (DIF) refers to the fact that defined groups may respond differently to particular test items for reasons unrelated to bias. Students in school may consistently score poorly on a set of questions, not because the items are biased against them, but because they were not taught the material. Chapter 12

distracter analysis is a procedure for examining the distracters in a multiple-choice item to determine which students (high versus low scoring) are selecting particular choices when the item is scored incorrectly. Chapter 7

distracters in multiple-choice test items are those choices that are incorrect. The distracters are constructed so that they will be plausible to someone who lacks the skill, or lacks an understanding of the content. Item difficulty can be thought of as a function of the similarity between the distracters and the correct choice(s). Chapter 7

dynamic assessment refers to an assessment system that constantly monitors student performance such that a trajectory of learning can be documented. It is in contrast to static assessment. Chapter 11

equating scores is the process of determining whether assessment scores, which may reflect different means from group to group, provide the same level of measurement validity for each group. Chapter 11

error is that element of a score which is actually peripheral to what one intended to assess. Error can be systematic, as it is when an instrument employs items that reflect a bias toward a particular group, or random, as occurs when someone is sick during an assessment and unable to perform as well as usual. Chapter 7

ETS refers to the Educational Testing Service in Princeton, New Jersey. It is perhaps the largest testing organization in the world. Chapter 11

evaluation is the process of making judgments about the adequacy of a product.

Excel is the popular spreadsheet marketed by the Microsoft Corporation. See **spreadsheets.** Chapter 6

exhibitions are procedures that the student uses to demonstrate learning. They are common in authentic assessment settings. Oral reports and laboratory demonstrations are examples of exhibitions. Chapter 4

face validity is the appearance of validity. It might be termed "apparent validity." It is relevant in all types of educational assessment but becomes a particular issue in authentic assessment because consistency between the assessment activity and the real-world experience for which the student is being prepared is so important. Chapter 4

factor analysis is a mathematical data reduction technique for determining the number of distinct characteristics that may be reflected in a group of scores. Ordinarily, a test with 20 items actually indicates the measurement of something fewer that 20 separate characteristics. Factor analysis can demonstrate this mathematically. It is one of the tools used to establish construct validity. Chapter 8

false negative. See **beta error.**

false positive. See **alpha error.**

fidelity continuum represents a range of assessment examples. It stretches from situations in which assessment tasks are completely disconnected from their real-world applications, to the other extreme where the task is assessed in exactly the environment for which the learner is being prepared. Chapter 4

field dependent defines a cognitive style. Such learners tend to recognize the patterns in the whole without being attentive to the specific components or details of a situation. Chapter 2

field independent learners tend to have a more analytical style, compared to field dependent people. They recognize the component parts of complex situation and intricate problems. Chapter 2

formative assessment is conducted while instruction is still in the formative stages. Data from formative assessment allow one to make adjustments that will benefit the student during the teaching process. Formative assessment is not a mechanism for grading students. Chapter 5

formative decisions are decisions based on assessment data that will serve as the basis for altering ongoing educational programs. Chapter 2

formula scoring is any of several procedures that allow one to systematically adjust scores on objectively scored tests so as to take into account the probable number of items students scored correctly by guessing. Chapter 7

FORTRAN is an acronym that stands for "formula translation." It represents one of the earlier programming languages widely used among a select few scientists and technicians when only mainframe computers were available. Chapter 11

Gaussian distribution, sometimes called a Gaussian curve, is the familiar bell-shaped curve associated with normal distributions. Mathematician Karl Gauss was the person who described its properties, which include one mode, and symmetry. Gaussian distributions are important in educational measurement because many mental characteristics tend to be normally distributed. Chapter 9

gender bias occurs when test data predict the performance of one gender with greater accuracy than the other. See **test bias.** Chapter 12

goals are statements of general intent. Chapter 2

grade equivalent scores are developmental-level scores rather than placement scores. The scores represent the student's performance in years and months. Whatever the intended grade level of the test, a score of 5.2 matches the score of an average fifth-grade student who is in the second month of the academic year. The score is not a recommendation for placement among fifth-grade students. Chapter 10

grading is an abbreviated representation of the evaluation. Chapter 5

Guttman scale is a specific type of cumulative attitude scale. The items in the scale are unidimensional, which means that they all measure the same characteristic. The items are organized such that a positive answer to one will likely be followed by positive answers to the other related items. Chapter 8

high inference behaviors may require several careful observations and some interpretation in order to establish their presence. Chapter 5

high-stakes tests are assessments for which the outcomes are important, or "the stakes" are very high, for the individual tested. High-stakes tests are such because the results serve as gatekeepers, defining which individuals may pursue a course of action or receive a service, and which may not. See **low-stakes tests.** Chapter 3

holistic scoring is the practice of scoring the entire work sample instead of scoring elements of the product independently and then aggregating the scores for a total. Chapter 4

impulsive cognitive style describes a learner who usually works quickly and makes decision without laboring over them at length. Impulsive students often finish assignments quickly and submit them without double-checking them for accuracy. Chapter 2

intelligence is a construct defined very differently by a variety of scholars. There is general agreement, however, that intelligence reflects the capacity of the individual for abstract thought and sound judgment. Chapter 8

interest inventories are a particular kind of attitude scale that help establish the respondents' interest in an activity. Interest inventories are usually conducted to scale interest relative to other, alternative activities. Chapter 2

internal consistency reliability is a measure of reliability based on a single administration of the test but with multiple scores derived by comparing either halves of the test, or individual item scores to total test scores. The advantage of internal consistency, of course, is that one derives a reliability score without the difficulty of multiple administrations of the test. Chapter 7

interrater reliability is the measure of consistency between separate measures of the same data. If two people score the same essay, inter-rater reliability is the degree to which their measures are in agreement. Chapter 4

interval data indicate the amount of a measured characteristic a subject possesses according to a scale that has equal intervals. When achievement data are reported in terms of the number of items scored correctly, they are nearly always interval data. The difference between a score of 7 and a score of 11 is the same difference in number of correct responses as the difference between a score of 22 and a score of 26. Chapter 9

item analysis is any of several different procedures undertaken to determine the quality of test items. The task is to analyze the performance of the test item in order to determine whether it yields the information one needs to make accurate judgments about the learners. Chapter 7

item bias occurs when some respondents to an item are at a disadvantage owing to the language or structure of the item rather than to the quality the designer intended to measure. Chapter 12

item characteristic curves define the probability that learners possessing varying levels of the particular trait will correctly score the item that calls upon that trait. See **item response theory**. Chapter 13

item difficulty is usually expressed in terms of the proportion of a given group that scored a dichotomously scored ("right" or "wrong") item correctly. If 15 of 20 people in a group score the item correctly, it has a difficulty of $p = .75$. Chapter 7

item discrimination is the degree to which a test item separates those who have a particular skill or knowledge from those who do not. If an item has high discrimination, those with the highest levels of the skill or knowledge that the item measures are most likely to score the item correctly. Possible item discrimination indices range from –1 (those with the least of the characteristic the item measures are most likely to score the item correctly) to +1. Chapter 7

item flexibility refers to the range of different levels of thought an item can be written to respond to. Some items, such as true/false, have a very restricted range. Others, such as the essay, have great flexibility. Chapter 6

item response theory or **latent trait theory** holds that the learners' abilities to choose, or to construct a correct response to a test item, depend upon their possession of a sufficient quantity of the mental trait assessed by the test item. Chapter 9

item stem is the initial part of the multiple-choice item, in which the problem is stated. The choices, including distracters, follow. Chapter 6

judgmental models are procedures for standard setting that establish the minimum allowable performance level on a test by analyzing the difficulty of the test items. Alternative standard-

setting models may include estimates of the test takers' ability. Chapter 13

judgment reliability reflects the level of agreement among multiple judges, or multiple judgments. The term is usually used in connection with authentic assessment, when the work sample evaluated is a portfolio or some other product that does not lend itself to traditional quantitative scoring. Chapter 4

Kuder-Richardson Formula 21 is a simple formula for calculating an estimate of test reliability. Chapter 7

Lake Wobegon effect is based on the mythical Lake Wobegon of radio fame, where "all of the children are above average." When current data are evaluated in light of outdated test norms, sometimes all of the subjects appear to be beyond the mean, a situation characteristic of state averages in the United States in the late 1980s and early 1990s. Chapter 12

Likert format is the approach employed by many test developers, which asks one to select a response that most closely matches one's feeling. "Strongly agree," "agree," "neither agree nor disagree," and so forth are examples of Likert format. Chapter 8

low inference behaviors. In contrast to high inference behaviors, low inference behaviors require little observation and little deduction in order to establish their presence. Chapter 5

low-stakes tests are assessments for which the outcome has a minimal impact on the test-taker's subsequent choices. See **high-stakes tests.** Chapter 3

mastery learning is an instructional approach based upon a philosophy stating that anyone can learn anything, if the time required to learn is allowed to vary as needed. Chapter 3

mean is a measure of central tendency used to describe interval and ratio data. It is the arithmetic average. It is symbolized with either $\bar{x}$, or M_n. Chapter 9

measurement defines assigning numbers to data according to rules. Chapter 2

measurement-driven instruction is an educational system in which what is taught is structured by what will be assessed. Traditionally, it was the opposite. What was assessed was dictated by what was taught, but because test results can have a great influence on the learner's options (see **"high-stakes tests"**), the instructional material is sometimes adjusted to reflect what will be measured. Chapter 3

measures of central tendency are descriptive statistics, such as the mean, median, and mode, that indicate which measure is typical of the group from which it is drawn. The appropriate measure depends upon the scale of the data and the characteristics of the distribution. Chapter 9

measures of dispersion are descriptive statistics, such as the range, variance, and standard deviation, that quantify the degree to which data spread out from some central point. Chapter 9

median is a measure of central tendency used to describe data that are measured at ordinal scale or beyond. The median (M_d) is the middle-most point in a group of scores. It is that point at which half the scores in the distribution are below, and half are beyond. Chapter 9

meta-analysis is a statistical technique that pools results from many independent studies in order to arrive at a common set of conclusions regarding the impact of some variable or procedure. The conclusions are more robust than would be possible from an analysis of any individual research experiment. Chapter 5

mode is the measure of central tendency used to describe nominal data. Mode (M_o) indicates what type of data is most common in the group. Chapter 9

nominal data have that characteristic that allows members of particular groups to be counted. Counting the number of males and females in a group or the number of students who belong to particular ethnic groups are examples of nominal data. Chapter 9

normal curve equivalent (NCE) scores are standard scores (see *z* **score** and *T* **score**) that reflect a distribution divided into increments identified by an integer from 1 to 99. Chapter 10

normal distribution is a collection of one such group of measures for a characteristic such as intelligence. Chapter 3

normally distributed means that if one were to measure a given characteristic throughout all members of a population, one would find the scores distributed in the familiar bell-shaped curve. Chapter 8

norm-references are employed when test scores are interpreted by comparing an individual student's score to the others in the group, or to the mean score in some comparable group, to determine the various grading and passing standards. Chapter 2

objectives are specific statements indicating how a goal is to be accomplished.

observed score is a student's raw test score. Chapter 2

ordinal data have that characteristic that allows subjects to be ranked according to whether they have more, or less, of a quality than other subjects. That is, ordinal data reveal information about the quality only in relative terms. Chapter 9

outcomes-based education places particular emphasis on the outcomes that learners must demonstrate before they can proceed to the next level of study. Chapter 3

parameter estimation is the process of determining the characteristics of a population by drawing inferences from a representative sample. In some educational programs, the parameter becomes the standard for evaluating individual students' performances. Chapter 3

Pearson correlation is named for the author of the formula, Karl Pearson. The correlation is symbolized as *r,* and quantifies the degree of relationship between two variables measured on an interval or ratio scale. Pearson correlations are linear, which means there is a constant relationship between the two variables—they are not positive in one instance and negative in others. Chapter 9

percentile scores identify where an individual score falls relative to the others who took the test. A percentile score of 43, for example, indicates that 43 percent of those who took the test fell below this score. Percentiles do not reveal how well an individual scored in any absolute sense. The data are purely comparative. Chapter 10

perceptual style describes one's dependence elements of the perceptual field. Field-dependent individuals develop global patterns of the perceptual field. Field-independent individuals tend to be more analytical, focusing on details of the perceptual field. Chapter 2

performance assessment is an approach to educational assessment that places particular emphasis on learning outcomes that have meaning beyond the educational setting as measures of student progress. See also **authentic assessment.** Chapter 3

personality measures are objective tests designed to assess personal and social traits in order to make more valid predictions about people. Chapter 8

portfolios are collections of relevant work samples gathered to represent some discrete learning period. In some instances they may be a better reflection of the student's knowledge and ability than alternative assessment methods produce. Chapter 4

positive correlation indicates that as measures of one characteristic increase, measures of a second tend to increase as well. For example, other thing being equal, children's height and weight have a positive correlation; as children grow taller, their weight increases. Chapter 9

preassessment is the assessment that precedes the development and delivery of instruction. Chapter 2

predictive validity is present when the data from one assessment predict the results of some future measure of the same characteristic. Entrance examinations are administered because of their predictive validity. Students who perform well on the SAT or the ACT, for example, generally perform better in college study than those who do poorly on those tests. Chapter 7

primacy effects occur when one allows what one sees initially during an observation to have an undue effect on any judgment made. Chapter 5

programmed comments are an automatically printed verbal explanation of the test-taker's score, often included as an option in computerized testing. Chapter 11

race-norming is a procedure developed in the 1970s to adjust individual's scores on high-stakes tests by a factor that neutralizes differences in ethnic groups' scores. One of the side effects of race-norming is that it has the effect of diminishing the predictive validity of the test data. It was abandoned in the 1990s. Chapter 12

range describes the dispersion of scores by subtracting the lowest score from the highest. Chapter 9

rater bias occurs when someone scoring a test is swayed by factors only tangentially related to the quality the item was intended to gauge. A scorer who responds to handwriting neatness or the richness of one's vocabulary, when those qualities are not the object of the measurement, is demonstrating rater bias. Chapter 12

ratio scale data have all the characteristics that interval data possess, in addition to a meaningful zero in the scale. In educational measurement, ratio data are rare since there are very few instances in which a zero actually indicates the complete absence of the measured quality. Chapter 9

readability tests are instruments that assist one to determine the grade level requirement of a particular reading selection. Chapter 2

recency effects occur when one allows what one sees last during an observation to have an undue effect on any judgment made. Chapter 5

reflective cognitive style defines the student who is very deliberate. Students who go over test questions time and again to check their accuracy, who think carefully before responding in class have a reflective style. Chapter 2

reliability is the degree to which measurement data are stable. When a test yields reliable data, further administrations will provide the same result when the relevant conditions remain unchanged. Chapter 7

reliability coefficients quantify test data's consistency. The coefficients range from 0 (no reliability) to 1 (perfect reliability). Chapter 7

rubric describes a rule for conduct. Within the assessment context, it describes the condition or the level of performance required for a particular score or grade. Chapter 6

scaling refers to the level of information provided by measurement data. The measurement scales range from nominal to ordinal, interval, and ratio scales. Chapter 9

scoring difficulty is one characteristic of assessment items. Scoring some assessment items requires nothing more than a simple key with which one compares the test taker's responses. Other items require a background in the content area, and perhaps also the ability to analyze the test taker's communication of the response. This latter is true of essay items. Chapter 6

scoring protocol is a guide prepared to help a scorer weigh the various elements of a response consistently. Scoring protocols are most commonly prepared for essay items. Chapter 6

scoring reliability is the degree to which a response that is scored at two or more different times evokes the same conclusion from the scorer. When the evaluation has a subjective element to it, this is often called **judgment reliability.** Chapter 4

selected response items are assessment items from which the learner chooses a response from among those provided. Multiple-choice, true/false, and matching items are examples of selected response items. Chapter 6

sigma is the symbol in statistical language for standard deviation when it is in lower case (σ), and the symbol for summation when it is in upper case (Σ). Chapter 5

skew is a term describing a distribution that lacks symmetry. When there are extreme scores in only one direction, called outliers, the distribution is skewed in that direction. "Positive skew" indicates that the higher scores are the more extreme, and "negative skew," the lower scores. Chapter 9

Spearman-Brown formula is designed to estimate the effect on reliability of manipulating a test's length (number of items). Chapter 7

Spearman's rho (ρ) is a correlation statistic for ordinal scale data. Chapter 9

speeded tests are timed because of the belief that there is a relationship between the characteristic measured and how quickly the respondent can complete the assessment. Chapter 7

split-half reliability, like other measures of internal consistency, determines reliability by comparing the students' scores on the halves of the test. Scores on the odd and even items, for example, take the place of scores from two separate tests. Scores from test halves are reliable only if both halves measure the same characteristic. Because test length affects reliability, split-half reliability measures typically underestimate data reliability. Chapter 7

spreadsheets are relatively easy to adapt to use for educational record keeping and for many of the calculation tasks that assessment requires. Originally designed for bookkeeping and accounting applications, spreadsheets' use of data columns and rows and their calculation and automatic recalculation functions make them excellent tools for managing and manipulating data sets. Chapter 11

standard deviation quantifies the degree to which the scores in a group typically deviate from their mean. Interval data are often reported in terms of their mean and standard deviation. The standard deviation is the square root of another measure of dispersion, the variance. A larger standard deviation indicates that the scores in the distribution described are relatively spread out. A smaller distribution indicates that the scores fall more tightly around the mean of the distribution. Chapter 5

standard error of measurement (SEM) is the standard deviation of all the errors in measurement that occur among the members of a group to whom a particular test has been administered. Chapter 9

standardized tests are those for which the conditions under which the particular test is administered are as consistent as possible. This is accomplished by using the same directions, by imposing the same limitations on learners regarding time and procedure, and by evaluating all test data in the same fashion. The advantage that standardized tests offer is the promise that variations in scores reflect differences in the characteristic one is measuring rather than differences in the conditions under which the test is taken. Chapter 10

standard normal distribution describes a frequency distribution that matches the bell-shaped curve called a Gaussian distribution. Furthermore, the distribution has a mean of 0, and a standard deviation of 1. Chapter 11

standards in education indicate what learners of a specified level should know or be able to do. Chapter 3

standard scores are the product of reformulating raw test scores so that they fit a defined distribution of scores whose characteristics remain constant. They allow one to compare scores from dissimilar tests because the scores are recalibrated in terms of a common metric. The z and T scores are common standard scores. Chapter 10.

standard setting is the process by which standards are established. Groups that include several different constituencies typically determine standards. Chapter 3

stanines is a shortened name for "standard nine-point scale." Like the z and T scores, stanines are standard scores. They represent a distribution divided into 9 segments. Chapter 10

static assessment is an assessment procedure that periodically assesses student performance, but which leaves one to extrapolate the data beyond assessments in order to develop a picture of student performance over the learning period. Static assessment is in contrast to dynamic assessment. Chapter 11

stem is the area in which the problem is presented in multiple-choice items. The stem should be framed in a complete sentence rather than completing the statement in each of the item choices that follow. Chapter 6

stem cue is some word in the stem of the item that prompts the learner to select a particular choice. At best, the cue has only an ancillary relationship to the characteristic measured by the item, but test-wise learners will allow it to guide them to a choice. Chapter 7

Strong Campbell Interest Inventory (SCII) is a standardized interest test designed to indicate where an individual's occupational preferences lie. Strong developed an instrument that allows one to indicate preference, neutrality, or nonpreference for a variety of activities unrelated to the particular occupation. However, the degree to which one's preferences match those of people who are happy in their field can be an important indicator of one's occupational preference. Chapter 8

summative assessment, in contrast to formative assessment, occurs at the conclusion of the instructional program when the students have had a maximum opportunity to learn. It is conducted for grading purposes. Chapter 5

summative decisions are those that one makes at the conclusion of a learning exercise about the students' levels of performance. Chapter 2

systematic errors occur in assessment when some condition results in test scores that are consistently too high or too low for some of the students. When only some students are test-wise, their scores tend to be higher than their command of the material will justify. There may also be test examples, unrelated to the subject tested, which favors one cultural or gender group over another resulting in biased items. Chapter 7

table of specifications is used to classify test items according to particular criteria such as the type of item and the topic the item addresses. Chapter 7

task analysis is a procedure by which one determines the skills and knowledge that are prerequisites to an activity. One begins by identifying the abilities that are immediately subordinate to the end product, and then those abilities that are necessary at the next level of

subordination, and so on until a complete hierarchy of subordinate knowledge is produced. Chapter 2

Teacher Performance Appraisal Instrument (TPAI) is the instrument used for assessing teachers' performance in the State of Georgia. It has served as the model for many other teacher assessment instruments. Chapter 5

teaching the test. See **coaching.** Chapter 10

test bias indicates the presence of *systematic* error in a set of scores. In such instances, some condition of the test or of the testing consistently places some one or some group at a disadvantage in a way unrelated to the characteristic measured. The error must be systematic, however, rather than the random type of error that occurs when someone is sick or distracted during the test and so does not perform well. Test bias is revealed when the data have lower predictive validity for some groups than for others. Chapter 9

test coaching. See **coaching.** Chapter 10

test-retest reliability is a measure of reliability taken by administering a test, administering it a second time under similar circumstances, and comparing the results. Chapter 7

tests of discrete competencies are the assessment techniques used in authentic assessment to gather data on specific abilities. Rather than a multiple-choice test of spelling ability, however, one might ask the student to spell the word aloud, choose words for the student based on the student's responses, probe the student with questions about spelling rules, and so forth. Chapter 4

test specifications define both the purposes and the context for an assessment before it is actually developed. They define for whom the assessment will be developed, why it was developed, how it will be used, and what limitations there will be in the assessment data. Chapter 7

test-wiseness reflects test takers' ability to determine the correct response to a test item even when they lack the knowledge or ability the item was designed to measure. Students are test-wise when they know that the teacher favors "c" responses or the more lengthy choices more often than random probabilities suggest that they should. Chapter 7

true score is a theoretical score representing what the measure of some mental trait would be if the measurement were taken without error. One can estimate true score but never establish it with absolute certainty. Chapter 7

T **score** is a standard score. In order to allow for meaningful comparisons, raw test scores are sometimes recalibrated to fit a particular distribution of scores called a *T* distribution, in which the mean of the distribution is always 50 and the standard deviation is always 10. The *T* score is an alternative to the *z* score, sometimes preferred because half of the *z* distribution's scores are negative, a characteristic absent in *T* distributions. Chapter 10

t-**test** is a statistical test used to determine whether the mean scores from two independent groups are sufficiently different that one could conclude that the difference is not random. This test is often used to determine whether some studied treatment or condition may be responsible for different scores. Chapter 11

two sigma problem is one of determining what combination of variables will have the same effect on student performance as tutorial instruction, which can boost student performance by two standard deviations. Chapter 5

type I errors are decision errors made when someone who lacks the characteristic measured is erroneously judged to possess it. Chapter 3

type II errors are decision errors made when someone who possess the characteristic measured is erroneously judged to lack it. Chapter 3

unimodal describes a distribution of scores in which there is just one area of most frequent scores. In the normal distribution, scores bunch toward the middle of the distribution and diminish in frequency as one moves from the middle in either direction. A bimodal distribution exists when scores collect with greatest frequency in two areas. Chapter 10

unitrait theories of intelligence are theories, such as those of Binet, Terman, and Spearman, that suggest that intelligence consists of one general intelligence characteristic. Unitrait theories are contrasted with dual-trait and multiple-trait theories. Chapter 8

validity is, at least in general terms, reflected in the extent to which one measures what one wishes to measure. Chapter 7

validity coefficients quantify data's validity. Validity coefficients range from 0 (no validity) to 1 (perfect validity). The validity coefficient's meaning depends upon the type of validity. For predictive validity, a coefficient of 1.0 indicates that the data predict some future quality or performance without error. Chapter 12

variance is a measure of the degree to which scores are dispersed around the mean of a distribution. A large variance means that scores are very spread out. The variance is the square of the standard deviation, another measure of dispersion. Chapter 7

$x = t + e$ is a symbolic expression of the following: Any observed score consists of a true measure of the trait or characteristic, and some component of error that has the effect of obscuring the measurement object. This understanding is the basis for **true score,** or **classical test theory.** Chapter 7

zone of proximal proficiency is a term Nitko (1989) used to describe the profile of the learners' ability that is the product of computer adaptive testing. Chapter 11

z **score** is a standard score. In order to allow for meaningful comparisons, raw test scores are sometimes recalibrated to fit a particular distribution of scores called a *z* distribution, in which the mean of the distribution is always 0 and the standard deviation is always 1. Chapter 10

Index